SUSTAINABLE
Transportation Planning

SUSTAINABLE
Transportation Planning

Tools for Creating Vibrant, Healthy, and Resilient Communities

Jeffrey Tumlin

WILEY

John Wiley & Sons, Inc.

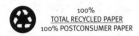
Copyright © 2012 by John Wiley & Sons, Inc. All rights reserved.

Published by John Wiley & Sons, Inc., Hoboken, New Jersey.

Published simultaneously in Canada.

For general information on our other products and services, or technical support, please contact our Customer Care Department within the United States at 800-762-2974, outside the United States at 317-572-3993 or fax 317-572-4002.

Wiley publishes in a variety of print and electronic formats and by print-on-demand. Some material included with standard print versions of this book may not be included in e-books or in print-on-demand. If this book refers to media such as a CD or DVD that is not included in the version you purchased, you may download this material at http://booksupport.wiley.com. For more information about Wiley products, visit www.wiley.com.

Library of Congress Cataloging-in-Publication Data:

Tumlin, Jeffrey.
 Sustainable transportation planning : tools for creating vibrant, healthy, and resilient communities/ Jeffrey Tumlin.
   p. cm. — (Wiley series in sustainable design ; 16)
 Includes index.
  ISBN 978-0-470-54093-0 (hardback); ISBN 978-1-118-11923-5 (ebk); ISBN 978-1-118-11924-2 (ebk); ISBN 978-1-118-12760-5 (ebk); ISBN 978-1-118-12761-2 (ebk); ISBN 978-1-118-12762-9 (ebk)
  1. Transportation—Planning. 2. Sustainable urban development. I. Title.
 HE151.T86 2011
 388.4—dc23

                                                                    2011016262

Printed in the United States of America

10 9 8 7 6 5 4 3 2 1

Contents

Acknowledgments

This book would not have been possible without the support and wisdom of many people, most prominently the following:

Julia Fremon, who kept me in the transportation field despite my better judgment, and who taught me everything I know about managing smart, creative, irrepressible people.

Bonnie Nelson, who believed in 1987 that it was possible to create a transportation consulting firm with a fun, egalitarian work environment and a sustainability focus, even before sustainability was a common word.

Patrick Siegman and Don Shoup, who taught me everything I know about parking.

Allan Jacobs, Jan Gehl, and Jane Jacobs, who helped me see cities through new eyes.

All of my colleagues at Nelson\Nygaard, whose ideas have shaped every page of this book, and particularly Tom Brennan, Brian Canepa, Mark Chase, David Fields, Michael King, Tara Krueger, Amy Pfeiffer, Patrick Siegman, Paul Supawanich, and Jessica ter Schure, who wrote substantial portions of the book, and Colin Burgett, Rick Chellman, Ed Hernandez, Lisa Jacobson, Ben Lowe, Carrie Nielson, and Michael Moule, who provided critical research and edits. I remain especially grateful to Steve Boland, who not only edited this entire book, but also helped restructure and rewrite entire chapters.

Many of our clients, who generously gave permission to have text and artwork from our previous work incorporated into this book, including the cities of Seattle, Santa Monica, San Francisco, Glendale, and Berkeley, and the Urban Planning Council of the Emirate of Abu Dhabi.

The folks at Wiley, including editor John Czarnecki, senior production editor Donna Conte, marketing manager Penny Ann Makras, and publisher Amanda Miller, who believed that it was time for a book like this one.

And finally, to Huib Petersen, who put up with me through the dark days of writing.

Foreword

One always hopes that competing forces can be brought together in creative ways that leave all or at least most of the competitors at rest, maybe even pleased, if not completely satisfied. Most important, with regard to the main subjects of this book, transportation and sustainable urbanism, is the underlying question: Does this bringing-together serve the basic interests of the people touched by the competing forces, and of the environment?

City planners and urban designers are very often in conflict with transportation professionals. Of course, that could be said in reverse: transportation professionals are often in conflict with city planners. But, for a long time (though less at present), transportation professionals may have barely noticed the planners. The position of transportation professionals, particularly the traffic engineers, has been long established: Early on, they collected lots of data about traffic volumes and presumed capacity of street types and lane widths; they were in the engineering departments of cities and states; they put together manuals on street design and adopted standards; they built predictive traffic models; they had numbers, and made more. They did a lot of good and, of course, they made some mistakes. Who didn't?

As a young city planner, working in Pittsburgh, I came to understand that those urban phenomena to which numbers could be attached were more likely to receive higher priority when it came to doing things as part of an urban plan than those that did not have quantitative data to justify their implementation. Streets and public rights-of-way got higher priority and were allocated more land more readily than other uses the values of which were less countable—like open space, for example, or housing, or—God forbid—urbanity. But I nevertheless tended to believe the data and projections (forgetting that trend need not forecast destiny), and tried to live by the standards.

Later, after years of experience, I began to question the data and projections, and certainly the standards set by the transportation profession, and often enshrined in city codes and ordinances. One only has to see many Vancouver streets, where three meters is the policy for lane widths, to begin to seriously and strongly question the twelve- and thirteen-foot lane standards that are so often the norm elsewhere. Narrower lanes on a commercial shopping street mean lower speeds than wider lanes, and thus fewer deadly accidents with pedestrians. On the best tree-lined streets, the trees come all the way to the corners; they don't stop some long distance from the corners to accommodate some sight-distance standard found in a manual.

A person can spend a lot of time gaining experience and learning lessons about how to design and arrange streets and roadways, from a citywide scale down to the smallest detail, in ways that will best meet the needs of the many planned-for users and of the environment itself. Would that it were easier! Would that there was an accessible, easy-to-understand source of both knowledge and methods that traffic professionals, planning practitioners, and the involved public alike could turn to in relation to transportation issues.

Jeff Tumlin does this; *Sustainable Transportation Planning* is a "how-to" guide for planning practitioners, transportation professionals, citizen activists, and people from a host of other professions and walks of life who want to understand transportation and land-use issues related to sustainable urbanism. His aims are to demystify common approaches to transportation matters, to help people challenge (and understand) traffic engineers when that is appropriate, and to help transportation professionals who want to do the "right thing," but lack training and appropriate texts. The book is concerned with resolving competing needs on a street, ways to reduce carbon dioxide emissions, the relationships between roadways and transit and economic development, social equity, quality of life, and much more.

Most importantly, this book is written in accessible language. It is a work that grows out of considerable experience. It does not contain a lot of theory. It is a book for general audiences and professionals alike.

In many ways Tumlin challenges the field from which he comes. One suspects that many of his brethren will take out after him, but hopefully not until they have read the book.

Jeff and I have consulted each other informally and worked together on projects in San Francisco and abroad. He is quick and sharp-witted at the same time that he is creative. He is interested in solving urban problems, not in making them. And, as any reader will soon find out, he knows his field (and others), is engaging, and writes very well.

Allan Jacobs

Chapter 1

Introduction

We transportation planning and engineering professionals are currently the most significant obstacle to sustainable urbanism in North America, Australia, and other growing regions around the world who seek to emulate us. Although transportation planning's related disciplines of land-use planning, architecture, landscape architecture, urban economics, and social policy have undergone major internal reform efforts over the past few decades, transportation remains largely stuck in a 1950s mentality, believing that there is an engineering solution to all problems—that we can literally pave our way out of our cities' congestion, mobility, and economic development problems. Our colleagues in other fields have recognized that sustainable urbanism is the most important environmental issue of the coming century, and that the challenges of sustainability can be met only by joining forces—witness interdisciplinary efforts such as LEED-ND. Meanwhile, transportation remains largely isolated, focusing on the details of systems efficiency while missing the big picture.

This book aims to reunite transportation with its sister fields to fill the largest remaining gap in urban sustainability strategies. Specifically, it seeks the following.

- First and foremost, this book is written to help non-transportation professionals understand transportation practice, so that they can more effectively guide it. Although grasping the details of highway engineering and bridge design requires years of technical study and professional licensing, the basic concepts of transportation are straightforward, if much misunderstood. Many elected officials and citizens are confused by the engineering jargon and black-box tools we use. Others are intimidated by our complex manuals, unaware that these tomes are often guidelines rather than standards, and that even our standards documents offer abundant flexibility.

- For planning practitioners, policymakers, and citizen activists, this book provides step-by-step instructions for implementing smart transportation concepts in their communities. For example, how does one actually implement Don Shoup-style parking reforms and address specific pitfalls? How can a downtown implement a productive circulator shuttle? On a main street, how should a local engineer allocate limited right-of-way among the competing needs of cyclists, through traffic, parked cars, sidewalk café tables, trees, and other demands? What are the most cost-effective tools for reducing the 30 percent of U.S. carbon dioxide emissions that come from transportation?

- For planning, design, transportation, and engineering students, this book offers an overview of where transportation fits in the overall study of urbanism.

- For transportation professionals, this book seeks to provide a better understanding of where our discipline fits in the larger context of sustainable urbanism. Transportation is not, after all, an end in itself, but rather a means by which communities achieve their larger goals. If we recognize that building roads and transit lines will never "solve the congestion problem," what is our role?

While this book has a clear perspective, and a goal of changing the industry itself and how it relates to other fields, it is not intended to be a polemical manifesto; others have already written those. It is not a work of academic research, though many academic texts are referenced throughout. It is also not an engineering or design manual; instead, it strives to help the reader understand how best to use existing manuals, and how to update local guidelines with a larger perspective (do not, under any circumstances, use this text alone to design your streets or transportation systems!). The aim of this book is to synthesize all of these objectives in language that general audiences will find accessible, and to offer implementation-focused guidance: Here is how to define your community's values as they relate to transportation; here is a summary of the current academic thinking in everyday language; and here is how best to use the various sets of guidelines and standards that exist, and to address the many contradictions and tensions among them. Simply put, this book is intended to demystify transportation for nonprofessionals and to act as a guidebook for avoiding the typical pitfalls of transportation for design and planning professionals.

In many ways, this book is a transitional document, aimed at helping auto-dependent cities and auto-oriented professionals find their way toward a post-carbon, health-oriented future (Figures 1-1 and 1-2). It is written with a North American perspective, so it will be of little use for cities such as Copenhagen, Freiburg, and the Dutch provincial capitals, all of which are already decades ahead of most places in the world. For the auto-dependent world, however, this book shows that it is not only possible to reduce automobile dependency, but also that doing so will help cities better achieve most of their goals—including the goal of making it easier to drive for those who need to do so.

Why Transportation?

Transportation is not an end in itself. Rather, it is an investment tool that cities use to help achieve their larger goals. Though most transportation planners and engineers focus their efforts on the efficient movement of people and goods, transportation touches all aspects of life in a city:

- **Economic development.** Although some politicians promote major transportation capital projects to "reduce congestion," in fact the prime motivation for most major transportation investments is economic development, because access drives real estate values. Places with excellent access by various modes of transportation tend to attract jobs and residences.

- **Quality of life.** In a poor economy, the leading citizen complaint is typically "jobs." But in a strong economy, "congestion" typically rises to the top of the list. Indeed, since Julius Caesar first tried to ban daytime use of wheeled carts to reduce traffic congestion in ancient Rome, congestion has been one of the greatest irritants in most great cities. Ancient Rome also suffered from another transport-related annoyance we hate today: noise, whether from freight deliveries,

Figures 1-1 and 1-2
Portland, Oregon, exhibits two key attributes of great places: pleasant places to walk and multimodal transportation options. *Source: Nelson\ Nygaard.*

airplane takeoffs, honking horns, or the hum of highways.[1] Done well, transport can be central to the quality of life of cities, and the source of both public enjoyment and tourism dollars. San Francisco's top tourist attractions include its cable cars, historic streetcars, and a spectacular Art Deco bridge.

- **Social equity.** Transportation policy is inevitably social policy, with specific winners and losers in any transportation investment decision. Projects to benefit higher-income motorists may harm lower-income pedestrians, whereas other investments may significantly expand mobility and job opportunities for those too young, old, or disabled to drive. Advocates for the winners in conventional transportation funding allocations sometimes argue that any adjustment in the current formula is "social engineering"—a criticism with some merit—but then, any public investment in transport, even and perhaps even especially those reinforcing the status quo, results in social impacts.

- **Public health.** Particularly for children and the elderly, there is no better indicator of overall public health (particularly measured by obesity, heart disease, and Type 2 diabetes) than rates of walking. Health science tells us that our bodies are uniquely designed for walking, and the proper functioning of many of our bodily systems requires a minimum of 20 minutes of sustained walking per day. Transport systems that do not make daily walking a pleasure for all citizens will tend to result in significant public health costs.

- **Ecological sustainability.** With 27 percent of United States greenhouse gas emissions[2] and 72 percent of U.S. petroleum use coming from transport,[3] transportation is inseparable from ecological policy—and, one might argue, from international relations.

The Big Picture: Mobility vs. Accessibility

To achieve cities' goals, transportation takes two key approaches: mobility and accessibility.

- **Mobility.** Mobility investments help us travel freely wherever we might want to go. Mobility investments are mainly capital facilities like an added highway lane, a rail extension, or a bicycle path. Mobility investments may also include measures that make the transportation system more efficient and productive, such as synchronizing traffic lights or improving transit speed, reliability, or frequency.

- **Accessibility.** Accessibility investments help us get the things we want and need. Rather than focusing on movement, accessibility may bring the product closer to the consumer. Locating a school and a retail main street in the middle of a neighborhood improves accessibility, reducing the need for people to move long distances and improving their choices. Accessibility investments include mixed-use zoning, delivery services, and high-speed Internet services that reduce the need for movement.

All transportation systems should invest in both mobility and accessibility, balancing the two. Systems that overemphasize mobility (Dubai, the exurbs of Los

Angeles County) tend to require excessive capital investment and result in dispersed land-use patterns. Mobility-oriented systems that emphasize only the automobile create all of the problems of automobile dependency addressed elsewhere in this book. Systems that overemphasize accessibility (monasteries, some resorts, some utopian communities) may result in close-knit communities isolated from the rest of the world, or levels of density too oppressive for most people. For more sustainable cities, the challenge for designers is to provide most of the needs of daily life within walking distance while maintaining the social and economic benefits of being tied to the larger region.

Structure of This Book

This book is in three sections:

In the first section (Chapters 2–4), the framework for the rest of the book is set. Chapter 2 introduces concepts of sustainability, including ecological, social, and economic elements of sustainability. Chapter 3 discusses issues of public health, which should be well understood by those who are interested in transportation planning. Chapter 4, "The City of the Future," sets out some broad principles by way of describing a vision for the future of our cities that is truly sustainable and healthy.

The second section (Chapters 5–10) provides practical advice for designing sustainable transport systems. Chapter 5, on streets, is an overview of the basic building blocks of all transportation systems; Chapters 6 through 10 address individual modes, including walking, biking, transit, and automobiles (which are addressed in separate chapters on cars and parking).

Finally, the third section (Chapters 10–15) covers other important topics in transportation planning: carsharing, transit station and station area design, transportation demand management, and performance measurement. These topics aim to help make the most efficient use of any transportation system. The final chapter of the book provides sources for more information.

Chapter 2

Sustainable Transportation

What Is Sustainability?

There is no common definition of *sustainability*, and certainly no standard definition for how it applies to transportation. Like so many once-powerful terms ("awesome," "unique"), *sustainability* is at risk of being rendered meaningless by the marketing industry, which uses the word to trumpet spectacularly unsustainable development projects from Las Vegas to Dubai, or defend the rapacious practices of the extraction industries in their shareholder reports. A good working definition of *sustainability* as it applies to cities was written by the Brundtland Commission of the United Nations in 1987: "sustainable development is development that meets the needs of the present without compromising the ability of future generations to meet their own needs."[1] Twenty-five hundred years earlier, the Buddha offered a more poetic definition, urging humans to build their household economy within nature's limits, as the bee treats the flower, gathering "nectar to turn into sweet honey without harming either the fragrance or the beauty of the flower."[2]

More complex definitions recognize that true sustainability must balance competing objectives, including the triple bottom line of "people, planet, and profit," or "equity, ecology, and economy." These definitions recognize that we cannot achieve an ecological objective, such as carbon neutrality, without simultaneously maintaining a stable society and productive economy (Figure 2-1). For example, though the use of petroleum—a polluting, finite resource—is

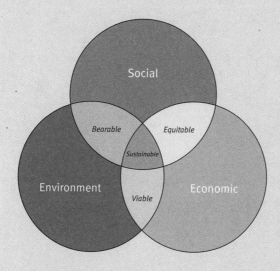

Figure 2-1
To determine whether your project is sustainable, you must analyze not only the triple-bottom-line issues of ecological, economic, and social sustainability, but also the intersections of these issues: Is your project viable, equitable, and bearable? Will it be loved?

unsustainable ecologically, an immediate ban on its use is unsustainable socially and economically. Today's economy is so dependent upon petroleum that a sudden ban would result in tremendous social upheaval and poverty, both of which would have dire ecological consequences. Sustainability, therefore, is never an end state, but a process of moving toward a better world.

Environmental Sustainability

Much of the current thinking about sustainability has its roots in the science of ecology. The word *ecology* is derived from the Greek, meaning "the study of the household"; in this case, the house being the entire planet, all things living upon and in it, and their myriad relationships. The word *economy* also comes from the Greek and means the "one who manages the household." Obviously, both the manager and the house are interdependent.

The science of ecology teaches us many principles that are useful in thinking about transportation.

WASTE AND LIMITS

In nature, there is no such thing as waste (Figure 2-2). In the wise words of children's author Taro Gomi, everyone does, in fact, poop.[3] In nature, however, one being's poop is another being's food. In a sustainable human food cycle, for example, human waste is eaten by fungi and bacteria, thereby enriching the soil, which is then "eaten" by plants, which then provide food for humans and the animals we

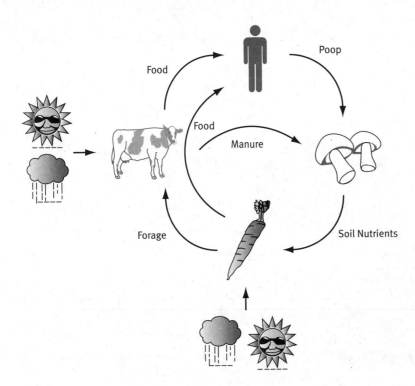

Figure 2-2
In the sustainable food cycle, there is no such thing as waste.

eat. The only inputs to this cycle are sunlight and water (usually the rain that the sun's energy enables). A sustainable cycle like this may run in perpetuity.

In a nonsustainable human food cycle, human excrement is seen as waste to be disposed of. To make up for the lost nutrients, chemical fertilizers must be applied to grow the plants and animals that support us. The sustainable cycle is broken, becoming dependent upon continued application of finite resources to support it. More importantly, the processes of disposing of human waste and producing and using chemical fertilizers generate compounds that are harmful to other natural systems (Figure 2-3). Waste, in the form of air, water, and soil pollution, builds up faster than biological systems can digest it. The result is a system that seems productive in the short run, meeting immediate human needs, but damages the larger natural systems and reduces future productivity.

In a sustainable transportation system, we need to make certain that biological systems have the capacity to process and digest any outputs. We must also ensure that biological systems can continue to support the inputs on which our transport systems rely. Sustainable systems must recognize and work within limits.

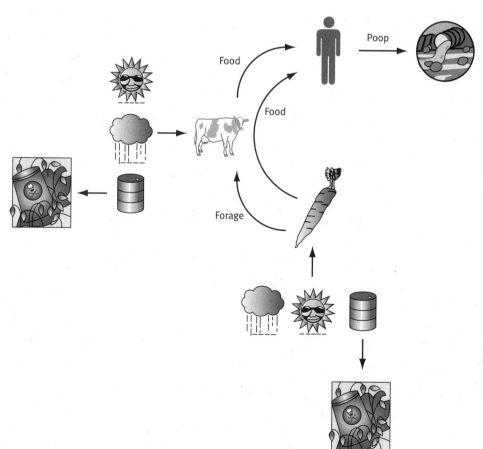

Figure 2-3
In a nonsustainable food cycle, the circle is broken, resulting in waste products that no being can use, which instead accumulate and destroy life.

The notion of limits is most easily understood (and ignored) by looking at water systems. For thousands of years, farms and cities have relied upon groundwater to grow crops and provide drinking water. If groundwater is extracted at a rate faster than it is replaced, the water table will drop. The result is that natural springs and aquifers will dry up, and the remaining groundwater may become increasingly saline and less able to support life. Thus, a farmer might pump a thousand acre-feet of groundwater a year and produce modest crop yields in perpetuity. But the same farmer could use ten thousand acre-feet of groundwater a year for ten years, producing spectacular yields until the water runs out or leaves a salty crust on the fields, effectively sterilizing the soil for decades. From the farmer's perspective, the latter option may be most profitable, provided there is another field to use once the first field must be abandoned.

In transportation, limits must be faced in many ways:

- Energy inputs, making sure that transport energy relies on renewable sources of energy
- Street capacity, using more space-efficient modes of transportation when capacity is constrained
- Finance, ensuring that there are sufficient resources to build and maintain our transportation infrastructure
- Politics, gaining broad support for transportation policies

COMPLEXITY, REDUNDANCY, AND ADAPTABILITY

Though we like to oversimplify natural systems with cartoonish diagrams (as in the preceding figures), nature is unfathomably complex, and in her complexity lies strength. As every farmer or gardener knows, nature abhors a monoculture. Plant too many tomatoes together in the same place for too long, and the tomatoes will do poorly, regardless of how much fertilizer and pesticide you add. In our gardens, crops do best when mixed and rotated. Overuse of pesticides may kill the tomato hornworms, but they also kill the parasitic wasps and other hornworm predators, clearing the way for a resistant hornworm to wipe out your crop.

Strategic redundancy is another key to survival in the natural world. If something is really important, nature produces more than one of it, because, as nature knows, stuff happens. Humans need only one kidney, a small but critical organ, but we have an extra in case one gets gored by a wildebeest. Plants produce an abundance of flowers, in case a few get munched by deer. Similarly, transportation networks that offer many routes are best able to withstand a fallen tree blocking a road, or a jackknifed big rig, or a utility replacement project.

Related to redundancy is adaptability. Humans have thrived on this planet in part because our digestive systems can accommodate a broad range of foods, and our opposable thumbs allow us to make clothing to accommodate a broad range of climates. Animals with a single food source are highly vulnerable; if their food source suffers from a new fungal disease or gets paved over for a new parking lot, they are done for. One reason for the extreme conservatism in transportation technologies—cars, trains, and ships are effectively the same technology as they were fifty years ago, with specific elements not much changed since the late eighteenth century—is that using the same technology as your neighbors offers ready adaptability. The Japanese imitated and improved upon German trains, which then allowed the Germans to imitate the Japanese improvements in their own technology. Technologically superior inventions often fail to catch on in the transportation world because their uniqueness makes them less adaptable, less able to take advantage of incremental improvements to conventional technologies.

Together, complexity, redundancy, and adaptability create something more simple and powerful: *choice*. The strongest cities in the world are those that offer a broad array of attractive transportation choices. Cities that rely entirely upon human-powered transport may be quaint, but they will be economically challenged and isolated due to the problems of handling freight and moving people and goods long distances. Cities that rely entirely upon automobile transportation may enjoy short-term economic benefits, but are vulnerable to petroleum price spikes and other resource constraints. In contrast, cities that offer many choices can be nimble enough to take advantage of economic trends, while reducing the risks of dependency on any one mode.

Social Sustainability

One shortcoming with strictly ecological or economic definitions of *sustainability* is that they are limited in their ability to inspire, turning over the measurement and envisioning of sustainability to scientists, economists, and other technocrats. Where does joy fit in these definitions? Belonging? The unique satisfaction we feel when among our family and friends?

To help expand our thinking about sustainability, we turn to American psychologist Abraham Maslow, who in 1943 developed his famous "hierarchy of needs."[4] Maslow described the highest level of human achievement as self-actualization, a position in which we can accept the facts of the situation and find creative, moral solutions to the problems that face us. To achieve self-actualization, though, we must first enjoy the esteem of others, and to enjoy the esteem of others, we must first have a sense of belonging. To have a sense of belonging, we must first have a sense of basic security, and our sense of security requires that we have our basic physiological needs met (Figure 2-4).

For your community to have a productive conversation about sustainability policies, in which the needs of future generations are considered, community members must be operating at the highest level of Maslow's pyramid. People who are worried about putting food on the table for their children today will have a hard time thinking about the needs of their great-grandchildren. People whose sense of social belonging extends no further than their three-car garage door will have a hard time finding sufficient shared purpose to work toward a stronger commonwealth.

Maslow's hierarchy is a useful tool for measuring the sustainability of your community's transportation investments, beyond simplistic measures like carbon dioxide (CO_2) emissions. If we plan our transit systems to offer only the most basic mobility to those who have no other choice—as do many bus systems today—voters will not see how transit helps them achieve their larger aspirations, and those voters will not pass tax measures to support better transit.

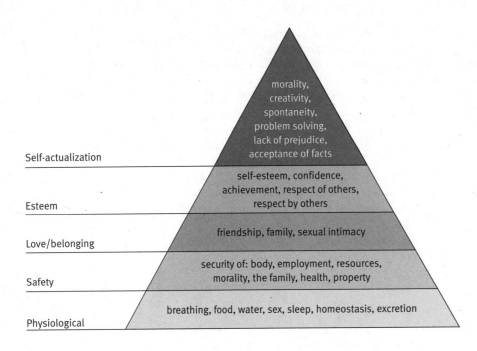

Figure 2-4
Maslow's famous hierarchy of needs reminds us that we cannot achieve ecological responsibility without first achieving a substantial degree of social sustainability.

A less hierarchical approach for explaining human needs and happiness is Clayton Alderfer's "ERG Theory," which reorganizes Maslow's divisions into three categories:[5]

● **Existence Needs**, merging Maslow's physiological and safety categories into all the basic needs of existence

● **Relatedness Needs**, merging social and external esteem

● **Growth Needs**, or self-esteem and self-actualization

Alderfer notes that as we move from meeting our Existence Needs toward meeting our Relatedness Needs, or from Relatedness to Growth, we experience satisfaction, but if we move in the other direction, we experience frustration. Moreover, if our Growth Needs are not being met, we redouble our efforts at Relatedness; for example, compensating for our lack of self-esteem by engaging in excessive sociability. If our Relatedness Needs are not being met, we compensate through excessive consumption. Alderfer's theory implies that oversized SUVs and McMansions are a reaction to our unmet Relatedness Needs.

What does all this mean for transportation? It means that sustainability is not just about emissions figures and energy cycles; it is also about human feelings. As planners, engineers, policymakers, and citizens interested in sustainability, our challenge is to push society toward the apex of Maslow's pyramid, so that we can see the impact of our actions today upon future generations, and also see the beauty of a more sustainable relationship with our planet and its resources. Indeed, *beauty* is more fundamental to sustainability than alternative-energy investments.

The human brain is hardwired to crave beauty, which unleashes the brain's dopamine reward circuitry in the same way as do sex, making money, and using cocaine.[6] Not only do we crave beauty, but we are also loyal defenders of it, as much with our beautiful spouses as we are with beautiful spaces. If something is beautiful, we will cherish it, maintain it, and continue to improve upon it. Maintaining and improving what you already have is almost always more sustainable than building something new.

The transportation world needs to learn from the makers of the iPod, the Coke bottle, or an Eames chair: when we see a bike, tram, or bus, we need to imagine it transforming us into our happier, sexier, more sociable, more glamorous selves. Strasbourg has done this with its gorgeous new trams. San Francisco's lovingly maintained array of antiquated transportation modes remains one of its biggest tourist attractions, and contributes significantly to the city's $7.85 billion tourism industry.[7] In the United States, People for Bikes has developed a sophisticated public service announcement campaign, which does not tell us to stop driving our cars because they're killing the planet. Instead, to upbeat music, a youthful narrator describes how riding her bike brings her a dozen small joys: "If I ride," she tells us with infectious promise, "people with thank me with flowers, and glaciers, and fireflies, and snow days off from school."[8]

Economic Sustainability

Conceptually, economic sustainability is easy: Does the activity or product generate more value than it costs? Can we continue paying for it over time? In practice, however, things are more complicated.

MARKET FAILURE

For almost every necessary commodity in our society—including food, clothing, and shelter—we use the free market to establish the price, ensure adequate production, and balance supply and demand. Transportation is the most prominent exception to this rule. For parking, roadways, and transit, the end user pays no more than a small fraction of the cost of providing those services. Instead, most transportation costs are bundled into the costs of other goods and services or borne by society at large. In part, this market dysfunction is the result of earlier technological limitations: How do you charge a fee on something as intangible as movement, without installing tollbooths everywhere? But the larger reason that movement remains unpriced is conscious economic and social policy.

Through the early twentieth century, most transportation was market driven. In the postwar era, the massive federal investment in automobile infrastructure, combined with more episodic investment in transit, resulted in a tremendous increase in mobility in America, which in turn produced systemic economic benefits. The rapid increase in per capita vehicle miles traveled also resulted in important improvements in quality of life for most Americans. These benefits, however, came at a price. Because people were not paying the full cost of their travel, the law of supply and demand kicked in, and resulted in scarcity—that is, congestion. What is more troubling, because travelers did not pay for the costs of noise and pollution, these problems had to be addressed through environmental regulation rather than pricing.

First described by Garrett Hardin, the "tragedy of the commons"[9] results when a group of individuals, each acting in their own self-interest, deplete a shared community resource because each individual has no incentive to use a sustainable share when the others can always use more than their share. The earliest example is a medieval sheep commons, which becomes overgrazed and useless because too many villagers graze their sheep there. The same effect occurs on the roadways, in the form of congestion, and in the skies, in the form of air pollution and CO_2 emissions. These are market failures, and they result from the absence of an appropriate price for the shared good.

VALUE CAPTURE

One reason that transportation did not require public subsidy in the early twentieth century was that it was not seen as an activity separate from land use. Rather, transportation investments were funded by real estate speculators who used transport to increase the value of land, which they then sold at a profit. Much rail investment in Japan is still done according to this model today.

In the United States, however, many transit agencies are expressly forbidden from capturing the value they create. Rather, public funds used to build new rail lines benefit lucky property owners along the way, with none of the value going back to the public that invested the funds. Key exceptions to this rule include the Portland and Seattle streetcars, which were funded largely using a self-imposed property tax by developers who owned land along the lines.

LIFE-CYCLE COSTING

Another routine economic failure in the transportation world is the firewall between transportation agencies' operating and capital budgets. Because of state and federal funding policies, it is generally much easier for transportation agencies to get capital dollars than operating dollars. As a result, rather than performing low-cost, ongoing street maintenance (an operating expense), many cities allow their street pavement to degrade to the point where the entire street has to be repaved (a capital expense), even though the latter costs an order of magnitude more money in the long run. Similarly, transit agencies may surround their rail stations with parking (capital expense, paid for by the federal government) rather than providing station access through a combination of feeder shuttles, bike and pedestrian improvements, and changes in land-use policy, even though it may be more cost-effective to use operating funds to invest in the latter.

FIXED VERSUS VARIABLE PRICING

To the extent that users do pay for transportation, many costs are fixed rather than variable. For example, purchasing a car, insuring it, and buying a monthly parking permit are all fixed expenses; they cost the same whether you drive the car one mile a day or two hundred. As a result, once these expenses are paid, the user has every incentive to get her money's worth, driving as much as possible to bring the per-mile cost down. If these costs were made variable, through carsharing programs, pay-as-you-go insurance, and hourly parking charges, people would drive significantly less.

Many of the costs of automobility are also "hidden," or paid on an automatic or infrequent basis rather than regularly at the point of use. Gas is a visible cost; we pay at the pump. However, vehicle and insurance payments, particularly those made automatically, are not part of the "everyday" cost of auto ownership and are thus often not included in conscious calculations of cost. Similarly, although repairs are inevitable, we tend not to budget for them, or be aware of just how much they can add up to over time. By contrast, many transit users pay on a per-use basis at the farebox.

Transportation and Environmental Sustainability

The starting point for achieving sustainability should be joy and beauty, but it is also necessary to understand the scientific facts of our current approach to transportation, and its impacts on ecological systems. Therefore, the relationship between transportation and environmental sustainability bears further exploration. Transport, after all, is driven largely by petroleum, and an array of air- and water-quality problems result from the extraction, processing, shipping, and consumption of petroleum. Transport also requires pavement, which creates stormwater absorption problems and agricultural land losses. Finally, transport affects human settlement patterns, which in turn have secondary ecological impacts.

ENERGY SOURCES

In the United States, about two-thirds of petroleum consumption is for transport[10] (Figure 2-5), so no analysis of sustainable transport is complete without examining this remarkable material.

Petroleum is a mix of hydrocarbons and other compounds, typically formed by the decay of algae and other microscopic organisms that were subjected to various geologic processes over millions of years.[11] Chemically, hydrocarbons are similar to carbohydrates, like sugars and fat. Both rely on the energy-intensive molecular bond between carbon and hydrogen atoms—bonds that were originally established largely through photosynthesis.

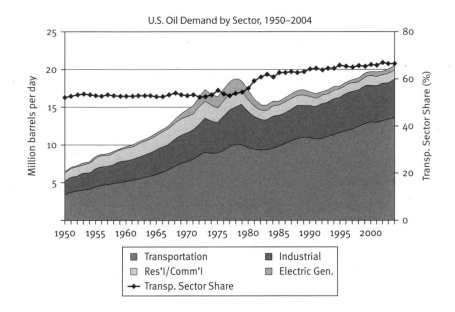

Figure 2-5
About two-thirds of U.S. petroleum consumption is used for transport.
Source: Annual Energy Review, Tables 5.12a and 5.12b, U.S. Energy Information Administration.

As you may recall from high-school chemistry, *photosynthesis* is the process by which plants use sunlight to convert carbon dioxide plus water into stored energy plus oxygen. The equation is:

$$6CO_2 \quad + \quad 6H_2O \quad \rightarrow \quad C_6H_{12}O_6 \quad + \quad 6O_2$$

| Carbon Dioxide | Water | Sunlight | Sugar | Oxygen |

Under the earth (especially under pressure) over long periods of time, these plant sugars are converted to hydrocarbons such as propane. When propane is heated in the presence of oxygen, it burns and releases energy in various forms, including heat and the expansion of steam. The equation is:

$$C_3H_8 + 5O_2 \rightarrow 4H_2O + 3CO_2 + Energy$$

Hydrocarbons are an extremely useful form of energy for transport for several reasons. Many are liquid at the temperatures found where most humans live, making the hydrocarbons easy to pump and ship. They are very stable compared to other energy sources. Most importantly, they have extraordinary energy density, creating a lot of propulsion with little volume or mass. Table 2-1 examines

Table 2-1: Energy by Mass and Volume of Common Fuels

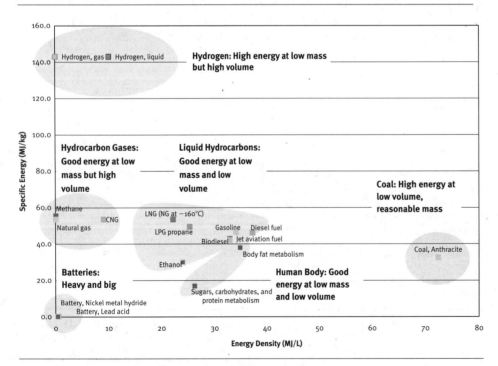

Specific references available at http://en.wikipedia.org/wiki/Energy_density.

a variety of common transport fuels and their *specific energy* (energy per unit of mass), measured in terms of megajoules per kilogram; and their *energy density* (energy stored per unit of volume), measured in megajoules per liter. In other words, the table tells us how much energy is available by mass and volume. Notice that gasoline and diesel fuel can move a heavy car a long distance on a modestly sized fuel tank. This energy density is what makes it sensible to spend tremendous amounts of energy refining petroleum and moving it halfway around the world to burn. Current battery-powered cars, in contrast, require such massive batteries that more energy is consumed moving the battery itself than moving the occupants of the car. Also notice why coal-powered locomotives and steamships transformed nineteenth-century economies, before the negative effects of coal burning reduced its use. One of the greatest challenges of the alternative energy movement is to identify fuels to replace gasoline that have a comparable energy density and gasoline's relative safety and ease of shipment. So far, few have even come close.

The chart also points out the remarkable efficiency of human metabolism, as we burn fat and sugars to walk or bicycle. If the food we eat to create those body fats and sugars derives primarily from plants grown locally, then the embodied energy density—counting all the energy it takes to extract, process, ship, and consume the energy source—of metabolized energy can dwarf that of petroleum.

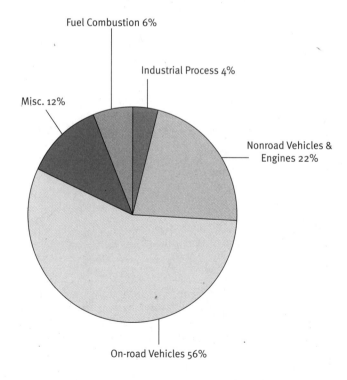

Fuel Combustion 6%

Industrial Process 4%

Misc. 12%

Nonroad Vehicles & Engines 22%

On-road Vehicles 56%

Figure 2-6
U.S. carbon monoxide emissions sources, 2002. *Source: U.S. Environmental Protection Agency.*

IMPACTS

AIR POLLUTION

Transportation results in a toxic blast of emissions, some of the most problematic of which include:

Carbon monoxide (CO), a colorless, odorless gas. According to the U.S. EPA,[12] motor-vehicle exhaust contributes about 60 percent of all CO emissions nationwide (Figure 2-6).

Nitrogen oxides (NOx), highly reactive gases that help form ozone. Nitrogen dioxide (NO_2) is a key cause of brown smog in urban areas.

Ozone (O_3), a gas composed of three oxygen atoms. It is a colorless compound that has an electric-discharge-type odor. It is a unique criteria pollutant in that it is exclusively a secondary pollutant. It is not usually emitted directly into the air, but at ground level is created by a chemical reaction between oxides of nitrogen (NO_x) and volatile organic compounds (VOCs) in the presence of heat and sunlight. The concentration of ozone in a given locality is influenced by many factors, including the concentration of NO_2 and VOCs in the area, the intensity of the sunlight, and the local weather conditions. Ozone and the chemicals that react to form it can be carried hundreds of miles from their origins, causing air pollution over wide regions.

Ozone has the same chemical structure whether it occurs miles above the earth or at ground level, and can be beneficial or harmful depending on its location in the atmosphere. "Good" ozone occurs naturally in the stratosphere and forms a layer that protects life on earth from the sun's harmful rays (ultraviolet radiation). In the earth's lower atmosphere, or troposphere, ground-level ozone is considered "bad." Ozone is the most prevalent chemical found in photochemical air pollution, or smog.

WATER POLLUTION

Just as transportation generates harmful air pollution, so does it result in a toxic stew of water pollution. In his publication, *Transportation Cost and Benefit Analysis II – Water Pollution,* Todd Litman summarized the key impacts of transport on water:[13]

- An estimated 46 percent of U.S. vehicles leak hazardous fluids, including crankcase oil; transmission, hydraulic, and brake fluid; and antifreeze.[14]

- 180 million gallons of lubricating oils are disposed of improperly onto the ground or into sewers.[15]

- Runoff from roads and parking lots has a high concentration of toxic metals, suspended solids, and hydrocarbons, which originate largely from automobiles.[16]

- Road de-icing salts cause significant environmental and material damage.[17]

- Roadside vegetation control is a major source of herbicide dispersal.

- Roads and parking facilities have major hydrologic impacts. They concentrate stormwater, causing increased flooding, scouring, and siltation; reduce surface and groundwater recharge, which lowers dry-season flows; and create physical barriers to fish movement.[18]

The costs of these pollution impacts and the costs of mitigating them are not insignificant. In Washington State, which has some of the most stringent water pollution control requirements in the world (due in part to its concerns about fish habitat), the state Department of Transportation estimates the costs of meeting these requirements at between $75 million to $220 million a year, or 0.2¢ to 0.5¢ per vehicle mile traveled.[19]

STORMWATER RUNOFF

When buildings and pavement cover the ground, rainfall is no longer able to percolate into the soil, and the result can be not only increased water pollution, but also flooding. One approach used in many cities is to require detention or retention basins for every development; essentially, this means digging a big hole in the ground next to each building so that rainwater from the roof and pavement can collect in the hole and slowly be absorbed into the groundwater. A more sustainable approach, however, is to design cities with less pavement.

In *Using Smart Growth Techniques as Stormwater Best Management Practices,*[20] the U.S. Environmental Protection Agency found that as density increases, so does the percent of impervious surface: Manhattan has a lot more concrete per acre than a leafy suburb. What's more important, however, is that as density increases, impervious surface *per household* drops significantly, largely because the amount of roadway per household shrinks (Figures 2-7 and 2-8). A community of 80,000 residents at 8 units per acre generates 396 million cubic feet of stormwater runoff a year, whereas the same community at 1 unit per acre generates 1.5 billion cubic feet—nearly a quadrupling of runoff.

GREENHOUSE GASES

Finally, it is important to recognize that transportation is a primary contributor to greenhouse gas emissions; in many locations, it is the biggest single contributor. Greenhouse gases consist of methane, nitrous oxide, hydrofluorocarbons, and other compounds, but because carbon dioxide (CO_2) contributes 85 percent of the warming capacity of all greenhouse gases, it gets the most attention.

Transport's share of CO_2 emissions varies largely by how a region handles electricity generation and heating. In locations that burn coal and other dirty fuels for electricity, electrical generation is the biggest CO_2 contributor. In places where there is low-carbon electricity, like hydropower, wind, and nuclear, transport accounts for by far the biggest slice of the pie.

Figure 2-9 shows California's CO_2 emissions, which are fairly typical among U.S. states. There, nearly 40 percent of total CO_2 emissions are from transportation. More importantly, of the transportation emissions, nearly three-quarters are from personal driving.

In the greenhouse gas reduction world, much attention has been paid to green buildings, evidenced by the development of elaborate rating and awards systems. Although green buildings programs are valuable and necessary, they are limited in two key ways:

- There is tremendous inertia in the built environment. In most cities, the vast majority of buildings that will exist fifty years from now are already here today.

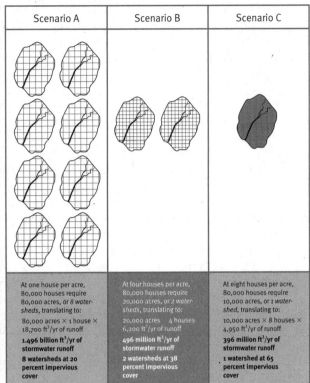

▲ Figures 2-7 and 2-8
Stormwater runoff and density at the site and community levels. *Source: U.S. Environmental Protection Agency.*

Scenario A — 1 house/acre
Impervious cover = 20 percent
Total runoff (18,700 ft³/yr × 8 acres) = 149,600 ft³/yr
Runoff/house = 18,700 ft³/yr

Scenario B — 4 houses/acre
Impervious cover = 38 percent
Total runoff (24,800 ft³/yr × 2 acres) = 49,600 ft³/yr
Runoff/house = 6,200 ft³/yr

Scenario C — 8 houses/acre
Impervious cover = 65 percent
Total runoff = 39,600 ft³/yr
Runoff/house = 4,950 ft³/yr

Scenario A	Scenario B	Scenario C
At one house per acre, 80,000 houses require 80,000 acres, or *8 watersheds*, translating to: 80,000 acres × 1 house × 18,700 ft³/yr of runoff **1.496 billion ft³/yr of stormwater runoff** **8 watersheds at 20 percent impervious cover**	At four houses per acre, 80,000 houses require 20,000 acres, or *2 watersheds*, translating to: 20,000 acres × 4 houses × 6,200 ft³/yr of runoff **496 million ft³/yr of stormwater runoff** **2 watersheds at 38 percent impervious cover**	At eight houses per acre, 80,000 houses require 10,000 acres, or *1 watershed*, translating to: 10,000 acres × 8 houses × 4,950 ft³/yr of runoff **396 million ft³/yr of stormwater runoff** **1 watershed at 65 percent impervious cover**

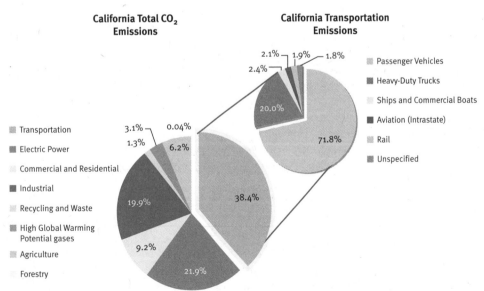

California Total CO$_2$ Emissions

- Transportation — 38.4%
- Electric Power — 21.9%
- Commercial and Residential — 9.2%
- Industrial — 19.9%
- Recycling and Waste — 6.2%
- High Global Warming Potential gases — 1.3%
- Agriculture — 3.1%
- Forestry — 0.04%

California Transportation Emissions

- Passenger Vehicles — 71.8%
- Heavy-Duty Trucks — 20.0%
- Ships and Commercial Boats — 2.4%
- Aviation (Intrastate) — 2.1%
- Rail — 1.9%
- Unspecified — 1.8%

◀ Figure 2-9
Specific California CO$_2$ emissions by source. *Source: 2006 California Air Resources Board Greenhouse Gas Inventory.*

- More importantly, the greenest building in a bad location produces more CO_2 than a leaky old building in a good location. This is because the CO_2 costs of driving to an isolated building in an auto-dependent community outweigh the CO_2 benefits of the green technology building investments.

The Jonathan Rose Companies have summarized the latter point in two simple graphs, shown in Figures 2-10 and 2-11. Figure 2-10 shows how a "green" detached suburban house can perform significantly better than a conventional

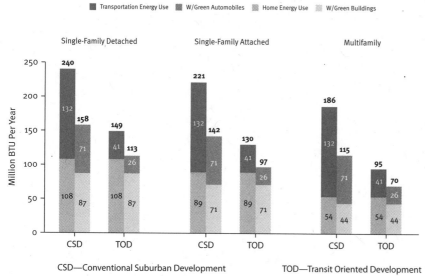

Location Efficiency: Household and Transportation Energy Use by Location

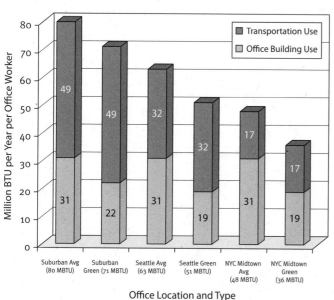

◀ **Figures 2-10 and 2-11**
Transportation and home energy use, by location. *Source: Jonathan Rose Companies.*

suburban house, but even the green suburban house (because of its larger size and exposed walls) performs worse than a conventional urban multifamily house, where shared walls and smaller floorplates mean less energy consumption. More importantly, in auto-dependent locations, the energy cost of getting to the building exceeds the energy the building itself uses. Figure 2-11 shows the same factors, but for office buildings.

Chapter 3

Transportation and Public Health

Over the past decade, some of the most powerful advocates for sustainable transportation have emerged from the health professions, who saw a hundred years of progress in improved medical techniques being undone by the sedentary lifestyles made possible (and in some cases, *required*) by the automobile. Much of the health professionals' power flows from their unassailable data, gathered over years of tracking the relationship between transportation and health in thousands of studies.

The Human Body

On Our Own Two Feet

Any discussion of the relationship between transportation and health should start with the human body. Since *Homo erectus* first stood up straight on her own two feet about 1.8 million years ago, our bodies have been defined by our unusual form of walking. For most of our history, we kept our bodies on the move much of the day, hunting, gathering, and making regular nomadic voyages. All of our bodily systems—digestion, healing, immunity, thinking—are designed to function optimally while walking. Among our distant ancestors, those who stopped walking became a significant burden to their tribe, so it's no wonder our bodily systems start slowing down as we stop walking. Indeed, the minute we stop walking, we start dying. Among older adults, the mortality rate of those who walk less than a mile a day is nearly twice that of those who walk more than two miles.[1]

Innumerable studies show a positive correlation between walking and an array of health benefits. Googling "walking" and "mortality" generates about 2 million results. In fact, after major surgery, one of the first tasks nurses force patients to do is shuffle down the hall in a flimsy gown, trailing the IV pole. Taking things further, the Japanese have long promoted "Manpo-kei" or "ten thousand steps a day" as the foundation of longevity and fitness, and this program has spread around the world. Adopting the "ten thousand steps" strategy requires only the purchase of a pedometer and building walking into all aspects of your daily life.

Don't Shoot 'Til You See the Whites of His Eyes

Another unique feature of the human body is our eyes. First, they are long in the horizontal direction, making it easy for us to look from side to side and enabling peripheral vision from both sides; we have to move our heads to look up. More importantly, the sclera (the white of the

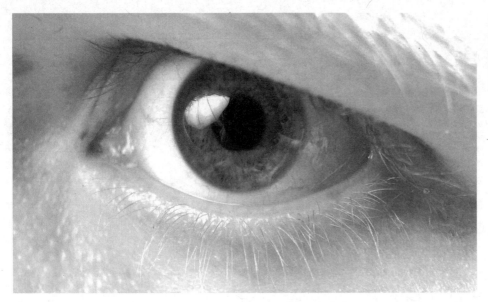

Figure 3-1
The human eye is unique in its sharp contrast between the sclera (white) and the iris. *Source: Tobias Hoffman (used under Creative Commons license: http://creativecommons.org/licenses/by-sa/2.0/).*

eye) is huge, and it has the greatest contrast of any mammal with the adjacent iris (Figure 3-1). This iris–sclera contrast is important, because it allows us to get a huge amount of social information by looking others in the eye.[2]

While walking, we constantly send signals with our eyes to the other humans around us. We establish social status with a haughty gaze or submissive downcast. We flirt. We appreciate and scold, bolstering the social contract. For New Yorkers, a firmly set, straight-ahead focus tells more casual strollers to get out of the way. On a Paris street, the right glance invites conversation.

In his book *Cities for People*,[3] Jan Gehl describes how the physical limitations of the human eye define the social interactions that occur in urban spaces (Figure 3-2). Specifically:

- At distances of 1,000 to 1,600 feet (about a quarter of a mile, or about three city blocks), we can generally identify people as human, as opposed to animals or other shapes.

- At around 300 feet, we can identify gender and estimate age. According to Gehl, this is a critical dimension, the maximum distance at which humans can feel comfortable and engaged in their space. Public squares should generally not be larger than 300 feet by 300 feet, and those that are bigger should be subdivided into more manageable "rooms."

- At 160 to 230 feet (less than a block), we can see hair color and body language and generally identify a person we know. We can also hear shouts for help at this distance.

- In theaters and opera houses around the world, 115 feet is the maximum distance at which we can perceive emotion, with the experience increasing greatly in intensity in seats closer to the stage—hence, the higher ticket prices.

Figure 3-2
Jan Gehl demonstrates how much
information we get from the human
face up close, and how little we
recognize as distance grows. *Source:
Jan Gehl/Gehl Architects.*

- At 70 to 80 feet (the distance from your front lawn to your across-the-street neighbor's), we can read facial expressions and understand dominant emotions. We can also shout to be heard, like yelling "Hello!" Gehl warns that very little of social interest in the city happens at distances greater than 80 feet. Within this 80-foot boundary, however, urban magic happens, and the intensity of human experience increases geometrically as distances shrink below 80 feet.

- Actual conversation is not possible until 23 feet, the length of a parking space.

- Intimate conversation happens at about a foot and a half, at which point all of our senses are also fully engaged in human interaction.

The scale limitations of the eye are in direct conflict with the requirements of the automobile. First, the automobile's geometry forces city planners to create streets and spaces that violate our basic habitat needs, with street dimensions starting at our maximum social limits. It is no wonder Americans spend billions a year visiting foreign countries and theme parks that offer a different scale experience. Leaving aside Canada and Mexico, the most visited international destinations for Americans are, in order, the United Kingdom, Italy, France, Germany, and Japan,[4] also among the most urbanized places in the world, but places full of the streets and squares we love. Why do Americans love the skinny streets and intimate squares of Venice? Because we are social primates, and our senses evolved make us most engaged at the scales Venice offers—a scale that is lost in automobile-dependent places (Figure 3-3).

Figure 3-3
Cities built before the car became ubiquitous offer a scale appealing to the human eye. *Source: Nelson\ Nygaard.*

Does This McMansion Make Me Look Fat?

Environments that discourage walking foster significant human health impacts, directly and indirectly. Direct impacts include the 34,000 Americans who are killed and over 2 million who are maimed by automobiles every year.[5] Of greater concern are the indirect impacts, including obesity and cardiovascular disease. Too much driving is not the sole cause of these health problems, but the correlations are startling.

The Centers for Disease Control (CDC) has compiled a variety of disturbing statistics, tracing worsening health in the United States. Obesity was not a serious problem in the 1980s and early 1990s, but reached epidemic proportions in the past decade, with 36 percent of Americans classified as overweight and 28 percent classified as clinically obese. The same body of data show how a steady reduction in regular physical activity correlates strongly with the increase in obesity.[6]

Obesity and cardiovascular ailments are not the only health problems that result from excess driving. Driving also creates air pollution, and from air pollution come other problems, including lung cancer and asthma. As reported by Dr. Michael Friedman and his colleagues in the *Journal of the American Medical Association*,[7] acute care visits for children's asthma dropped significantly during the Olympic period, when Atlanta's typically severe traffic also dropped dramatically. During the same time period, children's hospital visits for other conditions stayed the same.

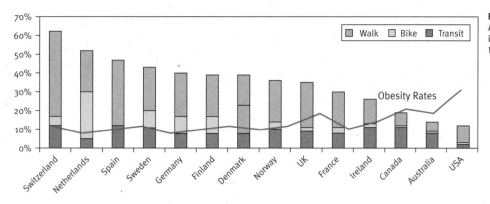

Figure 3-4
As walking decreases, obesity increases. *Source: Todd Litman, Victoria Transport Policy Institute.*

Comparing the obesity rates and primary travel modes of industrialized countries, Dr. David Bassett noted the strong correlation between rates of driving and rates of obesity (Figure 3-4).[8]

This data set indicates that transportation mode split is highly variable even among economically developed countries, and national obesity rates are inversely related to rates of active transportation (walking and cycling).

Danger, Will Robinson!

All told, nearly half of the years knocked off American lives are due to excess driving, either directly as a result of crashes, or indirectly through pollution exposure or sedentary lives. Todd Litman summarized the data available from the National Center for Injury Prevention and Control's 2009 data (see Figure 3-5).[9] Although the newspaper headlines may be filled with images of the victims of gunshots, tornadoes, fires, plane crashes, and shark attacks, driving is by far the most dangerous activity that most Americans will ever engage in.

These dangers are not only disturbing, but also expensive. In 2010, the University of California–San Francisco calculated the direct medical costs of treating pedestrians injured in auto crashes at San Francisco's public health hospital (see Table 3-1).[10] Over the five-year study period, the public hospitalization cost averaged $15 million a year, more than the city was spending on injury prevention, and excluding any social costs such as lost wages.

Table 3-1: Costs of Treating Pedestrian Injuries, San Francisco General Hospital

Collision Year	Total Cost (2008 Dollars)	2008 Population	Cost Per Capita
2004	$11,257,143.03	840,462	$13.39
2005	$13,480,653.08	840,462	$16.04
2006	$16,574,112.85	840,462	$19.72
2007	$17,673,296.91	840,462	$21.03
2008	$15,358,023.35	840,462	$18.27
All Years	$74,343,229.22	840,462	$88.46

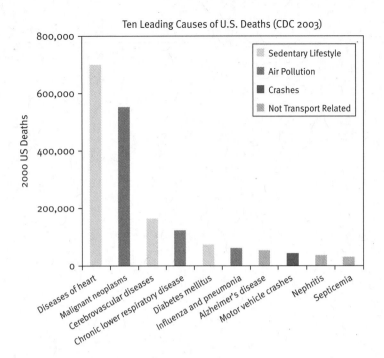

Ten Leading Causes of U.S. Deaths (CDC 2003)

Legend:
- Sedentary Lifestyle
- Air Pollution
- Crashes
- Not Transport Related

Y-axis: 2000 US Deaths (0 to 800,000)

X-axis categories: Diseases of heart, Malignant neoplasms, Cerebrovascular diseases, Chronic lower respiratory disease, Diabetes mellitus, Influenza and pneumonia, Alzheimer's disease, Motor vehicle crashes, Nephritis, Septicemia

Figure 3-5
Too much driving and too little walking are Americans' biggest health problems. *Source: Todd Litman, Victoria Policy Institute.*

Anger, Will Robinson!

Driving not only makes our bodies sick, but also makes our minds sick. The unique type of anger associated with driving even has its own clinical diagnosis: *road rage*, a type of "Intermittent Explosive Disorder" or IED.

Dr. Mark Fenske, Associate Professor of Neuroscience and Applied Cognitive Science at the University of Guelph, has studied the effects of road rage on brain chemistry.[11] Dr. Fenske notes that driving can have negative impacts on three key brain centers:

- The amygdalae, a pair of almond-shaped neuron centers in each half of the brain, are responsible for triggering the fight-or-flight response. Continued over-activation of these centers by, say, daily stressful driving, "can alter the physical shape and mode of functioning of these structures, which is often accompanied by increased anxiety."

- The nearby hippocampus, which helps turn experience into memory, is especially vulnerable to stress.

- Stress also affects the prefrontal cortex, damaging both memory and the ability to differentiate between good and bad, predict outcomes, and control one's antiso-cial tendencies.

Together, too much driving will make us anxious and stupid. These symptoms persist after we stop driving, too; after repeated exposure to these stressors, our brains are permanently altered and impaired.

The National Highway Traffic Safety Administration (NHTSA), which spends most of its time studying crash-test dummies and child safety seats, recognizes that road rage and aggressive driving are serious problems, directly contributing to killing about 1,800 people a year.[12] The NHTSA, presumably under pressure to "do something" about road rage, produced a handy brochure[13] that advises angry drivers to:

- **"Relax.** Tune the radio to your favorite relaxing music. Music can calm your nerves and help you to enjoy your time in the car."
- **"Avoid Eye Contact.** Eye contact can sometimes enrage an aggressive driver."

Avoid eye contact? Why would the federal government advise us to avoid eye contact with other drivers when we need more communication on the road, not less? Tom Vanderbilt, in his remarkable book *Traffic: Why We Drive the Way We Do,* eloquently describes how the evolutionary biology that works so well in our interactions on foot fails us on the road. Vanderbilt's interviews with UCLA biology professor Jay Phelan explain how our ancestral adaptations serve us poorly in our cars. Phelan explains the origins of "reciprocal altruism," necessary in hunter-gatherer societies with scarce resources: "You scratch my back, I'll scratch yours; we each do it because we think it will benefit us 'down the road.'"[14] In a car, however, speed, distance, and the concealing shell of the vehicle all hamper a brain attuned to nonverbal, body-language signals. When a motorist kindly lets us merge into a lane in front of him, our brain encodes the action as "the beginning of a long-term reciprocal relationship." In contrast, when someone unintentionally violates our sense of order on the highway, we may fly into a rage far out of proportion to the offense, largely because of the deep frustration we feel when our social messages are not heard, combined with the anonymity and easy escape offered by the car. In short, we avoid eye contact while driving, because speed and distance make it too easy to misinterpret the signals, and for a casual glance to be taken as aggressive posturing.

Health and Equity

At the root of these health and safety problems are state and federal funding formulas that prioritize driving over other modes, and that achieve safety goals through additional armoring—of cars, not of pedestrians. In fact, less than 1.5 percent of federal transportation funds have been spent on pedestrians and bicyclists under SAFETEA-LU ("Safe Accountable Flexible Efficient Transportation Equity Act: A Legacy for Users"[15]) even though pedestrians comprise 11.5 percent of all traffic deaths and trips made on foot account for almost 9 percent of all trips (Figure 3-6). Minority communities, children, and the elderly disproportionately bear the brunt of this inequitable investment.

Walkable neighborhoods will be increasingly important as the baby boomers continue to age—the coming "silver tsunami"—and more of the U.S. population becomes unable to drive and yet find themselves living in places that were not designed for walking. How do these folks get around? Unlike previous generations,

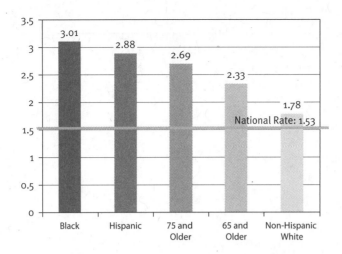

Figure 3-6
Pedestrian fatality rate per 100,000
persons. *Source: NHTSA, adapted by
Surface Transportation Policy Project
and Transportation for America in
Dangerous by Design, 2009.*

who accepted being shipped off to Shady Acres to live their last years in lonely
irrelevancy, older adults today are demanding full participation in society, as
demonstrated by ample research by their powerful lobbying group, the American
Association of Retired Persons (AARP).

AARP calculated that adults age 45 and over comprised 58 percent of the
voter turnout in the 2008 general election, and about two-thirds of the 2010
midterm elections. As that percentage grows (Figure 3-7), older adults will have
tremendous political power, not just in the United States but also throughout the
industrialized world.[16]

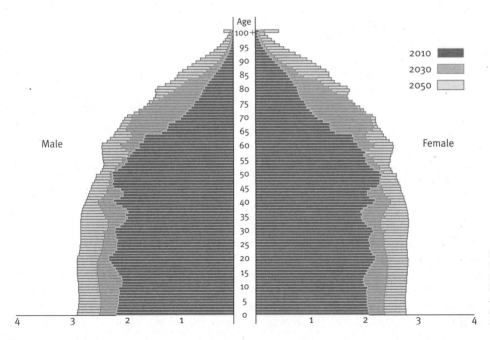

Figure 3-7
U.S. population projections by age,
2010–2050. Note the big increase
in adults over the age of 65 in 2030.
*Source: United States Population
Projections: 2000 to 2050 (U.S. Census
Bureau, 2008).*

For children, the situation is even worse. According to the U.S. Federal Highway Administration, about half of all students in 1969 walked or bicycled to school.[17] In 2010, however, fewer than 15 percent of all school trips were made by walking or bicycling; one-quarter were made on a school bus, and more than half of all children arrived at school in private automobiles.

Both children's health and their sense of independence are harmed by automobile dependency. Children who must be chauffeured by their parents miss considerable informal exploration of the world around them. More importantly, walking to school enhances academic performance, particularly when it comes to the stress of exams.[18]

Driving and Social Health

In his seminal book, *Livable Streets*, Donald Appleyard described how residents' social lives varied depending on the amount of traffic on their street.[19] Conducting detailed surveys of residents of three San Francisco streets, physically identical but with different traffic levels, Appleyard found:

- On the lightly trafficked street (200 vehicles in the peak hour), residents had an average of 3.0 friends and 6.3 acquaintances on their block. This street "was a closely knit community whose residents made full use of the street … Front steps were used for sitting and chatting, sidewalks for children playing … and the roadway by children and teenagers for more active games like football."[20]

- On the medium trafficked street (550 vehicles in the peak hour), residents had an average of 1.3 friends and 4.1 acquaintances on their block. On this street, "most activity was confined to the sidewalks where a finely sensed boundary separated pedestrians from traffic."[21]

- On the heavily trafficked street (1,900 vehicles in the peak hour), residents had an average of only 0.9 friends and 3.1 acquaintances on their block. This street "had little or no sidewalk activity and was used solely as a corridor between the sanctuary of individual homes and the outside world. Residents kept very much to themselves."[22]

In the twenty-first century, when social and business success is more about social networks than ever before, residents of heavily trafficked streets are at a significant disadvantage. More importantly, residents of high-traffic streets are much less likely to be engaged in their communities, fighting for community improvements and seeking a sustainable future for their city.

Transportation and Trust

Although the negative effects of automobile dependency on brain chemistry are disturbing, transportation also creates powerfully positive effects on the brain. Among the more socially powerful brain chemicals, oxytocin is perhaps at the top of the list, with academic research on it beginning to spill over into public policy.[23]

In *The Oxytocin Factor,* Dr. Kerstin Uvnas Moberg explains the primary functions of oxytocin:[24]

- In women, it is an essential component of breastfeeding and childbirth.

- In all mammals, it helps shut down the fear, anxiety, and social-control centers of the brain to allow for orgasm.

- It increases pair bonding and maternal attachment.

- It lowers blood pressure and other stress-related responses in the brain, contributing to overall health and healing.

- Most interestingly, it increases positive social behavior such as friendliness and trust.

In other words, this neuropeptide released by the pituitary gland is not only central to sex, but is also the biological basis for certain types of social trust (Figure 3-8). Trust is an essential element of family structure, friendship, politics, and business negotiations. Dr. Michael Kosfeld of the University of Tilburg points out: "In the absence of trust among trading partners, market transactions break down. In the absence of trust in a country's institutions and leaders, political legitimacy breaks down. Much recent evidence indicates that trust contributes to economic, political and social success. . . . Oxytocin [is] a biological basis of prosocial approach behavior."[25]

So, what releases oxytocin in our brains? Touch, sex, and breastfeeding, most prominently. But so does exercise, such as walking, cycling, and swimming. Doctors Jo Barton and Jules Pretty have researched how outdoor exercise affects oxytocin production,[26] and how even short periods of outdoor exercise lead to higher self-esteem and better mood. Interestingly, the greatest effects were found when exercising outdoors near water. In other words, though the encouragement of more frequent orgasms perhaps exceeds the rightful scope of government, governments can foster greater levels of trust and a stronger social contract by designing cities where outdoor walking, cycling, and swimming can be a regular part of daily life.

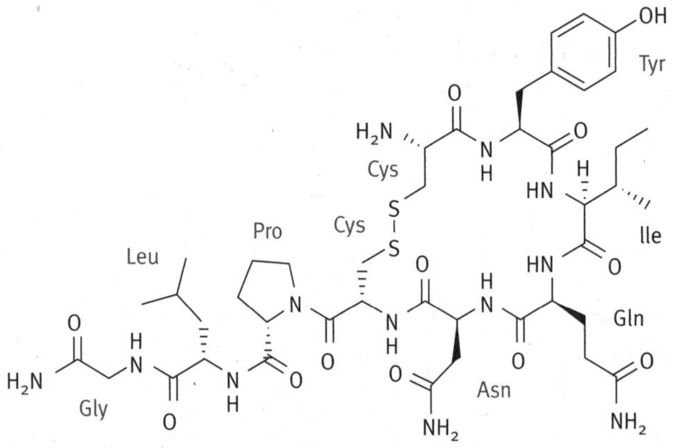

Figure 3-8
The oxytocin molecule is the biological basis for trust.

Conclusions

It is clear that moderate amounts of driving at moderate speeds do not create deleterious health impacts. Nevertheless, the data from the medical professions unequivocally show that too much driving does make us:

- Fat
- Sick
- Die early
- Poor
- Stupid
- Angry
- Mistrustful

At the same time, regular daily walking makes us:

- Fitter
- Smarter
- Able to handle complex reasoning
- Sexier
- More loving
- More trustful

It makes one wonder what would happen to our transportation priorities if public health outcomes were factored into transportation decisionmaking. Why don't we compare health outcomes against auto Level of Service (LOS) when evaluating the success of a street? Why aren't health outcomes a factor in prioritizing transportation spending?

Chapter 4
The City of the Future

Yesterday's Tomorrowland

One of the greatest obstacles for advocates of sustainable cities is the absence of a commonly held, compelling vision of the city of the future. If asked to create a picture of their city of the future, most people will inevitably draw from images resembling those from the 1933, 1939, and 1964 World's Fairs, or from the 1962–1963 Hanna-Barbera cartoon, *The Jetsons*: buildings on stilts, upward-thrusting architecture, roads and paths on many levels, and various bulbous transport devices that make a satisfying "whoosh" sound.

It is difficult to understate the impact these World's Fairs had on American culture, particularly during the Great Depression. The 1933 World's Fair was attended by nearly 49 million people at a time when the entire U.S. population was only 126 million. World's Fairs have always been largely corporate exhibitions, showcasing the latest technologies from major manufacturers, covering agriculture, consumer appliances, and (most prominently) transportation. The biggest attractions at these three fairs were their transportation and city-of-the-future exhibits; among these exhibits the biggest hit was "Futurama," sponsored by General Motors. According to General Motors' press release following the 1964–1965 fair, Futurama attracted more than 29 million visitors, setting the attendance record for any industrial exhibit at any World's Fair and eclipsing the 24 million visitors to GM's earlier "Highways and Horizons" exhibit at the 1939–1940 New York World's Fair.[1]

To understand how compelling Futurama was, search for "futurama" and "world's fair" on YouTube and watch the videos from 1939 and 1964. Aerodynamically designed cars glide through gleaming white interchanges. Pedestrians walk happily along skybridges, protected from the traffic below. Towers connect to elevated plazas filled with greenery. Cars, complete with tiny GM logos, are everywhere, but of course there is no traffic congestion. Today's audiences may find these images to be quaint and familiar—in part, because so much of the postwar world was shaped by them—but to visitors in 1939 through 1965, they were radical and thrilling.

As Futurama drove the design of urban renewal projects in cities around the world, designers began to notice problems not evident in the shiny 1:100 scale models. One was a problem of success. While the massive investment in superhighways and parking lots promised to eliminate congestion and create an easy-motoring utopia, the speed, convenience, and glamour of the car proved exceedingly popular. So many people bought cars, and affordable new houses in auto-dependent locations, that the new highways were rapidly beset with the same traffic congestion problems of the old cities' streets.

Another problem was largely about building arrangements, resulting from designers' fundamental misunderstanding of human habitat needs. Much criticism has been written about modernist architecture, but the buildings themselves were not the problem; rather, the issues arose from the relationships among the buildings and how they shaped the public space between them. Indeed, most cities have modernist buildings that are widely loved and remain vibrant to this day. Danish architect Jan Gehl wrote, "Modernists rejected the city and city space, shifting their focus to individual buildings."[2] In her classic book, *The Death and Life of Great American Cities*, Jane Jacobs went further, linking the Modernists' desire to strip away superfluous architectural ornamentation to a darker desire to tame the "disorder" of cities: "There is a quality even meaner than outright ugliness or disorder, and this meaner quality is the dishonest mask of pretended order, achieved by ignoring or suppressing the real order that is struggling to exist and to be served."[3]

If anyone could have made this modernist vision of cities work, it would have been the creative geniuses at Disneyland. They made a valiant attempt with Tomorrowland, both in its 1955 original and 1967 remodel (Figure 4-1). Tomorrowland was a celebration of transportation technology, including a monorail, peoplemover, submarine, and various rides simulating spaceflight, each sponsored by a different corporation. The 1955 Autopia ride, which remains popular today, highlighted the joys of the then yet-to-be-built interstate highway system (Figure 4-2).

Yet, despite Disney's half-hearted 1998 effort to "modernize" Tomorrowland with features like edible landscaping, fansites such as Micechat.com continue to worry that Tomorrowland has devolved into a kitschy "Yesterdayland," a quaint, midcentury vision unconstrained by inconvenient consequences. Disney's failure to help us visualize a compelling, engaging, and sustainable future is indicative of the

Figure 4-2
Autopia. *Source: Loren Javier, used under Creative Commons license* http://creativecommons.org/licenses/by-nd/2.0.

challenges all professions face in moving cities toward sustainability. If the "imagineers" at Disney can't do it, how can we?

Imagining the Sustainable City of the Future

So, if today's sustainable city of the future does not look like yesterday's tired vision, what *does* it look like? It is our belief that cities of the future will look a lot less like George Jetson's Orbit City and a lot more like today's Portland, Oregon; Boulder, Colorado; Melbourne, Australia; and Barcelona, Spain. Pulling together themes developed elsewhere in this book, we suggest the following defining principles, focusing on the transportation aspects of the city.

Walking Is a Pleasure for Everyone, Everywhere, at All Times of the Day

Sustainable city design starts with the human body and its needs. As described in detail in Chapter 3, on public health, the human body depends on walking—10,000 steps a day, by some estimates—to maintain optimal functioning. Thus, the first principle of a sustainable city, perhaps more important than all the others combined, is that walking must be delightful. It is not enough that walking be safe and comfortable. Cities must be designed so that people of all ages and abilities walk for the sheer joy of it.

Walking is fundamental not only to our bodily health, but also to the health of our psyches. We are social primates, and our sense of where we fit in the group is governed by a set of complex interactions that work only at the scale and pace permitted by in-person meetings on foot. Remove frequent eye contact and touch, and we get irritable and mistrustful.

Designing a pleasant walking environment is easy, and designers should have no excuses for creating places that are uncomfortable to walk in, even in intemperate climates. We all know the places where we like to walk, so establish your city's design rules to build upon the successful examples. Consider the following:

- Some of the best places in the world are comprised of mediocre buildings that enclose beautiful spaces. Ensure the right proportions of buildings in relationship to the street.

- Focus on the bottom 30 feet of buildings, ensuring the right relationship to the sidewalk, richly textured materials, and plenty of transparency. Inspire curiosity.

- Remember Jane Jacobs's rule of putting "eyes on the street,"[4] including occupied windows that look down on pedestrian ways and lots of people out and about. Humans find nothing more interesting than other humans.

- Moderate temperature extremes by putting shade and directing wind where it's hot and by putting sun and wind shelter where it's cold.

- Plant trees. Humans are creatures of the savannah, and we are drawn to places with trees.

- Maintain things to make it look like someone cares.

Bicycling Is Safe and Comfortable for People of All Ages

Although we start with walking in city design, bicycles come in a close second. Bicycles dramatically expand the territory we can cover under our own locomotion, providing more mobility with many of the same health and social benefits as walking. Bicycling is also the most energy-efficient mode of transportation ever invented, translating almost all of our metabolic energy into motion. For older adults and people with joint disorders, bicycling, particularly with adult tricycles, can continue to provide mobility and health benefits even as walking becomes more difficult.

Tools for making bicycling delightful can be found in Chapter 7, "Bicycles." Key measures include:

- Build a network of bikeways, separated both from pedestrians and motorists, which connect most major destinations.

- Use traffic calming, education, and other tools to ensure that motorists do not dominate cyclists on shared streets.

- Provide convenient, sheltered, and secure bicycle parking everywhere.

- Find creative solutions for addressing the limitations of cycling, particularly barriers due to steep grades and poor weather.

The Needs of Daily Life Are All within Walking Distance

The city of the future will continue to have cars, but no one will be dependent upon the car for the needs of daily life. Instead, all basic services will be within walking distance, including groceries, schools, child care, dry cleaning, and sundries. To be successful, retailers require a certain number of people within their catchment area. This means that there are minimum density requirements for a sustainable city, and that retailers need to be clustered in a walkable format. Fortunately, we already know how to do that. Almost all neighborhoods built before 1945 follow this pattern, including the streetcar suburbs of Los Angeles; Midwestern small towns with their Main Streets running perpendicular to the railroad; many beautiful older town centers like Savannah, Georgia; and most cities on anyone's list of "Best Places to Retire." The greatest urban places in the world—Paris, Barcelona, Vancouver, Rome, St. Petersburg, Melbourne—offer not only the basic needs of daily life within walking distance but all of life's extravagances and pleasures as well.

To eliminate automobile dependency in your city:

- Create a retail main street for every neighborhood, and design each neighborhood to create a sufficient market for retail success.

- Concentrate retailers in a walkable, park-once arrangement.

- Plan for the right mix of retailers. In boom-bust economies, consider limits on some types of retail to maintain a complete array of services.

Transit Is Fast, Frequent, Reliable, and Dignified

The dominant transit technologies of the twenty-first century will look a lot like more refined and efficient versions of late nineteenth-century transit, and less like General Motors' vision from the mid-twentieth century. In massive new town developments, like those already built in China and India, designers will experiment with emerging transit technologies, some of which will prove marketable and others of which will become curiosity pieces. The fact is that most great cities of the future will simply be retrofitted cities of the past, requiring incremental upgrades to existing transit services. For example, although maglev offers potential for greater speed and comfort than conventional steel-on-steel, high-speed rail technology, maglev requires that new systems be built all at once, using new rights of way. Upgraded conventional technology allows for incremental expansion. New high-speed trains can operate well, though at lower speeds, along old track, making it possible, for example, to provide direct rail service from Paris to London long before England completed its dedicated high-speed rail tracks to St. Pancras Station in the heart of London (Figure 4-3).

To be attractive to people who have a choice of modes, transit must meet certain basic requirements: It must be convenient—relatively fast, frequent, and reliable—and it must be comfortable. It should also be generally affordable, while not being considered solely as a social service for those who have no other mobility options. See more details in Chapter 8, "Transit."

Everyone Knows and Loves Their Neighborhood

Humans are tribal, territorial primates. We are apparently programmed to have a sense of belonging to a geographic zone of a certain size that ranges from the tiny,

fiercely independent *contrade* of Siena (Figure 4-4)—some just 500 feet square—to the "20-minute" neighborhoods of Portland, Oregon, where everything is within a 20-minute walk. Even mass-production homebuilders know the power of the neighborhood, and while they may offer only two floorplans, different districts are assigned different names, and may offer different façade treatments so that residents of "Tuscan Village" can tell from their stucco walls and tile roofs that they're part of a different tribe from the vinyl clapboard siding and black faux shutters of adjacent "Colonial Estates."

To cultivate a sense of neighborhood:

- Use natural topography, drainages, and trees to your advantage, to help residents define "defensible" territories.

- Create edges, using rivers, parks, railroads, and major roads.

- Create centers, with retail, schools, and community spaces.

- Provide places for neighbors to meet each other, including parks, post offices, and front yards.

Residents Have a Strong Sense of Ownership of Their Home and Their City

Throughout history, visions of the city of the future were driven by some One Great Man, who imposed order and a unifying style upon the chaotic city. Even visions of the sustainable city, such as Paulo Soleri's Arcosanti, Richard Register's Ecocity, and Sir Norman Foster's Masdar in Abu Dhabi, all bear the stamp of a godlike master

Figure 4-4
The *contrade* of Siena are real Tuscan villages, and their dimensions match our territorial needs as social primates. *Source: Phillip Capper (used under Creative Commons license:* http://creativecommons.org/licenses/by-nd/2.0/.)

architect. Such schemes often gain the passionate support that acolytes shower on a charismatic leader, but so far none has gotten very far. Besides the challenges of financing megastructures, these unified utopias are also limited by the human need to own and alter our immediate habitat. Living in Arcosanti is more an act of master worship or social experimentation than the putting down of roots. To truly feel like home, we must feel superior to our houses, capable of and permitted to alter them to suit our purposes.

Owners instinctively defend their properties, and will fight to ensure that their property increases in value. This powerful sense of ownership is available equally to renters and deed-holders, provided that renters are offered stability and a sense of control over their space.

To foster ownership:

- In all neighborhoods, encourage an array of housing types so that households of all income levels can afford to purchase a home.

- Establish protections for renters so they can develop the same sense of community investment as owners.

- Encourage residents to extend their sense of ownership into public spaces, through street tree-planting programs, community gardens, and programs that encourage private citizens to invest in underutilized public spaces.

Energy Is Local, Sustainable, and Precious

Past visions of the city of the future relied on hyperabundant, cheap energy that would power our hovercraft and personal jetpacks. Although some as-yet-unperfected new technology (cold fusion? safe disposal of nuclear waste? photovoltaic paint?) may one day salvage or resurrect those visions, it is more likely that energy will be scarcer and more costly in the city of the future, and that the externalized costs of energy production and distribution will be internalized. For transport, this means a lot more walking and biking, along with more efficient versions of ground transportation.

Cars of the future will run on new batteries and fuel cells, but these cars will be limited by the rare materials needed to build those batteries and fuel cells, the costs of electricity generation needed to charge them, and the sheer geometric problems of cars addressed in Chapters 9 and 10. Regardless of their fuel source, cars will be smaller, lighter, and more automated. Highly efficient, though almost forgotten, technologies like the electric trolleybus of the mid-twentieth century will be reinvented, with overhead wires designed not just for engineering performance, but urban elegance as well. Once-abandoned nineteenth-century rail corridors will enjoy reinvestment as intercity high-speed rail lines, regional commuter and freight rail, or urban light rail. In cities committed to carbon neutrality, we may even see a return of the urban horse pulling ultralight carbon-fiber carriages, oxen pulling ever-sharp ceramic plows, and trans-Pacific freight once again shipped by wind power on speedy, oversized catamarans. At first, these portmanteau nineteenth-century technologies will be the playthings of steampunk urban artists and nostalgists, but when the true costs of carbon dependence are factored into future transportation economics, they may also emerge as the most cost-effective.

Social Networks Are More Important Than Ever

The economy of the sustainable city of the future will not be based upon agriculture or industry, but upon networks: networks of information, networks of people, networks of capital. People who have ambition, creativity, and a choice of places to live will be drawn to locations that are richly networked. These creative individuals will drive the new economy. *New York Times* columnist David Brooks described the situation well:[5]

> Howard Gardner of Harvard once put together a composite picture of the extraordinarily creative person: She comes from a little place somewhat removed from the center of power and influence. As an adolescent, she feels herself outgrowing her own small circle. She moves to a metropolis and finds a group of people who share her passions and interests. She gets involved with a team to create something amazing.
>
> Then, at some point, she finds her own problem, which is related to and yet different from the problems that concern others in her group. She breaks off and struggles and finally emerges with some new thing. She brings it back to her circle. It is tested, refined and improved.
>
> The main point in this composite story is that creativity is not a solitary process. It happens within networks. It happens when talented people get together, when idea systems and mentalities merge.

Anne-Marie Slaughter, director of policy planning at the U.S. State Department, put it more succinctly: "In a networked world, the issue is no longer relative power, but centrality in an increasingly dense global web."[6]

To encourage the development of networks:

- Invest in technology, so that geographically isolated towns can tap into the global flow of ideas.

- Foster spaces where people can meet, talk, and, most importantly, flirt. As geographic proximity becomes less important to productivity, social proximity rises in importance. Cities that support flirtation will thrive. This means creating high-quality, convivial spaces and paying attention to critical details like good lighting.

- Invest in art, but less as a collection of objects to be consumed, and more as a participatory experience.

Style Is Local but Beauty Is Ubiquitous

Most of our images of the city of the future have to do with *style*, like Jules Verne's steampunk, the Jetsons' Googie, Le Corbusier's modernism, and the over-the-top visions of the Russian constructivists. Modernism sought a universal, global style, the "International Style," replicable in any location around the world. But if a sense of ownership is central to sustainability, then style will likely remain fiercely local. Overly rigid local style enforcement can result in dull uniformity and kitsch, but the development of a particular local character can help make residents loyal to a particular place and eager to make social investments there.

Far more important than style, however, is beauty. If a thing is not beautiful, it is not sustainable.

Chapter 5
Streets

Conceptualizing Streets

Streets play many roles. They are for more than just moving cars; they are for movement of pedestrians, bicycles, transit vehicles, and goods. They allow people to move through or within an area, provide access to properties, and accommodate utilities. They are also part of the neighborhood, offering open space for socializing and recreation.

The following chapters detail specific requirements for each mode of travel, including walking, cycling, transit, and autos. This chapter discusses street design in an integrated, holistic way, balancing the following factors:

- **Land-Use Context**. Each street should support adjacent land uses. Neighborhood retail streets, for example, should attract and accommodate shoppers by ensuring that traffic flow remains slow but steady, and that on-street parking is available. On downtown streets, movement of transit vehicles and pedestrians may be prioritized over movement by cars, whereas on local residential streets, traffic must be slow enough that drivers can safely stop for a child chasing a ball. Additionally, frontages should be considered as well as uses: streets lined with ground-floor retail, for example, have design imperatives different from streets that are also commercial, but are lined by service docks.

- **Priority for the Movement of Each Mode**. Streets with high-frequency transit service should allow transit to progress at speeds that allow it to compete with autos. Automobile priority streets, like arterials, should allow motorists to progress well enough to keep through-trips off parallel residential streets. Bicycle boulevards are designed to facilitate bicycle travel while discouraging through-trips by motorists. All streets must accommodate pedestrians comfortably, but on some streets an especially high level of investment is necessary.

- **Relationship to Other Streets in the Network**. Some streets have to carry more cars because they connect directly to freeways. On others, transit or cycling may be prioritized so that overall capacity is maximized in terms of total person movement, or so that the broader system can provide quality through-routes for every mode. All streets should accommodate pedestrians safely and comfortably, but some streets may be designed primarily for pedestrians.

- **Available Right-of-Way**. Many cities are more or less built out, with limited space available for street widening. Improvements for one mode, such as a wider sidewalk, may come at the expense of accommodations for other users, such as travel lanes for bicycles or autos and transit.

Complete Streets

A "complete" street is designed for safe, comfortable, and convenient movement both along and across the right-of-way by people of all ages and abilities, using multiple modes.

Since World War II, roads in America and elsewhere have largely been designed around the automobile, and this approach has resulted in unintended consequences. Roads designed primarily for private vehicle movement may be entirely lacking in accommodations for pedestrians, cyclists, or transit riders. Such streets don't just fail to account for whole user groups—pedestrians, cyclists, and transit riders, seniors and children—they actively present barriers to use by these groups, intentionally or otherwise. This singular focus on moving cars has become so ingrained in our habits of thought that any mode other than the automobile may now be described as an "alternative" mode.

Complete-streets policies seek to move beyond mere vehicle throughput and integrate routine consideration for all road users into every street design project. Many jurisdictions have adopted policies and codes that promote design of and investment in complete streets (for example, San Francisco; Seattle; Portland, Oregon; and Boulder, Colorado).

BENEFITS OF COMPLETE STREETS

Research has shown that more people walk, bike, and take transit when well-designed facilities are available, and this can result in an array of livability and other community benefits. The not-for-profit organization *Complete the Streets* has outlined several such benefits, summarized in the following list:

- **Safety**. Complete streets can reduce accident rates and accident severity. Studies have shown that as the number and proportion of people biking and walking increases, deaths and injuries from vehicle crashes decline.

- **Health**. Complete streets encourage walking and biking, and to the extent that emissions from autos are reduced, can further improve public health.

- **Children's Health and Safety**. Complete streets allow children to more safely explore their neighborhoods on foot or by bike, thereby gaining independence while engaging in physical activity.

- **Mobility**. Complete streets provide alternatives to traffic congestion and increase the overall capacity of the transportation network.

- **Climate Change Prevention**. Among other vehicle emissions, carbon emissions are also reduced.

ELEMENTS OF A COMPLETE STREET

Complete streets should be tailored to their unique contexts (Figure 5-1). Still, all complete-streets policies and projects share a focus on accommodating the full range of mobility options and considering the entire right-of-way. Complete-streets elements may include (but are not limited to):

- General travel lanes (in terms of both design and operation)
- Parking lanes

◀ Figure 5-1
A complete street suits its land-use context, and accommodates all users with equal comfort. In Seattle, 12th Avenue was rebuilt with bike lanes and improved sidewalks. *Source: Nelson\ Nygaard.*

- Bicycle lanes

- Sidewalks (including amenities such as landscaping and lighting)

- Off-street paths or trails

- Additional pedestrian and bicycle elements (such as crosswalks or "bike boxes")

- Loading zones

- Wheelchair ramps and other Americans with Disabilities Act (ADA) accommodations

- Transit stops and stations

- Transit-only lanes

- Traffic signal improvements

Street Typologies

A framework of street typologies is a tool for categorizing streets based on their most important characteristics.

Under the conventional approach used in automobile-oriented places (Figure 5-2), streets are defined by the degree to which they emphasize through movement for autos versus local access. This is known as *functional classification*. Streets designed for through movement are called *arterials*, streets designed for access are *locals*, and those in between are *collectors*.

▼ Figure 5-2
Conventional street typologies assume a tension between the needs of cars and the needs of buildings along the street. Better street typologies are driven by land-use context and consider all modes.

PROPORTION OF SERVICE

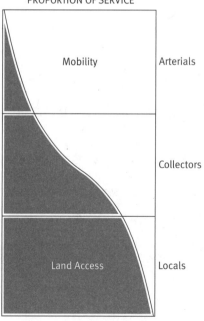

Mobility — Arterials

Collectors

Land Access — Locals

Table 5-1: Sample Street Typologies Based Upon Land-Use Context

| Land-Use Context | "Arteriality" or Former Functional Classification | | | |
	Arterial	Collector	Local	Alley
Downtown	Downtown arterial	Downtown collector	Downtown street	Service alley
Neighborhood	Main street	Neighborhood main street	Neighborhood main street	Service alley
Commercial	Commercial arterial	Commercial collector	Commercial street	Service alley
Residential	Residential arterial	Residential collector	Residential street	Residential alley
Industrial	Industrial arterial	Industrial collector	Industrial street	Industrial alley

In more multimodal and sustainable cities, however, streets serve many functions, and street design is most concerned not with automobile throughput but with pedestrian safety and comfort. In these places, typologies should take into account land-use context and other characteristics.

In places such as North America and Australia, where the auto-oriented "functional" classification system still dominates, the simplest way to transition toward a more comprehensive street typology may be to use a matrix with current street types on one axis and common land-use types along another (see Table 5-1, for an example).

To tailor names of street types to your community, use terms that are more meaningful in a local context. For example, a downtown arterial could simply be called a *boulevard*, whereas a local residential could be called a *residential lane*. Naming conventions for street classifications should also incorporate multiple modes, so a major street where transit is the highest priority might be called a *transit boulevard*, while a street designed mainly for bicycles might be a *bikeway*. Special characteristics may also be noted; for example, an extensively landscaped street might be called a *parkway*.

In some U.S. states, some types of maintenance funding are available only for specific types of streets, such as arterials. For this reason, U.S. cities that abandon the use of terms such as *arterial* and *collector* may wish to adopt policy language defining their terminology (e.g., transit boulevard) as meeting the requirements of an arterial.

Principles of Street Design

The following broad principles address design for individual streets as well as street networks; they also address design for new streets as well as redesigns of existing streets. Mode-specific design features are more fully addressed in later chapters dealing with individual modes.

Reflect the Landscape

First, consider environmental conditions:

- Sensitive areas that should be avoided.

- Topography, including bodies of water, waterways, and slopes that may serve to shape the street network. Streets might be aligned to accentuate topography, as

Frederick Law Olmsted did with sinuous curves in his residential neighborhood and park designs, or as Jasper O'Farrell did by laying straight streets over San Francisco's hills. Natural corridors formed by creeks and waterfronts, meanwhile, can serve as multiuse paths (often within a linear park) providing off-street walk and bike "trunk" routes connecting at various points to the street network and major destinations.

- Views that should be preserved, by aligning streets toward them. This rule applies to the built environment as well as the natural environment; many of Washington, D.C.'s diagonal avenues, for example, are designed to terminate at major buildings and monuments.

- Wind patterns, to capture breezes in hot climates or provide shelter from them in cold climates.

- Sun patterns, to maximize sunshine or shade.

Integrate Transportation with Land-Use Planning

The best transportation plan is a good land-use plan. With this in mind, the following land-use considerations should be applied to design of a street network:

- Always create small blocks (200 to 400 feet long). By providing more paths of travel, traffic can be better distributed; wide, pedestrian-hostile streets can be avoided; and the number of destinations within walking distance can be increased.

- Mixed-use neighborhood centers should be within walking distance of all homes and businesses, so that all of the basic needs of daily life are within walking distance. Small blocks will help to ensure this.

- Primary schools should be located within walking distance of all residences. Secondary schools should be within bicycling distance of all residences, and along transit corridors.

- Dense land uses (especially commercial nodes and corridors) and major activity centers (such as schools, universities, hospitals, and civic institutions) should be served by frequent transit, and connecting and adjacent streets should place a high priority on transit.

- To accommodate transit lines, streets should generally be straight, and streets suitable for transit service should be about a half-mile apart.

- Except in the most urban and pedestrian-oriented places, retailers should be visible from a major road.

- Successful retail demands a street that is busy with traffic yet is narrow enough that pedestrians on one side of the street can see storefronts on the other side. Retail streets work best when they are one travel lane in each direction, so they can function well as a single retail space. At more than two lanes in each direction, retail on each side of the street will tend to operate independently, with less mutual support of retailers across the street.

- If a major road would create too much of a pedestrian barrier for successful retail, retail streets should be located perpendicular to the road. Avoid locating retail centers on a street that will get little vehicle traffic.

- Unlike retail centers, parks and elementary schools are best located far from major streets. Key exceptions are high schools and major athletic facilities, which are major destinations and should be placed along transit lines.

- When modeling motor vehicle traffic demand for a new street network, ensure that the model is sensitive to land-use density, mix of land uses, transit availability, position in regional transportation networks, transportation demand management programs, and other factors. As density increases, vehicle trip generation rates decline (Figures 5-3 and 5-4).

More detail on street design can be found throughout the chapters on individual modes.

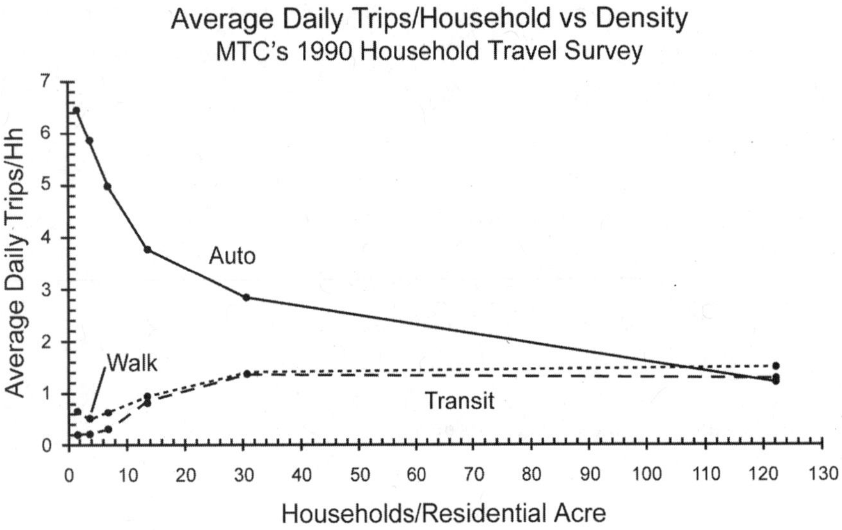

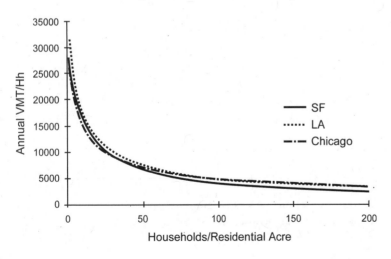

Average Daily Trips/Household vs Density
MTC's 1990 Household Travel Survey

Driving vs Residential Density

◀ **Figure 5-3**
As density increases, vehicle trips decrease. *Source: San Francisco Bay Area Metropolitan Transportation Commission 1990 Household Travel Survey.*

◀ **Figure 5-4**
Data show the same relationship between density and travel behavior in all regions. Note the big reduction in vehicle travel around 15 to 30 units per acre; this typifies the compact, low-rise development characteristic of many small city downtown neighborhoods. *Source: "Location Efficiency: Neighborhood and Socio-Economic Characteristics Determine Auto Ownership and Use—Studies in Chicago, Los Angeles and San Francisco."* Transportation Planning and Technology, *Volume 25, Number 1, 1 January 2002, pp. 1–27(27).*

Chapter 6
Pedestrians

with Amy Pfeiffer

Introduction

This chapter is a how-to guide for planners who are interested in making their streets delightful for pedestrians. It focuses on the principles and design techniques most often missing from other manuals. For more information, see more thorough pedestrian design manuals, such as San Francisco's *Better Streets Plan*, or New York City's *Street Design Manual*.

Pedestrian Planning Principles

The intent of this chapter is to supply easily accessible, understandable, and implementable ideas to create better environments for walking. To do so, pedestrian planners may consider the following fourteen areas of focus as priorities. All of these focus areas are necessary for successful projects.

The best pedestrian plan is a good land-use plan.
Pedestrian planning starts by ensuring that most of the needs of daily life are available within walking distance. This means:

- Zoning for neighborhood centers no more than about a mile apart from each other, so that almost everyone is within a half-mile walk.
- Require sufficient density to support retail success.
- Create mixed-use districts around neighborhood centers that allow an array of land uses.
- Forbid auto-dependent land uses and forms within pedestrian-oriented areas.

Make sure buildings relate to sidewalks rather than parking lots.
In your zoning code, pay attention to the following details:

- Establish build-to lines along the primary street frontage so that buildings are not set too far back from the street. For retail buildings, the build-to line will likely be zero feet.
- Forbid the placement of parking between the building's front door and the street.
- Require the primary front door to open onto the primary street frontage.
- In residential areas, require parking access from an alley.
- In commercial areas, require that parking be shared and carefully managed (see Chapter 10 for more detail regarding parking).

Make sure buildings are a pleasure to walk past.

In your zoning code, pay careful attention to how the fronts of buildings are designed, focusing especially on the first 30 feet:

- Consider establishing a form-based code, providing clear guidance to developers about how buildings should look and how they should relate to nearby buildings.

- Require frequent front doors along commercial streets, and set minimum spacing standards.

- In commercial areas, require that inactive buildings, like parking garages and big-box stores, be wrapped in active ground-floor uses or in-line shops.

- Set minimum requirements for the spacing and size of windows, particularly on the ground floor. These are called *fenestration* requirements.

- Require clear windows and forbid the use of opaque roll-down gates or screens that block pedestrians' view into shops and offices.

- Require the use of stoops or porches in residential areas, to encourage both community building and more informal surveillance of the street.

- Establish materials requirements and other standards to make sure building façades are richly textured and support your community's local character.

- Forbid parking entries along retail streets, and minimize the width of garage doors along all streets, except alleys.

- Where parking lots edge along a sidewalk, establish a minimum setback line and require landscaping and/or a low wall (typically, about 3 feet high) in the setback area.

Provide attractive, consistent lighting of the pedestrian realm.

Adopt lighting standards and invest in light fixtures to:

- Provide a consistent level of lighting of the pedestrian realm, without glare or shadow. This will mean more and lower light fixtures than those used to light the roadway, with the light typically about 15 feet high, so that it is not blocked by tree canopies. Lights can be building mounted or strung in trees.

- Use full-spectrum lighting, particularly in commercial areas, so that pedestrians can see colors accurately and feel attractive.

- Celebrate the street with artful lighting.

Make streets leafy.

Few investments can make a bigger difference in pedestrian quality at a lower cost than landscaping.

- Establish street tree standards, identifying the best trees for your local conditions. Provide for a mix of trees, including trees that grow to considerable size, producing a full canopy over the street.

- Establish planting standards to ensure healthy trees and minimize damage to pavement and utilities.

- Establish special funding districts to pay for tree maintenance and ensure adequate funding to address added pavement maintenance. Large trees add significantly to property values, but your public works department will oppose large canopy trees unless a portion of their real estate benefit is allocated to cover added maintenance costs.

- Ensure that your street design manual does not require unnecessary auto "clear zones" on urban streets or excessive sight triangles at controlled intersections. These concepts are, however, appropriate on highways and uncontrolled intersections.

- On residential streets and in commercial areas where there is no on-street parking, require a landscape strip between the sidewalk and the roadway; these are typically a minimum of five feet wide.

Design streets with pedestrians in mind.

Develop and adopt a street design manual that puts pedestrians first (see more in Chapter 5):

- Establish street typologies that account for different pedestrian needs in different land-use contexts.

- Establish minimum dimensional requirements for sidewalks in different contexts. Establish guidelines for the edge, furnishings, throughway, and frontage zones of the sidewalk.

- Minimize pedestrian crossing distances by tightening up the dimensions of intersections wherever practicable.

- Set standards for maximum distances between protected pedestrian crossings.

- Set standards for how driveways cross sidewalks, with the sidewalk taking priority.

Calm traffic.

The most effective tool to ensure pedestrian safety is to keep motor vehicle speeds at less than 18 mph (the design tolerance of the human body). To manage traffic speeds:

- Time synchronized traffic lights for an 18-mph-or-less progression speed. In downtown Portland, Oregon, most of the city's one-way streets are timed for about a 12-mph progression. As a result, downtown Portland has one of the lowest pedestrian fatality rates in North America.

- Provide only as many traffic lanes as are necessary, reallocating unnecessary lanes to bike lanes, parking, or wider sidewalks. Examine your congestion thresholds and fine-tune the designs, allowing for some additional peak-hour congestion if traffic speeds are too high in the off peak.

- Adopt traffic calming guidelines and fund corrections to streets where traffic goes too fast.

- Adopt street design guidelines that accommodate low speeds.

Promote Safe Routes to Schools.

Children are among the most vulnerable pedestrians, and one of the leading causes of morning traffic congestion results from parents chauffeuring their kids to school, for fear of them being run down by cars. To allow children to walk to school safely:

- Focus traffic calming efforts around schools, identifying the safest routes to access the schools from surrounding neighborhoods.
- Work with parents to educate children on safe walking, and to organize "walking school buses," programs in which parents volunteer to gather children from a given neighborhood and walk together to school.
- Conduct classroom education about safe walking and bicycling.

Partner.

Because everyone walks, the best pedestrian programs involve partnerships with a wide variety of departments and organizations. Organize partnerships for funding and implementing walking programs among:

- Recreation and parks programs
- Public health programs, hospitals, and advocates
- Schools and parent-teacher associations
- Disabled-rights and older adult programs and advocates
- Businesses, business improvement districts, and chambers of commerce
- Regional, state, and federal programs and funders
- Private foundations and individual donors

Measure success.

Pedestrians will never be taken seriously unless they are factored into your street performance measures and transportation funding formulas:

- Ensure that pedestrian quality cannot be sacrificed to improve auto Level of Service in your traffic impact guidelines, concurrency standards, and congestion management plans.
- Establish pedestrian quality standards and targets for different types of streets and contexts.
- Conduct pedestrian quality audits of your streets.
- Collect data on pedestrian activity, using, for example, the approach that Gehl Architects uses in their "Public Life and Public Spaces" surveys;[1] map pedestrian injuries and fatalities.
- Map missing or inadequate pedestrian facilities, including missing or overly narrow sidewalks, and inadequate paths of travel for people in wheelchairs or with visual impairments.

Create a welcoming public realm that invites lingering.

From a pedestrian perspective, sidewalks, plazas, and parks are all a part of the same public realm, and they should be designed as an integrated whole, celebrating the pleasure of urban life.

- Create a sidewalk furnishings plan that includes movable benches and chairs.

- Invest in public art, and focus on art that is best appreciated from the pedestrian scale.
- Particularly in retail areas, program sidewalk space with performances, public art, sidewalk vendors, and food carts.

Establish and fund priorities.

No city has enough money to build and maintain every sidewalk to the highest level of quality. To help figure out what to do first:

- Map the desired level of pedestrian quality on all streets in your city.
- Map the existing conditions, including missing or inadequate sidewalk segments, curb ramps, sidewalk width, tree canopy, landscape buffer, building frontage, and so on.
- Examine the difference between what is desired and what exists, and establish clear priorities for bridging the gap.
- Create a funding plan that implements your priority project on a specific timeline, and revisit it every year.

Make wayfinding intuitive.

For the most part, navigating sustainable cities should be intuitive: Downtown and the rail station are where the taller buildings are. The river is downhill. Main Street is the one with the fancy pavement and light fixtures. As cities get more complex, however, additional strategies are needed.

- Identify important vistas and protect them in your zoning code.
- Mark important locations with tall buildings and monuments.
- Bring in a wayfinding expert to help you use art, landscape, color, pavement, lighting, and other tools to help visitors find their way around your city.
- Once you have done all of this, have your wayfinding expert develop a signage strategy.

Make it feel safe.

Even if your city has no reported crimes, people will still not want to walk there if it does not *feel* safe—and the perception of safety is only somewhat related to the actuality of safety.

- Study "Crime Prevention Through Environmental Design," such as by reading Oscar Newman's seminal book, *Defensible Space*.[2]
- In your zoning code, ensure that there are requirements for active windows facing onto all sidewalks.
- Invest in a high level of maintenance, including regular sweeping and graffiti removal within 24 hours of reporting.
- Attract more pedestrians to places that feel unsafe, through programming or vendors.
- Bring in experts in Crime Prevention Through Environmental Design to address specific trouble spots.

Pedestrian Planning Tools

An array of tools is available to help make your city more walkable. This section summarizes some of the most common.

Walkability Audits

A wide variety of audit tools is available to help planners identify and solve pedestrian problems. Two useful sources are the following:

- The Federal Highway Administration Road Safety Audits program has detailed guidelines, available online (safety.fhwa.dot.gov/rsa/), that focus on traffic safety, including details on pedestrian safety. It provides much useful advice, but it is limited in that it does not examine the quality of the pedestrian experience, and it tends to limit pedestrian behavior in order to improve safety, such as by restricting midblock crossings rather than designing them in such a way as to be safe for all roadway users.

- Active Living Research has more than a dozen pedestrian audit tools available online (www.activelivingresearch.org), many of them complex and qualitative. Some of the tools include free software to graph and map the results in your community.

Your tool choice depends on the priorities of your city and the resources you have to invest in data collection and data processing. Because of the complexity of the pedestrian environment, the data needs may be formidable. A more effective approach may be to have actual pedestrians record their perceptions of specific walking environments. Perceptions may be ranked so that they can be quantified and averaged, producing results that can be weighed against such calculated performance measures as the automobile Level of Service.

Tracking Surveys

A simple but powerful tool for intersection design is called a *tracking survey*. Use a small team of observers to record, over a few hours, actual pedestrian walking patterns, then aggregate the information into a single map, like that shown in Figure 6-1. The map in Figure 6-1 resulted from observations conducted at a difficult intersection in the Harlem neighborhood of New York City.

This method makes it easy to understand where new pedestrian signals or crossings should be installed; where traffic calming measures, such as medians and curb extensions, are best placed; and where existing asphalt might be built out to absorb pedestrian and vehicle flow more safely.

Pedestrian Plans

Full pedestrian plans are concerned with much more than just sidewalks. People need to know where they are going (signs and wayfinding); want to get there without incident (traffic calming); need access (Americans with Disabilities Act requirements); don't like too much jostling (effective sidewalk width, curb edge use,

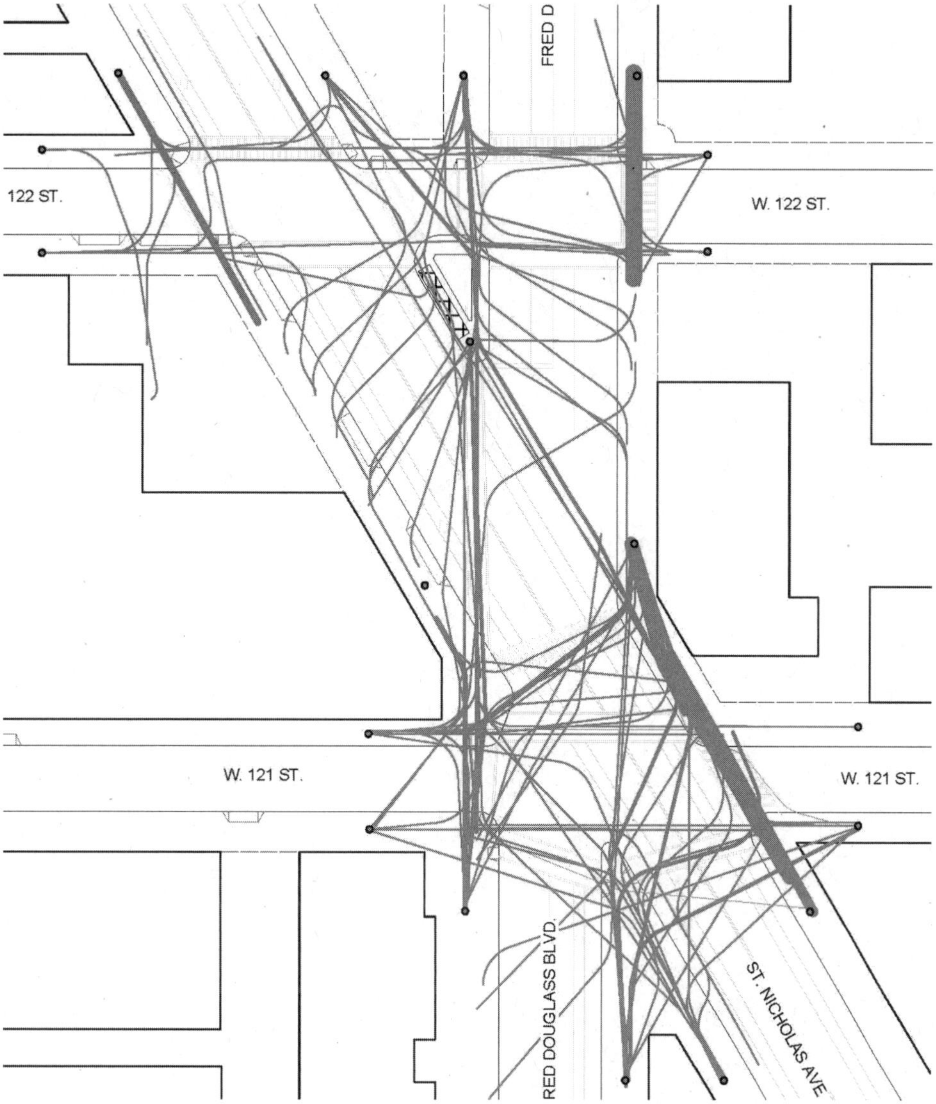

Figure 6-1
Harlem tracking survey. *Source: Nelson\Nygaard.*

building edge); are discouraged by poor lighting, recessed storefronts, and noise; and like places to sit (street furniture).

Figure 6-2 shows the area around the main rail station in Trenton, New Jersey. This image shows the key links in a network, and compares the difference between the one-third-mile easy-walking-distance radius (as the crow flies) and the actual walking distance.

Figure 6-3 provides an inventory of the available sidewalks around the station.

Together, maps like these helped policymakers in Trenton prioritize investments in pedestrian improvements, and allowed them to recognize that it was more cost-effective to fix pedestrian obstacles than to improve station access by other modes or means.

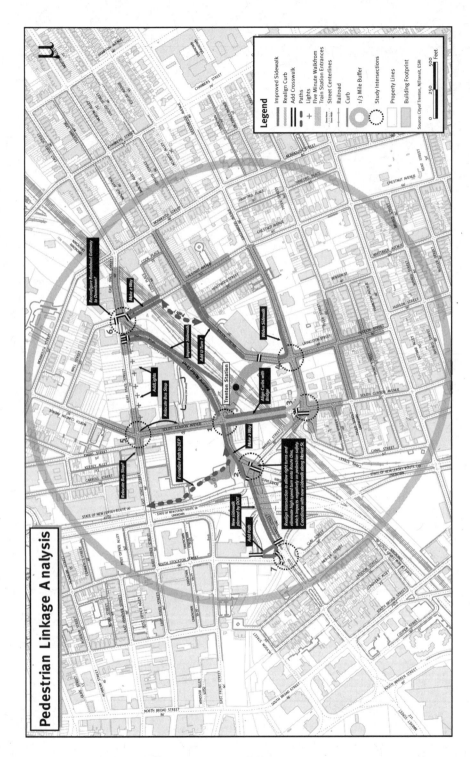

Pedestrian Linkage Analysis

Figure 6-2
Trenton links and actual walking distances, as compared to airline radius. *Source: Nelson\Nygaard.*

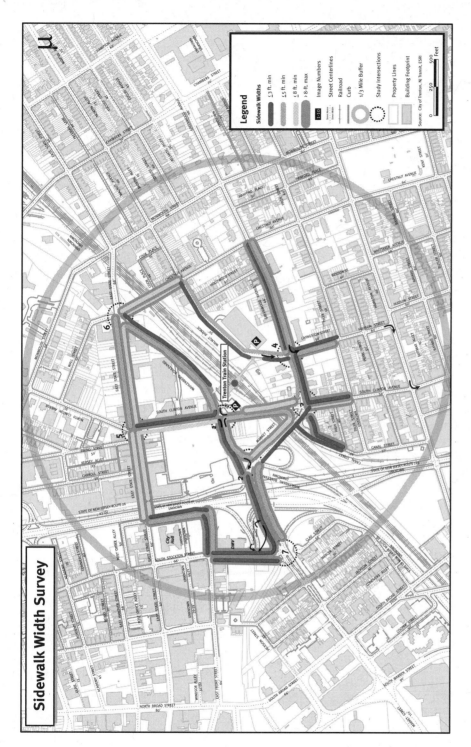

Figure 6-3
Trenton sidewalk quality inventory.
Source: Nelson\Nygaard.

Pedestrian plans also often include street classification systems, allowing pedestrian networks to be organized against street networks.

Pedestrian Design Tools

This section describes a few of the most important tools for design of pedestrian spaces in the public sphere, and focuses on sidewalks, street crossings, and special spaces such as flexible spaces in the parking lane and shared spaces. Much of the language in this section is adapted from San Francisco's *Better Streets Plan*.[3] Many details important for pedestrians are also covered in Chapter 9 of this text, standard street design manuals, and the Americans with Disabilities Act *Accessibility Guidelines for Buildings and Facilities* (ADAAG).[4]

Sidewalks

OVERALL WIDTH

Table 6-1 (adapted from the San Francisco *Better Streets Plan*) shows minimum and recommended sidewalk widths for different street types.

SIDEWALK ZONES

It is not just total sidewalk width that matters. Sidewalks aren't just for walking; indeed, much of a typical urban sidewalk is, practically speaking, unavailable to pedestrians. Figure 6-4 shows one way to think about sidewalk cross-sections (as well as the parking lane into which sidewalks or sidewalk elements may be extended in places). Edge and furnishings zones are sometimes combined, and the extension zone is not often considered separately, but at a minimum, urban sidewalks consist of three zones, only one of which is truly available for walking.

This section includes design guidelines for all zones. It should be noted that these guidelines are general; appropriate dimensions can vary depending on overall width, pedestrian volumes, adjacent land uses, presence of driveways, and other factors.

Table 6-1: *San Francisco Better Streets Plan* Sidewalk Specifications

Land-Use Context	Street Type	Minimum Sidewalk Width (in feet)	Recommended Sidewalk Width (in feet)
Commercial	Commercial throughway and neighborhood retail	12	15
Residential	Urban residential	12	15
	Low-density residential	10	12
Other	Industrial	8	10
	Parkway	12	17
	Alley	6	9

Source: *San Francisco Better Streets Plan*, Courtesy the San Francisco Planning Department.

FRONTAGE ZONE

Pedestrians tend to shy away from edges, even more so from walls, and especially from walls featuring doors that may open at any time. However, there are many appropriate uses for the *frontage* zone, including café or restaurant seating, benches, merchandise displays, plantings, and architectural elements such as awnings, canopies, and marquees (among others). On sidewalks that are not wide enough to accommodate a large furnishings zone, elements that would normally be sited in the latter, such as newsracks, trash cans, and poles, may occupy the frontage zone to keep the throughway zone clear.

On all street types, the frontage zone should be at least 18 inches wide. On commercial streets, the frontage zone should be a minimum of 2 feet to allow for seating and other amenities, as well as window shopping and frequently opening doors.

THROUGHWAY ZONE

The *throughway* or pedestrian clear zone should be free of obstacles, including changes to the cross-slope such as driveway aprons. The walking surface should be constructed of material that is durable, comfortable, and safe for pedestrians and persons in wheelchairs to use in all weather. Overhanging elements such as awnings, store signage, and bay windows may occupy this zone as long as they are at least 80 inches above the sidewalk, as required by ADA accessibility standards.

Americans with Disabilities Act regulations require a clear path of travel at least 4 feet wide, widening to a minimum of 5 feet at least every 200 feet. However, on streets other than alleys, and in particular on streets with relatively high pedestrian volumes, a minimum of 6 feet—enough for a pair of pedestrians walking side-by-side to be passed—is recommended. Where adjacent frontage or furnishings zones are kept clear of obstacles, they may be included in the clear space, as may ADA-compliant tree grates.

FURNISHINGS ZONE

The *furnishings* zone acts as a buffer between the throughway zone and the roadway. Street trees and other landscaping, benches, newsracks, streetlights, parking meters, signs, trash cans, utility boxes, fire hydrants, and other furnishings should be consolidated in this zone. The furnishings zone may be further identified as a place for lingering outside of the pedestrian path of travel by treating it in a different surface material.

Wherever street trees or sidewalk landscaping are provided, the furnishings zone should be at least 3 feet wide. However, where there is no on-street parking to provide a buffer from traffic, it should be wider: at least 4 feet, plus an additional

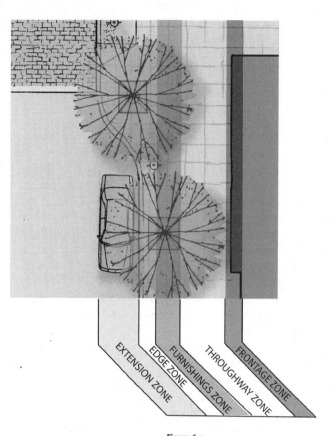

Figure 6-4
Functional zones of a sidewalk. *Source: San Francisco Better Streets Plan, Courtesy the San Francisco Planning Department.*

foot for every 5-mile-per-hour increase in the average speed of traffic over 25 mph. The furnishings zone may also be made wider to accommodate extensive landscaping and additional seating. Where there is a continuous planted strip, the furnishings zone should be connected to the edge zone every 20 feet using a 3-foot path aligned with the midpoint of the adjacent parking space.

EDGE ZONE

The *edge* zone is the interface between the roadway and the sidewalk, and is designed for use by people getting in and out of cars parked at the curbside. Because many of the elements found in the furnishings zone can often be placed in the edge zone while still leaving room to access parked cars, those two zones are sometimes combined.

On streets with parallel parking, the edge zone should be at least 18 inches wide (as measured from the face of the curb). On streets with diagonal or perpendicular parking, the edge zone should be a minimum of 30 inches.

EXTENSION ZONE

The *extension* zone includes those parts of the parking lane occupied by "bulb-out" curb extensions, as well as parking-lane "flexible uses" such as bike parking and off-curb tree basins (parking-lane flex uses are described in greater detail later in this chapter). Where there are substantial bulb-outs, elements typically found in the furnishings zone may be consolidated to allow for a wider throughway zone.

Where the pedestrian realm is expanded into the extension zone, it should take up the full width of the curb extension or parking lane.

SPECIAL ZONES

Figure 6-5 shows some of the additional special-use areas that sidewalks can be divided into when one thinks in linear terms, rather than simply of the cross-section.

CORNERS

Ideally, on streets with relatively high pedestrian or traffic volumes, corners of intersections should be "bulbed out," or extended to a point near the edges of adjacent travel lanes, in order to reduce crossing distances and increase visibility for pedestrians (Figure 6-6). This can be prohibitively expensive due to subsurface vaults or drainage requirements. In the latter case, it might be possible to provide "interim" bulbs consisting of raised islands connected to the sidewalk via grates, which can be removed to allow gutter sweeping.

Figure 6-5
Special areas of a sidewalk. *Source: San Francisco Better Streets Plan, Courtesy the San Francisco Planning Department.*

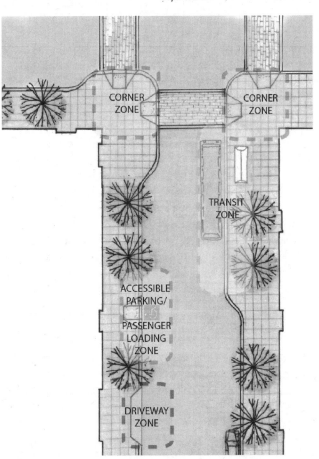

Figure 6-6
In Portland, Oregon, corner bulb-outs in residential areas are extended some linear distance to allow for porous planted strips. *Source: Nelson\Nygaard.*

To the extent possible, corners should be kept clear of obstructions, and should be designed so as to ensure clear views of one another for drivers and pedestrians. Furniture and amenities, including landscaping, can be clustered near corners, but not immediately adjacent to the corner itself. Corners should always include ADA-compliant wheelchair ramps with detectable warning surfaces for the visually impaired, aligned to provide direct access to crosswalks.

TRANSIT STOPS
For guidelines related to transit stops, see Chapter 8 on transit.

DRIVEWAYS
Where sidewalks cross driveways, the surface of the throughway zone should remain level, with no change in cross-slope, and detectable (high-contrast, tactile) warning strips should be provided. Minimum widths for the throughway zone are detailed in the previous section of this chapter.

DISABLED AND LOADING SPACES
Where disabled parking or passenger or delivery loading spaces are adjacent to the curb, street trees, furnishings, and other obstructions should be set back to allow a minimum of 8 feet of clear sidewalk width.

Given a choice between providing a median and other elements such as bicycle lanes, a sustainable street designer might lean toward the latter, as medians can encourage faster driving and thus be counterproductive. However, medians also add greenery, provide permeable surfaces, and (if they are at least 6 feet wide) pedestrian refuges. Extra-wide medians (more than 12 or so feet) might even offer opportunities for unusually large trees with broad canopies and for additional seating and gathering areas, and they can be cut out at intersections to provide left-turn pockets.

Streets

This section does not specifically address crosswalks, as crosswalk designs are described in detail in most other transportation planning guides. In general, however, crosswalks should be (1) available (crossings at corners should never be restricted), (2) highly visible, and (3) protected by traffic signals (either on a fixed cycle or pedestrian actuated).

STOP AND YIELD LINES

Stop (or limit) lines are solid white lines one to two feet wide, extending across approaching travel lanes in advance of stop signs or signals, that serve to reduce vehicle encroachment into crosswalks and improve motorists' views of pedestrians. The *Manual on Uniform Traffic Control Devices* (MUTCD)[5] allows their use from 4 to 50 feet in advance of crosswalks, depending on variables such as speeds, street width, on-street parking, potential for visual confusion, nearby land uses with vulnerable populations, and demand for queuing space.

As an alternative, yield lines consisting of a single row of white triangles can be used to indicate the point at which vehicles must stop to yield. These can be especially effective at reducing "multiple-threat" collisions, which occur when motorists in inside lanes fail to see pedestrians stepping out from in front of vehicles in outside lanes.

PEDESTRIAN SIGNALS

Pedestrian signals should be used at all traffic signals, and should consist of international symbols rather than text. They should be timed so as to allow sufficient time for all pedestrians to cross the street, including seniors, children, and people with disabilities.

Historically, a standard walking speed of 4 feet per second has been used to calculate the minimum clearance interval (the flashing red hand plus yellow and any all-red). The new federal standards, however, have reduced this to 3.5 feet per second. The pedestrian clearance interval plus the walk time should be long enough to allow someone to cross at 3.0 feet per second.

PEDESTRIAN "SCRAMBLES"

All-way pedestrian phases may be used where there are high pedestrian volumes and crossing distances are short.

Pedestrian "Head-start" Signals

Leading pedestrian intervals, which give pedestrians a head start before vehicles are given the green, may be used at intersections with a high incidence of pedestrian conflicts and right-of-way violations by vehicles.

Pedestrian-actuated Signals

Because many pedestrians fail to notice or use pedestrian-actuated signals, and because such signals send the psychological message that pedestrians have lower priority than cars, fixed signal cycles should generally be used rather than pedestrian push-buttons. However, pedestrian actuation can be used where pedestrian crossings are intermittent, at locations with relatively long clearance times that can result in excessive delay to transit vehicles, and to activate audible pedestrian signals or provide an extended walk phase. Timed progression of traffic signals should be used to ensure that sufficient time is allocated per cycle for pedestrian crossings.

Pedestrian Countdown Signals

Surveys show that many pedestrians misinterpret the meaning of the flashing hand in a traditional pedestrian cycle in much the same way drivers often misinterpret yellow lights: as a signal to hurriedly cross rather than coming to a stop before entering the intersection. By providing more precise information, countdowns can discourage this practice, or encourage pedestrians to use a median refuge. It could be argued that countdowns might encourage more reckless behavior; however, they have been shown to reduce injury collisions by 25 percent.

Flexible Use of the Parking Lane

Unlike auto travel or bicycle lanes, curbside parking lanes are inherently flexible. They are used not for through movement, but for storage, and are divided into units typically around 20 feet long. Parking lanes consist of *spaces*, and some of these spaces (or spaces *between* spaces) might be allotted to other uses. This practice has existed for some time overseas, and has recently been introduced in U.S. cities, including New York City and a number of cities in the San Francisco Bay Area.

Curbside parking spaces are immediately adjacent to sidewalks, which are used for a variety of purposes, so they too might be put to diverse uses, including landscaping, bicycle parking, café and restaurant seating, or simple benches. Parking lanes, of course, are adjacent to traffic lanes, at the level of the roadway rather than the sidewalk, so if they are to be used for seating, barriers from traffic such as planters or raised platforms should be provided. Eventually, it might make sense to convert flex spaces to permanent, bulb-out sidewalk extensions.

PASSIVE USES

To provide additional sidewalk space, as well as a visual cue for motorists to drive calmly, planters or trees can be placed between parking spaces at regular intervals. Tree basins should be a minimum of 4 feet by 6 feet, and care should be taken to ensure that canopies are kept clear of passing vehicles by pruning them to a minimum overhang of 14 feet.

Planters or basins in the parking lane introduce issues of drainage, cleaning, and maintenance. To maintain a gutter, they can be separated from the curb, with the gap potentially covered by a grate.

ACTIVE USES

On active commercial streets, parking spaces may be used for café seating, benches, or bicycle parking on a temporary or semipermanent basis. Flexible use of parking lanes should be prioritized in commercial areas with high pedestrian volumes, light to moderate traffic volumes, and numerous cafes and restaurants (Figure 6-7).

Flexible uses may be installed by individual actors, such as café owners, or as part of a street redesign. In either case, flexible use of parking lanes generally requires additional parking management, as well as sidewalk and flex-space maintenance, by a city or a third party such as a merchants association, business improvement district (BID), or individual permit holders.

In general, flexible uses of the parking lane should take up the full width of the parking lane and at least one full parking space. Flexible spaces should be designed to instill a sense that the space is intended for people, and dispel the sense that pedestrians or cyclists are infringing on auto space. Bollards, railings, planter boxes, and other materials can be used to provide a buffer from adjacent parking lanes while maintaining sightlines between drivers and flex-space users

Figure 6-7
Permanent flexible lane on Castro Street in Mountain View, California.
Source: Eric Fredericks (used under Creative Commons license: http://creativecommons.org/licenses/by-sa/2.0/deed.en.)

and visually and physically breaking the parking lane down into independent, distinct spaces.

Flex-use spaces can be nonpermanent in nature, such as those consisting of platforms raised to the level of the sidewalk (which might even be put away every evening) or simply of bicycle parking at street grade, or they can be more permanent (Figure 6-8). Where flexible use of the parking lane will occur as part of a street redesign, design elements should include:

- **Curb Extensions and Permanent Landscaping:** Landscaped curb extensions or parking-lane planters or tree basins should be located at least every five parking spaces (a maximum of 100 feet apart).

- **Special Paving Treatment:** Colored and textured paving materials should be used to differentiate these areas from the roadway.

- **Level Change:** A level change of 1 to 2 inches should be introduced between the roadway and the parking lane to differentiate these two areas. The curb between the parking lane and the sidewalk should be designed to include a stepped change in grade, rather than the standard 6-inch grade change. Flexible space should be made accessible to pedestrians with disabilities using ramps.

Flexible spaces should not conflict with other uses:

- Accessible parking spaces should not be converted to flexible use.

- Flexible uses of parking lanes should not obstruct the safe travel of bicycles in an adjacent bike lane.

- Flexible uses of parking lanes should not obstruct the safe travel of transit vehicles or the ability of passengers to board or alight from vehicles.

Figure 6-8
Semipermanent flexible space on Divisadero Street in San Francisco.
Source: Jeremy Shaw.

Shared Spaces

Shared spaces are rights-of-way in which the pedestrian and vehicle realms are at the same grade, or are not separated at all. In effect, they should function as linear plazas with occasional traffic (Figure 6-9).

Generally, for right-of-ways less than 15 feet wide, there is no need to provide separate zones. On wider rights-of-way, there should be pedestrian-only zones differentiated using detectable cues.

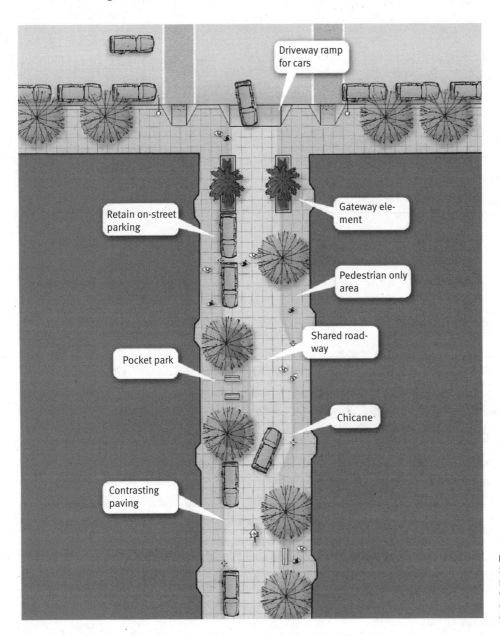

Figure 6-9
Shared streets allow cars and pedestrians to mix safely and comfortably. *Source: San Francisco Better Streets Plan, Courtesy the San Francisco Planning Department.*

Shared spaces should provide the following pedestrian-oriented elements:

- Alternative paving materials and/or patterns distinguishing them from traditional streets. Textures should be relatively smooth. Where surface materials are coarse enough to impede wheelchair circulation, a continuous 4-foot pedestrian path of ADA-compliant smooth material must be provided.

- In wider shared spaces, pedestrian-only spaces alternating from side to side to create chicanes, or interspersed among passenger loading zones, driveways, or parking spaces.

- Landscaping, seating, and other streetscape furniture and amenities.

- Vehicle closures on an intermittent or temporary basis for events, restaurant seating, markets, and the like.

Additionally, visual and tactile cues should be provided to identify the space as shared by pedestrians and vehicles, distinct from a traditional street, and to delineate between pedestrian-only and shared zones. Visual/tactile cues should be provided at all edges between pedestrian-only and shared zones. Visual/tactile cues should not impair the potential use of the entire right-of-way by all users. A variety of materials, treatments, and objects may be incorporated into visual/tactile cues. Combinations of elements may be used to create a more vibrant environment. Acceptable visual/tactile cues include, but are not limited to:

- Changes in texture (rougher surfaces in shared zones, or tactile bands between pedestrian-only and shared zones)

- High-contrast changes of color (light on dark or dark on light)

- Half-inch maximum ridges

- Landscaping and planters

- Street furniture

- Temporary or movable objects, such as swinging gates, movable planter boxes, or retractable bollards.

Measuring Pedestrian Success

True pedestrian Level of Service (LOS) consists of a long list of variables, each of which interacts with the others in complex ways. One measure included in the widely used *Highway Capacity Manual*[5] is pedestrian crowding, which is useful at specific locations, such as rail terminals and stadiums, but is not appropriate in most locations, as a modest amount of pedestrian crowding is helpful for personal security and urban vitality. Instead, consider measures that aggregate the most important factors for pedestrians in your city, such as the five following factors:

- **Distance to crossings** measures the average distance between designated pedestrian crossings, including signalized intersections and midblock crossings.

- **Crossing delay** focuses on how long a pedestrian must wait at a signalized intersection for a green phase. (At unsignalized crossings, omit this measure.) It is calculated according to the equation in Figure 6-10.

$$d_p = \frac{0.5(C-g)^2}{C}$$

where

d_p = average pedestrian delay(s),
g = effective green time (for pedestrians) and
C = cycle length(s).

Figure 6-10
Crossing-delay equation. *Source: Equation 18-5 from the* Highway Capacity Manual, *Transportation Research Board, Washington, D.C., 2000.*

- **Comfort** is a critical factor, but one that resists universal definition. In hot climates, the most important issue may be shade, particularly where pedestrians may be waiting for transit or waiting to cross the street; in such cases, percentage of shade or tree canopy could be a useful measure. In locations where personal security is a major concern, it may be best to create measures of "eyes on the street," such as maximum gap between occupied windows that face directly onto the street (that is, you may be able to fix the perceived pedestrian security problem by moving buildings closer to the street and ensuring a mix of residences and businesses so that people are observing the street at all times of day and night). In places where the quality of urban design is the biggest issue, use measures such as the frequency of doorways that open onto the street, percentage of the sidewalk that is edged with buildings (rather than parking lots), and/or the percentage of the ground floor of buildings that is windows and doors, rather than blank walls.

- **Crossing exposure** considers number of travel lanes to cross and the presence of a pedestrian refuge median.

- Finally, **conflict-free crossing time** considers the total percentage of crossing time when motor vehicles are not allowed across the crosswalk, including leading pedestrian interval, all-pedestrian phase, and no turning traffic.

To calculate the aggregate pedestrian LOS, measure each of the components, assign the numerical score that matches the LOS rating, and take the average. For example, a street that scored B on distance, C on delay, A on shade, C on lanes, and B on crossing time would get an aggregate LOS of B (4 + 3 + 5 + 3 + 4 divided by 5 = 3.8). Table 6-2 shows one approach toward aggregating pedestrian LOS.

Table 6-2: Aggregate Pedestrian Level of Service for Street Design

LOS	Score	Average distance to adjacent designated crossings (meters)	Crossing delay (seconds)	Comfort index	Number of lanes to cross and presence of pedestrian refuge median	Conflict-free crossing time
A	5	30 or less	5 or less	greater than 5	1 lane (one way)	100%
B	4	31–60	6–15	4–5	1+1 lanes	60–99%
C	3	61–90	16–25	3–4	2+2 lanes with refuge	30–59%
D	2	91–120	26–35	2–3	3 lanes (one way)	10–29%
E	1	121–150	36–45	1–2	3+3 lanes with refuge	1–9%
F	0	>150	>45	Less than 1	Any crossing more than 10 meters without a refuge or any street more than 3+3 lanes	0%

Case Study: Marin County Safe Routes to Schools

The Safe Routes to Schools program developed by Marin County, California, seeks to decrease rates of driving alone to schools using a combination of classroom lessons, contests and promotions, pedestrian and traffic calming improvements, enforcement, and regular evaluation. Surveys conducted in the fall of 2004 and spring of 2005 found that over the course of the school year, the program had resulted in a reduction in drive-alone mode-share of 13 percent (17 percent at private schools), a reduction in countywide vehicle miles traveled (VMT) of close to 2.6 million miles, and a reduction in carbon emissions amounting to more than 1,000 tons (Figure 6-11).

Engineering improvements are developed collaboratively, starting with a "walkabout" by members of a school task force (including parents, school staff, and community volunteers), local public works staff, law enforcement personnel, and elected officials. Once deficiencies are identified, an engineer works with each school's task force to develop potential short- and long-term improvements.

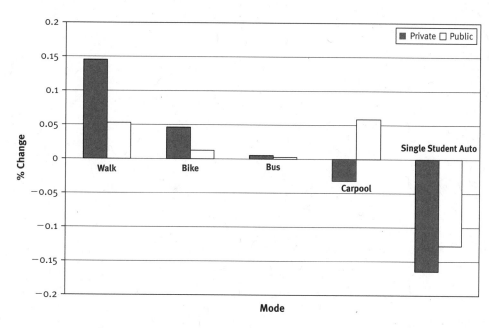

Figure 6-11
Marin County mode distribution, showing percent change in how children commuted to their public and private schools after implementing a Safe Routes to Schools program.
Source: Nelson\Nygaard.

Chapter 7

Bicycles

by Michael R. King

Introduction

Plenty of manuals, guidebooks, and white papers have been written for maintaining the bicycling status quo in North America. This is not one of them. Rather, this chapter reviews the key principles and design approaches necessary to make cycling an integrated part of sustainable city planning, and an attractive transportation choice for people of all ages and abilities. The audience of this chapter is not current cyclists—the stalwart types willing to endure the current state of bicycle infrastructure—but, rather, those who like the idea of cycling but find little pleasure in its current practice.

Why Invest in Cycling?

Aside from walking, bicycling is the most sustainable form of transportation:

- **Ecological Sustainability**. The bicycle is the most energy-efficient form of transportation ever invented, given the limited resources required for its manufacture, the minimal maintenance needed, and the human metabolism needed for its operation. It is also one of the most space-efficient, allowing a remarkable amount of mobility in a small amount of space. Most bicycle parts can be refurbished or recycled. No toxic substances are required for maintenance or operation of a bicycle. Provided the cyclist enjoys a sustainably harvested diet, bicycles are carbon neutral, thus far unique among commonly marketed mobility devices.

- **Social Sustainability**. As described in Chapter 3 on public health, bicycling supports humans' physical and emotional health. They are also cheap—almost anyone can afford to buy and maintain a bike.

- **Economic Sustainability**. As the price of carbon climbs, bicycling becomes the economic salvation for lower-density suburbs. As described in Chapter 8, transit is largely dependent upon density for its success. As density drops, so does the potential market for transit. As the transit market declines, transit agencies become unable to invest in high-frequency services. Because travelers place a high value on their time, people with a choice of modes rarely choose infrequent transit. Bicycling, however, works at all densities. Where bicycling and transit are planned together, low-density places can be linked—via bikeways—to higher-frequency transit lines. Rather than placing one hourly bus line every half-mile, transit operators can place a 15-minute route every 2 miles, so that almost everyone is within an easy one-mile bike ride to transit. Of course, making such a system work requires completely rethinking suburban roadway design and transit planning.

Increasing Cycling

In the past decade or so, there has been a semi-revolution in the world of cycling in North America, particularly in cities where the economic development strategy is to attract and retain the "creative class." There is something about cycling that appeals to the young, creative, and upwardly mobile.

Portland, Oregon, is an interesting example. There, city officials have noted significant increases in cycling for three years in a row. In some Portland neighborhoods, bike commuting is as high as 9 percent. Portland has installed more than 300 miles of bicycle lanes, bicycle boulevards, and off-road trails, resulting in a tripling of its bicycle network since 1991. During the same period, the number of bicycle trips across Portland's four bicycle-friendly bridges has increased over sixfold (Figure 7-1); meanwhile, corresponding auto counts have remained stable at zero growth. Here, relatively low-cost investments in cycling infrastructure are saving money by stabilizing auto travel as the population continues to grow rapidly (in fact, per capita vehicle miles traveled have dropped). Moreover, as the number of cyclists has increased, the bicycle crash rate has declined, as shown in Figure 7-2.

Of course, all of these numbers pale in comparison to the northern European capitals, such as Copenhagen and Amsterdam, where despite poor weather, bicycle trips exceed automobile trips (Figure 7-3).

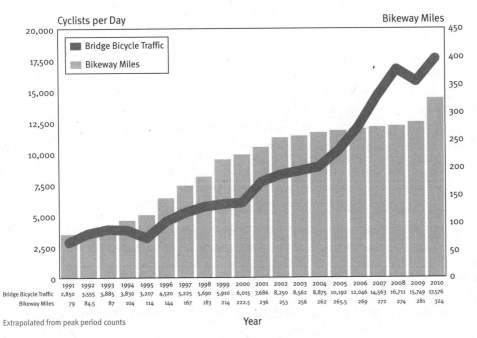

	1991	1992	1993	1994	1995	1996	1997	1998	1999	2000	2001	2002	2003	2004	2005	2006	2007	2008	2009	2010
Bridge Bicycle Traffic	2,850	3,555	3,885	3,830	3,207	4,520	5,225	5,690	5,910	6,015	7,686	8,250	8,562	8,875	10,192	12,046	14,563	16,711	15,749	17,576
Bikeway Miles	79	84.5	87	104	114	144	167	183	214	222.5	236	253	256	262	265.5	269	272	274	281	324

Extrapolated from peak period counts

Figure 7-1
Average daily bicycle traffic on the four main Willamette River bridges (Portland, Oregon). *Source: City of Portland Bureau of Transportation, Bicycle Count Report 2010.*

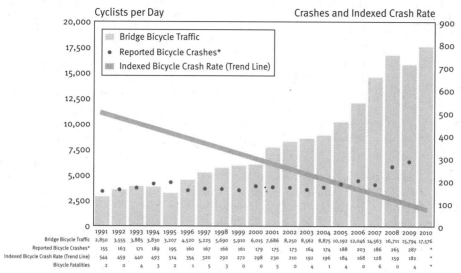

Cyclists per Day | Crashes and Indexed Crash Rate

Legend:
- Bridge Bicycle Traffic
- Reported Bicycle Crashes*
- Indexed Bicycle Crash Rate (Trend Line)

	1991	1992	1993	1994	1995	1996	1997	1998	1999	2000	2001	2002	2003	2004	2005	2006	2007	2008	2009	2010
Bridge Bicycle Traffic	2,850	3,555	3,885	3,830	3,207	4,520	5,225	5,690	5,910	6,015	7,686	8,250	8,562	8,875	10,192	12,046	14,563	16,711	15,794	17,576
Reported Bicycle Crashes*	155	163	171	189	195	160	167	166	161	179	175	173	164	174	188	203	186	265	287	*
Indexed Bicycle Crash Rate (Trend Line)	544	459	440	493	514	354	320	292	272	298	230	210	192	196	184	168	128	159	182	*
Bicycle Fatalities	2	0	4	3	2	1	5	3	0	0	5	0	4	1	4	0	6	0	4	*

Extrapolated from peak period counts

"Crash-Rate" represents an indexing of annual reported crashes to daily bicycle trips across the four main bicycle bridges.

*2008, 2009 Reported Bicycle Crashes data reflects increased crash reporting requirements.

Year

Figure 7-2
As cycling increased, the bicycle crash rate has declined sharply (Portland, Oregon). *Source: City of Portland Bureau of Transportation, Bicycle Count Report 2010.*

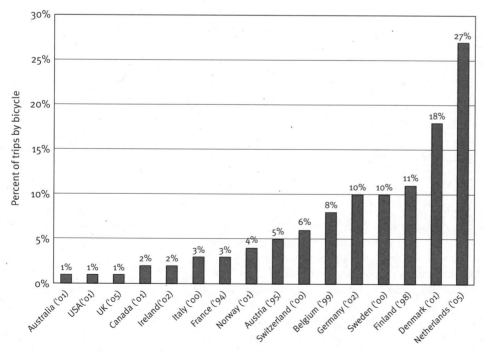

Figure 7-3
Bicycle share of trips in Europe, North America, and Australia (percent of total trips by bicycle). *Sources: John Pucher and Ralph Buehler. "At the Frontiers of Cycling: Policy Innovations in the Netherlands, Denmark, and Germany." Bloustein School of Planning and Public Policy, Rutgers University 2007. Original data from European Conference of the Ministers of Transport (2004); European Union (2003); U.S. Department of Transportation (2003); Netherlands Ministry of Transport (2006); German Federal Ministry of Transport (2003); Department for Transport (2005).*

Key Cycling Principles

Safety in Numbers

The more people cycle, the safer cycling becomes. Conversely, the fewer people riding in a community, the more dangerous their cycling becomes. Thus, the primary goal of a cycling program should be to increase ridership.

In the past decade, the *safety in numbers* phenomenon has been well researched and documented,[1] beginning with Peter Jacobsen's research in 2003. He found that:

> A motorist is less likely to collide with a person walking and bicycling when there are more people walking or bicycling. Modeling this relationship as a power curve yields the result that at the population level, the number of motorists colliding with people walking or bicycling will increase at roughly 0.4 power of the number of people walking or bicycling. . . . Taking into account the amount of walking and bicycling, the probability that a motorist will strike an individual person walking or bicycling declines with the roughly −0.6 power of the number of persons walking or bicycling.[2]

The conclusions to be drawn from Jacobsen's and others' research are counterintuitive but clear: The most effective strategy for improving cyclist safety is not the conventional approach of helmets and law enforcement, but rather finding out what would entice more noncyclists to ride. This is not to say that conventional safety approaches are unimportant, merely that they focus on the wrong audience.

Increasing Cycling Numbers

If cycling becomes safer with more cyclists, then increasing ridership will increase safety. So, how does one do that? By focusing on people who do not ride.

The first step is to find out why they don't. A survey of Americans found the number one reason for not cycling was lack of access to a bike.[3] Surveys of commuters who do not ride in Amsterdam, Montreal, and Seattle list distance and danger as the top reasons.[4] Other reasons include wanting to ride with others (like when you take a walk or drive with a friend), and needing to carry packages. In sum, potential cyclists need bikes, a place to park their bikes, a reasonable trip length, a safe bicycling route, and some storage space, each of which is covered in this section.

A BIKE FOR EVERYONE

Yes, you need a bike to ride a bike. It does not have to be yours, but if it is, you need someplace to keep it. This suggests that homes, offices, and shopping locations should have bike garages, or at least bike parking, incorporated into their designs (Figure 7-4). Hence, building and zoning codes should require bike parking, in much the same way they require auto parking, a number of toilets, accessible design, and so on.

As with any mode of transport, the more universal it is, the more accepted it is. In locations where the buses, trains, taxis, and so forth are all integrated into

Figure 7-4
Sheltered bicycle parking alongside house (Berlin, Germany). *Source: Nelson\Nygaard.*

one system, including the payment therefor, transit usage is higher. If there is a system, either organized or organic, where everyone has access to a bike, then bike usage will be higher. Bike share programs are an example. These operate like bike rental programs, but as cooperatives. Hotels and workplaces can offer bikes to their customers and employees—and some cities *require* shared bikes in new development. Bikes can be integrated into the train system so that people can use a bike for the last (or first) leg of the journey.

BIKEABLE DISTANCES

Trip length is a critical component of cycling. Using the rough guide of a 20-minute commute at 10 miles per hour (a "no sweat" pace), cycling has a range of 3 miles. Ergo, cycling will be most competitive in locations that have a 3-mile average trip length. In places where people must travel farther to work, school, and play, bicycling can work as part of the trip to a rapid transit line.

A BIKEWAY THAT FEELS SAFE

If your goal is improving bike safety by increasing the number of cyclists, the perception of safety is more important than the actuality of safety. It is not necessarily safer—in terms of actual crash statistics—to ride in a bicycle lane or cycle track than it is to ride in the middle of the outside travel lane of a major arterial. But only the hardiest of cyclists is willing to share the road with high-speed cars and trucks.

The research is clear, however, that when cities provide high-quality, dedicated bikeways, people use them.[5] "Bike Route" signs and pavement markings are insufficient. To create many cyclists, it is necessary to provide physical separation between vulnerable cyclists and motor vehicles, and design junctions to prioritize cycling. This tells cyclists that they do not have to rely on the goodwill of distracted drivers, and that someone is interested in their safety. When developing designs that increase perceived safety, it is critical also to address real safety by carefully considering how cyclists and motorists interact at intersections, as discussed later in this chapter.

A SOCIABLE BIKEWAY

While walking or driving a car, we can chat with the person next to us. Why does most bicycle infrastructure assume that biking is a solitary activity?

Even dedicated, lifelong cyclists are confronted with a challenge when they have kids. First, they buy a child seat and use it until the little ones are old enough to start pedaling themselves. Then they are faced with a predicament: How does one ride with a child?

If the child rides on the sidewalk, does the parent follow? Maybe not, because this is generally illegal. So, the parent is in the street and the kid is on the other side of the parked cars? If the child rides in the street, then the parent can join her, but not side-by-side—most bike lanes are just wide enough for one, and most jurisdictions forbid riding two abreast. So who goes first, the mom or the daughter?

If there is a cycle track of sufficient width, they can ride together. They can talk about cycling. They can talk about safety. These are teachable moments.

Fortunately, many jurisdictions (e.g., New Mexico, Washington) allow cycling two abreast.[6] Perhaps this is not the solution at all times and in all places, but furthering the life cycle of the cyclists seems to be an optimal way to increase ridership.

Great cycling communities have numerous events that celebrate those who ride, allow families to ride safely together, or pay homage to dedicated cyclists. Some common events include organized and supported rides; Sunday Parkways activities, where local streets are closed to cars and cyclists are free to ride; bike commute month (or week), during which local companies can compete for the highest cycling rates; and bicycle carnivals or events that showcase numerous types of cycling. All these events can help to build a cycling culture.

A PLACE TO CARRY AND STORE STUFF

Like everyone else, cyclists have stuff. They go shopping and buy stuff. They take stuff to work. They carry stuff to their friends' houses. With cars, we have trunks for our stuff. Something as simple as promoting better baskets and panniers—including lightweight lockable baskets—for cyclists can eliminate one of the major obstacles to cycling.

A COMFORTABLE RIDE

In the design of bicycle facilities, much is said about type, width, surface, location, traffic volume, and usage. Not much has been written about comfort.

The photos in Figures 7-5 through 7-8 show four different bike path treatments. They run alongside either the same or similar roadways in terms of speed, volume, and number of lanes. When shown these images, people who live in hot summer climates invariably choose Figure 7-7—the one with the most shade.

Figure 7-5
12 feet wide, good separation from road, good sightlines, no trees. *Source: Nelson\Nygaard.*

Figure 7-6
12 feet wide, good separation from road, satisfactory sightlines, trees with some shade. *Source: Nelson\Nygaard.*

Figure 7-7
6 feet wide, good separation from road, poor sightlines, good shade, dirt covering path. *Source: Nelson\ Nygaard.*

Figure 7-8
6 feet wide, no separation from road, good sightlines, trees but little shade. *Source: Nelson\Nygaard.*

Figure 7-9
Vehicular cycling: cycling amidst buses, trolleys and cars (San Francisco, California). *Source: Nelson\Nygaard.*

Even though this path is the narrowest, has poor sightlines to traffic, and has dirt covering it, it seems the most pleasant place to ride. Some people choose Figure 7-8, probably because it has some shade. Almost no one chooses Figure 7-5, even though it is the widest and has the best sightlines. Hardened cyclists choose Figure 7-9, probably because they are used to riding with traffic.

Design So That Everyone Will Enjoy Biking

Creating streets for use by bicycles is as much a question of attitude as of design. By its very nature, cycling challenges street design. Cyclists are adept at using all available surfaces to move—from roadway to walkway. Cyclists disregard any regimen given to a street, creating a more fluid and more efficient movement. Cyclists come in a variety of skill levels and purposes, from children to commuters, each of which demand a variety of facilities. The accomplished designer accepts these possibilities and creates streets that accommodate, encourage, and protect cyclists, especially the most vulnerable riders.

Cycling Types

Typical literature classifies cyclists into categories, such as advanced, beginner, and child; or leisure and utility; or commuter and recreational. Although such categorization is helpful, it may be more useful to focus on the type of cycling, not the type of cyclist. As Transport for London has discovered:

It is also important to remember that individuals may belong to more than one group: for example, a single person may commute to work, use cycling as an escape activity with their family, and sometimes cycle with their children to the shops. . . . Cycling is not a single, homogeneous activity, but a number of different activities that have in common the use of a two-wheeled unpowered vehicle.[7]

Most cyclists are covered in a range between two poles:

- **Vehicular cycling** (see Figure 7-9), when cyclists ride in traffic and follow the same patterns that cars do, such as merging into a left-turn lane to turn left. Vehicular cycling is accommodated on all roadways, and in such on-road facilities as bike lanes. In the United States, less than 1 percent of the population is comfortable with vehicular-style cycling on all roads, and another 7 percent is comfortable with typical bicycle lane conditions; these figures are typical around the world.[8]

- **Nonvehicular cycling**, when cyclists behave more like pedestrians than motorists. Nonvehicular cycling allows cyclists to navigate space in more complex ways than motorists, so that opposing flows of cyclists can intersect without any intersection controls and still avoid crashing, just as pedestrians do. Nonvehicular cycling is accommodated in paths, cycle tracks, and other facilities not shared by high-speed or high-volume motor vehicles. When nonvehicular cyclists use bike lanes, rather than merging to turn left, they tend to make a "box turn," using the crosswalks to cross first one street, then the other. About 60 percent of the population would like to be cyclists, but would mostly ride in a nonvehicular style.

To allow people to cycle in large numbers and make bicycling safe and comfortable for all, streets and paths must be designed to accommodate both types of cycling. As in the preceding examples, junctions must allow for cyclists turning with traffic, and cyclists turning with pedestrians. Programs have to address the needs of those riding in traffic, and those who simply will not—no matter how skilled they are.

Comprehensive Network

A bicycle network consists of much more than just bike lanes. A *bicycle network* is the same as the regular street network, save limited-access highways, plus paths, trails, and promenades. Bikes can go most places cars can, and most places pedestrians can. Thus, it is imperative for all streets to at least anticipate occasional use by cyclists, if only for a short stretch. Similarly, dedicated bicycle facilities that link together other routes are invaluable in creating a comprehensive network.

A bicycle facility network is:

- Cohesive, making connections throughout the community, including all major destinations

- Direct, without unnecessary circuitousness

- Understandable, with clear destination-oriented signage for cyclists

- Integrated, with particular care given to intersections, ensuring that cyclists can safely cross boulevards and other major streets (a bicycle network is only as good as its weakest link)

◀ Figure 7-10
Kiosk with bike map (Madison County, Illinois). *Source: Nelson\Nygaard.*

▼ Figure 7-11
Sharrow marking (Brooklyn, New York). *Source: Nelson\Nygaard.*

- Enforced, so that cycleways are free of parked cars and debris
- Clear, so that both motorists and cyclists know whether they have shared or separate spaces

Wayfinding

Knowing where you are going by bike is important. Positive route identification can help to embolden prospective riders (Figure 7-10). Highlighting popular destinations can expand the universe of cycling. Wayfinding tools help stitch together a network of various bicycle facilities. Wayfinding programs take a variety of forms:

- A series of signs and symbols on the road can be used to demarcate routes, distance to particular destinations, and upcoming turns.
- Bike lanes and "sharrows" can help guide cyclists (Figure 7-11).
- Colored bike lanes can self-identify routes, especially through complex intersections and turns (Figure 7-12).

Facilities

TYPES

Bicycle facilities can be classified into four general types:

- Off-street path
- Cycle track
- Bike lane
- Narrow lane

OFF-STREET PATHS (AND TRAILS)

Off-street paths (and trails) are cycle routes not part of the regular street network, commonly called "shared-use paths" in most U.S.-based design and planning documents. They include paths along rivers and railroad tracks,

▼ Figure 7-12
Bike lane colored green only through intersection (Seattle, Washington).
Source: Nelson\Nygaard.

▼ Figure 7-13
Typical bike path configuration.
Source: Nelson\Nygaard.

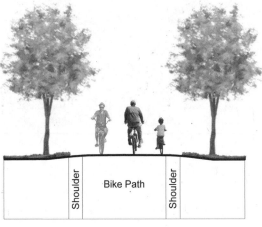

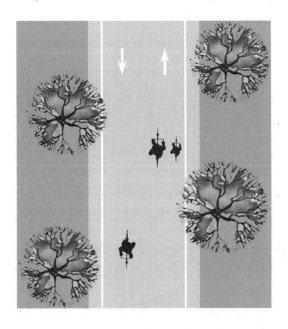

trails through parks and fields, promenades, and other places where people ride. They can take a variety of shapes and sizes, but should be at least 10 feet wide so that two cyclists can ride comfortably together and pass another cyclist. They should also be generally straight, level, and shaded. In most instances, the paths will be used by cyclists, joggers, skaters, and walkers, so where high volumes are expected, provide separate space for nonwheeled users (Figures 7-13 and 7-16). Cyclists can attain fairly high speeds on paths, so paths must be built using roadway engineering principles. Particular care must be taken when paths cross driveways or roads, to ensure that right-of-way is clear for both cyclists and cross traffic, and to ensure that cyclists can cross safely (Figures 7-14 and 7-15). At crossings of major roads, a traffic signal is usually necessary, with automatic detection of cyclists on the path. At minor crossings, a 6-foot median refuge may suffice, allowing cyclists to cross first one direction of travel, then the other, rather than waiting for a single gap in both directions.

CYCLE TRACKS (SEPARATED BIKE LANES)

When a bike lane is physically separated from the other lanes in the street, it becomes a *cycle track*. Cycle tracks are generally one-way and wide enough (6 to 7 feet) for two people to ride together (or one to pass another); see Figure 7-17. Care must be taken to maintain visibility for cyclists and motorists at intersections and driveways (Figure 7-18). Cycle tracks also require a specific maintenance plan, including small-scale street sweepers that can fit into them and clean them regularly.

Michael King

Figure 7-14
Bike path crossing rural roadway (Madison County, Illinois). *Source: Nelson\Nygaard.*

Figure 7-15
Bike path with both tunnel under
roadway and access to roadway above
(Madison County, Illinois). *Source:
Nelson\Nygaard.*

Figure 7-16
Bike path crossing a walkway (Santa
Barbara, California). *Source: Nelson\
Nygaard.*

Furthermore, cycle tracks must be designed to be clearly distinct from the sidewalk, or people will walk in them.

BIKE LANES

A *bike lane* is a travel lane for bicycles and other nonmotorized vehicles. They are generally 4 to 6 feet wide and placed between the parking and travel lanes (Figures 7-19 and 7-20). Wider bike lanes tend to be used as auto lanes unless separated from traffic and turned into a cycle track. Cyclists tend to be more afraid of being hit from behind by a car—a rare, but often fairly severe crash type—and less concerned about a car door suddenly opening in front of them—a common crash type and one that can also be severe and possibly fatal. To reduce "dooring," a 2- to 4-foot-wide buffer can be striped between the bike and auto lanes. In any case, where there is parallel parking, the minimum dimension between the curb and the inside bike lane stripe should be 13 feet.

On one-way streets, bike lanes may be placed on either the right or left side. Right-side bike lanes are more expected by cyclists, but left-side placement can be used to avoid bus stops, parking, or heavy right-turn movements, and will perform better when bike lanes on one-way streets are used (illegally, but inevitably) as counterflow bike lanes. Some bike lanes are used only during rush hours and parking is allowed in that space at other times. To highlight important bike lanes or note conflict points, many cities paint their bike lanes green, as seen in Figure 7-21, in New York City.

Where on-street parking occupancy is high, bike lanes may be blocked by double parking, rendering them useless. To reduce this problem, cities can designate loading spaces, make a dedicated double parking zone, or create a cycle track. The best solution is to manage parking so that spaces are always available on every block—see Chapter 10 on parking.

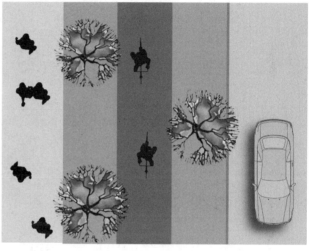

Figure 7-17
Typical cycle track configuration.
Source: Nelson\Nygaard.

NARROW LANES

If a street is too narrow to install a bike lane, one solution is to narrow it further to ensure that a driver cannot pass a cyclist except very slowly (Figure 7-22). "Narrow" lanes should be no more than 10 feet wide and should be traffic calmed to maintain low speeds (less than 20 mph).[9]

Narrow lanes are not "shared" lanes, which are typically 13 to 14 feet wide—wide enough for a driver to pass a cyclist but not wide enough for a bike lane (Figure 7-23). Shared lanes cause problems for all but the most intrepid cyclists, except where motor vehicle speeds are low.

▶ **Figure 7-18**
Cycle track (New York, New York).
Source: Nelson\Nygaard.

▼ **Figure 7-19**
Typical bike lane configuration.
Source: Nelson\Nygaard.

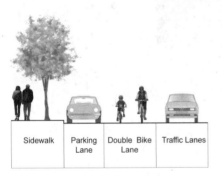

Sidewalk	Parking Lane	Double Bike Lane	Traffic Lanes

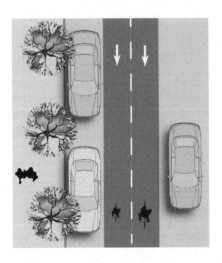

◀ **Figure 7-20**
Typical bike lane (Minneapolis, Minnesota). *Source: Nelson\Nygaard.*

▶ Figure 7-21
Applying green paint (thermoplastic
to a bike lane (New York, New York).
Source: Nelson\Nygaard.

▼ Figure 7-22
Typical narrow lane configuration.
Source: Nelson\Nygaard.

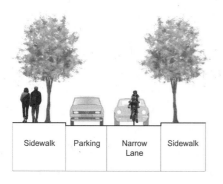

| Sidewalk | Parking | Narrow Lane | Sidewalk |

▼ Figure 7-23
Narrow, low-speed street—no need for
bike lane (New Orleans, Louisiana).
Source: Nelson\Nygaard.

BIKE BOULEVARDS

Bike boulevards are low-volume and low-speed streets optimized for use by cyclists, especially those too timid to ride on larger streets. Bike boulevards are typically traffic calmed and organized to create a continuous route for cyclists (Figure 7-24). They are ideal for use in a "safe routes to school" scheme, on quiet streets adjacent to commercial strips, and as an alternative to riding on a larger road.

Figure 7-24
Typical bike boulevard organization.
Source: ILS Schriften 21: Radverkehrskonzept Troisdorf, Fallstudie zu Niederkassel, 1989, ISBN 3-8176-6021-9. http://www.opengrey.eu/item/dIsplay/10068/86794 page 129.

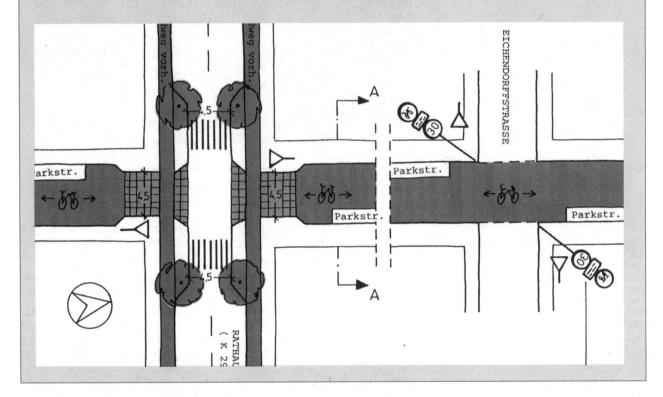

DE FACTO AND AD HOC BIKE FACILITIES

Much of what makes a city's bicycle network comprehensive is not cycle tracks and bike lanes, but rather the de facto and ad hoc bicycle facilities that make the rest of the streets amenable to cycling (Figures 7-25, 7-26, and 7-27). These include:

- Low-speed (20 mph or less) zones. These typically do not need designated bike facilities, especially if the volume is less than 3,000 vehicles per day.

- Bicycle access at dead-end streets. Where streets are discontinuous, it is important to provide connectivity for cyclists. This increases the options for cyclists, as cul-de-sacs often have low speeds and volumes—perfect for cycling.

- Ramps on stairs for bikes, especially at highway overpasses and transit stations.

SELECTING THE RIGHT FACILITY

The difference in speed between autos and cyclists can be used to choose the best facility type. Cyclists typically ride between 5 and 20 mph. Where the speed differential is less than 12 mph, cyclists can use the road without special provisions (a narrow lane). Where the differential is greater than 25 mph, a cycle track or buffered bike lane is desirable. In between, normal bike lanes are acceptable. Table 7-1 illustrates the preferred type of bicycle facility given motor vehicle speed.

Intersections and Junctions

Routing bicycle facilities through intersections is a complex task that requires more care than facility selection. Junctions, by their very nature, are where most conflicts occur, and the goal of any junction design is to reduce the severity of those conflicts. Happily, good design for autos and pedestrians is also good design for bicycles—intersections can be made safe for all.

The safest way to treat large intersections is to break them into smaller parts that can be navigated sequentially (Figures 7-28 through 7-32). Turn lanes, medians, and refuge islands all contribute to more manageable junctions. Signal systems that prioritize vulnerable road users (cyclists) can make those users more visible and provide conflict-free crossings.

Cyclists at smaller junctions should operate with normal traffic, albeit with prioritization techniques. Providing specialized facilities for all the turns that a cyclist might make will create a overly complicated junction. It is better to calm all traffic and ensure eye contact between driver and cyclist.

Key intersection design points and elements include:

- *Visibility.* Ensure that cyclists are visible at junctions by maintaining clear sightlines and routing facilities adjacent to auto traffic.

- *Turning speed.* Ensure that drivers turn slowly and can see cyclists so that they might yield.

Figure 7-25
Median is wide enough for cyclist to wait while crossing the street (Amsterdam, Netherlands). *Source: Nelson\Nygaard.*

Table 7-1 Bicycle Facility Selection Based on Speed Differential

Auto Speed	Narrow Lane	Bike Lane	Cycle Track
≥40 mph		X	XX
30 mph		XX	X
≤20 mph	XX	X	

Source: Adapted from *Guide to Traffic Engineering Practice*: Part 14: Bicycles. Austroads, Australia, 1999.

Figure 7-26
Bicycle shortcut (Davis, California).
Source: Nelson\Nygaard.

Figure 7-27
Pedestrian- and bicycle-only railroad
crossing (White Haven, Pennsylvania).
Source: Nelson\Nygaard.

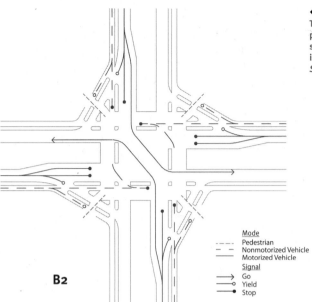

◀Figure 7-28
The separation principle comes into play at large intersections, including signal operations. Note the numerous islands defining the traveled way. *Source: Nelson\Nygaard.*

Mode
- - - - Pedestrian
- - - Nonmotorized Vehicle
——— Motorized Vehicle

Signal
→ Go
—○ Yield
—● Stop

B2

▼Figure 7-29
One option to route a cycle track through a junction. The cycle track bends outward and cyclists ride adjacent to auto traffic. *Source: Nelson\Nygaard.*

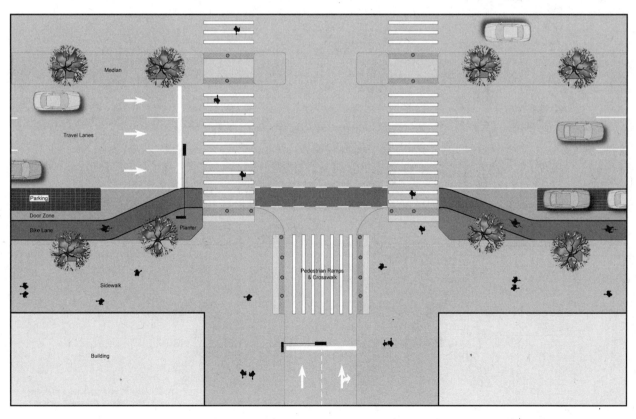

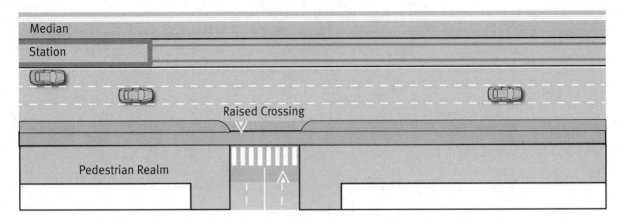

Median

Station

Raised Crossing

Pedestrian Realm

▲Figure 7-30
Routing a cycle track through a minor junction. The cycle track is given priority and is on a raised crossing. A similar treatment is recommended for driveways. *Source: Nelson\Nygaard.*

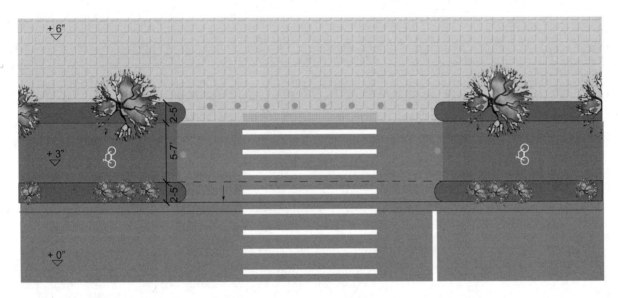

+ 6"

+ 3"

+ 0"

2-5'

5-7'

2-5'

▲Figure 7-31
At a midblock crosswalk, the cycle track or bike lane ends, as pedestrians have priority.. *Source: Nelson\Nygaard.*

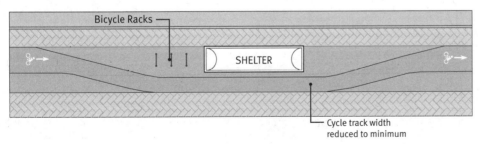

Bicycle Racks

SHELTER

Cycle track width
reduced to minimum

◀Figure 7-32
Routing a cycle track behind a bus shelter. *Source: Nelson\Nygaard.*

- *Intersection-only bike lanes and advance stop lines (bike box).* Reserve space for cyclists at the intersection, so that they may queue ahead of motor vehicles, especially if they are turning left. Placing cyclists ahead of drivers at junctions increases safety (Figure 7-34).[10]

- *Queue space at intersections.* Many cyclists make left turns by proceeding straight at the right side of a junction, then queue at the far corner until the signals change. Demarcating this area for cyclists both informs them of the proper place to queue, and also lets drivers know that cyclists are waiting there for a purpose (Figures 7-33 and 7-35).

- *Limiting right turn on red.* Many of the techniques (bike box, queue space) used to increase safety for cyclists at junctions are not otherwise possible.

- *Permit cyclists to treat stop signs as yield signs, and red signals as stop signs.* This is the law in Idaho and can address a common complaint among drivers that cyclists do not respect stop signs and red lights.[11]

- *Bicycle signals.* At complex intersections, it may be helpful to provide cyclists with their own signal; for example, to provide separate phases for right-turning motorists and through bicyclists (Figure 7-36).

- *Separation.* If the bicycle facility is separated from the main traffic flow, intersection design must be addressed very carefully to provide adequate sightlines between bicyclists and motorists, and provide special signalization to reduce

Figure 7-33
Corner of intersection is painted green to indicate location where cyclists are to queue (Changzhou, China).
Source: Nelson\Nygaard.

Michael King

Figure 7-34
Bike lane only at the intersection
(Santa Barbara, Califórnia). *Source:*
Nelson\Nygaard.

Michael King

Figure 7-35
Area between stop line and crosswalk
is demarcated with bike stencils to
indicate to drivers and cyclists that
cyclists turning left should queue
in this area (Manhattan, New York).
Source: Nelson\Nygaard.

conflicts between bicyclists and other modes (Figures 7-37 through 7-39). Some aspects of pedestrian facility design may be useful in addressing these intersection designs.

Bike Parking

Bicycle parking is a necessary component of a bicycle network. Simply put, one needs a place to leave one's bike at one's destination, and one needs to be assured that it will be there for the next ride (Figure 7-40). The following are guidelines for good bike parking.

LOCATION

For bicycles to be fully integrated into the transportation system, parking has to be located where people work, study, shop, play, live, and accomplish life's myriad errands. Consider the following:

- Observation
  - Locate parking where bicycles are currently parked ad hoc
  - Survey cyclists, bicycle clubs, and advocacy groups for desired locations
- Access
  - Locate parking as close as possible to building entrances (within 50 feet) without obstructing pedestrian flow (one of the major benefits of cycling is the ability to ride right up to the front door)
  - Avoid locations that require cyclists to carry their bikes up or down stairs, through narrow passages, or across other surfaces they cannot ride on
  - Where there is not room on the sidewalk, convert car parking spaces (10 bicycles can easily be parked in the space of one car)
- Visibility, security, lighting, weather
  - Locate parking in highly visible places to discourage theft and vandalism
  - Locate parking within view of passers-by, retail activity, or office windows
  - Explore opportunities to site bike parking within view of any security personnel nearby, especially if they have been hired to watch parked cars
  - Install security cameras if other measures are insufficient to deter theft and vandalism
  - Ensure that facilities are well lit
  - Protect parked bikes from inclement weather conditions, especially for commute cyclists

Figure 7-36
Bicycle signal (Davis, California).
Source: Nelson\Nygaard.

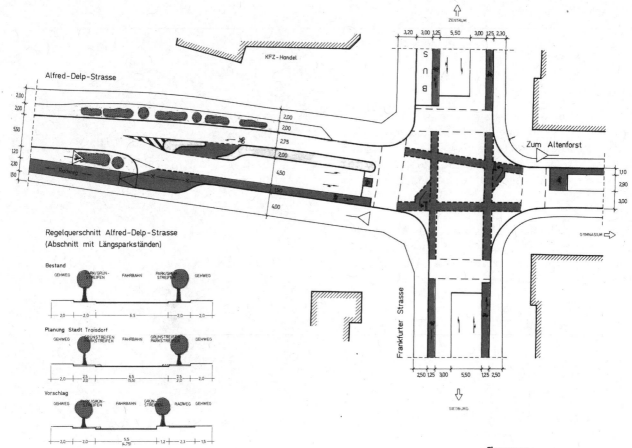

Figure 7-37
Organization of bike lanes through an intersection. Note how the bike path joins with the street to the left of the junction. *Source: ILS Schriften 21: Radverkehrskonzept Troisdorf, Fallstudie zu Niederkassel, 1989, ISBN 3-8176-6021-9, page 119.*

PARKING TYPES

RACKS

Often unprotected from weather conditions, bicycle racks are the most abundant type of parking facility and generally the least expensive to install. Spatially, they are the most efficient and can accommodate the greatest number of bicycles. There are many different styles and forms of racks, many of which were apparently designed by non-cyclists. Even in nonstandard forms like Figure 7-41, the most effective racks:

- Support the bicycle
- Are securely anchored and cannot be dismantled
- Allow the bike frame to be locked to the rack with a common U-lock and allow both wheels to be secured to the rack with a cable

LOCKERS

Bicycle lockers provide a higher level of security than racks and protect bikes from weather (Figure 7-42). Users can also store clothing, helmets, and other bicycle

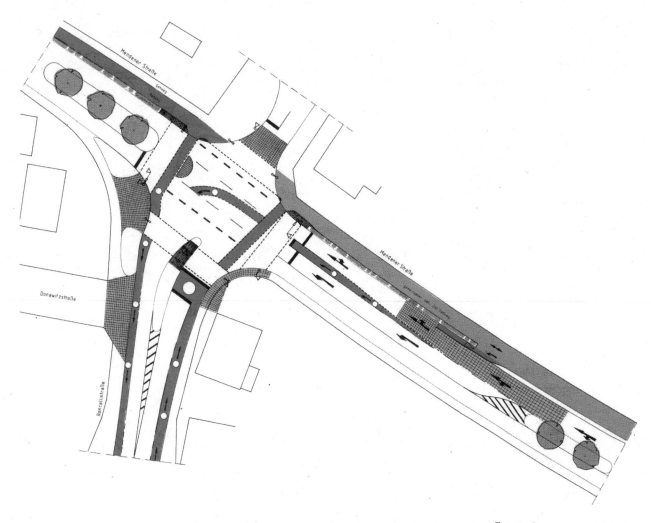

Figure 7-38
Organization of bike lanes through an intersection. Note how the two-way cycle track remains at the top of the street, while cyclists wishing to turn left transition into a turn lane. *Source: ILS Schriften 21: Radverkehrskonzept Troisdorf, Fallstudie zu Niederkassel, 1989, ISBN 3-8176-6021-9, page 135.*

accessories in lockers. Access to lockers varies, from single-key individual long-term use, to electronic card locks that allow for multiple users over an extended time period, to hourly rental lockers.

SHELTERS/GARAGES/INDOOR

Bicycle shelters and garages require more space than racks and have higher installation and maintenance costs, but provide a significantly higher level of security, especially if a guard is present. Shelters generally consist of rows of bicycle racks protected underneath a structure that is either fully or partially enclosed (Figure 7-43).

QUANTITIES

The amount of parking should vary by land-use type and geography, with more bike-friendly areas having more bike parking. Table 7-2 details some sample requirements.

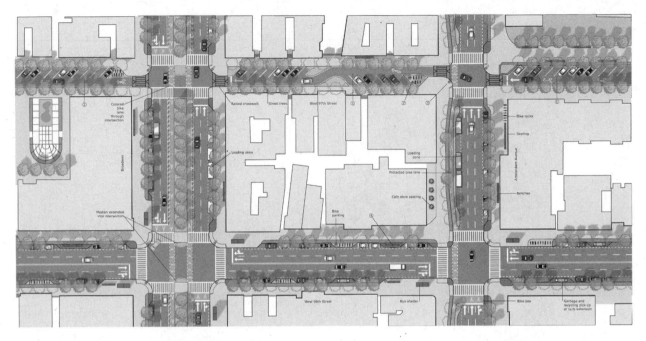

▲ Figure 7-39
Rendering of model block showing various bike lane permutations, including buffered bike lane along median, bike lane along left side of one-way street, no lane where there is diagonal parking that calms traffic along the minor street, bike boxes, and raised crossings. *Source: Nelson\Nygaard image created for Blueprint for the Upper West Side: A Roadmap for Truly Livable Streets. NYC Streets Renaissance, 2008*, http://transalt.org/files/newsroom/reports/UWS_Blueprint.pdf.

◀ Figure 7-40
Bike hung and locked on a fence indicates a need for bike parking (Newark, New Jersey). *Source: Nelson\Nygaard.*

Table 7-2: Bicycle Parking per Land Use

Land Use	Number of Bicycle Parking Spaces/Land-Use Unit	Who Would Provide This?
Residential (multifamily)	1 space per 3 units	Private developer
Commercial/retail	1 space per 4,000 square feet of leaseable space	Private developer
Office	1 space per 5,000 square feet of leaseable space	Private developer
School	1 space per 10 students	City/school board
Park	2 spaces per acre	City
Recreation center	1 space per 1,000 square feet of usable floor area	City

Measuring Bicycle Success

Bicycle Level of Service (LOS) can be used to locate routes and choose facility type. LOS is largely a function of motor vehicle speed and volume, plus available width. Figure 7-44 illustrates this relationship. For example, on a 30-mph street with 9,000 vehicles per day, a bicycle lane yields LOS-C for cyclists. If a higher LOS is desired, the following can be done:

- Reduce vehicle speeds
- Lower vehicle volumes
- Construct a cycle track

A higher-quality facility will produce a higher level of service for cyclists, which will encourage additional ridership. In addition, a higher number of cyclists on a certain route would necessitate wider facilities.

Figure 7-41
Bike rack in the shape of a dog (New York, New York). Note that both wheels can be locked to the rack, the rack is secured to the sidewalk, and one can lean the bike against the rack while locking it. *Source: Nelson\Nygaard.*

Further Information

The AASHTO *Guidelines for the Development of Bicycle Facilities* is the standard document for bikeways in the United States. It emphasizes on-street bicycle lanes in typical U.S. suburban contexts, but it is weak on more creative approaches, such as shared streets and cycle tracks.

The Dutch *Design Manual for Bicycle Traffic* takes a very different approach from AASHTO, with an emphasis on integrated bicycle design, traffic calming, and separated facilities. It is available in English, and may be ordered online at www.crow.nl.

In 2011, the National Association of City Transportation Officials (NACTO) published its *Urban Bikeway Design Guide*, which includes design and planning recommendations for emerging best practices for new bikeway designs. It is available free at www.nacto.org.

Figure 7-42
Typical bicycle locker (Los Angeles, California). *Source: Nelson\Nygaard.*

Figure 7-43
Bike parking in car parking garage (Minneapolis, Minnesota). *Source: Nelson\Nygaard.*

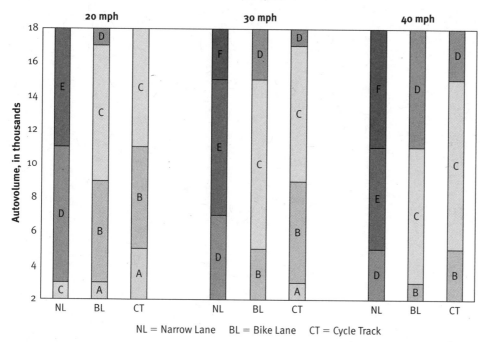

Auto Speed

Figure 7-44
Bicycle facility selection based on
motor vehicle speed and volume, plus
roadway width. *Source: Values based
on Harkey, D. L., Reinfurt, D. W., &
Sorton, A. (1998). The Bicycle
Compatibility Index: A Level of Service
Concept, Implementation Manual
Washington, D.C.: Federal Highway
Administration.*

Chapter 8

Transit

by Tara Krueger Gallen

Introduction

Mass or public *transit*—including subways, commuter rail, light rail, streetcars, buses, shuttles, and an array of other technologies and service types—is a catch-all term for shared, publicly available transportation services. Transit may run on a schedule, or it may come when you call it, as with dial-a-ride or taxis. It may be decrepit and overcrowded, or it may be luxurious, like New York's Grand Central Terminal. Regardless of the type of transit, you don't have to drive yourself, leaving you time to focus on other matters. Because you can't control the vehicle, however, you also must deal with the potential downside of transit: You can't leave exactly when you want to, and you can't necessarily go exactly where you want to go.

Why Invest in Transit?

Why not just let everyone drive their own cars? According to the American Public Transit Association, there are at least six important reasons:

1. **Productivity**: Efficiently run transit moves a lot of people in little space—more than ten times as many people per unit of roadway space than by car. In urban areas, it is often more cost-effective to invest in transit to create roadway capacity than it is to invest in added roadway capacity.

2. **Environment**: One person's switch to public transit can save as much as 20 pounds of carbon per day.

3. **Economy**: Transit can stimulate development and commercial revitalization, as well as raise property values. For every $1.00 invested in public transit, an estimated $4.00 in economic returns is generated.

4. **Financial**: Transit is a cost-effective means of transportation not just for cities, but also for individuals. According to Fannie Mae, the cost savings from giving up one car can allow a family to afford an extra $100,000 on a 30-year, fixed-rate house mortgage.

5. **Equity**: Transit provides transportation options for the roughly 30 percent of Americans who are too old, too young, too poor, or too disabled to drive.

6. **Health**: Transit requires some walking, and reduces obesity.

Why Take Transit?

Policymakers, including many planners, typically think about the decisionmaking process for each trip in terms of:

- Factors they can control (for example, quality of service)
- Factors they may be able to influence over time (for example, land use and urban design)
- Factors that are beyond their control (for example, fuel prices)

Customers, however, tend to base their trip-making decisions on a somewhat different set of factors:

- Rational or conscious factors, such as a cost-benefit analysis (for example, transit will take X number of minutes longer than driving, but will save X amount of money)
- Social, psychological, subconscious, emotional, or "irrational" factors, such as:
  - The "image" of transit vs. autos, or bus vs. rail
  - Perceived vs. actual safety
  - Perceived vs. actual cost (people tend not to think about the hidden or sunk costs of auto ownership, such as monthly car or insurance payments that might be automatically deducted from one's account)

In planning transit service, one should always try to bear in mind both perspectives—because members of the public will ultimately be the ones using the service, but also because a limited focus on transit will result in a certain myopia about the door-to-door nature of the whole trip, which also includes pedestrian legs and may include other modes.

Planners should also keep in mind that in addition to the "carrot" of quality transit service, "sticks" such as expensive parking can have a powerful effect on mode choice. These broader contexts, even when beyond the direct control of planners, should always be incorporated into planners' thought processes, as they can be a factor in key decisions such as alignment and stop placement, level of service that should be provided, and level of investment that should be made.

Transit Modes

"Well, sir, there's nothing on earth
Like a genuine,
Bona fide,
Electrified,
Six-car
Monorail!"

—*The Simpsons*, "Marge vs. the Monorail"

Certain transit technologies can be so compelling that some communities start with the choice of technology and then figure out where to put it. A classic example is *The Simpsons* episode in which snake-oil peddler Lyle Lanley attempts to sell Springfield on a new monorail system; unfortunately, similar (if less humorous) examples can be found in the real world.

In planning a transit project, a few basic questions should always be asked and answered:

- What are our objectives?
- Given these objectives, how should we measure performance?
- Applying these measures, what sort of service might be the best fit for this market?
- Applying these measures, what sort of infrastructure, right-of-way management, and vehicles might be the best fit with this service?
- What can we afford (what is the optimal level of investment to maximize cost-effectiveness)?

If there is only one thing you, as a prospective planner of transit, remember from this chapter, make it this: *Select a technology based on the need for service and not on a desire to have a particular technology*. Avoid putting the proverbial cart before the horse, and avoid "Flying Car Syndrome"—the idea that the future has promised us sleek technology and we shall have it, regardless of context. Ultimately, it is process that matters most. If one starts not with a vehicle, but with an understanding of the market to be served, a set of objectives, and related performance measures, the choice of mode is likely to be the right one.

When developing transit systems, one should always start small and build up. It is easy to become enamored with the idea of light rail, Personal Rapid Transit, or streetcars without thinking first about whether it would be the best fit. After all, these technologies are symbols of many successful, thriving cities, from Portland, Oregon, to Amsterdam. But technology for technology's sake is foolish.

Defining *Mode*

Transit vehicles are distinctive, so most of us tend to refer to transit vehicles and modes interchangeably. However, a transit *mode* consists of several elements, to be discussed throughout this chapter:

- Right-of-way design and management
- Stop/station design and access requirements
- Service model/operating plan
- Vehicle type

Although modes can generally be clearly defined based on typical or recommended parameters—and indeed, this chapter does so—one should be careful not to become too rigid or narrow in one's thinking about mode. Lines between modes can become blurred; for example, a streetcar could be coupled with right-of-way, stops, and an operating model typical of light rail (and in fact, some have argued for wider use of such a "rapid streetcar" mode). Moreover, performance can vary: Though, as Figure 8-1 illustrates, light rail generally costs less to operate on a per-passenger basis than local buses, this is largely due to capacity, and dependent on ridership. In San Francisco, where light rail trains are lower capacity than in many other cities (as they consist of only one or two cars) and where 60-foot articulated buses are used on many busy routes, light rail costs more to operate on a per-rider basis than buses.

The Role of Right-of-Way and Stops

Although different types of transit vehicles are generally associated with types of right-of-way and stops, both are to some extent independent of mode. For instance, buses or trains can operate in traffic, or in their own rights-of-way, and can use simple stops or more elaborate stations.

The ability of transit to compete with the car in terms of speed and reliability is critical to attracting ridership, and delay occurs both while buses are in motion—in traffic, from congestion, or at stop lights or signs—and at stops, through unnecessarily long "dwell" times.

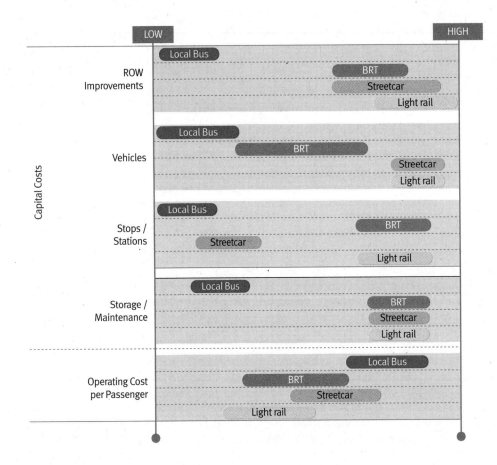

Figure 8-1
In terms of both defining elements and performance, lines between modes can sometimes become blurred. *Source: Nelson\Nygaard.*

Transit vehicles operating in traffic are not just slower; traffic-caused delay can also have a severe impact on reliability, as vehicles that fall behind schedule tend to fall ever further behind as more people have time to arrive at downstream stops, and more people must be loaded and unloaded (Figure 8-2). Sometimes transit vehicles fall so far behind schedule that they block the vehicle behind them, a phenomenon known as *bunching*.

Considerations in right-of-way design and management include:

- **Person Delay**: Travel times should be thought of in terms of *person* delay, as opposed to traditional standards of *vehicle* delay, which equate a single-occupant vehicle with a bus carrying sixty passengers.

- **Future Reliability**: Even where there is little existing congestion, dedicated right-of-way can provide a hedge or insurance policy against increasing congestion.

- **Strategic Investments**: Over the length of a long corridor, relatively modest transit priority treatments (such as traffic signal preemption and queue jump lanes) can lead to significant improvements in speed, reliability, and ridership.

- **Cost Savings**: Because speed is directly related to frequency—when transit vehicles are slower, more of them are required to maintain the same frequency—transit delay caused by traffic congestion carries a huge price tag in terms of operating cost.

- **Permanence**: Highly visible, permanent transit infrastructure, including both right-of-way and stations or stops, can provide a sense of clarity and security for

Figure 8-2
Chicago Transit Authority bus in urban operation is impeded by congestion. This is an operating reality of the local bus mode. *Source: Nelson\Nygaard.*

both potential riders and developers who might respond to a public investment with private investment.

Considerations in stop and station design include:

- **Level Boarding**: Doing away with stairs, either through low vehicle floors, high platforms, or some combination thereof, can reduce the time it takes to load and unload a passenger in a wheelchair by minutes, as wheelchairs can be rolled on and off using ramps or plates rather than relying on cumbersome lifts.

- **All-Door Boarding**: Simultaneous boarding through all doors is enabled by off-board payment or prepaid boarding policies using ticket vending machines at stops. Operating savings should exceed lost fare revenues, as evasion rates on proof-of-payment systems are typically in the low single digits.

- **Stop Placement**: In-line stops using bulb-out sidewalk extensions do not require transit vehicles to merge back into traffic. Likewise, far-side stops beyond intersections allow transit vehicles operating in mixed flow to pull into stops without waiting for traffic queued at a signal to clear, and allow vehicles to pull away from stops without waiting for a green light or for passengers who have just gotten off the vehicle to cross the street in front of them.

- **Stop Access**: Along with the quantity of destinations within the walkshed—a quarter- or half-mile distance, or a five- or ten-minute walk to or from a stop—the quality of pedestrian paths is among the most important factors in determining the success of a transit service. Pedestrian paths to and from stops are, unfortunately, often beyond the control of transit planners, at least beyond the immediate area. Over time, however, high-quality transit can encourage the development of dense, walkable neighborhoods.

Relationship to Land Use

A certain level of population and/or employment density is required to ensure cost-effectiveness and justify investment in different transit modes (Figure 8-3). Although density is just one of several land-use factors contributing to a transit-supportive environment—including pedestrian-oriented design and a diversity of uses—it can act as a useful shorthand for determining what level of service and investment might be warranted.

One important caveat: Rail modes have been shown to shape land-use context over time. Robust bus rapid transit featuring dedicated right-of-way and light-rail-like stations might also have the same effect, although so far data proving this effect are limited. In general, however, it seems that the more visible, permanent, and extensive the infrastructure, the greater the attraction for transit-oriented development, which can create a virtuous cycle of mutually supportive land use and transit service.

Buses

Buses offer unparalleled flexibility and cost advantages over rail. However, with the exception of trolleybuses, they emit more pollutants; they are smaller than

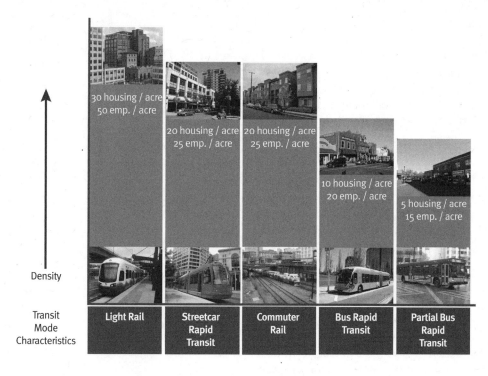

30 housing / acre 50 emp. / acre	20 housing / acre 25 emp. / acre	20 housing / acre 25 emp. / acre	10 housing / acre 20 emp. / acre	5 housing / acre 15 emp. / acre

Density

| Transit Mode Characteristics | **Light Rail** | **Streetcar Rapid Transit** | **Commuter Rail** | **Bus Rapid Transit** | **Partial Bus Rapid Transit** |

Figure 8-3
A minimum density threshold must be met before it makes sense to invest in a more intensive transit mode. *Source: Nelson\Nygaard.*

railcars; they do not offer as comfortable a ride because of lateral sway and bumps from rubber tires and pavement; and they generally suffer from an image problem. Nonetheless, buses can provide a relatively high quality of *trunk* or major corridor service in emerging transit markets, and essential feeder services in more mature markets.

For buses in particular, mode is not the same thing as vehicle, as the differences between bus modes have largely to do with right-of-way design and management and stop design and access.

LOCAL BUS

Local bus service is the workhorse of most transit systems. It is defined by relatively close stop spacing (in some systems, 800 feet or less, although access must be balanced against speed), curbside stop placement, and mixed traffic operation. Frequencies vary widely.

Although most local buses operate on a fixed route, "deviated fixed route" or "flex" services can deviate up to a quarter- or half-mile in response to customer requests (by phone or on the bus). This type of service can expand coverage in lower-density areas where resources are limited.

EXPRESS AND LIMITED BUS

Express services are sometimes referred to as *commuter routes*, and indeed many express services use commuter buses, operate during peak hours, and stop at suburban park-and-ride lots before continuing downtown via freeway high-occupancy vehicle lanes.

Limited-stop routes, in contrast, typically operate in urban trunk corridors, often as an overlay supplementing local service along the same alignment. Limited services are defined by their stop spacing—generally a half-mile or more, at least outside of central business districts—and generally operate relatively frequently and do not operate outside of weekdays or peak hours.

SHUTTLE

Shuttles are similar to local buses, but tend to serve distinct markets: "last-mile" connections, or as circulators within small areas. They are also more likely to use smaller, cutaway vehicles, and are often funded (if not operated) by cities or business associations. (A few special service-design rules for shuttles are provided later in this chapter.)

BUS RAPID TRANSIT

According to the Transit Cooperative Research Program, bus rapid transit (or, in the three-letter-acronym world of transportation planning, BRT) is "a flexible, rubber-tired rapid-transit mode that combines stations, vehicles, services, running ways, and Intelligent Transportation System (ITS) elements into an integrated system with a strong positive identity that evokes a unique image."[1] In other words, BRT is not so much a traditional mode associated with a vehicle as a package of tools designed to make buses faster, more reliable, and higher *quality* (thus the occasional name "quality bus"). BRT can also be implemented at far less upfront cost than rail, for which capital costs range from a few hundred thousand dollars a mile to tens of millions of dollars per mile.

Because BRT is a relatively new mode, and is not a mode in the traditional sense, a great deal of confusion (and controversy) remains about the meaning of the term. BRT consists of a range of elements, a spectrum or menu of options, and in some communities, implementations featuring only a few of these components are described as "rapid bus." The line between the two is not always clear, however, and many rapid-bus projects are described by their promoters simply as BRT.

This has resulted in much skepticism among rail advocates, some of whom see in BRT a shadowy conspiracy to stop rail projects in their tracks. Though there may be some truth to this in certain cases, planners should avoid getting caught up in "rail vs. BRT" debates, which tend to deal in broad generalities rather than the specific circumstances of each corridor and community, and neglect the value of both as potentially complementary tools in the same planners' toolbox. Instead, planners should follow the process described previously: identify goals and performance measures, *then* identify mode.

In any case, BRT implementations have been deemed successful in South America, Australia, Europe, and North America. BRT projects have consistently reduced travel times, improved reliability, and attracted many new riders, all in a relatively short period of time and for relatively less initial cost than rail lines. To date, international BRT systems have tended to be more extensive than North American applications, often featuring off-street transitways, some with multiple lanes for passing, and stations with fare-controlled areas.

BRT strategies commonly used in North America include:

- **Right-of-Way**: One of the advantages of BRT over rail is its ability to respond to different contexts within individual segments of an alignment by operating in mixed traffic where it is not possible to provide transit-only lanes, but where railcars would be blocked by traffic. Right-of-way treatments include:

  - **Bus-only lanes**, either in an off-street or median transitway or in side lanes that can be accessed by cars to turn right or access curbside parking (in some cases, taxis and bicycles may be allowed to share bus lanes). Lanes that are not physically separated from traffic may be painted to provide an additional visual cue to drivers that these areas are not for general use.

  - **Queue jump lanes**, which allow buses to bypass cars that are queued at intersections and go ahead of traffic using a special signal phase.

  - **Transit Signal Priority (TSP)** systems, which allow green lights to hold a few seconds more for an approaching bus, or (in some cases) allow a red light to turn green early.

- **Stops**: BRT stops or stations are generally spaced one-half mile to one mile apart and offer customer amenities such as more shelter, seating space, and information, including real-time wait times. Stops in more robust BRT systems feature raised platforms and ticket machines for all-door, level boarding.

- **Vehicles**: BRT buses are typically branded with distinct liveries or logos and paint schemes, and are sometimes designed to look like railcars, with sleek exteriors. They are generally 60-foot articulated buses with low floors and three or more doors.

- **Service**: BRT lines provide walk-up frequencies (in other words, service so frequent that schedules are not needed) of every 15 minutes or even less, and many are headway based, meaning that operators are instructed to simply go as fast as is safely possible, and not hold back in order to avoid arriving at stops ahead of schedule. Lines are also generally relatively direct and simple, although some transitways are used by multiple lines, which operate as local service outside of the transitway.

BRT may be a first stage of development toward rail, or an end in itself. Often BRT lines are themselves implemented in phases, either incrementally over a whole corridor (rapid bus leading to BRT) or by segment.

One area in which BRT is inherently inferior to rail is capacity. Even though some international systems have been able to achieve truly impressive throughput using massive transitways and stations, buses cannot be coupled together as railcars can to form trains, so BRT systems cannot serve very high levels of demand without incurring significant labor and long-term operating costs.

CASE STUDY: LOS ANGELES METRO RAPID

The Los Angeles Metro Rapid system is perhaps the most famous BRT implementation in the United States—yet it is actually a classic rapid-bus system that generally forgoes more expensive and politically challenging elements such as bus-only lanes in order to provide relatively significant benefits quickly and at low cost (less than $250,000 per mile to date).[2] (See Figure 8-4.) The system relies primarily on branding, limited stop spacing, direct routes, enhanced amenities at stops, low-floor buses, and signal priority, yet it has achieved time savings of up to 31 percent and an increase in ridership of up to 40 percent.[3] Established in 2000, by 2010 the system included twenty-eight lines and was close to 440 miles long.

Figure 8-4
Los Angeles's Metro Rapid BRT system has greatly improved travel times and ridership at very low cost. *Source: Fred Camino (used under Creative Commons license:* http://creativecommons.org/licenses/by-sa/2.0/)

Rail

Whatever else it may be, rail transit is permanent—North America's failed midcentury experiment in removal of streetcar lines aside. Prospective passengers can see tracks and overhead wires (or, in the case of metro rail and some light rail systems, subway station entrances), and know where trains will go. Likewise, developers see rail as a major public investment in a place, and often respond with private investment. Railcars provide a smoother ride, and trains offer higher capacity than buses, which can reduce operating costs in high-demand corridors. Finally, urban trains (though not most commuter rail lines) tend to be quieter and cleaner than buses, and use of electricity rather than diesel fuel can protect transit agencies from rising fuel costs. All in all, rail is a superior mode of urban transport—but one that can come at a high capital cost, of tens or even hundreds of millions of dollars per mile.

In this section, rail modes and vehicles are treated interchangeably. However, certain caveats apply (see the previous section on "Defining Mode").

STREETCAR
Prior to World War II, the streetcar was the driving force in urban development. Recently, something of a revival has taken place. Light rail (see the next section)

was the preferred mode of planners and policymakers looking to return rail transit to North American cities in the 1980s and 1990s, but less expensive (if slower and lower-capacity) streetcar lines have recently become an attractive option, either as a complement to other rail modes or as an alternative. Although streetcar costs vary, they are typically in the tens of millions of dollars per mile, whereas light rail regularly exceeds $50 million per mile and can cost more than $100 million per mile.

As a mobility option, streetcars offer few (if any) advantages over buses. However, they can increase *access*, or the number of destinations within reach, by driving economic development (see the accompanying case study). They also have a proven track record of attracting new riders: one study in Toronto found a 15 to 25 percent increase wherever streetcars replaced otherwise nearly identical bus services.

Because streetcars tend to operate in mixed traffic and stop relatively often, they can be fairly slow. For this reason, they tend to operate over short distances within downtowns and in adjacent neighborhoods. Their smaller size—streetcars are both somewhat smaller than light rail vehicles, and generally operate as single cars—makes them a good fit for urban streets. They are also lighter than light rail vehicles, and thus streetcar lines are faster and cheaper to build, as they require shallower foundations and less utility relocation. They are most successful where there is strong all-day, bidirectional demand rather than unidirectional, peak-oriented demand, and where there is relatively little traffic.

There are a few basic types of streetcars, all powered by overhead wires:

- **Restored vintage cars**: These vehicles are often President's Conference Committee (PCC) cars from the prewar period (Figure 8-5). Because car

Figure 8-5
PCC in San Francisco. *Source: Steven Weller/Nelson\Nygaard.*

CASE STUDY: PORTLAND STREETCAR

The Portland Streetcar has been credited with increasing property values along the line by 40 percent, and attracting up to $3 billion in private investment. Though much of this investment might have happened without the advent of the streetcar, the line expedited and shaped redevelopment in the formerly industrial Pearl District and is now enabling high-rise development in the South Waterfront (Figure 8-6). The streetcar line has already been extended twice, and a third, much longer extension across the Willamette River is now under construction.

Figure 8-6
Streetcars have expedited and shaped redevelopment in Portland. *Source: Nelson\Nygaard.*

manufacturing was discontinued in the 1950s, only a limited supply is available. Heritage vehicles are also not readily accessible to persons with disabilities, as they have high floors and no wheelchair lifts. They generally cost around $1 million each.

● **New "replica" cars**: These vehicles are built from blueprints of vintage vehicles, but can be modified to include wheelchair lifts.

- **Modern streetcars**: These vehicles have low floors and provide a more comfortable, quieter ride than their historic counterparts (Figure 8-6). They also provide higher capacity, of as much as 170 passengers both seated and standing. Maintenance is simpler, as parts are more widely available. Additionally, it is easier to acquire a fleet of modern streetcars. However, they are relatively expensive: recently costs have approached $4 million per vehicle.

LIGHT RAIL

Light rail transit, or LRT, has been the favored mode of North American rail planners for more than a generation. This is because it can provide many of the advantages of heavy or metro rail at significantly lower cost, usually less than $100 million per mile (and sometimes significantly less). LRT infrastructure is less expensive because it is less extensive, with smaller and simpler stops and, typically, some at-grade operation in freight rail corridors or on city streets. Light rail vehicles can reach speeds of up to 65 miles per hour, but can also quickly decelerate to make stops every few blocks.

Light rail vehicles are 80 to 90 feet long, with a total capacity of more than 200 passengers. Light rail *consists*, or trains, are generally one to four cars long, and where demand is high, this can result in substantial returns in reduced operating costs, as a single operator can serve several hundred passengers at a time.

The flexible, hybrid nature of light rail has resulted in widely varying applications, from European trams and pre-metros; to streetcar-derived systems in American cities (including Boston, San Francisco, and Philadelphia) that operate alternately in tunnels and on streets; to commuter rail-like systems in mid-sized American cities connecting outlying suburbs to central business districts. The first generation of newer light rail systems in the United States, including systems in Sacramento and San Diego, relied heavily on available rights-of-way and cost-cutting measures, such as single tracking to limit costs. More recent systems, such as the one in Seattle, are more elaborate and expensive, with long tunneled and elevated segments.

CASE STUDY: SAN DIEGO TROLLEY

The San Diego Trolley, launched in 1981, demonstrated that rail transit can attract large numbers of riders even in a sprawling, heavily automobile-oriented American city. Although average weekday boardings have declined somewhat since inception of the system, they reached almost 120,000 in recent years—and this despite significant gaps in the system, which still does not connect to the airport or such popular destinations as La Jolla and Mission Bay.

COMMUTER RAIL

Commuter rail is heavy rail, typically powered by diesel-fueled locomotives (although systems in New York, Chicago, and overseas run on overhead wires that supply electrical power) and serving mostly to deliver suburban workers to downtown jobs. Commuter rail may share track with freight and long-distance passenger rail (such as Amtrak). Cars are configured for long-distance comfort, and most stations include large park-and-ride lots. At a few million dollars per mile, commuter rail is relatively inexpensive to implement (if somewhat expensive to operate) and can play an important if limited role in a regional transit network by reducing congestion in major corridors during peak periods.

Recently, diesel multiple unit (DMU) lines have been established in Austin, Texas; near Portland, Oregon; in San Diego County, California; and in suburban New Jersey. DMU is a sort of hybrid of commuter and light rail, with smaller cars, shorter trainsets, and (in some cases) relatively frequent all-day operation. Capital costs are generally somewhat higher than for traditional commuter rail lines. In the United States, Federal Railroad Administration (FRA) guidelines restrict the light-weight DMUs common in Europe from sharing tracks with freight trains; however, operations can be temporally segregated, with freight movements taking place overnight when passenger trains are not in service, and heavier (if more costly) DMUs are available.

METRO RAIL

Metros, or *subways* as they are generally known in North America, are the top of the line in urban transit. They are discussed here only briefly because so few U.S. cities can justify the expense of new metro construction: hundreds of millions, or even billions of dollars, per mile. Generally speaking, however, one gets what one pays for: high speed (due to complete grade separation, either in subways or above ground), high capacity, safe, clean, and quiet transport. Metros typically provide a web of coverage in dense urban areas, and in some cases lines extend into the suburbs. Stations are generally multimodal hubs, served by feeder bus and sometimes other rail lines. For the purposes of this book, it is the design of metro and other station *areas* (see Chapter 12) that is of most interest, as this is the arena where much of the important transportation planning to be done in North America over the coming decades will take place.

Ferries

Like metros, ferries are of limited application. Uniquely among transit modes, their rights-of-way cost nothing to build or maintain and are freely available; however, on a per-passenger basis, ferry operating costs can be substantial, typically more than $10 per trip, compared to a few dollars for bus or urban rail modes. Ferry riders are generally willing to pay higher fares (in some cases they have no choice, as auto alternatives are unavailable), and ferries can attract a substantial tourist market, driving economic development. However, the waterfront locations of their landings hold only limited potential for transit-oriented development because of geography and, in some cases, environmental regulations; and these locations always create special access requirements: Outside of downtown terminals, pedestrian access is often limited, and auto ferries can cause severe, and severely peaked, congestion (Figures 8-7 and 8-8).

Figures 8-7 and 8-8
Vancouver's Aquabus water taxi provides short trips between destinations along Vancouver's downtown waterfront and the southern shore of False Creek. Its Seabus service is an active component of services provided by TransLink, the local transit operator, and provides a redundant transit service complement for access over a highly congested bridge.
Source: Aaron Donovan.

In addition to commuter ferries, waterborne transit services include *water taxis* that provide short-hop service between smaller terminals in urban areas, and excursion or tourist-oriented service, which is often seasonal.

Flexible Modes

PARATRANSIT

Paratransit is demand-responsive, curb-to-curb or door-to-door service. Customers generally make reservations in advance by phone, and vehicles are generally smaller cutaway vehicles, vans, or sedan cars rather than standard buses. Paratransit is sometimes thought of primarily as service for seniors and persons with disabilities, and indeed, U.S. fixed-route transit providers are required by the Americans with Disabilities Act (ADA) to provide paratransit service to those who can prove they are unable to use fixed-route services. General public "dial-a-ride" services, however, are also relatively common in low-density areas where fixed-route service would be inconvenient for riders and expensive to provide. Although such services are still relatively expensive on a per-passenger basis, total costs are lower than they would be for comparable fixed-route services, making dial-a-ride an attractive transit option for exurban and rural areas.

TAXICABS

Taxicabs are not usually thought of as public transit, yet they play an important role in ensuring mobility, either as an essential lifeline service or as a convenient supplement to other means of travel. Regulation of taxicab systems is generally outside the purview of transportation planners; however, planners should provide for taxi access wherever possible, including taxi stands at rail stations and, if practical, taxi access to transit lanes. Some public agencies also provide taxi vouchers as part of paratransit programs or reimburse Guaranteed Ride Home (GRH) program participants for select taxi rides as part of Transportation Demand Management (TDM) programs.

Related to taxis, but far less common in the United States and other developed countries, are *jitneys*, or group taxis. Airport shared-ride services are a form of jitney, and many free-market advocates have promoted widespread use of private jitneys in the United States as an alternative to traditional (and in their view, wasteful and unjust) public transit. However, equity, safety, and other concerns have prevented their broader acceptance to date.

Other Modes

Finally, a number of other transit modes exist, but are not covered in detail here because they are less common. These include:

- **Alternative fixed-guideway modes**, including automated light rail transit (ALRT), monorail, and people mover
- **Terrain-based modes**, including aerial trams, cog railways, and funiculars
- **Personal Rapid Transit (PRT)**
- **High-speed rail (HSR)**, including standard HSR and magnetic levitation (maglev)

Design for Transit

Regardless of demographic, transit riders and potential passengers value their time, convenience, comfort, safety, and money. Transit cannot compete with the auto for all trips; however, even in the most auto-oriented cities, transit can make auto use less necessary, serving as a sort of second car for households. It can provide a higher quality of service to transit-dependent riders while at the same time attracting so-called *choice riders*.

That said, in practice, designing a successful transit service often means confronting difficult tradeoffs among conflicting goals:

- Primarily serve the transit-dependent, or try to grow ridership by attracting discretionary riders?
- Cover a wide geographic area, or provide higher-quality service to a few corridors?
- Stop often so riders don't have to walk far, or speed up service?
- Provide more direct, one-seat rides between destinations at lower frequencies, or try to make transfers less of a hassle so that the system can offer higher frequencies?

The most fundamental tradeoff is between *productivity* and *coverage* (Figure 8-9). Transit agencies tend to want to locate stops within walking distance of as many people as possible, but the most cost-effective way to deploy resources is to provide a higher level of service in the busiest corridors.

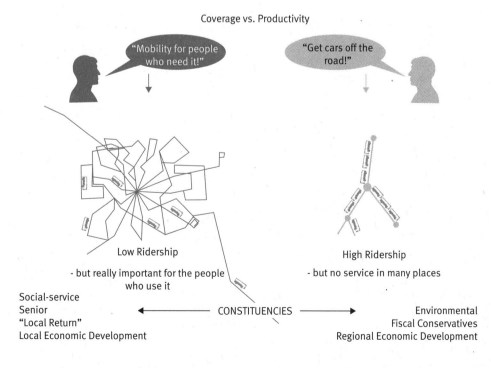

Coverage vs. Productivity

"Mobility for people who need it!"

"Get cars off the road!"

Low Ridership
- but really important for the people who use it

High Ridership
- but no service in many places

Social-service
Senior
"Local Return"
Local Economic Development

← CONSTITUENCIES →

Environmental
Fiscal Conservatives
Regional Economic Development

Figure 8-9
There is no one right answer in the tradeoff between productivity and coverage—it's up to each community to decide. *Source: Nelson\Nygaard.*

In all of these decisions, there is no single right choice. The only thing that is certain is that making active, conscious choices is crucial to designing a service that provides optimum utility, has a strong identity, and achieves maximum success.

This section explores best practices that can help a city or region get the most out of transit system investments. Application of these principles will, of course, vary depending on the unique characteristics of each place.

The Most Important Factors

In designing a new transit service or seeking to improve an existing one, three elements are most important:

Speed: Again, reducing delay (especially on the busiest routes) is important, not just to reduce travel times, but also to improve reliability and reduce operating costs, or to allow more service to be provided at the same cost: If a bus can be sped up by 25 percent, frequency can be improved by 25 percent—for example, from every 20 minutes to every 15—at no additional cost.

Even where it is not possible to provide dedicated right-of-way, signal priority, or upgraded stops, delay can be reduced simply by optimizing stop placement. On some routes, buses spend more than half their time stopped, either at stops or signals, and all people—including transit-dependent people—value their time.

Frequency: Research has found that time spent waiting for transit, as opposed to time in the vehicle, *feels* two to three times longer than it actually is. Given this fact, 15 minutes should be thought of as the *minimum* frequency of service necessary to begin attracting riders who might make a spontaneous decision to use transit for a particular trip. Beyond that threshold, operating more frequently will attract more choice riders.

Customer Experience: In addition to time, people value their convenience, comfort, safety, and money. In this area, as with speed, transit must compete with the personal car. This means:

- Transit vehicles large enough to avoid consistent overcrowding
- All-day, evening, and weekend service
- Seamless transfers (timed and, if possible, not requiring a second fare transaction)
- Amenities such as shelter and seating at stops and stations
- Secure, well-lit waiting areas
- Comfortable pedestrian (and bicycle) access paths
- Clean stops and vehicles
- Convenient ticket-purchase locations
- Uniform and simplified fare structures
- Discounted transit passes tailored to individual needs

- High-quality passenger information, including clear signs, and clear and widely available schedules and maps

- Real-time information for customers, at stops, on the Web, and on personal communications devices

Design for Bus Routes

Many bus routes have a story that goes something like this.

In the beginning, a group of people get together and decide that service is needed in a particular area of town. So, the City starts a transit route (Figure 8-10).

Early on, things are good; as awareness increases, ridership increases, and the City adds some more service. Then, Mr. Albertson calls up and asks if the service can operate on the street just one block north, because it's closer to a home for seniors. "Sure," the City agrees. It's not far out of the way. Then, a community service organization calls and asks if the route can go just four more blocks further out to serve a big-box store. "Sure," the City agrees, but there aren't enough resources to bring all the trips there; only a third of trips can go that far. Then, Mrs. Jones calls; Mrs. Jones is blind, and could more easily use the service if it made a loop to her house. "Sure," the City agrees—but only on the morning and afternoon trip she really needs to use. Pretty soon, the route looks like the one in Figure 8-11.

This route tries to serve everybody and therefore serves nobody. This story seems outlandish, but in reality is depressingly common. Transit agencies are generally required to consider public requests for service changes, but there must be a rational basis for making these changes, or else routes end up looking like spaghetti.

Therein lies the challenge of bus transit: Its flexibility is both a blessing and a curse. Services can be easily changed to meet changing service needs, but sometimes too easily, and when the public makes a firm request it can be tempting to do so. Adhering to a set of standards for designing bus transit will make it much easier to check in periodically to see if a route is serving its purpose, and to have a rational basis for accepting or rejecting service change requests.

Here are some rules for success in designing bus transit systems that maximize quality, efficiency, and effectiveness.

- **Routes should operate along a direct path**. If a route requires any riders to make a significant deviation, they will not ride if they have another option, even if it doesn't take much travel time.

- **Route deviations should be minimal**. Service should operate using a single set of service patterns: one inbound and one outbound. In some cases it may be

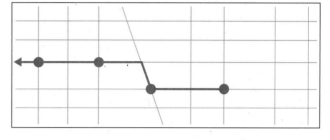

Figure 8-10
The City starts a transit route.
Source: Nelson\Nygaard.

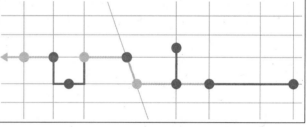

Figure 8-11
Pretty soon, the route looks like this.
Source: Nelson\Nygaard.

necessary to create different service patterns on a single route, but there must be a very compelling reason to do so. Alternatively, consider creating a separate route (perhaps a feeder route), or flex route service, or dial-a-ride. Routes should operate using the same path during the course of each day, and on every day of the week, if provided.

- **Routes should be symmetrical**. Customers from all areas should be able to use the route in both directions. Avoid loop designs, even if they operate in both directions.

- **Routes should serve a major destination at both ends**. Strong "anchors" promote ridership in both directions of a route, so that ridership is more balanced (think reverse commute).

- **Routes should serve a well-defined market**. A route should serve clearly defined markets, and routes should avoid competing with one another. Avoid operating more than one route of each type (e.g., commuter routes) in the same corridor unless multiple routes should logically operate through the corridor to unique destinations.

- **Use a service hierarchy**. Not all routes are created equal. Routes may have different orientations and purposes, such as commuter routes, rapid or limited routes, local routes, and so on. These may vary in a number of ways, such as span of service, headways, weekend operation, stop frequency, identity and branding, required stop amenities, and so on. Ensure that each route fits clearly within a defined hierarchy of services.

- **Maximize connectivity, and don't fear transfers**. Wherever possible, connect to other transit services. Riders will generally tolerate up to one transfer before they will switch to another mode given a choice. Long routes that overlap or operate in close proximity should be examined for conversion to trunk and feeder organization. Most riders will try to find another means of transportation if their desired trip would require two or more transfers.

- **Maximize the ease of transferring**. Transfer distance and route clarity are important. If customers are forced to walk more than a block or two to transfer between services, or if clear wayfinding does not exist, the extra time and inconvenience spent transferring could be enough to prevent them from using transit to make the trip. One option for transit scheduling that works well in lower-density environments is the *pulse* system, in which buses are timed to meet simultaneously at a transfer center, thereby reducing or eliminating transfer wait time. This system has drawbacks, such as challenges if certain routes cannot reliably meet the transfer, but they can be effective in the right conditions.

- **Provide direct service to major transit hubs whenever possible**. Most transit services converge at a few key transit hubs around the city, and any transit line is made more effective by serving one or more of these hubs.

- **Service should operate at regular intervals**. Routes should be timed and coordinated to depart on regular intervals so that passengers can remember what time the bus will pass their stop with minimal dependence on a schedule. When possible, routes should run on easy-to-remember "clockface" frequencies (such as every 10, 15, 20, 30, or 60 minutes).

- **Stops should be spaced appropriately**. In general, stops should be less frequent in low-density areas than in high-density areas, and stops should be less frequent on routes traveling long distances or focused on speed (such as commuter and BRT routes) than on local routes. Although topography and special-needs populations should be taken into account, stops on local bus routes should generally be at least 800 feet apart, and preferably close to a quarter-mile. Having fewer stops means that people converge at the stops that do remain, which can justify shelters and other amenities, and improves safety overall.

- **Service should maximize revenue hours and miles**. Routes should be designed to use as little time as possible pulling in and out of the garage, and layover time should be kept to a minimum.

- **Service should have adequate recovery time.** As a rule of thumb, a bus route needs 10 to 15 percent of the observed travel time for layover (operator break) and recovery, in case of congestion or other anomalies that impede the service.

- **Use vehicles and bus stops that dignify riders**. Opt for appropriate technologies that offer a comfortable ride—such as low-floor vehicles for urban service, or over-the-road coaches with cushioned seating for long-distance commuter routes. Bus stops should provide comfort and shelter wherever possible.

- **Integrate wayfinding and information**. Clear wayfinding leads riders between transit systems and points out nearby attractions and services, enhancing and simplifying the overall user experience.

A few additional rules apply to shuttle services for downtowns or other dense, mixed-use districts:

- **Serve multiple trip types**. Single-purpose "shopper shuttles" generally are not as productive as shuttles that serve many types of trips, including connections to work, shopping, and entertainment.

- **Stop often and quickly**. The shuttle should provide front-door service to key destinations. Dwell times should be reduced by using all-door boarding and low-floor vehicles.

- **Operate fare free.** Eliminating fares allows for all-door boarding, and encourages riders to hop on for short trips that would seem uneconomical for even a low fare.

- **Operate frequently and with a long service span**. Service can be initiated operating up to every 20 minutes, but a short-term goal should be to operate every 10 minutes or more frequently during peak periods. Frequent service allows people to hop on and ride without needing a schedule. Evening service allows people to stay in an area after work for dinner or entertainment and not worry about their return trips. Weekend service can be just as important as weekdays.

- **Market the area, not just the shuttle**. Using the shuttle is the means to an end—taking transit or parking once and taking full advantage of the opportunities available in the area. Marketing the shuttle should not be done in isolation, but rather should be an element of a larger marketing strategy.

- **Provide large door areas**. Shuttle riders tend to make very short trips. Riders should be able to enter and exit via all doors, getting on and off quickly.

- **Focus on comfortable standing room**. Because most trips are short, many riders never sit down. Seating is important, but the vehicle should emphasize comfortable standing room, with straps that allow riders to stand comfortably and safely.

- **Provide large window areas for high visibility**. Shuttle riders often need to be able to see where they are to get off at the store or restaurant of their choice. Because many shuttle riders are not regular riders who get off at the same stop every day, it is especially important that they be able to see where they are going.

- **Project a unique image**. It is important that riders not think of a shuttle as just another bus route. A unique vehicle can project an image that this route is something different to both commuters and occasional riders (Figure 8-12). The vehicle should be included in all marketing material and should become part of the image of the service. Even with little capital investment, buses can have a unique paint or wrap scheme, amenities can be improved, and a unique image can be created for the shuttle that will be enhanced over time with a unique vehicle type.

- **Use clean fuels**. In today's environment, many riders respond to "being green" as the primary reason for riding transit. To be successful, the vehicle must be clean, and must be perceived as clean.

Design for Stops

Again, riders perceive time spent waiting as several times longer than it actually is. For this reason, even along high-frequency routes, amenities matter. In reality,

Figure 8-12
"Art" shuttles in Englewood, Colorado, are uniquely branded. *Source: Nelson\ Nygaard.*

it is usually not possible to provide all amenities at every stop because of capital and maintenance costs and site considerations. Instead, provision of amenities can be prioritized based on usage. Table 8-1 sets out a classification scheme for stops developed by the Greater Cleveland Regional Transit Authority.[4] As it illustrates, stops that serve relatively few riders should provide a sign with route information, and if possible, a paved pad, lighting, and a trash receptacle. At the other end of the spectrum, major regional stops should be uniquely designed, and offer a full range of amenities, including local area information and real-time passenger information.

In designing a bus stop, the following principles should be applied:

- **Service should be obvious**. At a minimum, every transit stop needs a highly visible and clearly legible sign (Figure 8-13). For bus stops, signs should be at least 12 inches by 18 inches and mounted at least 6 feet off the ground. The sign should be placed perpendicular to the street so that it is visible from both directions and from the opposite side of the street. Each transit operator that serves the stop should be listed on the sign. Space permitting, the sign should also indicate the stop's ID number, route number(s), hours/days of operation, and a telephone number to call for more information.

- **Stops should be safe and clean**. The bus stop should be well maintained and well lit, and should provide a safe waiting area for riders. The stop should be visible from the street as well as from nearby buildings. The stop should be designed with adequate sightlines so that bus drivers have time to spot a waiting passenger and safely come to a stop.

Table 8-1: Greater Cleveland RTA Bus Stop Hierarchy and Amenities

	Type 1 Basic Stops	Type 2 Serving Moderate-Density Areas	Type 3 Serving High-Density Areas	Type 4 Community Destination Stops	Type 5 Regional Portals
Sign with route ID	√	√	√	√	√
Paved waiting pad	√*	√	√	√	√
Lighting	*	√	√	√	√
Trash can	√*	√	√	√	√
Bench		√	√	√	√
Landscaping		√	√	√	√
Bike rack		√	√	√	√
Shelter			√	√	√
Schedule information			√	√	√
Additional seating			√	√	√
Real-time schedule info				√	√
Public art				√	√
Transit system map				√	√
Local area info				√	√
Unique design elements					√

* Where possible.

Figure 8-13
Chicago Transit Authority bus stop sign listing routes servicing the stop and times of operation. *Source: Nelson\ Nygaard.*

- **Stops should be comfortable**. Waiting areas should provide sufficient space for passengers to sit or stand. They should serve as a refuge from traffic and other sidewalk activity. Protection from the elements should be provided to the extent possible. Where a full shelter is not possible, cover for waiting riders should be available under nearby awnings or trees.

- **Stops should be easily identifiable**. Stops should be highly visible, easily identifiable as transit stops, and carry the brand identity of the system. Elements should feel familiar, even if the exact amenities differ somewhat from stop to stop.

- **Stops should provide information**. For a new or even an experienced rider, the experience of waiting can produce ambiguity and anxiety: When will my bus arrive? Is it still running? How frequently do buses come at this time of day? Am I waiting in the right place? Is this bus accessible? Will there be a rack for my bike? Wayfinding elements such as standard flag signs displaying route information, system information (such as wheelchair and bike information), real-time wait-time displays, schedules, and route and system maps should be provided (Figure 8-14). Canisters make it relatively easy to provide a route map at any location that has a sign pole, and panels with system maps should be mounted wherever possible, including in hotels and at major tourist destinations near stops.

Figure 8-14
San Francisco Muni Metro system maps include tactile information readable by blind persons. *Source: Nelson\Nygaard.*

- **Stops should be accessible and integrated with their surroundings**. Stops should be accessible for passengers with limited mobility and should connect seamlessly to the neighborhood, with direct and complete pedestrian paths including both sidewalks and, if possible, signalized crosswalks. Bike racks should be provided. Stops should be placed near areas of activity, including shops and businesses.

At major stops, additional amenities may be desirable. These sorts of amenities are typical of rail and some BRT stations:

- Heating or air conditioning
- Public art (Figure 8-15)
- Newsracks and community kiosks
- Signs displaying the location of the stop (based on either cross streets or an adjacent landmark)
- Wayfinding signage pointing the way to nearby destinations
- Area maps
- Bike lockers

Passenger Information

When people are asked why they don't use transit more often, one of the most common reasons is a simple lack of understanding about how to use their local transit systems. Even many regular riders who are familiar with "their" routes may be uncomfortable going anywhere else by transit.

Figure 8-15
Bus shelters can be transformed into public amenities with art, such as this SEPTA stop in Philadelphia. *Source: Aaron Donovan.*

Transit is not as simple or obvious as driving one's own car (especially along roads that are lined by identical signs wherever one goes in America). A learning curve is required, and it can be daunting, frustrating, and offputting.

Legibility is the word used to describe the convergence of simple and well-defined transit services with readable and clearly understandable information on how to use those services. Though some transit agencies succeed in providing clear, easily understandable information about their services, most unfortunately do not. Informational materials are often produced for purely utilitarian purposes, without an eye toward design or use; in a time when resources are thinly spread, many agencies opt to focus on simply running the buses. In reality, transit systems provide customer services; thus, high-quality information is—or should be—a core part of their mission.

Following are some of the best methods of effectively demystifying a transit system.

WAYFINDING

Transit systems are easy to understand when it is clear where they are going. Surface rail, some bus rapid transit, and trolleybus lines have an advantage when it comes to wayfinding because riders can see where tracks, transitways (if clearly marked), and overhead wires go. Underground rail and most buses do not have this advantage, and this can add an element of uncertainty for riders.

However, easy-to-understand signs, maps, and even vehicles can provide guidance and a sense of security for new users. In Los Angeles, Metro buses are color-coded based on service type (e.g., rapid, limited, local, and express). All signage and printed materials should adhere to graphic design standards, and signs should be placed appropriately, at key "decision points" in stations and at the right heights and angles.

Although this book does not delve deeper into details of transit wayfinding, the importance of wayfinding should not be underemphasized. For some examples of best practices, see the signage, maps, and other materials produced by Transport for London (TfL), which are widely available online at www.tfl.gov.uk.

MAPS

System maps should do the following:

- Wherever possible, show routes as separate lines.

- Use colors, line thickness, or dashes to provide information about frequency and span of service. Many transit maps don't, and are analogous to road maps that don't distinguish between major and minor streets (or, in the worst cases, between a freeway and a neighborhood street).

- On lines with wide stop spacing, show stops.

- If possible, provide schedule information.

- Try to graphically represent details such as service changes by time of day, and avoid text bubbles, which can quickly clutter maps and may not be understandable to those with limited English proficiency.

- Show landmarks, including neighborhood shopping districts, if possible.

- Show connections to and major services within the service area by other transit providers. To the extent possible, provide information about other sustainable modes, such as bike share and carshare locations.

- To the extent possible without cluttering the map, create a map that can serve as a guide for getting around not just the system, but the entire service area. Showing streets, even as thin or faint lines, can help facilitate pedestrian connections.

Many rail and some bus systems use simplified diagrams, or schematic system maps, that do not provide much (if any) information about elements other than routes, stops, and major transit connections. This is acceptable and may be desirable in some cases where the system is especially complex. However, for simpler rail systems, or even for relatively large bus systems, geographically accurate maps are generally preferable, as they provide important navigational aids (such as landmarks and streets) for those using surface transit. In all cases, the right balance must be found between providing too much and too little information.

Route maps may be diagrams showing only major stops (or all stops on lines with relatively few stops), transit connections, and major destinations that are adjacent to the route. In addition to system and route maps, some agencies have begun to provide supplementary maps, such as frequent-service maps, which show only those routes with walk-up frequencies. Such maps can add value not just by clarifying the system for less-experienced users, but also by encouraging experienced users to take additional, spontaneous trips (Figure 8-16).

Increasingly, transit mapping is being transformed by new media. Maps produced by transit agencies primarily for print (and often provided on websites only as a PDF rather than the easier-to-load GIF or JPG file) are being supplemented—and in some cases supplanted—by maps produced by third parties, including private companies such as Google Transit as well as for-profit and volunteer developers of applications for mobile phones. Although transit agencies may fear a loss of control (and not long ago, tended to react defensively to such efforts), most have come to realize that making route, schedule, and real-time arrival information available to Internet developers can add value for themselves and their customers at little cost. Online maps also have the virtue of being relatively easy to update.

NEW MEDIA AND REAL-TIME INFORMATION

In recent years, newer media outlets, such as websites and mobile phone applications, have greatly simplified the process of distributing transit information.

The most transformative strategy to attract riders is to provide real-time arrival information (e.g., "Route 1 arriving in 5 minutes"). The cost to disseminate real-time information has been reduced dramatically by the advent of widespread mobile phone use, even among riders of limited economic means.

Even where transit vehicles are consistently on schedule—which is, unfortunately, all too rare in the United States—real-time information on wait time can greatly increase customer security and satisfaction and virtually eliminate a significant barrier

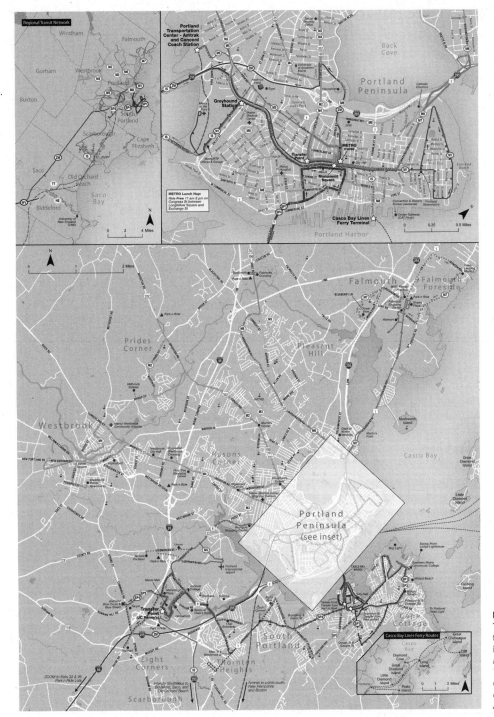

Figure 8-16
The Portland, Maine, regional transit map shows stops and other important details. *Source: Nelson\ Nygaard, Portland Area Comprehensive Transportation System (PACTS) Transit Committee, Greater Portland Council of Governments, Federal Transit Administration.*

to attracting new users. Such information should be available not just to users of mobile devices, but also, where possible, through displays at stops and stations.

New media outlets that can be used to provide transit information include:

- Agency websites, which should adhere to standards of good user-interface design (including both visual and organizational simplicity) and which should prominently display service alerts and trip planners (although increasingly, trip-planning tools developed in-house are being replaced by third-party trip planners) on their home pages. Many agency websites dedicate valuable home-page real estate to "news" of interest primarily to agency staff rather than customers.

- Collaborative websites, such as the "511.org" service in the Bay Area, which serves as a clearinghouse for information on all regional transit operators.

- Third-party map and scheduling websites such as Google Transit.

- Mobile applications, typically developed by third parties.

- Text-messaging services, which can be used to "push" service alerts to customers who have voluntarily subscribed for updates.

- Social networking websites, such as Facebook and Twitter, which can both provide useful information and serve to make transit services feel friendlier and more accessible.

- Interactive kiosks at stations and major stops.

Here are some things to keep in mind about using new media to promote transit:

- **Consistency**: As with other elements of branding strategies, information provided via new media outlets should be uniform in design to the extent possible. Consistency in message and tone is also important.

- **Quality control**: The emergence of third-party information providers has proven something of a mixed blessing. Though agencies should not shy away from making information available to third parties, care should be taken to ensure that such information is presented accurately and in keeping with applicable agency standards.

- **Added value**: Just because a new media outlet exists does not mean that it must or should necessarily be used, or that extensive resources should be devoted to its use. Though agencies should not be afraid to be early adopters of promising new technologies, they should do so with an eye toward potential long-term value, and should always bear in mind that even in our increasingly digital age, many riders and potential riders continue to prefer old-media printed or broadcast information.

Transit-First Strategies

The transit-first concept refers to a comprehensive and coordinated set of strategies that mandate or encourage land-use and transportation decisions to favor transit (and by extension, bicycling and walking, as these modes are used to get to and from transit) over automobiles. Transit-first policies include policy initiatives (in the form of regulations, ordinances, and laws), financial incentives, design guidelines, and capital improvements. Transit-first land use consists of relatively dense, mixed-use, transit-oriented, and pedestrian-oriented development.

ADVANTAGES OF TRANSIT-FIRST PLANNING

Existing development patterns and planning policies tend to strongly discourage transit and favor automobiles. Free parking is often provided by employers and businesses; transportation funds are directed primarily toward roads; streets are designed to expedite traffic flow; and zoning regulations insist on strict segregation of land uses, relatively low densities, and excessive amounts of parking. It is no wonder that use of public transit in the United States is still quite low, accounting for just 1.9 percent of all trips according to the 2009 National Household Travel Survey.[5] Transit-first policies can help break this dependence on the automobile, promote more compact development, and reintroduce transit, biking, and walking.

CHARACTERISTICS OF A TRANSIT-FIRST TRANSPORTATION SYSTEM

Changes in the design of the transportation system can take the form of physical measures that prioritize transit and nonmotorized modes on roads and highways. Where the inevitable conflicts between auto throughput and transit reliability or speed occur, transit-first planning requires that transit have priority. This is not simply a modal bias: transit-first effectively means prioritizing person throughput over auto mobility. Some opportunities for transit-first improvements include:

- Transit rather than traffic lanes
- Bulb-out curb extensions in place of parking, and allowing buses to stop in traffic lanes
- Signal priority for transit
- Complete-streets design for pedestrians and cyclists
- Policies to ensure that a percentage of infrastructure funding is directed to transit and nonmotorized modes
- Transportation Demand Management (TDM) strategies

Measuring Success

Finally, it is never enough to simply design effective service. One must also constantly monitor and refine service.

Planners often measure the success of transit services in terms of ridership. However, additional questions must be asked. Has transit mode share been increased? Have operating costs risen faster than ridership? Have quality-of-service factors, such as passenger amenities, which are less easy to measure, been improved? To what degree is transit helping the larger community meet its economic development, quality-of-life, social equity, and ecological sustainability goals?

There are a number of effective tools for assessing the success of transit:

Develop a system of performance metrics. Regular performance measurement can be relatively simple, but should be broad enough to capture the full range of service and other community objectives. As a starting point, consider measurement of factors such as:

- Productivity, expressed in terms of passengers per hour or other units

- Additional cost-effectiveness measures, such as subsidy per trip

- Speed (e.g., average speed including stops as a percentage of posted speed limit)

- Frequency and span

- Safety (e.g., miles between accidents)

- Transit mode share

- Vehicle miles traveled (VMT)

- Customer satisfaction, including on-time performance standards weighted to measure reliability as actually experienced by riders, and not independent of usage (as transit vehicles with the most people on them are those likeliest to fall behind schedule)

- Economic benefits

- Livability measures, including pedestrian and bicycle conflicts

- Environmental impacts, such as air quality and noise pollution

Measure by route. Some transit agencies subject routes that fail to achieve performance standards (consisting of either a minimum threshold, or performing in the bottom quintile) to performance audits on an annual or other basis.

Be conscious of equity and environmental justice issues. In the United States, Title VI requirements obligate federally funded transit agencies to consider environmental justice as a part of service operation. Demographic measurements compared with transit service provision levels in disadvantaged communities can be a useful tool to determine whether service is equitable.

Conduct surveys. In addition to customer satisfaction metrics that can be obtained using data provided by vehicle sensors, such as on-time performance (which, additionally, should be measured in terms of headway rather than schedule adherence on routes with walk-up frequencies), passengers and potential riders should be surveyed on a regular basis. This might take the form of on-board, online, mail-back, or intercept surveys.

Use peer comparisons to benchmark operations. Compare services with those offered in cities of similar size and form. Consider best practices from comparable peer cities as well as model cities to whose status your city might aspire.

CASE STUDY: BOULDER, COLORADO, COMMUNITY TRANSIT NETWORK

Transit ridership in Boulder, a modestly dense city of about 100,000, has experienced dramatic growth in recent years, from fewer than 20,000 daily boardings in the early 1990s to nearly 35,000 in 2009.[6] Boulder has employed several strategies: a downtown TDM program offering free universal transit passes, funded out of parking revenues, to all downtown employees; permanent subsidies of 25 to 30 percent (50 percent in the first year) to residents of neighborhoods participating in the transit pass program; and a Community Transit Network, or CTN, that builds on the basic service provided by the regional transit agency, the Regional Transportation District (RTD). The CTN consists of seven local routes operated primarily by RTD, but subsidized by the city so that frequencies of 10 minutes or less can be offered on all routes. The routes are simple and direct, and each is uniquely branded: They have colorful names—"Hop," "Skip," and "Jump"—and each has its own colorful scheme branded on cutaway vehicles that are neighborhood-scaled and come complete with on-board music. Finally, local sales taxes pay for capital improvements such as shelters, as well as an ongoing marketing campaign.

Transit Planning Resources

A number of excellent transit planning resources are available for free online. These include:

- **Transit Cooperative Research Program (TCRP) reports and syntheses**: TCRP publishes practical research studies on a wide variety of transit-related topics of interest to planners, operators, and others. Most research is available for free download at the TCRP website, http://www.tcrponline.org/

- **National Center for Transit Research (NCTR) reports**: NCTR conducts a variety of transit-planning and design research studies, and most are available for free download on its website, http://www.nctr.usf.edu/

- *Designing Printed Transit Information Materials: A Guidebook for Transit Service Providers*: From Principal Investigator Alasdair Cain at the NCTR (see previous list entry), this is a particularly handy guidebook for those designing transit maps, schedules, and other printed materials. The document is available online (http://www.nctr.usf.edu/abstracts/abs77710.htm) and supporting research is also available from the NCTR website.

- **The American Public Transportation Association**: APTA's website and other publications contain a wealth of information and news of practical value to transit planners: http://www.apta.com/

- *ITDP Bus Rapid Transit Planning Guide*: Published by the Institute for Transportation and Development Policy (ITDP) in 2007, this guide provides a detailed and practical examination of the ingredients for success in BRT systems. Available as a free download from the ITDP website: http://www.itdp.org/

Chapter 9

Motor Vehicles

Introduction

Since the discovery of fire, the wheel, and agriculture more than 7,000 years ago, no human invention has simultaneously shaped cities and captured the public imagination like the automobile. There are, of course, its practical advantages: The car allows us to come and go when we please, in any weather, at any time of day or night. We can travel vast distances in speed, comfort, and remarkable (if inadequate) safety. Compared to the earlier alternatives of saddling up a horse, or putting up with the limited schedule and company of strangers on the train, the private automobile offered enormous advantages of ease, comfort, and flexibility.

Far more powerful than its pragmatics, however, is the car's ability to shape our emotions. Sitting behind the wheel, we are wearing a suit of seemingly invincible armor. The car is not just a tool we use, but an extension of our selves. It is not just a protective carapace, but a means of projecting power and allure. Our cars are a form of costume, something we put on in order to craft a persona. If we're vulnerable, our cars can make us feel strong. If we're poor, our cars can make us feel wealthy. If we're feeling rejected, combining the right tunes on the stereo, the right exterior detailing, and the right curves on the highway, we can feel sexy beyond words, back in the center of our personal universe.

City planning textbooks may highlight Otis's invention of the elevator, Edison's electric light, or Willis Haviland Carrier's electric air conditioning in the shaping of cities, but the overall attraction of the car—combined with its scale of use—has caused it to be the dominant factor in shaping most urban forms for the past 60 years. In most cities, in fact, more land is given over to the habitat of cars than to the habitat of people (Figures 9-1 and 9-2).

Many authors have bemoaned Americans' "addiction" to cars as a defense of status quo policies, or as a reason for minor harm-reduction policy changes, much like needle exchange programs for heroin users. Indeed, many people have strong emotional ties to their automobiles. Many of us behave irrationally, treating our cars less like a conveyance tool and more like a beautiful mistress, something we feel a little guilty about, but could easily destroy a successful marriage over.

Indeed, more than 70 years before manufacturers convinced tame suburbanites to buy oversized, overpriced SUVs with the promise that it would introduce regular wilderness adventures into their humdrum, predictable lives, a 1923 ad in the *Saturday Evening Post* promoted the new Jordan Playboy (less subtly named than Nissan's 1984 brilliant rebranding of its feminine Silvia into the "200SX," after which "SX" became the standard trim designation for several manufacturers' sportier models). The ad copy set a new standard for promoting automobiles:[1]

Figures 9-1 and 9-2
San Ramon, California, a typical
auto-oriented suburb. *Source: Google
Earth/Nelson/Nygaard.*

SOMEWHERE west of Laramie there's a bronco-busting girl who knows
what I'm talking about.

She can tell what a sassy pony, that's a cross between greased lightning
and the place where it hits, can do with eleven hundred pounds of steel and
action when he's going high, wide and handsome.

The truth is—the Playboy was built for her.

Built for the lass whose face is brown with the sun when the day is done of revel and romp and race.

She loves the cross of the wild and the tame.

There's a savor of links about that car—of laughter and lilt and light—a hint of old loves—and saddle and quirt. It's a brawny thing—yet a graceful thing for the sweep o' the Avenue.

Step into the Playboy when the hour grows dull with things gone dead and stale.

Then start for the land of real living with the spirit of the lass who rides, lean and rangy, into the red horizon of a Wyoming twilight.

Many people also have strong emotional attachments to video games, pets, stuffed animals, Hummel collectibles, and local sports teams, but indulging in these attachments does not kill 40,000 Americans a year, as driving does. Motor vehicle deaths are caused by so-called "accidents"—as if they were beyond our control—and rarely make the news. By contrast, about 3,000 innocents were killed in the September 11, 2001, terrorist attacks, 62 people in the San Francisco Bay Area Loma Prieta earthquake of 1989, and about 2,000 people in the New Orleans flooding that resulted from Hurricane Katrina. Why do we tolerate so many driving deaths? What makes driving different from other activities?

There are two key reasons.

First, we equate our freedom of mobility with personal liberty, in a "give me liberty, or give me death" sort of way (with many unfortunate motorists ending up with death when they thought they were choosing liberty). As a matter of public policy, there is little we can do about this delusion, except learn from antismoking campaigns, which have done so much to expose the falsities of the tobacco industry, and change perceptions of smoking from something glamorous to something dirty.

Lesson number one: *Never insinuate that motorists are bad people.* Rather, motorists are good people who have been duped by the auto and real estate industries into an auto-dependent lifestyle that doesn't serve their needs.

Lesson number two: *Don't go to extremes.* Just as it's OK to smoke, provided you do it in a place that doesn't harm others, so is it OK to drive—but not through crowds of pedestrians, and not excessively.

Lesson number three: *Focus on the positive.* Take a page from Fresno, California's "Biking = Joy" campaign to help people imagine how much more fulfilling, happy, and sexy their lives will be if they can arrange their lives to do more walking and biking and require less driving.

The costs of providing for the automobile are largely hidden, or they are sunk costs that, once paid, encourage more driving. From a public policy standpoint, revealing the hidden costs of driving is the highest priority, and the simplest fix. Thus, bringing these hidden costs to light is arguably the highest priority for any planner interested in sustainable cities.

Todd Litman at the Victoria Transport Policy Institute has done more than anyone in cataloging the hidden costs of driving. He has summarized these costs in his encyclopedic *Transportation Cost and Benefit Analysis: Techniques, Estimates and Implications*, available free at www.vtpi.org. Litman's primary factors are summarized in the following list.

- **Vehicle ownership**: Fixed costs of owning a vehicle
- **Vehicle operation**: Variable vehicle costs, including fuel, oil, tires, tolls, and short-term parking fees
- **Travel time**: The value of time used for travel
- **Crash**: Crash costs borne directly by travelers, and costs a traveler imposes on others
- **Parking**: Off-street residential parking and long-term leased parking paid by users and others
- **Congestion**: Congestion costs imposed on other road users
- **Road facilities**: Roadway facility construction and operating expenses not paid by user fees
- **Land value**: The value of land used in public road rights-of-way
- **Traffic services**: Costs of providing traffic services such as traffic policing, and emergency services
- **Air pollution**: Costs of vehicle air-pollutant emissions
- **Greenhouse gas pollution**: Life-cycle costs of greenhouse gases that contribute to climate change
- **Noise**: Costs of vehicle noise-pollution emissions
- **Resource externalities**: External costs of resource consumption, particularly petroleum
- **Barrier effect**: Delays that roads and traffic cause to nonmotorized travel
- **Land-use impacts**: Increased costs of sprawled, automobile-oriented land uses
- **Water pollution**: Water pollution and hydrologic impacts caused by transport facilities and vehicles
- **Waste**: External costs associated with disposal of vehicle wastes

With each of these costs, some are borne by the motorist (*internalized*) and others by other people or the economy at large (*externalized*). Costs that are externalized are inefficient to the economy and harmful to others; these costs tend to be small, but are numerous. Internalized costs can be further divided into fixed and variable costs. *Fixed costs* include the purchase of the car itself, along with such annualized costs as insurance. Once the car is bought and insurance is taken out, motorists have every incentive to "get their money's worth" on their purchase. *Variable costs* include items such as gasoline, for which there is a close relationship between cost and use. Motorists who drive less see an immediate reduction in how much they spend on gas.

Summarizing all these costs, Litman produced the chart shown in Figure 9-3. This figure shows average car costs per vehicle mile, ranked by magnitude.

Here, we see that the costs of driving are split into fairly even thirds, with 35 percent externalized and paid for by others, and about 28 percent paid for by the

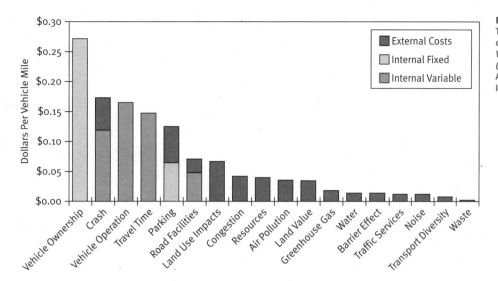

Figure 9-3
The internalized and externalized costs of driving. *Source: Todd Litman, Victoria Transport Policy Institute (from* Transportation Cost and Benefit Analysis: Techniques, Estimates and Implications, *Figure 1, Page ES-4).*

motorist but fixed. Only 37 percent of the costs of driving are paid for by the motorist and vary according to rates of driving. In total, Litman estimates that rural driving costs about $0.94 per mile and urban peak-period driving costs about $1.64 per mile—but once they've bought their cars, motorists only pay 37 percent of this cost, with the remainder being borne by society.

From an economic efficiency and public policy standpoint, this is a disaster. How can we possibly complain about congestion and air pollution, yet at the same time *subsidize* motorists to drive more? Much as children would complain if government suddenly halted a national free ice cream program, so will motorists complain if they have to take on the full costs of driving. Shifting that burden must be done gradually, and should be done through a change in tax policy rather than in the form of new taxes and fees. Motorists should also be made to understand that the current policy of subsidizing driving through property and income taxes is inefficient and socially unjust.

Cities and states should also work to make the fixed costs of driving variable, so that motorists who drive less pay less. One of the most powerful ways to do this is to promote carsharing programs, as detailed in Chapter 11. Another useful tool is pay-as-you-go or pay-at-the-pump insurance, where insurance rates are paid per mile rather than at a fixed price based largely on the type of car and owner's zip code.

Designing for Cars

There are four simple rules for gracefully accommodating the automobile in sustainable cities. Understand these, and everything else is easy:

1. Design follows from context.

2. Speed kills.

3. You cannot build your way out of congestion.

4. Making cities work for cars first requires making cities delightful for pedestrians.

Each of these concepts is described in detail in the following subsections.

Design Follows from Context

Proper street design varies more by land-use context than it does by any other factor, yet most conventional street design manuals force a one-size-fits-all approach upon cities. It is obvious to any motorist that travel lanes on a high-speed highway should be wider than on a low-speed residential street, and that sidewalks on a retail main street should be designed differently from those in an industrial area. As a rural highway enters the city, the highway itself must urbanize, just like the buildings alongside it.

To define how changing land-use context affects design decisions, several urban design and street design manuals borrow the idea of the *transect* from the Congress for the New Urbanism. The concept of the transect was developed in biology to describe the ranges of various plants and animals as habitats transitioned from one type to another. For example, biologists would draw a straight line from the intertidal zone of the sea, inland through coastal dunes, brackish estuary, marshland, grassland, oak woodland, and evergreen woodland, and count all of the species within a certain distance of the line. They would discover that limpets are found only in the intertidal zone, but crabs cover both the intertidal zone and the coastal dunes. The only crabs in the grassland were the leftover snacks of the seagulls.

Similarly, in human habitats, we can draw a line from wilderness to the downtown, with varying degrees of rural and suburban development in between. In the suburbs, we expect to see white picket fences, front porches, and low buildings, but these would probably look ridiculous downtown. An ornate Victorian light fixture may look great on Main Street, but it would look silly in farm country. Andres Duany and his colleagues at Duany Plater-Zyberk closely examined this human habitat transect and divided the resulting line into six zones, from T1, the Natural Zone, to T6, the Urban Core Zone (Figure 9-4).

Figure 9-4
A typical rural-urban transect, with transect zones, from SmartCode version 9.2. *Source: Duany Plater-Zyberk & Company.*

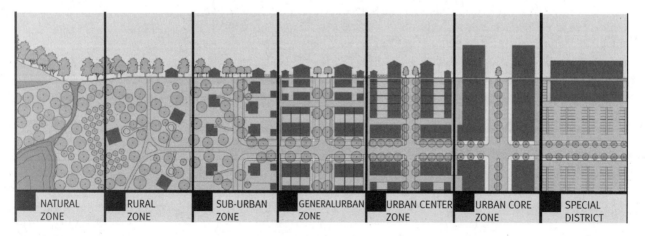

NATURAL ZONE | RURAL ZONE | SUB-URBAN ZONE | GENERALURBAN ZONE | URBAN CENTER ZONE | URBAN CORE ZONE | SPECIAL DISTRICT

Duany and others use this transect system to develop urban design codes, with building height and placement, architectural details, landscape treatments, and other factors all varying by transect zone. In the SmartCode, they also apply the transect to street design, with travel lane width, turning radius, parking configurations, and other factors adjusted by context zone. Figures 9-5 and 9-6 summarize the key street design guidance from the SmartCode.

Other street design manuals use context zones in different ways, as described in the next section.

Speed Kills

Besides the practical advantages of getting from A to B faster, there is a certain giddy thrill to speed. Humans simply like to go fast. According to the International Association of Amusement Parks and Attractions, we spent $12 billion at more than 400 U.S. amusement parks in 2007,[2] mainly to be accelerated to dizzying speeds.

In a crash, however, speed is our enemy. Isaac Newton tells us that the force of impact in a crash varies by the mass of the object involved, times the square of its velocity. That is, kinetic energy $(E_K) = \frac{1}{2} mv^2$. So, as speed doubles, the energy involved in a collision increases fourfold. Most of the critical elements of the human body have a specific design tolerance to withstand a trip-and-fall at our peak sustained running speed. While Usain Bolt can do a 100-meter sprint averaging 23 mph, most of us peak at about 18 mph. If we fall at such a speed, we can generally pick ourselves up, patch up the scrapes, and keep going. The same forces come into play if we are stationary and we are hit by a car at 18 mph.

As our speed or looming vehicle speed increases beyond this threshold, however, the effects on our bodies become dire. Whereas a crash at 18 mph may result in mere scrapes and bruises, as speeds increase, bones are broken and organs are damaged; at about 37 mph, the crash will likely be fatal (Figures 9-7 and 9-8).[3]

DESIGN SPEED	TRAVEL LANE WIDTH	T1	T2	T3	T4	T5	T6
Below 20 mph	8 feet	■	■	■	□		
20-25 mph	9 feet	■	■	■	■	□	□
25-35 mph	10 feet	■	■	■	■	■	■
25-35 mph	11 feet	■	■			■	■
Above 35 mph	12 feet	■	■			■	■

■ BY RIGHT
□ BY WARRANT

DESIGN SPEED	PARKING LANE WIDTH	T1	T2	T3	T4	T5	T6
20-25 mph	(Angle) 18 feet					■	■
20-25 mph	(Parallel) 7 feet			■			
25-35 mph	(Parallel) 8 feet			■	■	■	■
Above 35 mph	(Parallel) 9 feet					■	■

DESIGN SPEED	EFFECTIVE TURNING RADIUS	T1	T2	T3	T4	T5	T6
					(See Table 17b)		
Below 20 mph	5-10 feet			■	■	■	■
20-25 mph	10-15 feet	■	■	■	■	■	■
25-35 mph	15-20 feet	■	■	■	■	■	■
Above 35 mph	20-30 feet	■	■			□	□

Figure 9-5
Vehicle lane dimensions, from SmartCode version 9.2. *Source: Duany Plater-Zyberk & Company.*

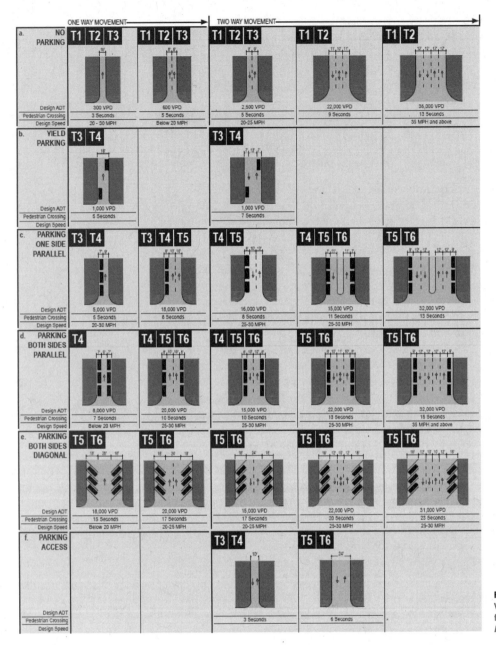

Figure 9-6
Vehicular lane/parking assemblies, from SmartCode version 9.2. *Source: Duany Plater-Zyberk & Company.*

Speed complicates safety in another way, by increasing the distance that is covered before reaction time and braking bring a vehicle to a stop. Say you are driving a car and a child runs into the street in front of you, chasing after a ball. At 20 mph, you'll cover 70 feet as you realize that there is a danger and move your foot from the gas pedal to the brake, and another 40 feet as your car comes to a stop. At 40 mph, the distance covered is 150 feet for the reaction and another 150 feet to stop (Figure 9-9).[4]

146   Motor Vehicles

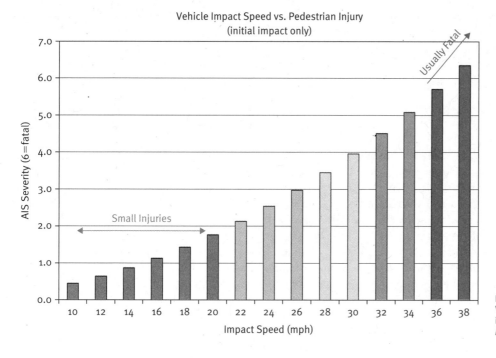

Figure 9-7
Vehicle speeds versus pedestrian
injury and fatality risk. *Source: Nelson\
Nygaard.*

You Cannot Build Your Way Out of Congestion

Congestion is the equilibrium point of the transportation market, balancing roadway supply and demand. In a growing economy, congestion is the constant in any
traffic analysis—not a variable—except where congestion pricing or other market
tools are applied. Congestion will result regardless of how many or few travel lanes
you provide. If you build more travel lanes, people will adjust their travel patterns
to take advantage of them and the real estate market will respond
with more auto-oriented development. If you build fewer travel lanes,
travel patterns and real estate markets will adjust accordingly.

For traffic engineers, accepting the futility of maintaining
congestion-free Level of Service (LOS) thresholds should come as a
relief, but it is unnerving unless replaced by other measures of success. To develop the right measures, traffic engineers need to partner
with land planners and real estate economists to develop the optimal
accommodation for the car. To reduce infrastructure costs and increase
residential land values, the real estate people may advocate for skinnier streets. To handle the traffic, the engineers can offer better street
connectivity, and the land planners can concentrate employment and
retail around transit. But if the market doesn't support urban development, the economists can shrink the project or reduce its density.
Transportation planning is a balancing act, part of an ongoing negotiation with economists, designers, and other city planning professionals.

Figure 9-8
Pedestrians' chances of death at
different speeds. *Source: Nelson\
Nygaard (data drawn from U.S.
Department of Transportation,* Killing
Speed and Saving Lives).

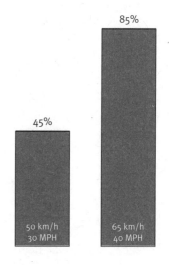

Oversizing your roadways won't solve your congestion problem, so choose the right balance between walkability and easy motoring that best suits your community's values.

Making Cities Work for Cars First Requires Making Cities Delightful for Pedestrians

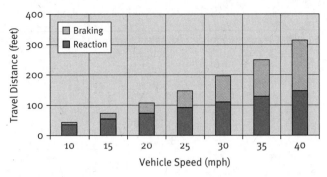

Figure 9-9
Reaction time and stopping distance by speed. *Source: Nelson\Nygaard.*

This last point is the most important and also the most counterintuitive. Places that are designed largely for driving a car often end up being no fun to drive in. Although the speed and spacious comfort of the car may be its greatest advantages, when there are too many other drivers on the road, these assets quickly become liabilities. Aside from the unfortunate side effects of burning petroleum, most of the car's problems are rooted in its geometry. Cars are big. On the road, they consume more than 10 times as much roadway space per traveler as any other mode of transportation. More troubling, they require enormous terminal space at the beginning and end of every trip—also known as *parking*. In most cities, minimum parking requirements for cars consume more area than occupiable floor area in the buildings themselves.

Places that are designed largely around the car, with a dedicated parking space for every trip at every destination, and roadways designed to accommodate a free flow of traffic at all times of day, end up requiring a lot of driving. All that parking reduces density, spreading uses out beyond walking distance of each other. The wider roads make walking, bicycling, and transit useful primarily for those who have no other choice. Kids can no longer walk to school or soccer practice, requiring parents to become chauffeurs. Employees drive to lunch, or bring a brown bag to the corporate break room. Walking is still required, but it is the dreary walk from the outer edge of the parking lot toward the store (assuming that one has not circled around for 15 minutes waiting for a motorist in a nearer space to pull out).

In more balanced communities, the car is accommodated, but never at the expense of the pleasure of walking. Towns and neighborhoods developed in the 1920s and 1930s exemplify this balance, as do newer neighborhoods in places like Vancouver, British Columbia. The rules are fairly simple:

- Parking is shared and managed so spaces are readily available.
- Streets are never too wide to walk across comfortably; this requires an interconnected grid of closely spaced streets.
- Protected pedestrian crossings are available at least every 300 to 400 feet.
- Sidewalks are gracious, landscaped, and buffered from fast-moving traffic.
- Buildings orient to the street, not the parking lot.
- Density is increased to the point at which the needs of daily life are available within walking distance, but not so great that the urban intensity become uncomfortable.

Put these factors together, and the magic happens. People walk more, and they do it with pleasure. Vehicle miles traveled drop by around 50 percent.[5] Property values rise, and air pollution, water pollution, noise, and infrastructure costs all drop.

Design Manuals That Build upon Context

In the United States, the American Association of State Highway and Transportation Officials (AASHTO) maintains a document called *A Policy on Geometric Design of Highways and Streets*, colloquially known as the "Green Book" because its hardback cover was once plain green. It is the Talmud of street design, comprehensive yet subject to debate and interpretation. A great strength of the Green Book is its flexibility—it accommodates a wide range of dimensions for all situations—but it is weak in that it provides little guidance to the designer about when to use the upper or lower end of a range of dimensions, and especially weak in providing context as to *why* one might use different approaches.

To address the Green Book's ambiguities, the Institute of Transportation Engineers published its *Designing Walkable Urban Thoroughfares: A Context Sensitive Approach* as a recommended practice in 2010. The book is the result of a three-year collaboration by the ITE, the Congress for the New Urbanism, the Federal Highway Administration, and the U.S. Environmental Protection Agency.

Adapted from the ITE document and elsewhere, Table 9-1 shows the key differences between walkable and vehicle-oriented thoroughfares.[6]

Table 9-1: Walkable versus Vehicle-Oriented Thoroughfares

Characteristic	Walkable Thoroughfares	Vehicle-Oriented Thoroughfares
Target speed range	20–30 mph	35–50 mph
Pedestrian separation from moving traffic	Curb parking and streetside furnishing zone	Optional, typically separation achieved with planting strip
Streetside width	Minimum 9 feet (residential) and 12 feet (commercial) to accommodate sidewalk, landscaping, and street furniture	Minimum 5 feet
Block lengths	200–660 feet	Up to ¼ mile
Protected pedestrian crossing frequency (ped signals or high-visibility markings at unsignalized crossings)	200–600 feet	As needed to accommodate pedestrian demands
Pedestrian priority at signalized intersection	Pedestrian signals and pedestrian countdown heads, adequate crossing times, shorter cycle lengths	Vehicle priority; may have longer cycle lengths
Pedestrian crossings	High-visibility crosswalks shortened by curb extensions where there is on-street parking	Full street width
Median width	6 feet minimum width at crosswalk if used as pedestrian refuge plus 10 feet for left-turn lane, if provided; 14-foot total width for left-turn lane if no refuge needed	14–18 feet for single left-turn lane; 26–30 feet for double left-turn lane
Vehicular access across sidewalks	24 feet or less unless specific frequent design vehicle requires added width	As needed
Curb parking	Normal condition except at bus stops and pedestrian crossings	None
Curb return radius	10–30 feet; low-speed channelized right turns where other options are unworkable	30–75 feet; high-volume turns channelized

Crucially, the ITE manual recognizes that the optimal dimensions and characteristics of several parts of the street vary depending upon the urban context. The ITE manual uses the same definitions as the SmartCode's context zones, but calls them C (for "Context") 1–6 rather than T (for "Transect") 1–6. It also recognizes that within a given context zone, certain street design characteristics vary depending upon whether the land-use frontage is primarily residential or primarily commercial.

The ITE manual is available as a free PDF at www.ite.org, and the SmartCode is available at www.transect.org.

For smaller, lower-volume streets and residential streets, the UK's *Manual for Streets* is an excellent resource, as is the ITE's *Residential Streets*. *Residential Streets* offers the following guidance for local streets:

- "A 24- to 26-foot-wide pavement is the most appropriate width." This provides either two parking lanes and a single two-way traffic lane, two parking lanes and a one-way traffic lane, or two traffic lanes and a single parking lane.

- "For lower volume streets with limited parking, a 22- to 24-foot wide pavement is adequate."

- "For low volume local streets where no parking is expected (for example, large-lot, rural communities), an 18-foot pavement is adequate."[7]

The 24-foot, two-way street with parking on both sides is a particularly interesting type. It is called a *yield* or *queuing* street, because motorists going in opposite directions must negotiate with each other in order to pass. Though it may seem dangerous to put opposing traffic in the same lane, in fact these are among the safest streets ever designed, largely because it is impossible for motorists to achieve sufficient speed to create a severe injury crash. Yield streets work best on small blocks where there are occasional driveways or where on-street parking is not 100 percent occupied, as motorists may need to pull into the parking lane to allow opposing traffic to pass.

Adopting the Right Manual

There are certainly many qualities that make your community special and unique—and the needs of your streets probably are not near the top of the list. Though the exercise of developing a street design manual can help educate recalcitrant municipal engineers, it is not necessary for each city to develop its own manual. Instead, copy someone else's manual, perhaps amending it to address the particular characteristics of your city, such as snow removal considerations, historic light fixtures, flagstone pavers, and so on.

There are two steps, both of which are critically important:

1. Forbid the use of a *highway* design manual for urban streets. This is a major problem in most U.S. states and Canadian provinces, where historic main streets connect to rural highways and are under the jurisdiction of state or provincial highway authorities. Along rural highways, design techniques that accommodate driver error through more generous dimensions tend to improve roadway safety. In urban areas, however, where pedestrians are present, more generous dimensions tend to result in higher speeds and greater driver distraction, resulting in

worse safety. This topic is addressed well in *Flexible Design of New Jersey's Main Streets*,[8] which provides guidance about how to make the transition from a rural highway environment to urban streets.

2. Formally adopt a manual that provides the best guidance for your streets and keep it updated. The adoption process is particularly important in some U.S. jurisdictions where traffic engineers can be held personally liable for crashes that occur on the streets they design, except when the design follows adopted guidelines. For example, in some conventional guidelines, where a standard highway travel lane dimension of 12 feet is provided, along with an allowable range of 9 to 14 feet, engineers may feel pressured to use the "standard" dimension unless the text is clear about the conditions under which a smaller or larger figure is suitable.

Adoption of better guidelines is useful at the municipal level, but it can be even more powerful at the state level. For example, the Texas Department of Transportation adopted the ITE *Walkable Urban Thoroughfares* manual for use on state-maintained roads.

Design Guidance

Regardless which manual your city chooses, it is important that the manual provide clear guidance on the following major topics.

Design Vehicles

Design vehicles are simply the typical vehicles designers have in mind when designing a street or intersection. Does the intersection have to accommodate a big semi-tractor trailer, or just a typical panel truck? Do buses have to turn right here? Is it OK for the fire truck or bus to cross the centerline in order to make it through? The notion of design vehicle is most important in intersection design, because bigger vehicles require a lot more space to make a turn. Proper intersection design involves at least four design vehicles:

- **Speed-control vehicle**. Because most pedestrian- and bicycle-related crashes occur at intersections, it is important to ensure that cars go slowly when making right-hand turns (left turns in places where cars drive on the left). That is, if your intersection design easily accommodates a big truck making a right turn, but doing so allows cars to turn at 25 mph, the result is an intersection that may be unsafe for pedestrians. So the *speed-control vehicle* is a typical passenger vehicle, and the designer's challenge is accommodating the larger design vehicle while ensuring that the smaller speed-control vehicle cannot travel unsafely fast.

- **Design vehicle**. The *design vehicle* is the vehicle that must be regularly accommodated without forcing the driver into opposing traffic lanes or over a curb. Deciding the appropriate design vehicle is a judgment call. On a typical downtown street, where really big trucks are rare, using a 40-foot panel truck as a design vehicle will accommodate most urban commerce. If and when a semi-trailer has to make a delivery, the driver may need to make three left turns in order to turn right, or make the delivery at night when traffic volumes are low enough to complete a turn into opposing lanes. On a major freight route, however, a larger truck may be the appropriate design vehicle. Similarly, on a primary emergency response route, a ladder truck might be the design vehicle, and on a transit route the bus will be the design vehicle. In contrast, on some low-volume residential streets, it may be fine for a passenger vehicle to cross the centerline to make a turn. A useful technique for accommodating right turns by trucks in a tight intersection is locating the stop bar on the street onto which the truck is turning 12 to 20 feet from the intersection. This allows the truck to make the turn slowly and cross into the far-side through lane on the adjoining street if necessary.

- **Control vehicle**. A *control vehicle* is one that occasionally uses the roadway and must be accommodated, but perhaps not with the greatest of ease. Control vehicles may have to cross the centerline into opposing traffic in order to complete their turns. In some cases, it may make sense to use rolled curbs at a median to allow occasional big trucks or fire engines to bump over the median. Designers may also use a low curb at the corner to slow the speed-control vehicle, and then use a line of bollards on a longer radius in the sidewalk to allow the control vehicle to bump over the corner curb and complete a right turn.

- **Nonmotorized vehicles**. In intersection design, it is important to consider how bicycle facilities affect the design considerations for the other modes. For example, bicycle lanes increase the effective turning radius—see more later in this section—requiring adjustments for balancing the needs of the speed-control vehicle and the design vehicle. Similarly, a projected cycle track through the intersection will alter considerations for the other design vehicles.

Generally speaking, the smaller the design vehicle, the safer the road will be for pedestrians, and the higher the value for adjacent land, largely because intersections will be smaller and operate more slowly. Setting the design vehicle too low, however, can result in major problems:

- Goods delivery may be delayed and result in significant traffic congestion, as trucks negotiate tight turns. In historic urban cores with narrow streets, such as Philadelphia or Quebec City, the combination of uniqueness and high real estate values allows merchants and delivery firms to work out arrangements to keep commerce continuing—though at an added cost. All else being equal, however, a tavern keeper is more likely to open shop on a street where it's easy to get beer deliveries than on one that involves extra hassle and cost.

- For emergency services providers—police, fire, ambulance—lost time equals lost lives. Perhaps the greatest challenge of any roadway designer is balancing traffic safety against emergency response time. Streets that offer no delays for fire trucks may also result in excessive speed for passenger vehicles—and therefore more pedestrian crash fatalities. See more about addressing emergency response later in this section.

- Even if there are no current plans for transit service on the street you are designing, you may not want to preclude future service by making intersections too tight. Think about logical future bus routes, paying careful attention to where buses may have to turn right.

Design Speed

The design speed concept is typically used in highway design, but it finds its way into urban street design as well, often inappropriately. *Design speed* is simply the speed at which most motorists would be expected to drive comfortably. To accommodate high design speeds on highways, designers will bank the roadway like a racetrack (this is called *super-elevation*) and offer sweeping curves. To enhance safety at high speeds, designers will also use shoulders and generous dimensions, so a driver who strays from the lane will not wreak havoc. On highways, the design speed is typically higher than the speed limit, so a driver who exceeds the speed limit by a bit will still be able to manage the roadway well.

On urban streets, however, accommodating higher speeds for motorists becomes a self-fulfilling prophecy: Drivers intuitively know the design speed and many will drive faster, regardless of the posted speed limit. As speeds increase in complex urban environments, safety decreases. So, tools that work well on rural highways have the opposite effect on urban streets.

In most urban street design manuals, including the ITE manual, the design speed is the same as the *target speed*—the speed at which designers want the roadway to operate, balancing motorist convenience with safety for all users. Maintaining appropriate urban driving speeds means incorporating the following concepts into road design:

- Travel lanes that accommodate the appropriate design vehicle at the target speed, but are no wider than they have to be. If there is excess roadway width, use this space to widen sidewalks, add on-street parking, or add bicycle lanes, rather than providing excessively wide travel lanes.
- No "shy" areas or shoulders between travel lanes and curbs.
- No super-elevation.
- On-street parking.
- Tight corner radii at intersections and elimination or reconfiguration of high-speed channelized right turns.
- Appropriate spacing of signalized intersections and synchronization to the desired speed.
- Gateway elements and other appropriate devices to gradually transition speeds from outer, higher-speed areas to the urban setting.
- Vertical shifts, such as raised pedestrian crossings and intersections.
- Curb extensions.
- Bicycle facilities.

Lane Width

The proper lane width on a road depends on a variety of factors, including the design vehicle, target speed, and lane position.

A typical 40-foot bus is 8 feet to 8 feet 6 inches wide, with mirrors that extend about a foot on either side, making the total vehicle up to 10 feet 6 inches wide. Panel trucks have similar dimensions and mirror widths. A 2009 Hummer H2 is 6 feet 9 inches wide, plus another 8 inches or so on each side for the fold-in mirrors, for a total width of just over 8 feet. Trucks and buses can operate in a lane narrower than their dimensions, but designers need to think about where the extra width will go. Will cyclists be struck in the head by a truck mirror? What about pedestrians waiting at the curb on a street with narrow lanes and no on-street parking? On a street with heavy truck and bus volumes, will mirrors get clipped, adding costs to the transit operators?

For optimal operations, streets with regular bus service and truck traffic should have travel lanes at 11 feet, at least in the lanes where trucks and buses are expected. If two 10-foot lanes are provided instead, understand that truck and bus drivers may sometimes straddle both lanes to ensure safe operation, reducing capacity. Also, be cautious about using the minimum dimensions for all roadway elements on major streets, especially when striping bike lanes, or motorists may ignore the bike lane stripe. On a typical four-lane street, use 10 feet for the inside lanes and 11 feet for the outside lanes to accommodate a usual mix of urban traffic.

On lower-speed streets and streets with little bus or truck traffic, 10-foot lanes are generally sufficient.

On low-speed residential streets and in side access lanes, 9-foot lanes may be sufficient, but will require drivers to slow when approaching oncoming traffic. On many low-speed, low-volume streets, the notion of "lanes" is irrelevant—opposing directions of traffic can use the same space, and cars can share space with pedestrians and cyclists.

How Many Lanes?

As a rule of thumb, never require a pedestrian to cross more than 40 feet at a time without a median refuge. Beyond that distance, it becomes nearly impossible to accommodate a slow-moving pedestrian crossing the full distance of the intersection without creating significant delay for all users or significant safety problems for slower pedestrians. Because of the need to accommodate pedestrian crossings, widening streets beyond a certain dimension will result in diminishing additional capacity. The maximum practical width for any street is three travel lanes in each direction, a left-turn lane, and a 6-foot center median. Wider streets become too great an obstacle for pedestrians.

Tests have shown that a single traffic lane in an urban environment can have a capacity of between 650 and 1,200 vehicles per hour,[9] largely depending upon how intersections are handled. When planning urban streets, you should not add more lanes than are needed.

Intersection Design

Intersections are junctions of streets where through-moving and turning pedestrians, bicyclists, transit vehicles, and motor vehicles all share the space, preferably

1. Undivided streets should be no wider than three lanes—one lane in each direction with or without a center-turn lane.
2. Streets that are divided by a raised median should be no wider than four lanes—two lanes in each direction, with left-turn lanes provided adjacent to a traffic separator at intersections; right-turn lanes may also be provided.
3. In exceptional circumstances, a divided street may be six lanes wide, but intersection design must be carefully managed to keep crossing distances short. At any intersection approach, only one left-turn lane may be added, small corner radii should be used, and right-turn lanes are discouraged and if used they must include channelizing islands to reduce pedestrian conflicts and crossing distance.
4. One-way streets should be no wider than three lanes.

at different times to minimize conflicts. The general rule of intersection design in urban areas is to make them as compact as possible with low vehicle speeds. There are many ways to design intersections. For example, an intersection of two narrow, local streets may best be served by a raised intersection with no traffic control. In this manner, vehicle speeds are kept low; drivers, cyclists, and pedestrians are forced to make eye contact; and conflicts are minimized.

At the other extreme, a large intersection is best served by separate lanes for the various vehicle flows, pedestrian refuge islands, distinct bicycle travelways, and traffic control devices. Travel speeds through large intersections can be moderated by design features and operations. Figure 9-10 depicts examples of properly designed urban intersections

Urban intersections are shared public spaces. They must be designed so that all users of the intersection are aware of the shared function of the intersection, and especially aware of the other users of the intersection. For best-practice design of intersections, apply the following principles:

- Accommodate the needs and accessibility of all modes; do not eliminate any mode.

- Design for a hierarchy of users: first for the most vulnerable (pedestrians) and last for the least vulnerable (motor vehicles).

- Minimize conflicts between modes, where *conflicts* are defined as sharing the same location at the same time by users crossing each others' paths in the intersection.

- Provide good visibility for all users, particularly between pedestrians and motorists.

- Avoid extreme intersection angles and complex intersections (more than four legs).

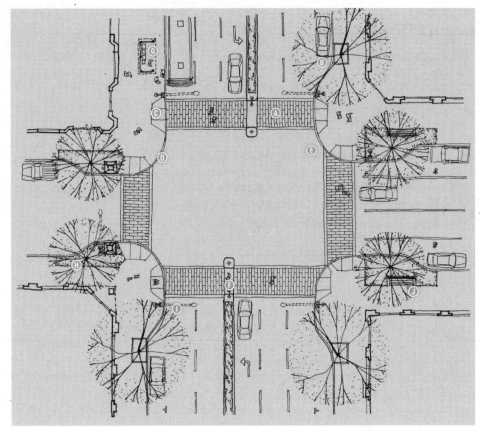

Figure 9-10
Elements of good intersection design:
A. Visible crosswalks
B. Parking restrictions at corners
C. Curb ramps
D. Tight curb radii
E. Curb extensions
F. Pedestrian refuge islands
G. Accessible transit stops
H. Street trees and landscaping
I. Street and pedestrian lighting
J. Seating and other site furnishings
Source: San Francisco Better Streets Plan, Courtesy the San Francisco Planning Department.

- Minimize pedestrian exposure to moving vehicles—design intersections to be as compact as possible, minimizing crossing distance and crossing time.

- Moderate vehicle speeds. Urban streets should have slower vehicle speeds than rural streets because the best urban streets are more complex and multifunctional.

Corner Sight Distance

Corner sight distance is a critical concept in highway design, ensuring that merges and turning movements can happen safely at high speeds. In urban places, where speeds are slower and intersections are controlled with signals or stop signs, the evaluation of proper sight distance changes significantly (Figure 9-11). It is important to apply highway sight distance requirements to highways, and to apply the proper urban street sight distance requirements depending on the type of intersection control.

Some rules to consider:

- Streets should generally intersect at 90-degree angles, which provide optimal sight lines and the shortest crossing distances. Avoid having streets intersect at

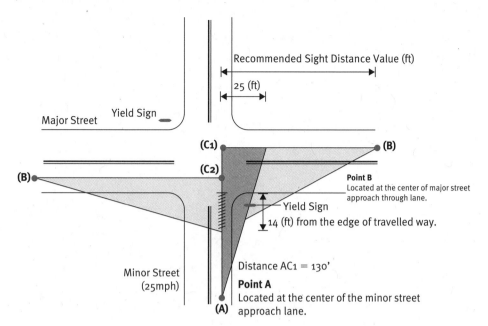

Major Street

Yield Sign

Recommended Sight Distance Value (ft)

25 (ft)

(C1)   (B)

(B)   (C2)

Point B
Located at the center of major street approach through lane.

Yield Sign
14 (ft) from the edge of travelled way.

Distance AC1 = 130'

Minor Street (25mph)

Point A
Located at the center of the minor street approach lane.
(A)

Figure 9-11
Sight triangles are much tighter in urban, controlled intersections than along highways.

less than 60 degrees, except at very low speeds, or when some movements are restricted. (At very low speeds, it is possible to use complex medieval street patterns that violate the rules of most street design manuals, but create some of the safest streets in historic town centers around the world.)

- At intersections controlled by stop signs, motorists stopped at the stop line need to be able to see vehicles arriving from the other three directions in order to know who has right of way. More importantly, motorists stopped at the stop bar need to be able to see pedestrians approaching along the sidewalk from all four corners, so they can yield to pedestrians crossing in any of the four crosswalks.

- At signalized intersections, motorists need to be able to see pedestrians and cyclists who may conflict with their left or right turn. In places where right turns are allowed on a red light, motorists must also be able to see a gap in traffic approaching from their left in order to turn right safely.

- At intersections, improve sight distances by using curb extensions to restrict on-street parking near the intersection, and to allow pedestrians to wait where they can see and be seen.

- At intersections, minimize sign clutter that distracts drivers from being able to see pedestrians crossing.

- Vertical objects near the corner, including sign poles, utility boxes, and trees, should generally be no wider than a pedestrian.

- Shrubbery, utility boxes, and other visual obstructions near the intersection should be kept lower than the height of a small child.

- At lower speeds and at controlled intersections, it may be possible to plant trees near intersections provided there are mechanisms in place to ensure that lower limbs and leaves are kept trimmed high, and the trunks do not grow wide enough to obscure pedestrians. Also be careful about planting tightly spaced rows of trees such that their trunks in alignment create a visual wall. When calculating the impact of trees on sight triangles, consider just the mature trunk, and not the entire canopy, again provided there is dedicated funding for tree maintenance.

- At very low speeds, the rules about sight distance become less important, and in an urban setting the same is true at signalized intersections.

Corner Radii

Corner radii and *turning radii* are not the same thing (Figure 9-12). The former is the actual dimension of the curb. The latter is the possible dimension of the motor-vehicle turn. Some general rules for corners include:

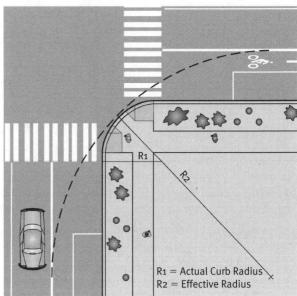

Figure 9-12
Difference between corner and turning radii. *Source: Oregon Department of Transportation.*

- Corner radii should be the minimum practical (typically, 6 to 15 feet, and 2 feet where there are no turns), to minimize motor-vehicle turning speed and minimize pedestrian crossing distances.

- Turning radii should be calculated to reflect "effective" turning radius and available space for turning, including the space for on-street parking, bicycle lanes, and all travel lanes on the receiving street (not just the nearest lane).

- Corners should be designed to accommodate the largest vehicle that will *frequently* use the intersection, including regularly scheduled transit service. Assume that the turning speeds of buses and trucks will be 5 to 10 miles per hour, and assume that large vehicles will use all receiving lanes when turning. It is acceptable for larger, infrequent vehicles (fire engines, large delivery trucks) to utilize opposing travel lanes when turning and/or cross over the centerline on the approach to a turn. Design options include moving the stop line back and mountable curbs.

- Computer software such as AutoTurn is a useful tool for designing and testing turning radii.

- Design turning radii to be as small as possible in walkable, urban settings, as shown in Table 9-2.

Right-Turn Lanes

The following are some rules of thumb about designing right-turn lanes:

- Dedicated right lanes are useful for expanding roadway capacity, because cars that are waiting to turn right can do so without blocking through traffic behind

Table 9-2 Radius and Turning Speed

Turning Speed (mph)	Vehicle Path Radius (feet)
10	18
12.5	30
15	46
17.5	74
20	103
22.5	136
25	185

Source: Based upon calculations from Formula 3-12 on p. 160 of AASHTO, *Policy on Geometric Design of Highways and Streets*, 2004 Edition.

them. This is especially true in places with high pedestrian volumes, as queued right-turning vehicles can completely block the travel lane for the entire signal cycle. In contrast, right-turn lanes add to pedestrian crossing distance and prevent curb extensions at the corner. So, start with the assumption that most urban streets don't need dedicated right-turn lanes, except where analysis determines that they would be helpful (Figure 9-13).

- Right-turn lanes are particularly helpful on streets with on-street bicycle lanes, because they reduce conflicts between turning motor vehicles and straight-through cyclists (Figure 9-14).

- Use traffic modeling software, such as Synchro, to test whether a dedicated right turn is necessary and whether it should be channelized. In all cases, use professional judgment about whether to accept the modeling tool's recommendation.

- If the traffic analysis and professional judgment say the turn lane should be channelized, be sure to design it according to modern standards, as shown in Figures 9-13 and 9-14.

Figure 9-13
Improper and proper right-lane design.
Source: San Francisco Better Streets Plan, Courtesy the San Francisco Planning Department.

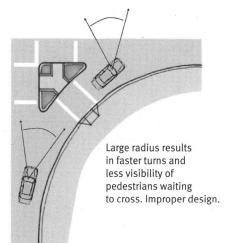

Large radius results in faster turns and less visibility of pedestrians waiting to cross. Improper design.

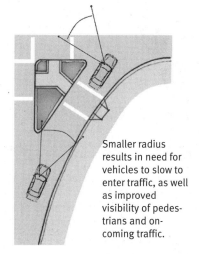

Smaller radius results in need for vehicles to slow to enter traffic, as well as improved visibility of pedestrians and on-coming traffic.

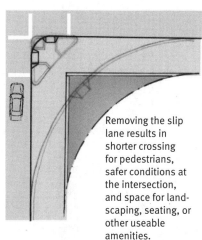

Removing the slip lane results in shorter crossing for pedestrians, safer conditions at the intersection, and space for landscaping, seating, or other useable amenities.

- Avoid using free-flow channelized turn lanes where traffic turns into a dedicated receiving lane.

Curb Extensions

At intersections and midblock crossings on streets where on-street parking is present, curb extensions should be provided (Figures 9-15 and 9-16). The width of the curb extension should typically be the same as the width of the parking lane, adjusted slightly for curb and gutter to ensure that the gutter does not encroach into the bike lane or travel lane. The appropriate corner radius should be applied, as discussed earlier in this chapter. Because of reduced road width, the corner radius on a curb extension will likely have to be larger than if curb extensions were not installed. Curb extensions have many benefits:

- Reduced pedestrian crossing distance, resulting in less exposure to vehicles and shorter pedestrian clearance intervals at signals.
- Improved visibility between pedestrians and motorists.
- Narrowed roadway, which has a potential traffic-calming effect.
- Additional room for street furniture, landscaping, and curb ramps.
- Additional on-street parking potential, because of improved sight lines at intersections. Curb extensions allow pedestrians to walk out toward the edge of the parking lane without entering the roadway, so they will be located where they can more easily see vehicles and motorists can more easily see them.

Right-Turn Slip Lane—Details

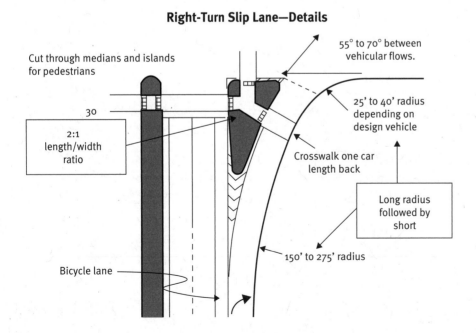

Cut through medians and islands for pedestrians

30

2:1 length/width ratio

55° to 70° between vehicular flows.

25' to 40' radius depending on design vehicle

Crosswalk one car length back

Long radius followed by short

150' to 275' radius

Bicycle lane

Figure 9-14
Right-turn slip-lane details.

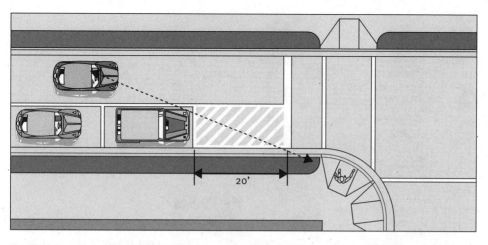

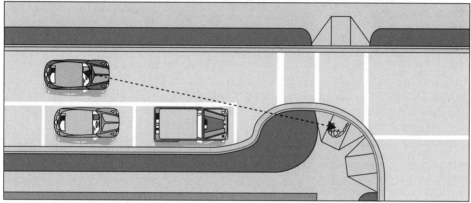

Figures 9-15 and 9-16
Curb extensions reduce crossing
distance and improve visibility
between pedestrians and motorists,
sometimes allowing for parking to be
placed closer to the crosswalk.

To create a better urban environment, the curb extension and parking area can be integrated into the sidewalk corridor (Figure 9-17). This technique involves using similar surface materials for the curb extension, parking area, and sidewalk. Instead of the curb extensions appearing to jut out into the street, the parking appears as parking "pockets" in the furniture zone. To reinforce this design where street grades permit, the gutter line and drainage grates should be placed between the travel lane and the parking lane/curb extensions. This creates a stronger visual cue separating the parking lane from the bicycle lane or travel lane, and can sometimes allow existing drainage infrastructure to be left in place.

Access Management and Driveway Design

Access management is a set of techniques usually intended to make cars go faster and improve motor-vehicle safety, but many of these strategies provide benefits for pedestrians as well. Too many driveways, for example, significantly degrade the pedestrian realm. Cities should severely limit or ban them on major boulevards and retail streets, providing access from side streets and the rear instead. Raised medians are another access-management technique that has significant benefits for

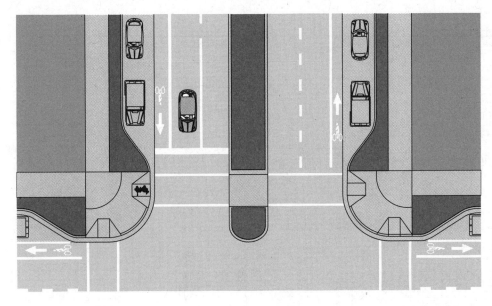

Figure 9-17
Integrating curb extensions and on-street parking into the sidewalk corridor enhances pedestrian safety and the walking experience.

pedestrians walking on the sidewalk or crossing the street. Figure 9-18 illustrates how controlled access and limited driveways reduce conflict points between pedestrians and motorists.

Principal access-management techniques include:

● Limiting the size, quantity, and frequency of driveways. Typically, this includes combining access points.

● Employing traffic-calming techniques to moderate motor-vehicle speed and driver behavior as motorists enter and exit main streets.

● Designing driveways and minor street crossings to favor pedestrians and cyclists. This means driveways ramp up to sidewalk height at the curb, and the pedestrian way continues with the same materials and other design treatments across the driveway. The design should say that the sidewalk is the main travelway, and that motorists using the driveway must yield to pedestrians.

Grade Separations

PEDESTRIAN BRIDGES AND TUNNELS

When confronted with the problem of helping pedestrians cross major streets, some designers may imagine that a pedestrian bridge or underpass is the solution, offering no waiting for pedestrians, no impacts on traffic, and greatly improved safety for everyone. Cities' real-world experience with pedestrian grade separations, however, reveals many disadvantages:

● Pedestrians like to travel in a straight line directly toward their destination. Research shows that most pedestrians will avoid using a grade separation if the time required to do so is 50 percent greater than crossing at grade.[10] To get over

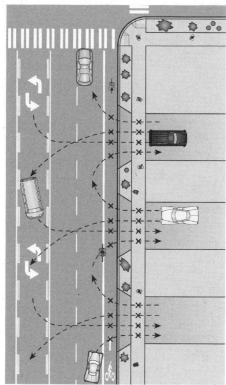

Uncontrolled accesses create 8 potential conflict points at every driveway.

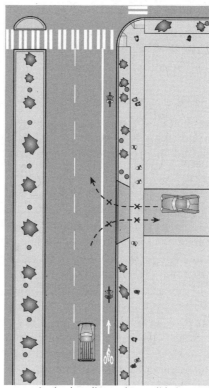

A raised median and consolidating driveways reduce conflict points.

Figure 9-18
Access management benefits pedestrians as well as cars. *Source: Oregon Department of Transportation.*

or under a roadway, a long, spiraling ramp is needed. At the 5-percent slope necessary to accommodate wheelchair users, it takes a full 380 feet of ramping to make the typical 16-foot highway clearance, plus 3 feet for the bridge structure. A typical six-lane roadway with a left-turn lane and 6-foot center median is only 83 feet, so crossing on a bridge takes ten times longer than crossing at grade! Even with stairs or an elevator, pedestrians still need to travel significantly out of direction to use the stairs, or wait for the elevator.

- Tunnels and bridges create entrapment places. The principles of Crime Prevention Through Environmental Design (CPTED) emphasize the need for clear sightlines in all directions and multiple escape routes in case people encounter a potential threat. These principles are important not only for preventing actual crime, but also for making pedestrians feel comfortable and secure. As humans, we don't like walking into places where we could possibly be trapped.

There are a few limited locations where grade-separated pedestrian crossings are appropriate in urban areas, such as:

- To traverse a major obstacle, such as a highway, railway, or waterway

- To provide a direct pedestrian route, such as between an elevated Metro station and a shopping mall or a park

- Where there are major pedestrian flows, such as at a stadium
- Where a continuous path is being provided, such as the Minneapolis Midtown Greenway, New York City's High Line, and the creeks paths of such cities as Boulder, Colorado, and Eugene, Oregon

MOTOR-VEHICLE GRADE SEPARATION

Motor-vehicle grade separations should be avoided in urban areas. In extraordinary circumstances, motor-vehicle grade separations may be built, provided cars and trucks are only placed in tunnels and underpasses rather than overpasses.

Emergency Service Vehicles

All streets should be designed to allow reliable operation of emergency service vehicles, including police cars, ambulances, and fire trucks. The precise degree to which designers should accommodate large emergency vehicles, however, requires careful consideration. In an emergency, seconds matter, so to improve fire safety, the first impulse is to design streets that are wide and straight. Streets that are designed for a big ladder truck to travel fast, however, also accommodate passenger vehicles driving even faster. The result is that fire safety is at odds with traffic safety (Figure 9-19). To address this dilemma, designers should take a life safety approach to street design, maintaining reasonable emergency response times while minimizing traffic injuries and fatalities. In most U.S. communities, there are more than ten times as many traffic injuries and fatalities as those related to fires (Figure 9-20).

For emergency responders, *response time* equals speed times distance. To increase emergency vehicle speed without increasing general traffic speed, cities should ensure that emergency vehicles can change traffic signals in their favor

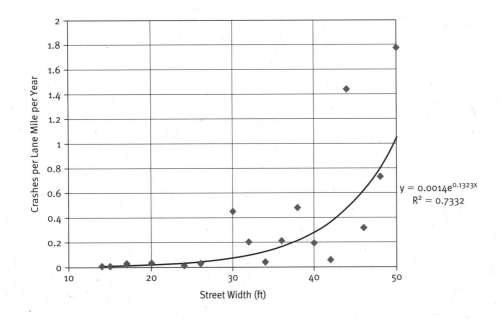

$$y = 0.0014e^{0.1323x}$$
$$R^2 = 0.7332$$

Figure 9-19
As streets widths increase, so do injury rates. *Source: Courtesy of Peter Swift.*

and use transitways, and they should use traffic management tools to ensure that primary emergency response routes are relatively free of congestion. To reduce distance, cities should provide an interconnected grid of streets. Where developers provide disconnected streets and culs-de-sac, they should be charged higher emergency response impact fees so that additional fire stations may be built.

An interconnected street grid is important to emergency responders in several ways. First, it offers the shortest possible distance from the station to the emergency. Second, it allows multiple backup routes if the primary route is blocked by construction or a double-parked delivery truck. Finally, it allows responders from multiple stations to approach a major emergency from several directions at once, minimizing interference.

With an interconnected grid, and clear standards for staging areas where there are tall buildings, it is possible to have streets narrower than 20 feet, while still maintaining excellent emergency response ability. To accommodate safer, skinnier streets, work with your fire marshal to set life safety standards for streets and specific conditions under which skinny streets may be allowed. For more information about how to balance traffic safety and fire safety, see the *Oregon Neighborhood Street Design Guidelines* and the Emergency Response and Street Design project of the Congress for the New Urbanism and U.S. Environmental Protection Agency, available at www.cnu.org.

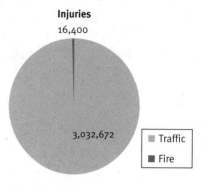

Injuries

16,400

3,032,672

- Traffic
- Fire

Figure 9-20
A life safety approach to street design considers traffic safety and emergency response times. *Source: Courtesy of Peter Swift.*

Traffic Calming

Properly designed streets usually do not need extra efforts to ensure that vehicles travel at safe speeds. If motorists are driving too fast, it usually means that the travel lanes are too many and too wide, the intersections are too big and too far apart, and the traffic signal timing is set to encourage faster driving.

If you find that motorists are driving faster than your community wants them to, it may be necessary to alter the roadway to slow traffic, using a series of techniques known as *traffic calming*. Traffic-calming projects have an impact on at least one of the following:

Vehicle speed. Vehicle speed is a significant determinant of severity of crashes.

Pedestrian and bicycle exposure risk. By making the distance to cross the street shorter, the time spent crossing the street is reduced and the exposure to risk is subsequently reduced.

Driver predictability. If other users can better predict how and where a particular vehicle will be driven, the street will be safer.

Vehicle volume. Reducing the number of vehicles reduces the impacts of those vehicles.

For a project to be considered true traffic calming, it must function every day, at all times of day or night (Figure 9-21). Closing a street to vehicles for a weekend market is not traffic calming. A school safety patrol is not traffic calming, for they are absent after school and on weekends. Detail on traffic-calming measures may be found in publications such as Reid Ewing's *Traffic Calming: State of the Practice*.[11]

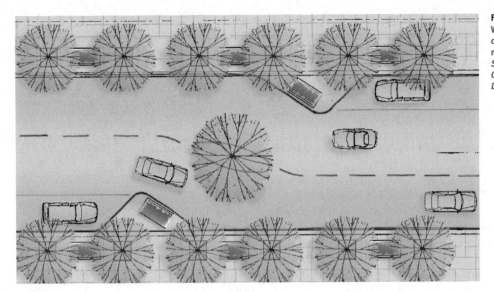

Figure 9-21
Where speeds are too high, streets can be retrofitted with traffic-calming measures such as this chicane. *Source: San Francisco Better Streets Plan, Courtesy the San Francisco Planning Department.*

Modeling Traffic

The Four-Step Travel Demand Model

For over half a century, the Four-Step Travel Demand Model has been a primary tool for forecasting future travel demand for transportation planning projects in the United States. These models use a series of calculations that forecast travel behavior based on assumed land-use patterns, socioeconomic data, and a given transportation system.

Four-step models were originally employed during the 1950s to forecast the future demand for highway infrastructure, focusing on the predicted number of automobile trips between regional activity centers. Over time, four-step models have evolved to include nonautomobile modes of travel and to address a number of related factors. These improvements were driven in part by the Clean Air Act Amendments (CAAA) of 1990, which required more rigorous regional analysis of air-quality impacts (primarily total vehicle miles traveled, travel speed, and time spent in congestion) and the Intermodal Surface Transportation Efficiency Act (ISTEA) of 1991, which required consideration of nonautomobile modes and land-use impacts.

In a typical travel demand modeling exercise, a study area is divided into geographic subareas called travel analysis zones (TAZ). These analysis zones can range in size from a few blocks in dense urban areas to several square miles in rural areas. The travel demand model predicts travel demand between these zones using four sequential steps:

1. **Trip generation**—determines the number of trips generated in each analysis zone based on land use and socioeconomic parameters. For instance, highly populated zones with affluent households in low-density developments tend to generate more automobile trips. Trip generation rates are based on an analysis of historical data.

2. **Trip distribution**—determines originating and destination zones of each predicted trip, looking at the relative attractiveness of individual zones. For example, zones with more retail space will attract more shopping trips. Also, all things being equal, trips will be distributed to closer zones, minimizing travel distance.

3. **Mode choice**—determines the travel mode used for individual trips based on cost, convenience, and travel-time comparisons between modes. In more robust models, travel-time parameters address in- and out-of-vehicle times, which include travelling to transit or the time required to park a vehicle. Up to this point in the process, all trips are analyzed as person trips. The mode choice component of the model can assign people to single-occupant vehicle trips, to higher-occupancy vehicle or transit vehicle trips, and to nonmotorized modes such as walking and cycling. For "work trips," mode choice data collected by the United States Census Bureau is useful for modeling purposes, although it is important to remember that work trips represent just a small portion of total daily trips.

4. **Route assignment**—determines which path each trip will take between its origin and destination. This step assigns automobile trips to specific roadways and transit trips to unique bus routes. This is an iterative process seeking to minimize travel time based on traffic congestion. For example, if too many trips are assigned to a given street, the resulting congestion causes excessive delays, so trips must be reassigned to alternate paths until the overall system is balanced.

Before being used to forecast future transportation system scenarios, model results are calibrated against known information and the estimated results are adjusted. Ideally, this is done at each step of the four-step process.

Four-Step Models and Transit Use

Four-step modeling has a number of inherent limitations, particularly in regard to dense urban areas where travel decisions are complex and many people use multiple modes each day. The following limitations can result in inaccurate results when analyzing transit use in and/or improvements to urban areas.

- **Trip purpose**—Historic four-step models focus on work trips that originate from home and return there afterward. This attention to commute trips is often a result of limited data on nonwork trips. However, the number of daily nonwork trips (shopping, school/college, personal errands, etc.) exceeds work travel. Data from the U.S. *National Household Travel Survey* show that up to 70 percent of evening peak-hour travel is not work related in many urban areas.[12] Some models are limited in that they use a limited number of trip purpose categories; also, data on nonwork trips may not exist in many locations.

- **Zone-based travel**—The model analyzes trips that start and end at centers of analysis zones. Many nonautomobile trips travel just across zone boundaries (not all the way to the center of a zone), with many remaining in a single analysis zone. As a result, trips can seem longer than they really are, and the use of walking and bicycling is often underestimated.

- **Homogeneity**—Demographic and land-use characteristics are considered constant across a single analysis zone. Those factors that facilitate or hinder the use of alternate modes can vary within even small zones.

- **Mode bias**—The basic model does not account for individuals' propensity to use bus rapid transit or rail transit over conventional bus service. In addition, few applications of the model account for land uses that facilitate walking and bicycling (such as sidewalk/street connectivity and/or short blocks) when making mode choice decisions.

- **Travel time**—Most models do not account for changes in peak-period travel. Trips are typically assigned to peak periods at the start of the modeling process and the process requires manual intervention to account for any changes in travel time to avoid congestion or in response to TDM measures.

- **Parking parameters**—Models may not be accurate if the cost of parking and/ or the out-of-vehicle time required to park and retrieve a car are not accurately represented.

Planning agencies, typically metropolitan planning organizations (MPOs), employ various model factors based on their local needs and/or available data. Most look at typical work-trip generators, including the number of households and jobs. However, very few incorporate factors related to the built environment or the cost of parking, leading to an overestimate of single-occupant automobile trips.

Improving on the Four-Step Model

Although the four-step model was conceived for regional automobile travel forecasting, it has been improved in functionality and application as a tool for developing demand estimates for more complex urban transportation projects. Many of these modifications represent industry-accepted model revisions; others are local patches to address specific conditions or policy directives. Modeling is a time-consuming and expensive undertaking. Because many agencies may have an interest in modeling efforts, significant process is often required to change model algorithms or assumptions.

A number of planning agencies have enhanced the four-step model to address the previously noted limitations, including:

- Use of more robust socioeconomic data in algorithms

- Use of smaller analysis zones to limit socioeconomic and land-use variations within zones, as well as to limit trip lengths within zones and to nearby zones

- Definition of a greater number of trip purpose categories

- Addition of built environment factors to account for transit, pedestrian-, or bicycle-friendly land uses

These adjustments improve the effectiveness of four-step models in forecasting demand of multiple modes and in urban areas; however, they do not fully resolve the inherent limitations of a four-step model. The trend in the industry is to look for an alternative to the four-step model. Activity-based models better address traveler behavior, as they look at individual and household travel choices. These alternative models better account for individual responses to TDM incentives, congestion, trip-chaining needs, vehicle/mode choices, seasonal or weather variations, and changes in fuel costs. They avoid the problems associated with aggregating all travel behavior to a single TAZ.

Freeways

Freeways offer tremendous advantages, allowing motorists to cover longer distances in speed, comfort, and remarkable safety. They accommodate efficient freight movement, and they allow metropolitan commuters to get to work quickly and with few negative impacts on nearby neighborhood streets.

Freeways also carry some disadvantages:

- **Lost capacity**. Freeway lanes can move about 2,000 vehicles per hour when flowing smoothly, whereas urban streets with signals, parking, and other obstructions move about 700 vehicles per hour. When a freeway cuts through an urban grid, it can eliminate as much capacity as it creates, by blocking streets along the way and providing only limited overpasses and underpasses.

- **Congestion chokepoints**. When high-volume freeways ramps connect with a fine urban grid, a big-pipe-to-small-pipe problem is created, resulting in congestion. It is challenging to spread out the high vehicle volumes associated with a freeway ramp into a matrix of narrow, pedestrian-friendly streets.

- **Dead zones**. Freeways are big, with even the tightest urban freeway consuming a full city block in width. In the best of situations, where freeways run below grade through urban areas, freeways still create a dead zone where there is an absence of activity along the sidewalk.

- **Noise and pollution**. Freeways are loud, and they concentrate emissions, especially of asthma-causing fine particulates. In California, the Bay Area Air Quality Management District requires builders to conduct air-pollution-control studies to reduce resident exposure to pollution if their projects are within 1,000 feet of a freeway.

- **Real estate value loss**. As a result of the problems listed here, urban freeways typically cut nearby real estate values in half, according to case studies of freeway removal projects in North America.[13]

- **Real estate value export**. By opening up rural areas to auto-dependent development that would otherwise not be marketable, urban freeways have the effect of shifting real estate value out of core cities and toward the suburbs.

Fixing Freeways

If your city is stuck with freeways, or a new freeway is going to be built, here are some tools for reducing their negative impacts:

- **Go under**. First, if at all possible, run the freeway below grade through urban areas, rather than elevating it. This dramatically reduces noise and visual impacts, and makes it easier to alleviate other problems.

- **Cap**. If your freeway is below grade, look for ways to cap it. Seattle, Mercer Island, and other cities have capped portions of their freeways with parks. In high-value urban areas, it costs about the same to construct a freeway cap as it does to buy land, at least for caps without major structures. It may make financial sense for a city to sell parkland for development, and move the athletic fields to a freeway cap.

- **Wrap**. Too many elevated urban freeways leave a dreary dead zone underneath them, creating a perceived barrier and personal security concerns. It's much better to wrap the freeway in a wall and use the space inside for storage.

- **Build under**. Better than wrapping an elevated freeway in a wall is wrapping it in active uses, putting shops in the space underneath and minimizing the barrier effect. Tokyo does this to great effect along portions of its Metropolitan Expressway near the Ginza, where the entire elevated freeway covers a series of elegant, two-story, linear shopping malls, including some of the finest restaurants in the neighborhood. The structure is so solidly built that truck noise and vibration are minimized, making pedestrians walking alongside it completely unaware of its presence (Figure 9-22).

Figure 9-22
In Tokyo, much of the elevated expressway system near the Ginza has shops and restaurants underneath it, making the freeway a part of the urban fabric, rather than a dead zone as in most U.S. cities. *Source: Nelson\ Nygaard*.

- **Build alongside**. High Street in Columbus, Ohio, is perhaps the best example of how to minimize the negative impacts of freeways on cities. Where a great neighborhood retail street, High Street, crosses I-670, the city widened the overpass and built chic shops above the freeway, so that pedestrians strolling along the street never know they're crossing eight lanes of busy highway beneath them.

Some tricks for addressing freeway ramps include:

One-way couplets. To help deal with the big-pipe-to-small-pipe problem, many cities use one-way couplets to help disperse freeway traffic within the urban grid. In this case, freeway off-ramps lead to one or two one-way streets heading in the same general direction as the freeway, allowing motorists to turn left or right efficiently into the grid. The reverse serves the on-ramps.

Gateways. Freeway driving and street driving require very different states of awareness. On the freeway, motorists focus attention straight ahead, covering a long distance, in order to manage speed and predict potential hazards well before arriving at them. In urban street driving, motorist attention focuses on shorter distances, and more directions, as hazards can approach from all sides. To help motorists adjust from one driving mode to another, it is helpful to use gateway treatments to shock motorists out of freeway complacency. Some of the most effective tools are vertical elements, such as trees and structures that gently constrain the visual field as a motorist leaves the freeway. Freeway off-ramps are perhaps the most challenging roadway element to design, because they mark the transition between the opposing rules of safety for urban streets and highways.

Multiway boulevards. To accommodate a major flow of traffic while maintaining a livable street, consider using a multiway boulevard. These streets have a central portion for higher-speed through traffic, and side access lanes for very low-speed access to properties alongside. San Francisco converted its elevated Central Freeway into a multiway boulevard, accommodating significant vehicle traffic while improving pedestrian conditions and increasing property values.

Beauty and pedestrian scale. So long as the street looks like a highway, motorists will drive on it like a highway. Pay extra attention to pedestrian design techniques near freeway ramps, to send a clear signal to motorists that they're in pedestrian territory now. This includes street lighting, landscape, buildings, maintenance, and other amenities at the off-ramp just as one would find them in the town center.

Accepting congestion. Finally, it is important to recognize that freeway ramps serve an important metering effect for managing congestion elsewhere in the city street grid. Do not allow any more cars off the freeway than your streets can manage.

Freeway Removal

Rather than accommodating urban freeways, cities around the world are removing them from their urban cores, recognizing that the benefits of walkable city centers exceed those of freeways. Although there are a number of examples of urban freeway removals in North America, certainly no two are exactly alike. Cities can learn a number of lessons, however, from studying other cities' efforts at reducing the negative impact of freeways (notably Chattanooga, San Francisco, Milwaukee, Seoul, and Portland). Lessons include the following:

- **Reduction of roadway capacity reduces the number of auto trips**. Also, to the extent that vehicle miles traveled can be reduced, a number of social and environmental benefits are derived: decreased energy usage and carbon emissions; improved air quality and public health; increased safety for motorists, pedestrians, and cyclists; a reduction in fumes and noise pollution; and more cost-effective use of existing transit capacity.

- **Spillover traffic can be absorbed**. Experience to date suggests that the ceiling of traffic volumes that can reasonably be accommodated through alternate routes, on all modes, with appropriate demand management and land-use strategies may be higher than previously believed. Gridded street patterns are especially effective at accommodating whatever traffic remains once capacity has been reduced. Studies have shown that the addition of capacity can actually increase congestion by funneling traffic into a single direct route, rather than distributing it over a network.

- **Freeway removal does not require a major shift to transit**. The experiences of other cities suggest that removal of an urban freeway will in and of itself change travel patterns significantly. Traffic will find alternate routes and travelers will choose the most convenient mode for their trips, or travel at different times or to different locations.

- **Freeway removal has a catalytic effect**. Excess right-of-way can often be redeveloped or converted into civic amenities such as open space, but even where this is not the case, the impacts of freeway removal tend to be felt over a broad area. Surrounding property values increase, neighborhoods become more attractive to investors and visitors, and crime can be reduced through increased foot traffic and the elimination of shadowy hiding places. Even if crime is not reduced, perceptions of safety often change. None of the cities studied noted any long-term negative economic impact, even to areas that had previously been directly served by the freeway.

- **Design is key**. It is not enough to merely replace a grade-separated roadway with an at-grade street. Complete-street design that seeks to accommodate all users, traffic calming, and other engineering techniques should be applied. Design decisions should be guided by concerns about equity and efficient, sustainable use of transportation supply.

- **Reductions of roadway capacity must be managed, mitigated, and monitored over time**. Freeway removal is not just a one-time demolition project. To be effective, it requires a long-term commitment and a willingness to adjust. It also requires a thorough, integrated approach, one that constantly observes conditions and designs solutions for all users, including not just motorists but also transit riders, pedestrians, and cyclists.

- **Freeway removal should be undertaken only after careful consideration of the tradeoffs**. Even under the most favorable circumstances, freeway removal is not a panacea for urban ills. Inevitably, it will require sacrifices for some. By displacing traffic onto at-grade roadways, it may prove challenging to pedestrians; to the extent that it reduces auto mobility, it may promote some types of businesses over others. Attempts to substitute access for mobility through mixed land uses may result in densities unacceptable to many. In any case, a civic conversation about competing values must take place: Reduced mobility may be acceptable if other values, such as quality of life and economic development, are prioritized.

- **Freeway removal should be part of a larger strategy**. Removals are most effective when they are one element of a comprehensive, clearly articulated civic vision for enhanced quality of life, sustainability, and economic development that leverages the opportunities made available by removal. For all of its potential benefits, freeway removal should not be seen as an end in itself, but as a means to advance greater goals and objectives.

Chapter 10

Parking

with Patrick Siegman and Brian Canepa

Introduction

In every city, sufficient automobile parking is necessary for the success of most businesses, and for the quality of life of car-owning residents. But how much parking is "sufficient"? How much is too much? Indeed, given the cost of building parking, too much parking may be just as bad as too little for economic success.

If your city wants to focus on one topic for reducing traffic congestion, improving housing affordability, cleaning the air, lessening climate change, making government more efficient, and enlivening the economy—all at the same time—then it should focus on parking.

Additional information on parking for rail stations can be found in Chapter 12, "Stations and Station Areas," and details on parking cash-out can be found in Chapter 13, "Transportation Demand Management." For even more information, consult Don Shoup's book, *The High Cost of Free Parking*,[1] which should be on all planners' bookshelves, alongside Jane Jacobs's writings.

Parking Is Destiny

Parking touches almost all aspects of a city's life and economy. Designers must understand all of these connections if they are to plan properly for parking:

Parking consumes land. A parking lot averages 100 spaces per acre or about 330 square feet per space, including typical drive aisles, ramps, and setbacks. Therefore, any city that requires more than 3 spaces per 1,000 square feet of building area is requiring more parking area than building area (Figure 10-1). At 5 spaces per 1,000 square feet—a typical minimum requirement for a suburban office—parking consumes nearly two-thirds of the developed area.

Parking is expensive. Building a new structured parking space can cost upwards of $40,000 in 2010 U.S. dollars—and about $30,000 to $60,000 underground once both hard and soft costs are included. Factoring in the high cost of land in most urban centers, a surface space can be even more expensive. Although it is important to have sufficient parking, building too much parking is wasteful. At these high prices, it is essential that all of a city's parking spaces be managed as a precious resource. Every empty parking space is $40,000 that could have been spent on street trees, traffic calming, shuttles, or other access improvements.

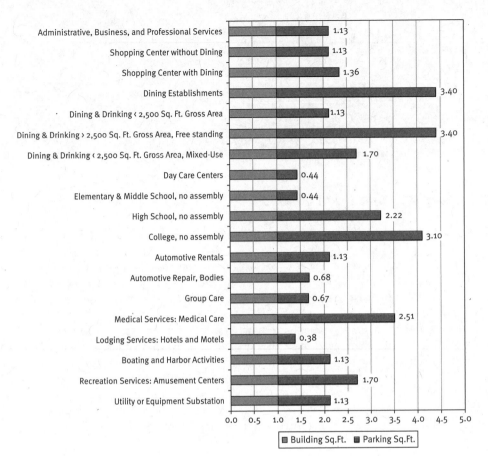

Administrative, Business, and Professional Services	1.13	
Shopping Center without Dining	1.13	
Shopping Center with Dining	1.36	
Dining Establishments		3.40
Dining & Drinking < 2,500 Sq. Ft. Gross Area	1.13	
Dining & Drinking > 2,500 Sq. Ft. Gross Area, Free standing		3.40
Dining & Drinking < 2,500 Sq. Ft. Gross Area, Mixed-Use	1.70	
Day Care Centers	0.44	
Elementary & Middle School, no assembly	0.44	
High School, no assembly	2.22	
College, no assembly		3.10
Automotive Rentals	1.13	
Automotive Repair, Bodies	0.68	
Group Care	0.67	
Medical Services: Medical Care	2.51	
Lodging Services: Hotels and Motels	0.38	
Boating and Harbor Activities	1.13	
Recreation Services: Amusement Centers	1.70	
Utility or Equipment Substation	1.13	

0.0   0.5   1.0   1.5   2.0   2.5   3.0   3.5   4.0   4.5   5.0

■ Building Sq.Ft.   ■ Parking Sq.Ft.

Figure 10-1
Comparing parking area to building area in typical minimum parking requirements reveals that cities require more parking than building. *Source: Nelson\Nygaard/City of Ventura, CA, Downtown Parking and Mobility report.*

Parking reduces housing affordability. Each off-street parking space, along with its share of necessary aisles and ramps, consumes about the same amount of building space as a studio apartment. According to the San Francisco Planning Department, each parking space added to a typical multifamily residential unit increases the price of that unit by about 20 percent and decreases the number of units that can be built by the same amount. According to Scott Bernstein of the Center for Neighborhood Technology, households that can give up ownership of one vehicle can afford an additional $100,000 in mortgage in 2008 dollars, or save $650 a month for rent, education, or other opportunities. While housing in central cities may be more expensive, residents there can save far more on parking and transportation costs than the added costs of housing (Figure 10-2).[2]

Parking worsens traffic congestion. Parking spaces—particularly commuter or visitor spaces—are like magnets for cars. There is no point in providing more parking than there is roadway capacity to access those spaces. Some cities, like Portland, Oregon; Cambridge, Massachusetts; and San Francisco, California, have used commuter parking constraint or pricing as a congestion management tool. Indeed, parking pricing is the most effective transportation demand management (TDM) tool. The worst kind of traffic congestion, however, is created by poor parking management. As available parking spaces become scarce, motorists end up driving around in circles looking for an empty space. Not only does this result in an increase in driving, but it also creates excessive turning movements and bad motorist behavior, all of which exacerbate traffic congestion far more than the addition of vehicle trips. In fact, available studies suggest that this "cruising" for parking represents between 8 percent and 74 percent of traffic in commercial areas.[3]

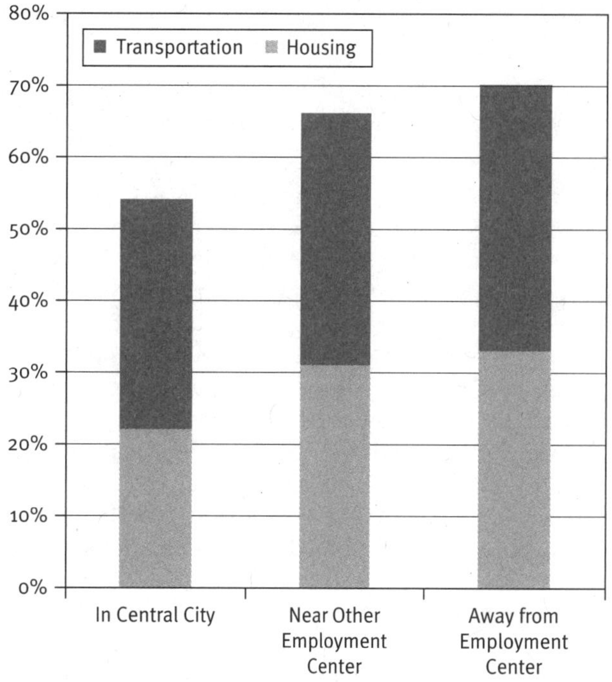

Parking results in greenhouse gas emissions. Providing free parking is the same as providing free gasoline or writing motorists a big check every time they drive. By removing parking subsidies and revealing the true cost of parking to motorists, we can cut vehicle miles traveled (VMT) by 25 percent in the United States.

Parking pollutes our rivers and seas. In most cities, rain that falls on parking lots washes directly into the storm drain system and then goes untreated into local rivers and streams, carrying with it a toxic brew of volatile organic compounds, brake dust, and other pollutants. In fact, parking lots are the single biggest source of water pollution in many cities, according to the U.S. Environmental Protection Agency. When parking is reduced, more land is available for stormwater to be absorbed into the soils, where pollutants can break down. Parking lots may also be designed with permeable pavements and systems that allow runoff to be treated before reaching natural waterways.

Parking can destroy walkable urbanism. Designed poorly, parking can be ugly, reducing the walkability of commercial areas or neighborhoods and increasing the likelihood that people will drive. Designed well, parking can accommodate cars while also improving conditions for pedestrians, bicyclists, and transit users.

Figure 10-2
Low-income households can reduce their transportation costs by living near transit and driving less. *Source: Center for Neighborhood Technology.*

Parking Economics 101

To solve a city's parking problems, it is important to think more like an economist and less like an engineer. Parking, after all, is simply a commodity, like ice cream, or a shirt, or an apartment, and is subject to Adam Smith's various laws of supply and demand. Economic theory teaches that there are limited tools a city or business can use to balance parking supply and demand:

- **Substitution** could increase the attractiveness of alternatives to driving, including all the tools covered in Chapter 13, "Transportation Demand Management."
- **Regulation** could restrict parking to a certain segment of users, such as employees or shoppers of a specific business.

- **Price** could encourage motorists to choose cheaper, less convenient parking over more costly front-door parking.

- **Queuing**—or standing in line—requires that motorists circle around to find a space or wait for another motorist to leave.

Many public goods, such as utilities and housing, combine some or all of these approaches, manipulating the free market to achieve larger social goals. For example, telephone companies are regulated to provide lifeline service to low-income families, deeply discounting the price of service, and they provide discount, off-peak, long-distance coverage in order to minimize the amount of time a caller cannot get through—the telephonic equivalent of a queue.

In the former Soviet Union, the central government mandated the production of specific numbers of housing units, to be given away free or at deep discounts, to ensure that all of its citizens were properly housed. The communist government reasoned that a free, equitable, and productive society required housing for everyone, and that it was efficient to tax production to achieve this social goal. Similarly, the government mandated production requirements for bread and distributed bread free to ensure that its citizens were happy and well fed.

In the capitalist West, we imitate the Soviet communists by establishing government mandates that ensure not free housing for all citizens, but rather free housing for all its cars. In fact, in the United States, there are between 3.5 and 8 government-mandated parking spaces for every car,[4] despite the fact that more than 640,000 citizens remain homeless.[5] Although we take a free-market approach for all other social goods, including food, clothing, and shelter, the car and not the citizen merits special treatment in our society.

What Happens If Parkers Pay for Parking?

Although the costs of parking are largely hidden in the costs of goods and services, or are borne by society at large, sometimes motorists do pay for the parking they use. In such cases, Adam Smith's invisible hand waves in welcome.

The price elasticity of demand helps economists predict how demand will change following a change in price. Many studies have found that parking is a fairly inelastic good—that is, compared to other goods for which there are ready substitutes, it takes a big increase in price to reduce parking demand. This makes sense: Automobiles themselves are highly elastic goods because consumers can choose among many makes and models, and they can postpone their purchase decision for many years. Parking is inelastic because it is a fairly small component of all the costs bundled into a driving trip, including the cost of gas, the wear and tear on the car, and, most importantly, the time cost to the driver and the comparative time cost of taking the trip by another mode of transportation.

Various studies have established a range of parking price elasticity of demand between –0.1 and –0.6, with the average at –0.3—that is, for every 100 percent increase in the price of parking, there is a 30 percent decrease in parking demand.

Parking Tools

Before looking at specific management techniques and tools, it is helpful to review a few of the tools available to help communities build and manage parking.

ITE *Parking Generation* Manual: Use Cautiously!

The most common tool communities use to establish their parking ratios is the *Parking Generation* manual published by the Institute for Transportation Engineers (ITE). This is a useful guide for building auto-dependent communities, but not for mixed-use and walkable communities without significant adjustment. As noted in its "User's Guide", most of the data in the ITE manual comes from isolated, single-use places, where there is no transit service or even pedestrian access.

It is also important to understand how to read the data in the manual. Even in auto-dependent areas, parking demand varies significantly for any land-use type. Be particularly cautious of figures with low statistical significance or a low R^2 value. The ITE figures represent a reasonable worst-case scenario for peak parking demand, so avoid using these numbers to establish minimum parking standards.

ULI Shared Parking

The Urban Land Institute (ULI) Shared Parking Model is embodied in a Microsoft Excel spreadsheet, and it is a useful supplement to the ITE manual for mixed-use and commercial areas that share parking. The spreadsheet compares the peaking characteristics of different land uses and calculates, for example, the degree to which a theater, which has its parking peak nights and weekends, can share parking with an office, which peaks during weekdays. The spreadsheet is a companion to the book *Shared Parking, Second Edition*, published by the Urban Land Institute and the International Council of Shopping Centers in 2005.

Like the ITE numbers, the ULI model data should be used with some caution. If the model is used with its default settings, it tends to overestimate the total parking needed, for several reasons:

- First, like ITE, the default assumption is that everyone is driving, so in walkable and transit-accessible locations, parking demand will have to be adjusted downward using other tools, such as URBEMIS.

- Secondly, the base parking ratios in the ULI Shared Parking Model are *not* intended to predict the number of vehicles that are likely to be parked at an average project. Instead, the base parking ratios represent the ULI's opinion about the number of parking spaces that should be provided; this model assumes enough parking to provide a cushion that will result in 85–95 percent occupancy at the peak hour. By contrast, using average peak parking ratios from the ITE's *Parking Generation* as the base parking ratios for the model is more likely to accurately predict need.

- Finally, the ULI spreadsheet primarily uses December as its default month for generating demand outputs, assuming that there is the highest parking occupancy during that month (Figure 10-3). The result is that users design parking for a potential three-week period before Christmas, even though many of those spaces will sit vacant for the other forty-nine weeks of the year.

Fortunately, the spreadsheet is readily adjustable so users can enter their own assumptions about mode split and target peak for planning purposes.

U.S. Census

Unlike the ITE data, which is from all over the country and dates back to the 1970s, the U.S. Census can provide accurate local data on household auto ownership and can help estimate employee parking demand. The census data has a few drawbacks:

- It is only collected every ten years, so it may be out of date.
- Because the source is the census long form, watch for very low sample sizes when analyzing data at the block group level.
- Though it is very useful for estimating residential parking demand, it is less precise for commercial demand.

To use the census data, go to factfinder.census.gov. The first step is to identify the census block groups for analysis. To do this, click on "Maps" and then "Reference Maps." Then, check "Census Tracts and Blocks" and enter the state and zip code for the study area. This brings up a map that shows census tract and block group boundaries for every community in the United States.

To find facts for these block groups, go back to factfinder.census.gov; click on "Data Sets," then "Decennial Census" and check "Summary File 3" and "Detailed Tables." In the pull-down menu under "Geographic Type," select "Block

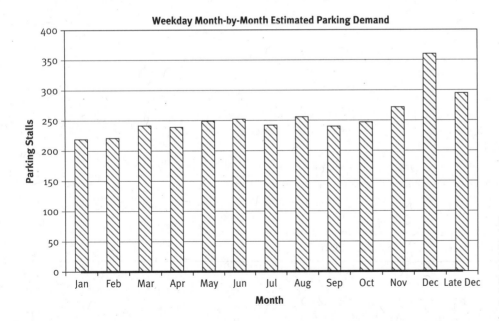

Figure 10-3
The ULI Shared Parking model shows how different land uses have peak parking demand at different times of day. *Source: Nelson\Nygaard, from Shared Parking model, Shared Parking, Second Edition, Urban Land Institute 2005.*

Group," then note the state, county, census tract, and block groups that you want data for. On the next page, select the data you are looking for. Two of the most interesting data sets include:

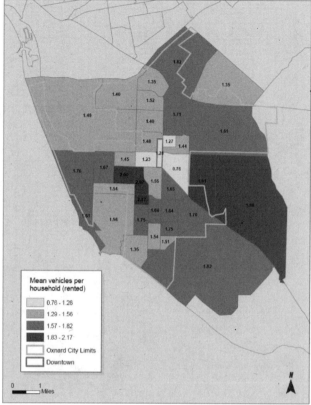

Oxnard Vehicle Ownership: Vehicles Per Household (Rented)

- P30. Means of Transportation to Work by Workers 16+ Years

- H44. Tenure by Vehicles Available

There is also a wealth of related information on income, race, population size, place of work, travel time to work, and so on, allowing a correlation of the transportation data and social data if you wish to conduct a social equity analysis. Clicking on any of these data sets results in a simple chart that can be copied into Excel or other software for more detailed analysis, including mapping in GIS.

Applying this data, it becomes clear that parking demand and auto ownership vary more by geography than they do by land-use type or even income. In most communities, households in walkable neighborhoods near transit and retail own far fewer cars than households in more auto-dependent neighborhoods in the same city (Figure 10-4).

U.S. DOT Census Transportation Planning Products

Whereas the U.S. Census website focuses on data about residents and their travel behavior, the U.S. Department of Transportation publishes data that focuses on employee travel behavior. To use this data, order the Census Transportation Planning Products (CTPP) Part 2 Place of Work Tables free (on CD) from www.fhwa.dot.gov/ctpp. The CD comes with software that describes how to select relevant data and complete simple analyses.

The tables identify how employee travel behavior varies from one location to another. For example, the data may show that employees in a downtown location are 40 percent less likely to drive than in the county as a whole, thereby providing a useful adjustment factor for the expected parking demand in a proposed downtown office building.

More interestingly, the data also show employee commute patterns for any given employment center. These patterns are very useful for planning all sorts of transportation investments. For example, Figure 10-5 shows the employee commute data for the small city of Oxnard, California, where planners had assumed that most employees were commuting long distances from remote rural towns or far-distant Los Angeles. To their surprise, the largest share of their commuters traveled only short distances within the city, with another major stream coming from nearby San Buenaventura. This analysis allowed Oxnard to prioritize local bicycle, pedestrian,

Figure 10-4
Using census data, it is easy to see how auto ownership patters vary in your city. Parking demand varies more by location than it does by land-use type. *Source: Nelson\Nygaard.*

Commuter Origins of Oxnard Workforce

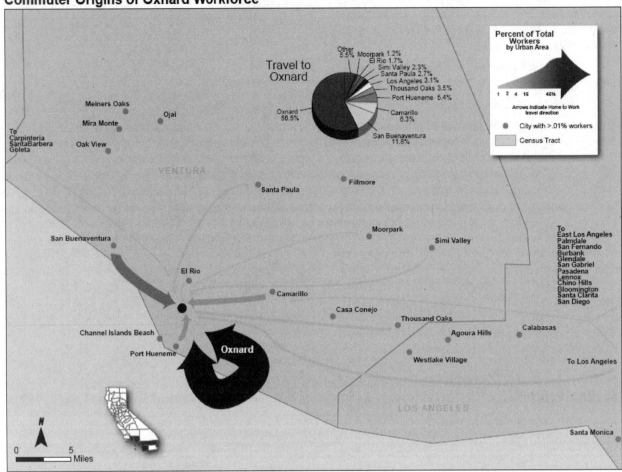

Figure 10-5
Using the Census Transportation Planning Products, you can see detailed travel patterns for your community, allowing you to invest in the right amount of parking, transit, and other access strategies. *Source: Nelson\Nygaard.*

and shuttle investments, plus more frequent transit service to San Buenaventura, to meet its congestion management goals.

URBEMIS

URBEMIS (an acronym drawn from the words *URBan EMISsions model*) is a free tool developed by the air-quality management districts of California to estimate pollutants resulting from urban development. To estimate pollutants and CO_2 emissions from cars, the model provides detailed adjustments to the ITE *Trip Generation* figures, taking into account area-specific characteristics to determine accurate trip rates. The number of trips generated by a development depends not only on the characteristics of the project itself, but also on the nature of the surrounding area. For example, neighborhood characteristics such as a good balance of housing and jobs, the presence of frequent transit service, and a highly connected, walkable street network are strongly associated with lower vehicle trip rates. High-density housing added to an existing central city neighborhood, where many shops, services, and transit lines already exist, will normally generate fewer trips than the same housing located close to a freeway interchange and surrounded by only low-density housing subdivisions. For this reason, URBEMIS requires data about the area within approximately a half-mile radius from the center of the project, or for the entire project area, whichever is larger.

The full model and instruction manual are available free at www.urbemis .com. Its use in adjusting trip generation factors was upheld by the federal district court in California in the case of *California Building Industry Association v. San Joaquin Valley Unified Air Pollution Control District*.[6]

Parking Management Principles

Well-designed parking policies are an essential prerequisite for vibrant commercial districts and livable neighborhoods. Without appropriate parking policies, mixed-use and transit-oriented development is often financially infeasible. Guiding principles for effective parking planning include the following.

1. *A one-size-fits-all solution never works for parking.*

   When planning for parking—like everything else—pay close attention to the unique strengths and characteristics of a particular place. Parking solutions that work in the suburbs often don't work downtown, and vice versa. Certainly, parking demand patterns vary more by location than they do by land-use type.

   In the past century, a common mistake in walkable, mixed-use centers was to impose suburban parking standards, with the mistaken assumption that downtown could not "compete" with suburban shopping centers unless it had the acres of free parking that shoppers find at the mall. In fact, we have found that if downtown tries to compete on the same terms as the mall, it will always lose. Rather, mixed-use places have to compete on their own terms, offering a high-quality, diverse, walkable environment, and emphasizing excellent parking management rather than excessive parking supply.

2. *Ensure that some parking is always available everywhere.*

   Motorists are not interested in the overall number of parking spaces in an area; what matters is how easily they can find an empty space. This means that parking facilities should be managed to achieve 85–90 percent occupancy, which represents the optimal balance between ease of finding a space and efficient use of resources. The target occupancy level can be higher for large, centralized facilities, or where sophisticated real-time information systems are available. Parking charges, time limits, and other restrictions should be used to maintain availability. This is particularly important for the most visible spaces on the street and close to garage entrances. If occupancy rises above 90 percent, it should trigger an increase in price, a reduced time limit, or another measure to increase availability.

3. *Ensure that the public perceives that parking is always available.*

   Economic success depends not just on the availability of parking, but on the public's perception of parking availability. Available spaces are of little use if they are invisible to motorists. Several strategies can be used to improve the public's perception of parking availability:

   - *Information.* At a minimum, roadway signs, information brochures, and websites can highlight the location of parking facilities where space is likely to be available. Ideally, real-time information signs can show the number of free spaces in different garages at that time, and direct motorists accordingly. Information on all area garages should be provided in all promotional materials, which will play a key role in directing visitors to underutilized garages.

   - *Differential pricing and demand management.* Perceptions are most influenced by occupancy of the most visible spaces, particularly on-street spaces and those on the lower floors of garages. Pricing and time limits are particularly important here, and generally these premium spaces should command a higher price and/or be subject to a shorter time limit.

   - *Education.* To leave the most convenient spaces free for customers, merchants and their employees should be encouraged to park in less visible spaces, such as on the top floor of a parking garage.

   - *Valet services.* Valet parking ensures that customers never have to worry about finding a space, if they are willing to pay a premium charge for help from an attendant.

4. *Ensure that parking facilities are shared.*

   Sharing parking spaces among different land uses maximizes the efficiency of the parking system, and allows the same demand to be satisfied with fewer spaces. This is so for two main reasons:

   - Different land uses have different times of peak demand. For example, residential demand is highest at evenings and weekends. Office demand peaks during the working day, whereas retail demand is highest on the weekends.

   - Shared parking moderates peaks in parking demand. A common parking pool allows the supply to serve multiple uses. Most parking facilities are oversized to cater to variations in demand and accommodate peaks of a single or primary use. As more uses with different peak parking demands share a parking facility, the service efficiency increases for the facility.

   Parking should be designed for shared use to take advantage of this potential. For example, pedestrian entrances should lead to the street, not solely to a particular building. Otherwise, security issues can hamper shared parking arrangements. Parking spaces should not be reserved for particular users. At the least, reserved parking spaces—for example, for residents—should be charged for at a premium rate.

   Parking spaces should be owned and managed on a common basis. Public parking facilities are the easiest to share, as institutional barriers are avoided. If private parking facilities are constructed, development agreements should make provision for public access and shared use. The creation of local business improvement districts (BIDs) can facilitate these efforts by creating an entity that leases parking from third-party owners and arranges to make it accessible to the public, thereby optimizing utilization to support economic productivity within the district.

5. *Put the customer first.*

Different users of parking facilities bring different economic returns and have varying abilities to use alternative modes. For example, employees generally travel at peak hours when transit is most frequent and, because they make the same trip every day, can research different transit options. They are also unlikely to choose a different job based on the availability and cost of parking alone.

Shoppers and visitors, in contrast, generally travel at off-peak times, make their trips less frequently, and have a greater choice of alternative destinations. They are also the most critical group to attract to achieve economic development goals.

Within mixed-use districts with constrained parking supply, parking facilities should prioritize users based on the following hierarchy:

- Customers and shoppers
- Other visitors
- Residents
- Employees
- Park-and-ride commuters

6. *Manage the entire parking supply as part of a coherent system.*

As far as possible, different types of parking—on- and off-street, public and private—should be managed according to the same set of principles. Pricing, time limits, and payment mechanisms should be standardized as far as possible, to increase understanding.

7. *Analyze alternatives before increasing the parking supply.*

Providing parking is just one possible—and expensive—way to accommodate new trips. Before constructing a new parking facility, determine whether the same number of trips could be accommodated at less cost through other means. Potential alternatives might include:

- *Improving information.* Better signage and real-time information can allow existing parking facilities to be used more efficiently.
- *Valet parking.* Particularly if peaks are short in duration, it may be cost-effective to employ extra staff to "stack" cars and eliminate aisles, rather than provide more parking. Parking lifts are another way to fit more cars into the same area.
- *Transit improvements.* Faster, more frequent transit service will attract more riders to transit, freeing up parking spaces for other users.

- *Bicycle and pedestrian improvements.* Bicycle parking, on-street bike lanes, and pedestrian crossing upgrades can encourage more employees and visitors to walk or bike.

- *Financial incentives.* In some cases, it may be cheaper to pay people not to drive than to construct new parking facilities.

- *Other demand management programs.* These include carpool matching and vanpool programs, as well as the pricing and permit strategies discussed earlier.

8. *Use parking as a tool to manage roadway congestion.*

Controlling parking is any city's most powerful tool for managing congestion. Although a wide range of demand management tools exist that can be used to manage congestion, many of these—such as gasoline taxes and charging for the use of road space—are not controlled by municipalities.

The amount of parking and the level of charges have a major impact on automobile traffic levels. For every automobile parking space added in a city, the potential for additional automobile trips is also added. Charging for parking is the single most effective strategy, meanwhile, to encourage people to use alternatives to the single-occupant vehicle.

The structure of parking charges also influences roadway congestion. Residential and shopping trips are more likely to take place at off-peak times, in contrast to the journey to work. Prioritizing spaces for shoppers, visitors, and residents (for example, through differential pricing) will therefore help to spread vehicle trips throughout the day and reduce peak-period congestion.

9. *Site curb cuts to avoid or minimize negative impacts on transit service and pedestrian access.*

To maintain transit running time, it is critical to limit the number of turning movements made by autos on transit priority streets. Left turns into off-street parking areas, in particular, have a significant negative effect on transit. New curb cuts should therefore not be allowed on transit priority streets (Figure 10-6). If off-street parking is necessary for a development project on a transit priority street, access should be from the side street, back alley, or other adjacent street.

10. *Maximize the contribution of parking to good urban design.*

Parking garages can be a blight on the urban environment. Blank garage doors and parking structure walls can have a significant negative visual impact on streets, make the pedestrian environment less attractive, and disrupt the character of neighborhood commercial districts. Surface lots also can have a blighting effect on neighboring properties.

There are a number of strategies, however, that can minimize the impacts of parking on the pedestrian environment and on neighborhood amenity:

- Prohibit garage doors and blank walls on neighborhood commercial streets and key pedestrian corridors.

FRONTAGES WHERE CURB CUTS ARE NOT PERMITTED

Map 10

Figure 10-6
In San Francisco's Market & Octavia Plan, curb cuts for parking are restricted along key streets. *Source: San Francisco Planning Department.*

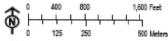

- Wrap all floors of above-grade parking with active uses (i.e., retail, residential, office).

- Provide access to parking structures via a side street or alley, rather than from the main commercial street.

- Screen surface parking lots from the street with vegetation and low walls.

- Minimize the width and number of entrances/exits to off-street parking to minimize conflict points with pedestrians, cyclists, and transit, and to reduce the amount of ground-floor space taken up by garage entries.

11. *Address spillover concerns.*

One of the most significant threats to infill development is the current residents' fear that new residents and jobs will translate into scarcer parking. Most cities have neighborhoods and commercial districts that were built before minimum parking requirements were introduced for residential uses in the late 1950s, and many rely on existing curbside spaces. If new developments in their neighborhoods are built without a full complement of off-street spaces, existing residents tend to become especially fearful about impacts on the nearby on-street parking supply.

Residential permit parking zones protect residents from spillover parking from employees and commuters. However, they are of limited value when the cause of parking scarcity is the number of residents themselves competing for scarce on-street spaces. In the long term, this problem could be addressed through the creation of a true market for on-street spaces (see discussion in the following section on residential parking).

12. *Involve the business community.*

Research shows the importance of involving businesses, whether they participate through actually running parking and transportation services, or in designing the parking policy strategies. It is critical that the city and businesses work together to develop a plan that everyone can support.

Top Ten Parking Management Strategies

All cities interested in sustainability should implement the following parking management best practices. These strategies are applicable in both small towns and urban centers.

Strategy 1: Park Once

Goals: Make efficient use of the parking supply by including as many spaces as possible in a common pool of shared, publicly available spaces. Build a small number of cost-effective, strategically located parking structures, rather than many small, inefficient, and scattered private lots.

Recommendation: Adopt a "Park Once" strategy for your downtown or any mixed-use retail area by (a) operating as many parking spaces as possible in a common pool of shared, publicly available spaces; and (b) encouraging existing private commercial parking to be shared among different land uses and available to the public when not serving private commercial use. This strategy should be implemented through the following policies:

1. Prohibit or discourage private parking in new development (except for residential spaces). Instead, make public parking lots available to downtown

shoppers and employees, and (when more exclusive parking arrangements are necessary) lease spaces in nearby public lots and garages to private businesses, for the particular hours and days of the week when the reserved parking is actually required.

2. Purchase or lease existing private parking lots from willing sellers, and add this parking to the shared public supply.

3. Facilitate shared and/or valet parking in existing private parking lots wherever feasible:

    a. Allow parking provided in all downtown development to be off-site within a quarter-mile of project site (about six blocks, a comfortable walking distance for most people).

    b. If commercial developments are allowed to provide on-site parking, require as a condition of approval that any such parking be made available to the public when not in use by the owner/occupant.

DISCUSSION

The typical suburban pattern of isolated, single-use buildings, each surrounded by parking lots, requires two vehicular movements and a parking space to be dedicated for each visit to a shop, or office, or civic institution. To accomplish three errands in this type of environment requires six movements in three parking spaces for three tasks. With virtually all parking held in private hands, spaces are not efficiently shared among uses, and each building's private lots are therefore typically sized to handle a worst-case parking load. Most significantly, when new and renovated buildings in an existing downtown are required to provide such worst-case parking ratios, the result is often stagnation and decline. Buildings are not renovated, because no room exists on the site for the required parking; new shops often demand the tear-down of adjacent buildings, generating free-standing retail boxes surrounded by cars, or pedestrian-hostile buildings that hover above parking lots. The resulting low-density fabric generates too few pedestrians to let downtown reach critical mass.

When the suburban practice of building individual private lots for each building is introduced into a traditional downtown, the result is also a lack of welcome for customers: At each parking lot, the visitor is informed that the vehicle will be towed if he or she peruses any place other than the adjacent building. When this occurs, nearby shopping malls gain a distinct advantage over the downtown with fragmented parking. Mall owners understand that they should not divide their mall's parking supply into small fiefdoms: they operate their supply as a single pool for all of the shops, so that customers are welcomed wherever they park.

Park once: Those arriving by car can easily follow a "park once" pattern. They park their cars just once and complete multiple daily tasks on foot before returning to their cars.

Shared parking among uses with differing peak times: Spaces can be efficiently shared between uses with differing peak hours, peak days, and peak seasons of parking demand (such as office, restaurant, retail, and entertainment uses).

Shared parking to spread peak loads: The parking supply can be sized to meet *average* parking loads (instead of the *worst-case* parking ratios needed for isolated suburban buildings), because the common supply allows shops and offices with above-average demand to be balanced by shops and offices that have below-average demand or are temporarily vacant.

Studies indicate that when a "park once" strategy is followed, the parking demand for mature mixed-use districts typically ranges from 1.6 to 1.9 spaces occupied per 1,000 square feet of nonresidential built space, or one-third to one-half that required for conventional suburban development. Table 10-1 shows that even in wealthy, suburban locations with low transit utilization and low prices for parking, peak cumulative parking occupancy is still remarkably low, largely because shoppers are parking once and doing multiple activities. Palo Alto, which had the highest observed parking demand, also has one of the highest-grossing downtown main streets in California, and parking meters are illegal there by statute.[7]

To implement a park-once strategy, parking in your downtown must be managed as a public utility, just like streets and sewers, with public parking provided in strategically placed, city-owned and -managed lots and garages. New development should be prohibited (or strongly discouraged) from building private parking (except residential spaces): When private developments, such as new offices, require a guarantee of a certain number of spaces at particular hours (e.g., Monday through Friday, 9:00 a.m. to 5:00 p.m.), they should be provided with the opportunity to lease those spaces in a nearby public lot or garage, with the exclusive right to use them during the desired hours. Such arrangements leave the parking available during evening and weekend hours for other users (e.g., patrons of dining establishments and entertainment providers), resulting in an efficient sharing of the parking supply and lower costs for all.

In addition, your downtown should work to make existing private parking lots available to the public when they are not actively serving nearby commercial uses. If your downtown has many private lots that forbid public parking, the existing

Table 10-1 Actual Parking Demand in Successful, Mixed-Use, Park-Once Downtowns

| | City Population | Mode Split[1] | | | | | | | Occupied Parking Spaces per 1,000 Sq. Ft.[3] |
		Drove Alone	Carpool (2 or More Persons)	Transit	Bicycle	Walked	Other Means	Worked at Home	
Chico, CA	59,900	61%	12%	1%	11%	13%	1%	1%	1.7
Palo Alto, CA	58,600	80%	9%	4%	3%	3%	1%	0%	1.9
Santa Monica, CA	84,100	74%	11%	11%	1%	2%	1%	0%	1.8
Kirkland, WA[2]	45,600	77%	12%	4%	0%	2%	1%	4%	1.6

[1] Source: Census Transportation Planning Package (CTPP) 2000.

[2] Commuter mode split for Kirkland, Washington, is not limited to the main-street district, but covers commuting to the entire city, due to lack of data from CTPP 2000.

[3] "Sq. Ft." refers to occupied nonresidential built area in Chico and Palo Alto and both vacant and occupied nonresidential built areas in Santa Monica and Kirkland.

parking supply is not being used as efficiently as it could be. By adding these existing spaces to the public supply, the city will be able to inexpensively add a significant amount of parking capacity to the downtown.

Overall, the benefits of fully implementing a park-once strategy for your entire downtown include:

- More welcoming of customers and visitors (fewer "Thou Shalt Not Park Here" signs scattered throughout downtown)
- Fewer, more strategically placed lots and garages, resulting in better urban design and greater redevelopment opportunities
- Construction of larger, more space-efficient (and therefore more cost-effective) lots and garages

Finally, and perhaps most importantly, by transforming motorists into pedestrians, who walk instead of drive to different downtown destinations, a park-once strategy is an immediate generator of pedestrian life, creating crowds of people who animate public life on the streets and become the patrons of street-friendly retail businesses.

Strategy 2: Create a Commercial Parking Benefit Area

Goals: Efficiently manage demand for parking while accommodating customer, employee, resident, and commuter parking needs.

Put customers first by creating vacancies and turnover of the most convenient front-door curb parking spaces to ensure availability for customers and visitors.

Generate revenues for desired improvements, such as upgraded security and enhanced streetscapes, in the blocks where the meter revenue is collected.

Recommendation: Install coin- and credit-card-accepting parking meters on any block face in commercial areas where parking occupancy routinely exceeds 85 percent. Set parking prices at rates that create a 15 percent vacancy rate on each block, and eliminate time limits. Dedicate parking revenues (a) to cover the costs of acquiring, operating, and enforcing the meters; and (b) to public improvements and services that benefit the blocks where the revenue was raised. Create a "Commercial Parking Benefit Area" to implement these recommendations.

DISCUSSION

Always-available, convenient, on-street customer parking is of primary importance for ground-level retail to succeed. To create vacancies and ensure availability in the best, most convenient, front-door parking spaces, it is crucial to have price incentives to persuade some drivers to park in the less convenient spaces (on upper garage floors or a block or two away): higher prices for the best spots, and cheaper prices for the less convenient, currently underused lots.

Motorists can be thought of as falling into two primary categories: bargain hunters and convenience seekers. Convenience seekers are more willing to pay for an available front-door spot. Many shoppers and diners are convenience seekers.

They are typically less sensitive to parking charges because they stay for relatively short periods of time, meaning that they will have to spend less than an employee or other all-day visitor. By contrast, many long-stay parkers, such as employees, find it more worthwhile to walk a block or so to save on eight hours' worth of parking fees. With proper pricing, the bargain hunters will choose currently under-utilized lots, leaving the prime spots free for those convenience seekers who are willing to spend a bit more. For merchants, it is important to make prime spots available for these people: those who are willing to pay a small fee to park are also those who are willing to spend money in stores and restaurants.

WHAT ARE THE ALTERNATIVES TO CHARGING A PRICE HIGH ENOUGH TO CREATE SOME VACANCIES?

The primary alternative that cities can use to create vacancies in prime parking spaces is to set time limits and give tickets to violators. The "time limits and tickets" approach, however, brings several disadvantages. First, enforcement of time limits is labor-intensive and difficult. Second, employees, who quickly become familiar with enforcement patterns, often become adept at the "two-hour shuffle," moving their cars regularly or swapping spaces with a coworker during the workday. Even with strictly enforced time limits, if the price incentive is not sufficient to persuade employees to seek out less convenient, bargain-priced spots, employees will probably still park in prime spaces.

For customers, strict enforcement can bring *ticket anxiety*, the fear of getting a ticket if one lingers a minute too long (for example, to have dessert after lunch). As Dan Zack, Downtown Development Manager for Redwood City, California, put it, "Even if a visitor is quick enough to avoid a ticket, they don't want to spend the evening watching the clock and moving their car around. If a customer is having a good time in a restaurant, and they are happy to pay the market price for their parking spot, do we want them to wrap up their evening early because their time limit wasn't long enough? Do we want them to skip dessert or that last cappuccino in order to avoid a ticket?"[8]

WHAT IS THE RIGHT PRICE FOR PARKING?

If prices are used to create vacancies and turnover in the prime parking spots, then what is the right price? An ideal occupancy rate is approximately 85 percent at even the busiest hour, a rate that leaves about one out of every seven spaces available, or approximately one empty space on each block face. This provides enough vacancies that visitors can easily find a spot near their destination when they first arrive. For each block and each parking lot, the right price is the price that will achieve this goal. This means that pricing should not be uniform: the most desirable blocks should charge higher prices, whereas less convenient lots and block faces should be cheaper. Prices should also vary by time of day and day of week. In Pasadena, California, for example, parking meters in Old Pasadena are in operation on Sunday through Thursday nights until 8:00 p.m., but until midnight on Fridays and Saturdays, when late-night demand is greater. Similarly, cities like Pasadena, Redwood City, and San Francisco charge higher rates on high-demand blocks and lower rates on low-demand blocks.

USE TIME-OF-DAY PARKING RATES, NOT "PROGRESSIVE PRICING"

The experience from cities that have adjusted parking rates with the aim of ensuring that parking is well used, but still readily available, shows that to achieve this goal, it is better to use rates that vary by time of day, rather than what is known as *progressive pricing*. With progressive pricing, motorists are charged higher parking rates for longer stays (e.g., $1.00 for the first hour and $2.00 for the second hour), with the goal of increasing turnover at curb parking spaces. *Turnover*, however, is not the key metric that customers care about. Customers care about *availability*. Customers want to find a space available near their destination when they arrive. As long as a space is available for the customer to use, he or she doesn't care how long other people on the block have been parked there.

To achieve the desired level of *availability*, particularly at busy hours such as lunchtime and dinnertime, rates that vary by time of day and by location have proven to be more effective than progressive prices. New York City's PARK Smart program, for example, has set parking meter prices in Greenwich Village at $3.75 per hour from noon to 4:00 P.M., and at $2.50 per hour at all other times. This rate structure responds well to observed curb parking demand, helping ensure vacancies when the lunch crowd and afternoon shoppers arrive.[9] By contrast, progressive pricing—with a low rate for the first hour or two—often does little to create vacancies during the lunch-hour rush.

Rate structures need not be terribly complicated: "good enough" should be the goal, not perfection. Along San Francisco's waterfront, for example, regular daytime prices (7:00 A.M. to 7:00 P.M.) vary from $3.00 per hour in the busiest section to $1.00 per hour in the quietest blocks. Evening rates (7:00 P.M. to 11:00 P.M.) are just $1.00 per hour in the busy blocks, and $0.50 per hour in the quiet blocks.[10] Using parking occupancy sensors at each stall, the Port monitors demand continuously, and will adjust prices in the future if its occupancy goals are not met.

THE RIGHT PRICES

Ideally, parking occupancy for each block and lot should be monitored carefully, and prices adjusted regularly to keep enough spaces available. In short, prices should ideally be set at market rate, according to demand, so that just enough spaces are always available. Professor Donald Shoup of UCLA advocates setting prices for parking according to the "Goldilocks Principle":

> The price is too high if many spaces are vacant, and too low if no spaces are vacant. Children learn that porridge shouldn't be too hot or too cold, and that beds shouldn't be too soft or too firm. Likewise, the price of curb parking shouldn't be too high or too low. When about 15 percent of curb spaces are vacant, the price is just right. What alternative price could be better?

If this principle is followed, then there need be no fear that parking pricing will drive customers away. After all, when the front-door parking spots at the curb are entirely full, underpriced parking cannot create more curb parking spaces for customers, because it cannot create more spaces. If the parking meter rate on a block is initially set too high, so that there are too many vacancies, a policy goal of achieving an 85-percent occupancy rate will require that the parking rate be lowered (including making parking free, if need be) until the parking is once again well used.

Rates need not change constantly or abruptly. When extending meter hours or changing rates, the safest way to reach the right price, without fear of over-shooting and accidentally driving away customers, is to increase or decrease rates slowly, with occupancy checks before and after each rate adjustment. For example, adjusting rates once per month initially, and considering rate adjustments once every three months thereafter, is plenty. The goal should be to adjust rates reasonably often, with the primary aim of serving customer needs for available spaces, rather than maximizing meter revenue. Again, "good enough" is fine. As long as the city adjusts rates more than cities like Los Angeles (where many meter rates have not been adjusted for 20 years) and Indianapolis (where meter rates have not been adjusted in 35 years), the city will be ahead of many municipal parking operations.

ELIMINATING TIME LIMITS

Once a policy of market-rate pricing is adopted, with the goal of achieving an 85-percent occupancy rate on each block, even at the busiest hours, then time limits can actually be eliminated. With their elimination, much of the worry and ticket anxiety for customers disappears (Figure 10-7). Redwood City, California, recently adopted such a policy, and Dan Zack, the city's downtown development manager, described the thinking behind the city's decision in this way:

> Market-rate prices are the only known way to consistently create available parking spaces in popular areas. If we institute market-rate prices, and adequate spaces are made available, then what purpose do time limits serve? None, other than to inconvenience customers. If there is a space or two available on all blocks, then who cares how long each individual car is there? The reality is that it doesn't matter.

Redwood City eliminated all time limits on its downtown streets in 2007. Previously, there was a one-hour time limit on Broadway, the main drag, and varying time limits on nearby blocks, but the time limits had failed to create a good vacancy rate. The *Wall Street Journal* reported on how the switch to pricing, rather than time limits, has affected downtown customers:

> In the past, Cheryl Angeles has had to jump up in the middle of a coloring treatment, foil in her hair and a black-plastic cape around her neck, to

Figure 10-7
All parking meters must be able to accept credit and debit cards, and they should be able to call motorists on their cell phones to ask if they want more time. *Source: Nelson\Nygaard.*

pop more quarters into the meter. Twice the self-storage company regional manager got $25 parking tickets when she didn't make it in time. Now that the time limits have been removed, she can pay once and return when the appointment is over.[11]

While customers like Cheryl Angeles can stay as long as they like (as long as they pay the going rate), the city's performance-pricing structure has succeeded nonetheless in ensuring vacancies, as employees and bargain hunters have moved to lower-price off-street parking nearby. The recommendations for pricing parking, eliminating time limits, and the creation of a commercial parking benefit district are discussed in greater detail in the following section.

BOUNDARIES OF METERED PARKING IN THE COMMERCIAL PARKING BENEFIT DISTRICT

Given a primary goal of creating vacancies on the blocks where parking is currently overused, and shifting some parking demand to underused parking lots, meters should be installed on blocks and in parking lots where occupancy routinely reaches 85 percent or more during the peak hours of demand. In addition, meters should be installed on immediately adjacent blocks, where demand is likely to shift and parking will become overcrowded if those blocks remain entirely free. Parking meter prices should be set to maintain a 15-percent vacancy rate, according to the Goldilocks principle: If occupancy rates are consistently above 85 percent, the parking rates are too low; if occupancy rates are consistently below 85 percent, the parking rates are too high.

WAYFINDING AND REAL-TIME INFORMATION SYSTEMS

As part of the process to install new technology, cities should consider installing real-time information systems for structures and larger public parking lots. It is extremely important that there be clear directions to these parking spaces, because they will provide cheaper or free parking to employees, residents, and long-term visitors. Poor information about off-street parking availability leads to motorists driving around looking for a place to park. Parking guidance systems alert drivers to off-street parking availability. The structures and lots should be equipped with add-and-subtract loop detectors that record the exact number of spaces left vacant in each facility.

The changeable message signs installed at the entries to downtown parking garages are designed to display the available number of spaces remaining (Figure 10-8), but they are not as accurate as they could be. Downtown parking management can be improved by ensuring that the signs display accurate information and by locating additional signs, possibly static ones, further from the garages so that drivers can make informed decisions about where to find parking.

ORDINANCE LANGUAGE

For samples of good ordinance-language text, search online for Downtown Redwood City Parking Ordinance (Ordinance 242 in 2005) or the Downtown Ventura Parking Study.

Strategy 3: Invest Meter Revenues in Areawide Improvements and Transportation Demand Management

Goal: Invest in the most cost-effective mix of transportation modes for access to the downtown, including both parking and transportation demand management strategies.

Recommendation: Invest a portion of meter revenues in transportation demand management strategies for downtown employees and residents, including transit, carpool, vanpool, bicycle, and pedestrian programs. Invest the remainder of net meter revenues in improvements to the area where the revenue was raised.

DISCUSSION

Net revenues from paid parking in a commercial parking benefit area (CPBA) should fund public improvements that benefit the blocks where the revenue is collected (*net revenues* means total parking revenues from the area, less revenue collection costs, such as purchase and operation of the meters, enforcement, and administration of the CPBA). If parking revenues seem to disappear into the city's general fund, where they appear to produce no direct benefit for downtown, there will be little support for installing parking meters, or for raising rates when needed to maintain decent vacancy rates. But when local merchants and property owners can clearly see that the monies collected are being spent for the benefit of their blocks, on projects that they have chosen, they become willing to support market-rate pricing.

To ensure such continuing support for a parking benefit district, and for continuing to charge fair market rates for parking, it is crucial to give local stakeholders a strong voice in deciding how parking revenues should be spent, and overseeing the operation of the district to ensure that the monies collected from its customers are spent wisely.

To accomplish this, consider establishing an advisory board; an example of this is the City of Pasadena's Old Pasadena Parking Meter Revenue Advisory Board, which advises the city on expenditures of meter revenue from the Old Pasadena parking meter zone. The advisory board should advise the city council or city managers how the community would like the meter revenue spent, although the city council/managers should retain final approval over all expenditures. Bonding against future revenue (i.e., issuing revenue bonds) can make it possible to fund larger capital projects.

Figure 10-8
All real-time information about parking availability not only helps motorists find the closest parking space, but also reminds motorists and merchants that there are always nearby empty spaces, even if some motorists whine about not being able to find a space. *Source: Nelson\Nygaard.*

Potential uses for parking benefit district revenues include:

- Additional police patrols to provide additional security
- Landscaping and streetscape improvements
- Street cleaning, power-washing of sidewalks, and graffiti removal
- Pedestrian-scaled lighting
- Transit, pedestrian, and bicycle infrastructure and amenities
- Purchase and installation costs of meters (e.g., through revenue bonds or a "build-operate-transfer" financing agreement with a vendor)
- Oversight and management of CPBA infrastructure and amenities
- Additional parking construction and/or facility replacement
- Marketing and promotion of local businesses
- Additional programs and projects as recommended by the community via an advisory board and approved by the city council/manager

USE PARKING REVENUE TO REDUCE PARKING DEMAND

A parking benefit district should also invest a portion of parking revenues (and other fees, grants, and/or transportation funds, when available) to establish a full menu of transportation programs for the benefit of all downtown residents and employers. These programs should include:

- **Universal transit passes.** A universal transit pass program can provide free transit passes for every employee and resident in a downtown. The annual passes would be purchased at a deeply discounted bulk rate by the parking benefit district from the transit operators. For many transit operators, universal transit passes provide a stable source of income while helping them meet their ridership goals.

- **Carpool and vanpool incentives.** Provide ride-sharing services, such as carpool and vanpool incentives, customized ride-matching services, a "Guaranteed Ride Home" program (offering a limited number of emergency taxi rides home per employee), and an active marketing program to advertise the services to employees and residents.

- **Bike/pedestrian facilities.** Centralized provision of bicycle facilities, such as clothes lockers, secure bike parking, and shower facilities, are a must if the city wishes to increase its rates of cyclists and pedestrians.

- **Transportation resource center.** A storefront office that provides personalized information on transit routes and schedules, carpool and vanpool programs, bicycle routes and facilities, and other transportation options. The center could also house the Transportation Improvement District's staff, and would take responsibility for administering and actively marketing all demand management programs. Parking operations and administration could be housed here as well.

For more detail, see Chapter 13, "Transportation Demand Management."

Strategy 4: Create Residential Parking Benefit Areas

Goal: Prevent spillover parking in neighborhoods adjacent to your downtown or other commercial area.

Recommendation: Implement residential parking benefit areas (RPBAs) in adjacent residential areas. RPBAs are similar to residential permit parking areas, but allow a limited number of commuters to pay to use surplus on-street parking spaces in residential areas, and return the resulting revenues to the neighborhood to fund public improvements.

DISCUSSION

To prevent spillover parking in residential neighborhoods, many cities implement residential permit parking areas by issuing parking permits to residents, usually for free or for a nominal fee. Conventional residential permit parking areas have several limitations. Most notably, cities often issue an unlimited number of permits to residents without regard to the actual number of curb parking spaces available in the area. This often leads to a situation in which on-street parking is seriously congested, and the permit functions solely as a hunting license, simply giving residents the right to hunt for a parking space with no guarantee that they will actually find one. (An example of this misuse comes from Boston, where the city's Department of Transportation has issued residents 3,933 permits for the 983 available curb spaces in Beacon Hill's residential parking permit district—a 4:1 ratio.[12])

An opposite problem occurs with conventional residential permit areas where there actually are many surplus parking spaces, especially during the day, when many residents are away. The permit area prevents any commuters from parking legally for longer than an hour or two in these spaces, even if demand is high and many motorists would be willing to pay to park in one of the surplus spaces. In both cases, conventional residential parking permit districts prevent curb parking spaces from being used efficiently, promoting overuse in the former example and underuse in the latter.

To avoid these problems, cities should implement residential parking benefit areas in residential areas adjacent to the downtown. This can prevent excessive spillover parking from commuters trying to avoid parking charges, while simultaneously raising revenue to benefit these neighborhoods.

COMMUNITY PARTICIPATION AND LOCAL CONTROL

Residential parking benefit areas should be implemented only if a majority of property owners in a proposed area support formation of the area. Once implemented, residents, property owners, and business owners in the district should continue to have a voice in recommending to the city council how new parking revenue should be spent in their neighborhood. This could occur via city staff attendance at existing neighborhood association meetings, mail-in surveys, or public workshops. Another option is to appoint advisory committees in each parking benefit district, and task them with recommending to the city council how the revenue should be spent in the subject neighborhood.

IMPLEMENTATION DETAILS

The following steps are recommended to implement each residential parking benefit area:

- Count the number of available curb parking spaces in the area where the RPBA is being considered. Counting the number of curb parking spaces available in an area where a RPBA is being considered is an essential first step for any parking manager. It is the equivalent of knowing how many seats are in a movie theater, for the manager of the movie theater. Just as the manager of a movie theater cannot know how many tickets to sell without knowing how many seats exist, parking managers cannot know how many parking permits to issue unless they know how many parking spaces exist.

- Make maps showing the results of the parking inventory.

- Count the number of residential units on each parcel within the same area.

- Compare the existing number of residential units in the area to the number of available curb parking spaces in the area. For the entire area, it is important to determine the ratio of curb parking spaces to residential units. (For example, if there are 1,000 curb parking spaces and 500 residential units, then the ratio is 2.0 curb parking spaces per unit.)

- Measure curb parking occupancy in the area during both daytime and evening hours. If the area is currently a residential parking permit area, distinguish between vehicles with and without valid parking permits.

- Decide, in close consultation with local residents, how many curb parking permits to issue to residents. Should it be unlimited, which may lead to shortages? Limited to ensure availability of curb spaces? Should existing permit holders be grandfathered in, with a wait list for newcomers? Moving from a practice of issuing unlimited permits per household to limited numbers of permits is often controversial, so we recommend being flexible in considering suggested solutions.

- Resident permits should be priced to balance multiple considerations, including: (a) the need to win acceptance for the program from existing residents (which is often best achieved by "grandfathering in" existing residents by providing them with free or nominally priced permits); (b) the need to fund the program's ongoing administrative costs; (c) the desire of local residents to raise funds for neighborhood improvements; and (d) the need for prices to balance supply and demand for the limited number of curb parking spaces. To reduce the price for residents, funding from nonresident sources, such as commercial parking benefit district revenues, fees charged for commuter parking, and fees on new development can also be used.

- Rather than entirely prohibiting nonresident parking, as is done in many conventional residential parking permit districts, the city should sell permits for any surplus parking capacity to nonresident commuters at fair market rates. However, these nonresident permits should generally be valid only during daytime hours, when residential occupancy rates are typically lower.

- One useful supporting approach is to reserve one side of every block exclusively for residents, to help ensure that some curb parking is always available for residents' use.

- Finally, the rates for nonresidents' parking permits should be set at fair market rates (i.e., at a price that maintains an 85-percent occupancy rate) as determined by periodic city surveys. All net revenues above and beyond the cost of administering the program should be dedicated to pay for public improvements in the neighborhood where the revenue was generated.

- Implement appropriate technology for charging nonresidents for parking: for RPBAs, the most efficient and least capital-intensive technology is likely to take the form of a strategy like that adopted by the Borough of Westminster in London. In Westminster's residential parking permit districts, visitors may pay by cell phone for parking (the number to call is posted on the residential parking signs), or by purchasing books of parking cards from local libraries.[13] In Pasadena, California, pay stations for purchasing visitor parking permits are located at each neighborhood fire station; visitor permits may also be purchased online and printed out at home.

BENEFITS OF RESIDENTIAL PARKING BENEFIT AREAS

Residential parking benefit areas have been described as "a compromise between free curb parking that leads to overcrowding and [conventional residential] permit districts that lead to underuse. . . . [Parking] benefit districts are better for both residents and non-residents: residents get public services paid for by non-residents, and non-residents get to park at a fair-market price rather than not at all."[14] Benefits of implementing RPBAs include:

- Excessive parking spillover into commercial adjacent neighborhoods is prevented.

- Scarce curb parking spaces are used as efficiently as possible.

- Need for construction of additional costly parking structures is reduced.

- Residents are guaranteed a parking space at the curb.

EXAMPLES OF RESIDENTIAL PARKING BENEFIT AREAS

Residential parking benefit areas have been implemented in various forms in the following jurisdictions:

- Aspen, Colorado (nonresident permits $5.00/day)

- Boulder, Colorado (resident permits $12/year; nonresident permits $312/year)

- Santa Cruz, California (resident permits $20/year; nonresident permits $240/year)

- Tucson, Arizona (resident permits $2.50/year; nonresident permits $200–$400/year, declining with increased distance from the University of Arizona campus)

- West Hollywood, California (resident permits $9/year; nonresident permits $360/year)

Strategy 5: Provide Universal Transit Passes

Goal: Increase transit ridership and provide incentives for downtown employees and residents to reduce parking demand by providing free universal transit passes to all downtown-area residents and employees.

Recommendation: Using deeply discounted group transit pass programs, provide free transit passes to all existing employees and residents. Fund this program using parking benefit area revenues and other sources as available. For all new developments, require that transit passes be provided to employees and residents.

For more detail on this strategy, see Chapter 13, "Transportation Demand Management."

Strategy 6: Unbundle Parking Costs

Goal: Increase housing affordability and housing choice, while reducing parking demand and vehicle trips from new development.

Recommendation: Adopt an ordinance to require new residential and commercial development to "unbundle" the full cost of parking from the cost of the housing or commercial space itself, by creating a separate parking charge for employee and residential spaces.

DISCUSSION

Parking costs are frequently subsumed into the sale or rental price of offices and housing, for the sake of simplicity, and because that is the traditional practice in real estate. But although the cost of parking is often hidden in this way, parking is never free. Each space in a parking structure can cost upwards of $40,000; in many cities, given land values, surface spaces can be similarly costly. Unbundling these parking costs from the cost of other goods and services is a critical step for reducing parking demand and vehicle trips, because providing anything for free or at highly subsidized rates encourages use and means that more parking spaces have to be provided to achieve the same rate of availability.

UNBUNDLING PARKING COSTS FROM HOUSING COSTS

For both rental and for-sale housing, the full cost of parking should be unbundled from the cost of the housing itself, by creating a separate parking charge. (The exception to this policy should be in any new residences with individual garages, such as townhouses, rather than common, shared parking areas.) This provides a financial reward to households that decide to dispense with one of their cars, and helps attract that niche market of householders who wish to live in a transit-oriented neighborhood where it is possible to live well with only one car, or no car, per household. Unbundling parking costs changes parking from a required purchase to an optional amenity, so that households can freely choose how many spaces they wish to lease. Among households with below-average vehicle owner-ship rates (e.g., low-income persons, singles and single parents, seniors on fixed incomes, and college students), allowing this choice can provide a substantial finan-cial benefit. Unbundling parking costs means that these households no longer have to pay for parking spaces that they may not be able to use or afford.

It is important to note that bundled residential parking can significantly increase per-unit housing costs for individual renters or buyers. Two studies of San

Francisco housing found that units with off-street parking bundled with the unit sell for 11 percent to 12 percent more than comparable units without included parking.[15] One study of San Francisco housing found that the increased affordability of units without onsite, off-street parking can increase their absorption rate and make home ownership a reality for more people.[16] In that study, units without off-street parking:

- Sold on average 41 days faster than comparable units with off-street parking

- Allowed 20 percent more San Francisco households to afford a condominium (compared to units with bundled off-street parking)

- Allowed twenty-four more San Francisco households to afford a single-family house (compared to units with bundled off-street parking)

Charging separately for parking is also the single most effective strategy to encourage households to own fewer cars, and rely more on walking, cycling, and transit. According to one study, unbundling residential parking can significantly reduce household vehicle ownership and parking demand.[17] These effects are presented in Figure10-9.

It is critical that residents and tenants be made aware that rents, sale prices, and lease fees are reduced because parking is charged for separately. Rather than paying "extra" for parking, the cost is simply separated out, allowing residents and businesses to choose how much they wish to purchase. No tenant, resident, employer, or employee should be required to lease any minimum amount of parking.

SAN FRANCISCO'S UNBUNDLING ORDINANCE FOR NEW RESIDENTIAL UNITS

San Francisco's citywide unbundling ordinance for residential developments—Ordinance 112-08—provides a good model. This language has the advantage of having been reviewed by the city attorney of a major California jurisdiction, and tested by numerous development projects.[18]

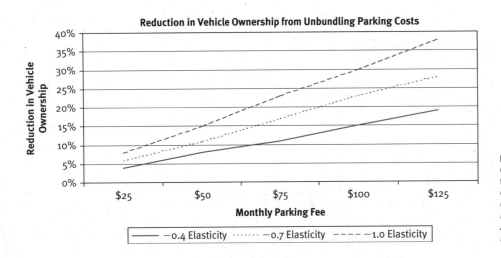

Figure 10-9
Charging separately for parking is also the single most effective strategy to encourage households to own fewer cars. *Source: Todd Litman, Parking Requirement Impacts on Housing Affordability, Victoria Transport Policy Institute, 2004.*

UNBUNDLING PARKING COSTS FROM COMMERCIAL LEASES

New commercial developments should be required to unbundle parking costs by identifying parking costs as a separate line item in the lease, and should be required to allow employers to lease as few parking spaces as they wish. Bellevue, Washington, for example, requires downtown office buildings of more than 50,000 square feet to identify the cost of parking as a separate line item in all leases, with the minimum monthly rate per space not less than the price of a two-zone bus pass.[19] This requirement for unbundling parking costs does not increase the over- all cost of occupying office space in a building, because the payment for the office space itself declines as a result. In other words, unbundling separates the rent for offices and parking, but does not increase their sum. This innovative policy has several advantages. It makes it easy for employers to cash out parking for employ- ees (that is, to offer employees the value of their parking space as a cash subsidy if they do not drive to work), because employers can save money by leasing fewer spaces when fewer employees drive. It also makes it easier to institute shared park- ing arrangements, because building owners can more easily lease surplus parking spaces to other users.

Strategy 7: Require Parking for Carsharing Vehicles

Goal: Support and enhance carsharing, thereby allowing downtown residents and
    employees to have access to shared cars when needed.

Recommendation: Adopt an ordinance requiring developers of large residential
    projects to offer carsharing services the right of first refusal to a limited number
    of parking spaces. Require that those spaces be provided to the carsharing
    services free of charge.

For more detail, see Chapter 11, "Carsharing."

Strategy 8: Require Parking Cash-Out

Goal: Subsidize all employee commute modes equally and create incentives for
    commuters to carpool, take transit, and bike or walk to work.

Recommendation: Require all new and existing downtown employers that provide
    subsidized employee parking to offer their employees the option to cash out their
    parking subsidy.

For more detail, see Chapter 13, "Transportation Demand Management."

Strategy 9: Remove Minimum Parking Requirements

Goals: Remove barriers to new development and renovation and reoccupancy of
    existing buildings. Create a healthy market for parking, where parking spaces
    are bought, sold, rented, and leased like any normal commodity. Increase
    housing affordability and housing choice, while reducing parking demand and
    vehicle trips from new development.

Recommendation: Remove all minimum parking requirements, at least within your
    downtown and mixed-use areas.

DISCUSSION

Minimum parking requirements have emerged as one of the biggest obstacles to many cities' efforts to encourage new residential and commercial development in their proposed transit-oriented districts. Moreover, minimum parking requirements work at cross-purposes to many cities' adopted goals for their downtowns. As UCLA professor Don Shoup describes it, "Parking requirements cause great harm: they subsidize cars, distort transportation choices, warp urban form, increase housing costs, burden low-income households, debase urban design, damage the economy, and degrade the environment. . . . [O]ff-street parking requirements also cost a lot of money, although this cost is hidden in higher prices for everything except parking itself."[20]

The effects of minimum parking requirements in decreasing housing affordability and reducing land values are particularly noteworthy. For example, a study of Oakland's 1961 decision to require one parking space per apartment (where none had been required before) found that construction costs increased 18 percent per unit, units per acre decreased by 30 percent, and land values fell by 33 percent.[20] This occurred partly because the space needs of residential parking spaces restricted how many housing units could be built within allowable zoning and building envelope. Developers also responded to the requirement by building fewer, larger, and more expensive units, to help defray the cost of this expensive new amenity required for each unit.

COMMUNITIES THAT HAVE ELIMINATED PARKING REQUIREMENTS

Examples of communities that have partially (in particular neighborhoods and districts) or entirely eliminated minimum parking requirements include:

- Coral Gables, FL
- Eugene, OR
- Fort Myers, FL
- Fort Pierce, FL
- Great Britain (entire nation)
- Los Angeles, CA
- Milwaukee, WI
- Olympia, WA
- Portland, OR
- San Francisco, CA
- Stuart, FL
- Seattle, WA
- Spokane, WA

The one useful purpose that minimum parking requirements do currently serve is to prevent *spillover* parking, the phenomenon of commuters filling up all of the parking spaces on a destination's streets, and then spilling over into adjacent areas. However, if the recommendations of this chapter are used, market-rate prices for on-street parking in the commercial areas will ensure that ample vacancies exist on the street. In the adjacent residential neighborhoods, the mechanism of residential parking benefit areas, together with improved enforcement made possible by license plate recognition systems, will ensure that unwanted spillover parking is prevented there as well. Once these two key policies have been implemented, imposing minimum parking requirements becomes superfluous.

Once on-street parking is properly managed, so that spillover problems are solved, it will become possible for a city to join the many communities and places (see preceding list) that have removed minimum parking requirements. Doing so will provide numerous rewards and reap numerous benefits, allowing the city to achieve its goals of a more walkable and transit-oriented district, a healthier economy and environment, lower housing costs, and better urban design.

Strategy 10: Fund Parking Facilities with User Fees and Revenue Bonds

Goal: Fund the development of new parking capacity in a way that furthers your city's goals of advancing economic efficiency, environmental sustainability, and social equity.

Recommendation: Finance off-street public parking facilities by issuing revenue bonds for the construction of lots and garages, and repaying the bonds with parking fees from those who park in the facilities.

DISCUSSION

The strategy of issuing revenue bonds and repaying them with parking fees may not be innovative or groundbreaking. However, this method does have many advantages beyond simply being a tried-and-tested approach to municipal parking finance. The advantages include:

Economic efficiency: Paying for parking facilities using direct parking fees helps balance parking supply and demand. When the true cost of parking is made visible through direct fees, employers and residents are able to save on parking by using less of it. Employers, for example, can institute transportation demand management programs to help employees leave their cars at home, and reap the savings by leasing fewer employee parking spaces. Similarly, residents, as discussed earlier, are able to save substantial amounts of money by owning fewer vehicles and leasing or purchasing fewer parking spaces. The result is that fewer parking spaces have to be built, and less motor-vehicle traffic is generated in the downtown. As a result, parking construction costs are substantially lower than if parking is funded in indirect ways, such as through taxes and other fees on downtown (or citywide) property owners, businesses, and residents.

Environmental sustainability: Because paying for parking through direct user fees reduces both motor-vehicle trips and parking construction, it substantially reduces air and water pollution and greenhouse gas emissions, compared to funding methods that hide the cost of parking in the cost of other goods and services. The principle is similar to the principle of charging for electricity through direct fees: When the cost is revealed, users have an incentive to conserve.

Social equity: Paying for parking facilities using fees from those who park in the facilities follows a principle that is widely accepted as fair: that the beneficiaries of a project should pay for the project. Moreover, because higher-income households, on average, own more vehicles, drive more often, and park more often than households of lesser means, the "user pays" approach means that higher-income households shoulder a greater share of the burden for parking facilities than if the cost of parking is hidden in the cost of other goods and services.

PARKING LEASES AND PARKING CONDOMINIUMS

The most common way of purchasing parking in public garages is through hourly fees or long-term leases. However, selling parking condominiums is another valid approach that is widely used in major cities.

Paying for parking through direct user fees does not preclude the development of public parking facilities that include dedicated spaces for residents of nearby buildings. In many urban areas, parking facilities have been developed as *parking condominiums*. The parking facility itself, or a portion of the facility, is held in a condominium form of ownership. Nearby residents and employees are able to purchase spaces. In the case of projects that have been converted entirely to condominiums, a condominium association is formed, and normally hires a parking operator to manage and maintain the garage.

In the case of a public garage, it is possible to sell a portion of the spaces in the garage, with the city retaining ownership of the remainder. In this way, the city could, for example, sell parking condominiums to a developer of a new downtown residential building (potentially in advance of actual construction), providing the city with substantial revenue up front for parking development and providing the developer with assurance that it will actually be able to obtain off-site parking for the new building. Once the new building is built and new residents purchase their units, the developer would normally resell the condominium parking spaces to the new residents.

Chapter 11
Carsharing

by Mark Chase

Introduction

We're taught to share at an early age. In kindergarten we may have learned to wait patiently while our friend was finishing with the color crayon that we wanted. Carsharing organizations (CSOs) take ordinary cars and add access technology and automated billing so that members can use a car when and where they need it. The CSO maintains the vehicles, pays for gas and insurance, and otherwise takes on the least palatable parts of car ownership.

Advances in technology and new business models are bringing carsharing to an ever-widening array of places, and its popularity is growing rapidly (Figure 11-1). For carsharing to succeed, members must be able to undertake the majority of their mobility needs without a car. Carsharing also provides members with the right vehicle for the right need: a truck to move furniture, a BMW for an important business meeting, or an electric vehicle for around-town driving.

Contemporary carsharing uses technology to facilitate reservations, ensure exclusive reservation-only access, and penalize members for bad behavior that may compromise the system for other members. Reservations are generally accomplished via the Internet, with a smart phone, or via text or interactive voice response systems. By automating all aspects of car reservation, access, and billing, CSOs are able to minimize their costs of doing business and keep member rates affordable.

Two factors of carsharing contribute to a sustainable transportation system. First, all the costs of driving are bundled into an hourly or daily usage rate. This encourages members to use the shared cars sparingly and rely on walking, transit, or bicycling for most of their trips. On average, a carshare member drives 44 percent less than a typical car owner.[1]

Second, more than a third of carshare members would otherwise own a car if carsharing were not available. Typically, shared cars serve between twenty and fifty members and result in between five and twenty cars being taken off the road.[2]

The combination of reduced parking needs and the reduced vehicle miles traveled (VMTs) of those who rely on carsharing has profound implications for cities and sustainable transportation planning (Figure 11-2). This chapter describes the various types of carsharing; the impacts of carsharing on parking, mode-share, and driving; and the policies that can foster successful carsharing programs.

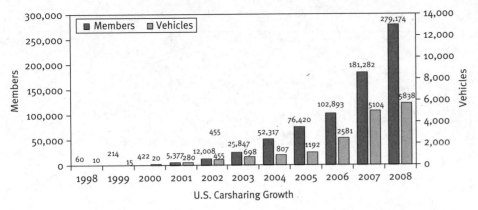

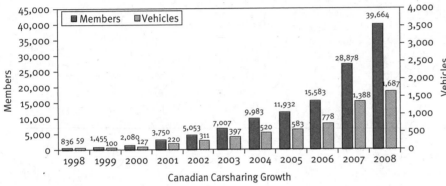

Types of Carsharing

Since the inception of modern carsharing in Europe in the early 1990s, the majority of successful carsharing operations have followed what may be termed a *traditional* carsharing model:

- Cars are leased or owned by the carsharing organization.
- Vehicles are spread across a geographic area rather than located at a central facility.
- Reservations are made using the Internet or by telephone.
- Once reserved, access to the car is restricted to the reserving member.
- Shared cars must be returned to the location from which they were taken.

Technology and business-model changes are bringing to market a new array of carsharing programs, such as peer-to-peer (P2P) carsharing. Given that most private vehicles sit idle for 75 percent of the time, P2P

▼ Figure 11-2
Carsharing's niche among travel options. *Source: Eric Britton.*

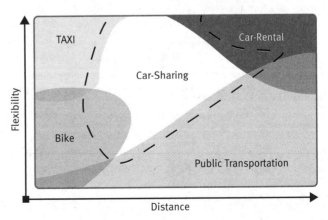

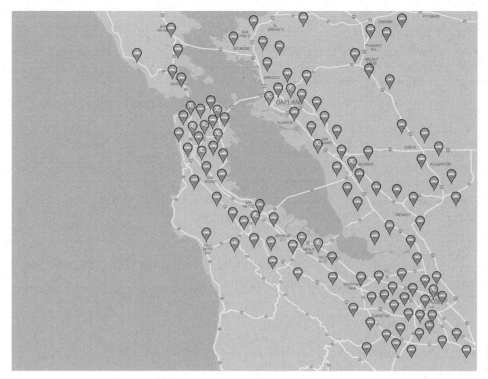

promises better utilization of an existing resource as well as an opportunity for vehicle owners to recoup some of the high costs of car ownership.

The general business model varies significantly from traditional carsharing. The primary beneficiary of P2P is the car owner, who stands to get significant rental revenue from his or her vehicle. By the same token, car owners are responsible for keeping the shared car in good repair. Peer-to-peer CSOs are more fully technology providers. This significantly reduces cost barriers that traditional carsharing organizations have faced: vehicle lease, parking, and maintenance costs.

By lowering the costs of deploying shared cars, it is likely that P2P carsharing will spread beyond the prime locations where carsharing now exists to areas where it was not previously feasible. Conceptually, a sole car owner could share her car with neighbors, allowing for carsharing to exist in smaller communities or less dense areas that might not otherwise support a traditional carsharing service. Figure 11-3 is a conceptual map showing how P2P provider Getaround supports and augments Zipcar's fleet in the San Francisco Bay Area.

Impacts

The American Automobile Association (AAA) estimates that the full cost of owning and operating a small sedan purchased in 2010 is $5,636 per year.[3] More than three-quarters of this amount ($4,381) are fixed costs that accrue to the car owners whether or not they drive their cars. For this reason, most vehicle owners perceive that the cost of driving is little more than the price of gas. In contrast to this, carsharing takes all of the costs of car ownership (including parking fees, which are not included in the AAA estimate) and bundles them into an hourly or daily rate charged to a carshare member. This pay-as-you-drive model has significant positive effects for the community.

Less Driving

Typical carshare rates vary from about $4 per hour to $12 per hour, based on the type of car used and whether per-mile fees apply. This pay-as-you-go fee structure results in members driving about 44 percent less than if they owned their own cars.[4] When members do drive, they are more likely to include multiple destinations in a trip (*trip chaining*), further improving the efficiency of their transportation dollars spent.[5]

As members drive less, they rely more on local resources to meet their needs. A local retail establishment, which may at first have appeared expensive when compared with a competitor reachable by driving, now seems like a bargain when the full transportation costs are included in the cost of the trip.

Less Parking

Carsharing programs can be seen as area-wide vacuum cleaners of cars. Underutilized private cars are sold and shared cars more efficiently take their place. Taking an average of eleven surveys conducted since 1999, carsharing members report that they sold (23 percent) or avoided the purchase (49 percent) of a car when they joined a carsharing organization.[6] Taking these averages as a baseline and a conservative member-to-vehicle ratio of 40 to 1, each shared car results in the removal of somewhere between nine and twenty private vehicles from the road.

Where Carsharing Is Most Successful

Carsharing is one element of a healthy transportation ecosystem. As noted throughout this book, healthy transportation systems incorporate land-use and urban design elements that support multiple modes of transportation. These same elements are critical to the success of carsharing. When considering where or whether to implement carsharing, you must consider several ecosystem elements in concert with each other.

Density and Mixed Uses

The importance of density and mixed uses cannot be overemphasized in relation to carsharing. The density needs of carsharing closely mirror those of transit. For transit, five units per acre is the desirable minimum for hourly service. Just as hourly transit service may be considered substandard by many, similarly, six units per acre would be a bare minimum for a carsharing location. A better situation is 10 units per acre (and up), which will adequately support carsharing as long as other supportive measures (discussed later in this chapter) are present. A sampling of some communities with healthy carshare programs and their respective densities are listed in Table 11-1.

Although density helps to ensure that carsharing (and transit) can succeed, mixed uses also play a crucial role in the viability of carsharing. A financially healthy carsharing system will be used by residents during nonworking hours and by businesses during the day Monday through Friday. The synergies of business and residential use are shown in Table 11-2.

The total number of potential reservable hours for residents is only slightly larger than those for business (53 vs. 45 reservable hours per week). The shared use of cars between businesses and residents models the same demand profile of shared parking and creates the same positive synergies.

Parking Cost and Availability

The cost and/or availability of parking may be the single most important determinant of the viability of a carsharing program. Parking costs should not just be measured in monetary terms; instead, they should also include the time and hassle of finding a parking space (where parking rates are artificially low). Given that many municipalities undercharge for on-street parking, private off-street parking rates can be an excellent metric for the viability of a carsharing program (see Table 11-3).

Table 11-1: Residential Density in Places Where Carshare Works Well

City	Households/Acre
Cambridge, MA	10
Yale Campus/New Haven, CT	12
Boston/Back Bay neighborhood	14
Hoboken, NJ	18
Center City, Philadelphia	39
Manhattan, New York City	43

Source: Mark Chase.

Table 11-2: Potential Reservation Hours by Residents and Businesses

Day/Time	Monday	Tuesday	Wednesday	Thursday	Friday	Saturday	Sunday
8 AM to 5 PM	9	9	9	9	9	9	9
5 PM to 10 PM	5	5	5	5	5	5	5
10 PM to 8 AM	10	10	10	10	10	10	10

Legend	Business	Resident	Low Use

Source: Mark Chase.

Table 11-3: Carshare Locations Graded Based on the Cost of Parking

Grade	Private Market Rate in Dollars/Month
A	More than $150
B	$100
C	$75
D	$50
F	Less than $50

Source: Mark Chase.

   High parking costs may encourage members to join, but also create a challenge for carsharing organizations. Parking costs increase the cost of running a CSO, which must be passed on to the members as a higher usage fee. To ameliorate this situation, municipalities and developers often offer subsidized and highly visible parking to CSOs to encourage carsharing. This type of assistance is addressed in more detail later in this chapter.

Transportation Modes That Support Carsharing

For carsharing to be cost-effective, members must be able to get to work without a car. The cost of a shared car sitting idle for the majority of a day makes it prohibitively expensive for commuting. Therefore, one metric to determine whether carsharing will succeed in a particular area is the percentage of residents who do not drive alone to work. Utilizing the American Community Survey, planners can use journey-to-work data to help determine optimal car placements. In general, ideal carsharing locations have in excess of 40 percent of trips to work in nonauto modes. Figures 11-4 and 11-5 demonstrate how car placement by Vancouver's Co-operative Auto Network mirrors patterns shown in the journey-to-work data available from the Canadian census.

Locating Potential Shared Car Locations

Integrating all of the measures discussed in this section can help maximize the opportunities for success of a shared car program. Table 11-4 summarizes key carsharing metrics that must be analyzed to determine the viability of carsharing in an area.

Table 11-4: Metrics for Success

Grade	Density of Households/Acre	Market Rate Parking per Month	Census Journey to Work (% non SOV)
A	14 or greater	$150 or more	0.4 or more
B	11	$100	0.35
C	8	$75	0.3
D	6	$50	0.25
F	Less than 6	Less than $50	Less than 0.25

Source: Mark Chase.

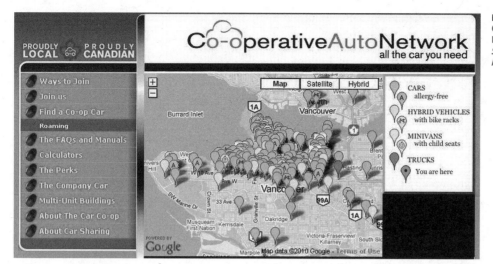

Figures 11-4 and 11-5
Cooperative Auto Network Vancouver
locations; Vancouver census data.
*Source: Map of carshare vehicles in
Metro Vancouver, Modo The Car Co-op.*

The more grade A and B metrics one has in each of the categories, the more likely it is that carsharing will succeed in the measured community.

Public Policies That Support Carsharing

Given all the economic, environmental, and community benefits of carsharing, many municipalities are developing policies and programs to support CSOs. Support can range from low-cost promotional efforts to important financial contributions to help kick-start a program. Furthermore, zoning laws frequently significantly affect carsharing. Tools, policies, and programs to support carsharing include providing parking, enacting supportive zoning codes, and taking advantage of local opportunities that can help to jump-start a program.

Parking (On- and Off-Street)

One of the more progressive approaches to carshare parking has been taken by the city of Hoboken, New Jersey, with its Corner Car program.[7] The city developed an agreement with Connect by Hertz to place forty-two cars at twenty-one corners around the city. These locations have excellent visibility and allow access by both residents and businesses. More than 90 percent of Hoboken residents now live within a 5-minute walk of a shared car. When fully subscribed, the city expects each shared car to take fifteen privately owned cars off the road.

Transit agencies can also provide parking to CSOs to help overcome the last-mile challenge: Transit riders arrive at a stop needing to get from the station to a remote destination. San Francisco's Bay Area Rapid Transit (BART) allows up to three parking spaces per carsharing operator at any BART station.[8] The CSO must pay the full permit rate for the parking space, which varies by station ($63 to $115 per month). This arrangement is a win-win for both CSOs and the transit system.

Other examples of municipal parking policy[9] include:

- Seattle, Washington; Portland, Oregon; and Arlington, Virginia, have parking stalls that are designated for carsharing vehicles as a class, similar to taxi zones.

- The Austin, Texas, city council passed Resolution 20060928-069, which establishes free parking spaces and exempts carsharing cars from parking meter charges. This facilitates the city's innovative Car2Go program that allows for one-way carsharing.

- The City of Cambridge deeply discounted parking for the first 3 years for fledgling Zipcar in 2000, after which the CSO paid full price for parking.

- Off-street municipal parking spaces have been allocated in numerous locales, including Philadelphia; Washington, D.C.; and San Francisco.

Zoning

In most communities, carsharing is neither permitted nor prohibited by zoning. Zoning regulations often do exist for car-rental operations, and communities must early on establish a definition for carsharing that differentiates it from traditional car rental.

The City of Seattle defines *carsharing* as a "system in which a fleet of cars (or other vehicles) is made available for use by members of the carshare group in a wide variety of ways. Carsharing provides an alternative to car ownership under which:

Persons or entities that become members are permitted to use vehicles from a fleet on an hourly basis;

Vehicles are available to members in parking spaces at dispersed locations or facilities; and

No separate written agreement is required each time a member reserves and uses a vehicle."[10]

Permit Carsharing by Right

Another key—and very basic—provision to support carsharing is to allow it by right in the municipal zoning code. A good example of zoning language for this was recently enacted by the National Capital Planning Commission in Washington, D.C. A simple text amendment was made that defined a *carsharing vehicle* and a *carsharing space* and allowed these in residential, mixed-use, and special-purpose districts:

The Definitions section of the code is amended by adding the following:
Car-sharing vehicle—any vehicle available to multiple users who are required to join a membership organization in order to reserve and use such a vehicle for which they are charged based on actual use as determined by time and/or mileage.
Car-sharing space—a parking space that is designated for the parking of a car-sharing vehicle.
Uses as a Matter of Right, is amended by adding the following new paragraph:
(v) Car-sharing spaces; provided that no more than two (2) spaces may be located on a single lot and the car-sharing space may not be a required parking space for the principal use.[11]

Development Code

The zoning code is an excellent place for measures to encourage or require carsharing programs to be integrated into new developments. Many developers understand that carsharing is a tenant amenity, carrying the same status as exercise facilities, on-site retail, and concierge services. Even so, spelling out requirements in the zoning code makes carsharing a public benefit that should be provided for in the development review process.

Zoning ordinances vary widely, from requiring shared-car parking in large developments to offering incentives and parking relief for on-site carsharing. Some national carsharing standards are detailed in the next subsection.

Shared-Car Parking Requirements

The City of San Francisco requires new residential developments of more than 49 units to provide one shared-car parking space, up to 200 units.[12] For 201 units or more, two carsharing spaces must be provided, with an additional shared space for every 200 units over 200 units. Furthermore, shared cars must be publicly accessible (not for exclusive use of tenants).

Nonresidential developments must provide one shared-car space for the first twenty-five regular parking spaces built and one additional shared-car space for each fifty regular parking spaces over fifty.

Relief by Right

Many cities (including Seattle, Austin, and Vancouver, BC) with minimum parking standards offer relief from parking requirements when an on-site carsharing program is included in the development. An agreement between the developer and the CSO is required to ensure that the developer is realistic in assessing the demand for carsharing in a project.

Public Access

In some cases, developers will seek to restrict access to shared vehicles for tenants only. However, carsharing systems have the broadest impact at a neighborhood level. Two shared cars that might serve 20 tenants in a development might serve 100 people in a neighborhood. Furthermore, tenant-only vehicles often require revenue guarantees to the CSO, which might not be needed if the cars are made accessible to an entire neighborhood. For these reasons, policymakers should require public access to shared cars (through unrestricted CSO membership).

State-Level Enabling Legislation

States also have an important role to play in enabling carsharing innovation. In 2006, California State Assembly Bill 2154 amended Section 22507.1 of the California Vehicle Code to allow a "city or county, by ordinance or resolution, to designate certain streets or portions of streets for the exclusive parking privilege of motor vehicles participating in a carshare vehicle program or ridesharing program in an exclusive designated parking area."[13] A city or local ordinance would then establish the criteria for a public or private company or organization to participate in the program.

California Bill AB 1871 was passed in 2010 to facilitate peer-to-peer carsharing.[14] The bill cleared up many of the ambiguities in state law that would potentially prohibit P2P sharing. The most important element is that owners will be able to share their cars without invalidating their auto insurance. Among the provisions are the following:

- Creates a new insurable class called "personal vehicle sharing."

- Exempts personal shared vehicles from laws pertaining to taxis and livery vehicles if revenues for the shared vehicles do not exceed costs (depreciation, interest, lease payments, auto loan payments, insurance, maintenance, parking, and fuel).

- Requires personal shared vehicle programs to provide insurance for the cars when used by members.

- Authorizes the insurer of the vehicle to exclude any and all coverage afforded under the vehicle owner's automobile insurance policy while the vehicle is being used by a person other than the owner as part of a personal vehicle sharing program.

Municipal Fleets

Many cities and towns have fleets of cars that employees use to conduct municipal business. Converting fleet cars to shared cars offers the opportunity for cities and towns to reduce their fleet expenses while giving residents access to the cars during nonbusiness hours. The ability of fleet cars to be used by both municipal staff and residents vastly increases the utilization and viability of the carsharing operation (Figure 11-6).

Cost savings accrue to municipalities because of the increased efficiency enabled by carsharing organizations, including:

- A reduction in fleet vehicles owned and maintained by the municipality. As with individual carshare members, a large fixed cost is replaced with small pay-as-you-go costs.

- Automated billing to relevant departments creates accountability at the departmental level. This results in more efficient vehicle use.

- The ability to have more reservations per day per vehicle because of the elimination of hand-to-hand key exchanges between an administrator and a member.

Figure 11-6
City CarShare is a nonprofit carshare provider in the San Francisco Bay Area, competing directly with the for-profit Zipcar. *Source: citycarshare.org.*

The City of Philadelphia, partnering with Philly-Carshare, was able to eliminate 310 city fleet vehicles. Cost savings attributed to the program are estimated to amount to more than $9 million over 5 years.[15] About half the cost savings were realized through reduced maintenance and fuel costs; additional savings came from avoided vehicle purchases. After the program started, departmental driving was also reduced, due to better cost allocations to the city departments using the cars.

Jump-Starting a Program

Carsharing programs clearly benefit the communities in which they are located. Some communities do not yet have the needed transportation infrastructure to support car-free living, even though they may be moving in the right direction. Even in the absence of ideal conditions, a community can help to start a carsharing program in several ways.

Revenue Guarantees

Carsharing operators, like any business, need to have more revenues than expenses to survive. Shared-car utilization is monitored to determine if membership and usage revenues support the associated expenses. Many CSOs have programs whereby a municipality, developer, university, or other entity can guarantee revenues in return for placing shared cars where they would otherwise not be viable.

The city of Davis, California, entered an agreement with a carsharing operator to place four vehicles in the city by guaranteeing a revenue stream if the service was underutilized. The CSO already had a successful program on the UC Davis campus, but the city wanted to offer the service in residential neighborhoods. In a worst-case scenario, the city would pay $76,800 per year if the vehicles were completely unused. The city is confident that any subsidy it ends up paying will be manageable.[16]

Federal, State, and Private Funding

Municipalities can also leverage federal monies to start carsharing programs. The City of Pittsburgh won a $200,000 Congestion Mitigation and Air Quality grant to set up a carsharing program in 2005. The $50,000 match was provided by Pittsburgh Downtown Partnership. The project met its goals and the city now has full self-sustaining carsharing service.[17]

Developers are also good candidates to fund a carsharing program. They can accrue cost savings from carsharing through zoning relief in the development permitting process, as a tenant amenity when the project is built, and as a parking management tool when a development finds it is short on parking. For example, the developer of the 144-unit Buckman Heights project in Portland, Oregon, agreed to pay the full costs of two carsharing vehicles to be available to tenants.[18] In return, the developer was allowed to avoid the requirement to build fourteen parking spaces.

Chapter 12
Stations and Station Areas

by David Fields, AICP

Introduction

In the vocabulary of a city, transportation is the verbs: *walk, ride, access, travel*. Transit station areas, though part of our transportation system, are different. They are the nouns: places and things, anchoring transportation services with locations. Planning for station areas is therefore different from planning for transportation systems, and it requires a different mindset about both access and activity.

The most successful stations evoke our grandest memories of travel experiences: Grand Central Terminal in New York City; the Union Stations of Washington, D.C. (Figure 12-1), Los Angeles, and Chicago; and 30th Street Station in Philadelphia. These are all more than tracks

Figure 12-1
Architecture, lighting, and retail transformed Washington, D.C.'s Union Station into an active space. *Source: Nelson\Nygaard.*

and platforms with waiting rooms—they are physical and mental icons. They are
buildings and surrounding areas that offer an opportunity for local development, a
landmark for visitors, and an anchor for the most elusive part of planning: creating
a place. Even without heavy rail and a memorable building, Mockingbird Plaza in
Dallas and Director Park in Portland (Figure 12-2) generate excitement and encourage travel, not simply to arrive, but to experience the station.

Conversely, poorly planned stations have become eyesores, places to travel
through quickly, if at all. They are difficult to walk to and uncomfortable to wait
inside. They provide access, but they discourage any other use, and minimize the
amount of time people will wait.

In between, there are stations that provide transportation functionality, but
are not supportive of the surrounding community. They make travel simple, but
their economic development potential is not realized. They are stations, but do not
effectively become station *areas* (Figure 12-3).

Station areas, like all elements of our built environment, can be planned to
invite people in and surpass or extend their primary purpose, or they can simply be

built and allow chance to decide their value. This chapter describes the key considerations for shaping a transit station into a community asset, offers a process to help you decide what you want your station to be, and provides case studies to illustrate how these opportunities have been applied.

Multimodal Access

Tracks are where trains run. Roads are for cars. Sidewalks are for people. Bike lanes are for bikes. A station has all of these, and deciding what mode goes where, how they connect, and what mode is the priority are the first steps in planning a station.

Pedestrians

Every trip via any mode starts and ends as a pedestrian trip, and each successive connection between modes adds additional pedestrian trips. Because one of the roles of transit stations is to offer people an opportunity not to drive, the pedestrian's accessibility and safety are even more important in a station area than throughout most of the rest of the town. To ensure that people who choose to ride transit can first safely and comfortably cross the street, the following six fundamental pedestrian conditions should be prioritized in station area planning:[1]

- **Safety**—pedestrians should be well protected from road hazards such as vehicles.
- **Security**—an environment where pedestrians are not susceptible to robberies or other crimes.
- **Directness**—a pedestrian path that minimizes the distance to be traveled.
- **Ease of entry**—the walk to/through the station does not involve onerous exertions, such as walking up steep inclines.
- **Comfort**—the capacity and quality of the pathway, as well as provisions for protection from inclement weather, such as wind, precipitation, and hot sun.
- **Aesthetics**—the walking environment is pleasing to the eye and inspires a person to use public transport.

These qualities are not necessarily always mutually compatible. For example, the most direct path may involve conflicts with vehicles, or the safest route may require climbing a difficult set of stairs. The challenge is to find a balance that optimizes the total package of characteristics.

SAFETY

Encouraging people to choose not to drive requires providing a safe space for pedestrians to walk, where they are protected from road hazards such as vehicles. Part of the solution is to provide a sufficient supply of space, in the form of adequate direct and wide walkways, but these must be coupled with measures to protect more vulnerable pedestrians from the potentially fatal operation of motorized vehicles. *Traffic calming* consists of a set of tools to reduce the speeds or volumes of motorized traffic and help to significantly increase the safety of adjacent pedestrian routes. In station areas, auto speeds should be kept low, both to increase pedestrian safety and to allow drivers to look around the station area. Slower speeds also convey a message to all that the station area is intended to be visited on foot.

SECURITY

A secure environment requires addressing both actual and perceived conditions. Any personal fears of walking to a transit station will be enough to nullify the whole system's use. Coordination with local police and community organizations may be the only way to accurately determine the actual security. If a location or route is actually unsafe, as verified by incident statistics, alternatives may be required. On the other hand, implementing security elements, ranging from lighting to providing security personnel, may be the only way to overcome perceptions of crime.

While security techniques are a subject unto themselves, there is much to be said for "eyes on the street" and "safety in numbers." The more people there are in an area, the safer it will be due to the number of potential witnesses to any crime. Witnesses can be other people walking, police officers on the corner, or simply shopkeepers or homeowners looking out from their windows and doors. By improving the physical and safety conditions on a route, more people will walk, which will make them more secure.

DIRECTNESS

While the shortest distance between two points is a straight line, the most important element of station access is time. Pedestrians will not want to significantly increase their travel time, especially when the train or bus is coming. Instead they will find different (possibly unsafe) routes or not use the facility at all.

When pedestrians are delayed 30 seconds or more of travel time, compliance is significantly reduced. For example, a pedestrian overpass that adds more than 30 seconds compared to crossing at street level will generally not be utilized.

EASE OF ENTRY

Accessibility is the ability to reach a station from an external origin and to travel from the station to the final destination. The dominant accessibility concerns include overcoming physical barriers (specifically for travelers with disabilities), avoiding excessive demand that may impede timely access, providing a safe route, and minimizing conflicts and detours (Figure 12-4).

The *Paved Accessible Route* (PAR) is the pedestrian accessway prescribed to conform to Americans with Disabilities Act standards. The PAR is not just a sidewalk or walkway but, rather, an entire system providing accessibility to all destinations.

Provision for a satisfactory PAR means that everyone can use the station area. The PAR should be a minimum of 5 feet wide (though greater width is recommended to provide enough clearance for two wheelchairs to pass each other). The surface of the PAR should be stable and firm and should consist of slip-resistant material.

Figure 12-4
Clear sidewalks make it easy to board transit. *Source: Eric Fredericks, used under CC license* (http://creativecommons.org/licenses/by-sa/2.0)

COMFORT

A safe environment for pedestrians is an important factor, but without viable access the facility may never be used. Accessibility is primarily based on the other demands for space compared to the amount of space available (volume and delay), as well as context and security.

Chapter 6, "Pedestrians," offers an array of ways to measure pedestrian quality, but does not focus on crowding. At station areas, however, crowding can be a problem. Walkway Level of Service (WLOS) is a scaled measurement that quantifies the flow of pedestrians in a given walkway width. It is most applicable to sidewalks, corridors, and bridges with high pedestrian volumes where the essential concern is the provision of sufficient space. Calculating WLOS requires two inputs: effective width and number of pedestrians per hour. A pedestrian facility has a high WLOS if few pedestrians are present.

Table 12-1 shows the range of area needed per person under average and platoon conditions. *Platoons* are created when a group of pedestrians is released en masse (such as when a bus or subway opens its doors). A platoon of walkers requires more space than if the same number of people were spaced evenly throughout a sidewalk. When two platoons meet each other, as when travelers are connecting between two trains, the spatial requirements are even greater.

AESTHETICS

Every station area has one major asset to anchor a visually pleasing design: the station building itself. Stations come in many shapes, sizes, and functions, but the

Table 12-1: Walkway Level of Service, Average and Platoon

	Average (Square Meters per Person)	Platoon (Square Meters per Person)
A	>5.6	>49.2
B	3.7–5.6	8.4–49.2
C	2.2–3.7	3.7–8.4
D	1.4–2.2	2.1–3.7
E	0.7–1.4	1.0–2.1
F	≤0.7	≤1.0

Source: Highway Capacity Manual 2000 (Transportation Research Board).

constant in all of them is a physical space that travelers can use as their visual reference. Regardless of the architectural style and design features incorporated into the building, the following considerations should enter into the design.

- *Articulation* refers to the concept of using street frontage design elements to make an interesting streetscape and break up building mass. Well-articulated station buildings should embody transparency, defined entries, and use of patterns and various materials. *Transparency* means making the inside of the building visible to pedestrians, and making the street visible to those on the inside. The use of visual cues, such as awnings or canopies, helps guide pedestrians to station entrances. Entries can also be defined through wayfinding and clearly defined ground-floor uses.

- Reduce expanses of solid walls on buildings, as they create a closed-off feeling to pedestrians. For those inside the buildings, blank walls also reduce light and air circulation. Connecting the inside and outside of the station with active uses, such as restaurants, creates spaces that improve the whole station.

- Outside of the station building, provide landscaping and walkways to break up the perceived size of large parking lots. Large parking lots around buildings create a sense of low density and long distances between destinations. Also, in summer months, parking lots become hot and unpleasant to walk through; landscaping helps to minimize this problem.

- Plant street trees at a minimum of 30 feet on center along long pedestrian paths. Trees have many benefits, including improved air quality, shade, and aesthetics. Trees also have a traffic-calming effect by focusing the driver's line of sight.

Transit

TRANSFERS TO OTHER TRANSIT MODES

Locating transit stations and alignments at key locations creates connections between origins and destinations. This may achieve the primary goal of providing local connectivity to significant trip generators, but there is more to the story. To maximize the effectiveness of any transit mode, it is imperative to offer system connectivity.

Transit stations are frequently where many transit modes meet; stations should therefore provide convenient transfers. Evaluation of rush-hour volumes may be the key to maximizing pedestrian convenience at transfer points. Whether alignments run east/west, north/south, or any combination thereof, most locations will have dominant flows. Connecting services will be rendered most useful by planning for the overall flow patterns.

Even after locations for transfer points are determined, the elements discussed earlier with regard to safety and access remain constant. Critical safety factors (e.g., reducing pedestrian crossing time and distance) and accessibility criteria (e.g., offering routes that have available sidewalk space) are as important to providing effective modal connectivity as is origin/destination connectivity.

Transferring between transit modes should be the easiest connection for passengers. Transit-to-transit transfers should be located closer to the station entrance than any other vehicle mode. Ideally, transit passengers should not have to cross any travel lanes to access the station entrance, although crossing in front of bus bays may be acceptable where volumes are low to moderate. At higher-volume transfer points, stairways or escalators to pedestrian underpasses or overpasses should be considered, if time-delay factors are properly taken into account.

BUS BAYS

Bus bays or berths are designed to accommodate more than one transit vehicle. Bays provide off-street service and staging areas that do not interfere with traffic movement. Bus bays are most common at transfer stations, where waiting areas for passengers are needed.

The number of bays required is based on the demand (number of vehicles to be served in the peak hour) and reliability of the operation (to provide protection for the overall system when individual vehicles are delayed).

According to *TCRP Report 100: Transit Capacity and Quality of Service Manual* (2nd ed., 2003), the following four factors should be used to determine the number of bus bays required:

- Dwell time: average amount of time a bus is stopped at the curb to serve passengers, including the time required to open and close doors.
- Clearance time: minimum time needed for one bus to clear the loading area and the next bus to pull into the loading area (dwell time plus clearance time gives average amount of time a bus occupies the loading area)
- Dwell time variability: the consistency of dwell times of buses in the loading area
- Failure rate: the probability that one bus will arrive at a loading area, only to find another bus already in the space (dwell time variability plus failure rate gives additional margin of time)

The sum of these factors produces the minimum *headway* between buses required. Dividing the headway into the number of seconds in an hour gives the number of buses per hour that can use the space (i.e., loading-area capacity).

Table 12-2 presents the maximum loading area, given the minimum time required for a bus to accelerate out of and clear the loading area and for the

Table 12-2: Maximum Buses per Hour Based on Dwell Time

Dwell Time(s)	Berth Capacity (buses/hour)
15	116
30	69
45	49
60	38
75	31
90	26
105	23
120	20
180	14

*Assumes 10-second clearance time, 25% failure rate, 60% coefficient of variation, and no traffic signal interference.

Source: TCRP Report #100, *Transit Capacity and Quality of Service*, 2003.

next bus to pull in. For larger bus stations, where individual routes are generally assigned individual berths, this table would not apply.

In general, routes with headways of less than five minutes need two bays; routes with headways of more than five minutes need only one bay. Washington, D.C.'s regional transit operator (WMATA) utilizes the following rule of thumb: one berth for six buses per hour with no more than two to three connecting services per boarding berth.

STRAIGHT CURBS VERSUS SAWTOOTH BAYS

Bus stops can be provided in two forms: straight curbs or sawtooth bays. The first type of bus stop is a straight curb where a bus pulls up to a straight length of curb.

Straight curbs are less efficient and are used most often when buses will occupy the berths for only a short time. Table 12-3 presents the amount of space required for a straight-curb bus stop, according to different operating requirements.

The second type of bus bay is a sawtooth bay, which is angled into a curb, thus requiring less linear frontage and providing access to the bus door within the curb. Sawtooth bus bays allow for independent arrivals and departures, increasing system capacity. The sharper the angle of the bay, the less linear frontage required, but the larger the overall area needed for the bay.

Table 12-4 presents recommended measurements for sawtooth bus bays. Figure 12-5 allows a comparison of bus-bay measurements for two different berth arrangements.

Table 12-3: Straight Curb Design Measurements

Operating Condition	Curb Length	Additional Length between Stopped Vehicles
No overtaking	Bus length	1 meter
Independent departures but not independent arrivals	Bus length	6–8 meters
Independent arrivals and departures	Bus length	8–11 meters between standard and 10–13 meters between articulated buses

Source: Vuchic, Vukan R. 2007. *Urban Transit: Systems and Technology*. Hoboken, NJ: John Wiley & Sons, Inc.

Table 12-4: Sawtooth Bus-Bay Design Measurements

Angle	Bus-Bay Length	Bus-Bay Width	Clearance in Front and Behind Bus Bay
45°	Length of bus plus one meter	3.25 meters	8–10 meters
60°	Length of bus plus one meter	3.50 meters	10–12 meters
90°	Length of bus plus one meter	3.75 meters	12–14 meters

Source: Vuchic, Vukan R. 2007. *Urban Transit: Systems and Technology.* Hoboken, NJ: John Wiley & Sons, Inc.

REAL TIME BUS-BAY ALLOCATION

When many bus routes serve a station, multiple bays are needed to accommodate vehicles arriving at the same time. Because routes operate on different headways, assigning each route to a specific bay will result in inefficiencies, as different bays will accommodate different volumes of buses at different times of the day. To alleviate this inefficiency, flexibility is needed to vary which vehicles use which bay. However, announcing which bay a route will arrive at as it is happening is confusing to waiting passengers, who cannot be ready for the bus to arrive until it already has.

The maturation of vehicle locator technology has provided a valuable solution. Transit operators and transit station managers can now utilize real-time location of buses and assign each vehicle to a bay in real time. In Spokane, Washington, every bus has been equipped with a transponder. As each bus nears the Plaza Transit Center, a transmitter receives the bus's signal and route number and automatically assigns the vehicle to a bay. That information is transmitted to the audio/visual

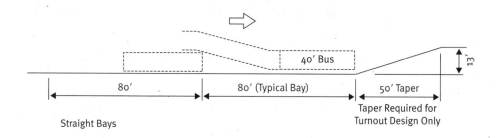

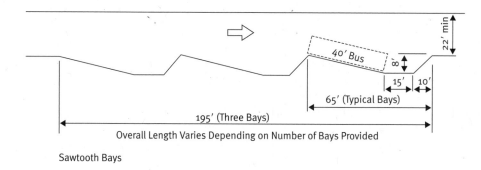

Figure 12-5
Comparison of bus-bay measurements.
Source: Vuchic, Vukan R. 2007. *Urban Transit: Systems and Technology.* Hoboken, NJ: John Wiley & Sons, Inc.

system, which flashes a notice on a screen directing passengers to the correct bus bay (Figure 12-6).

The value of the real-time bus-bay allocation system is not limited to operating efficiency. By using each bay more efficiently, transit stations can accommodate their operations plan with fewer bus bays. Fewer bays means less land needed, and reduced land needs mean lower capital, maintenance, and operating costs (Figure 12-7). Perth, Australia, is redeveloping its central transfer station to improve operation and management of its bus and rail facilities. One of the keys is an automated bus-bay allocation system that directs incoming buses to a bus bay in groups by common destination. Real-time allocation (also known as *dynamic allocation*) has reduced the land requirements for the bus portion of the station by more than 50 percent;[2] by the project's build-out year in 2031, the facility is anticipated to accommodate more than 200 buses per hour in seventeen bus bays.

ADJACENT MODES

One station cannot always accommodate all connecting modes on site. Modes that operate and stop within a travelway (such as many light rail and bus rapid transit systems) would require rerouting and additional travel time to enter a transfer station. In these cases, the adjacent mode should remain within the right-of-way, and be located along a straight path from the station area entrance. All of the pedestrian access standards described earlier should be considered, and clear wayfinding information should be provided at both the station and the adjacent stop (Figure 12-8). Where feasible, the connecting route should be weather-protected to facilitate the transfer.

Figure 12-6
Real-time bus-bay allocation (Mineola, New York). *Source: Nelson\Nygaard.*

Private Vehicles

KISS-AND-RIDE

Kiss-and-ride facilities are dedicated loading/unloading areas at stations that allow drivers to stop and park temporarily to drop off and pick up passengers, rather than use longer-term parking facilities. Kiss-and ride facilities generally provide access to private autos, taxis, paratransit vehicles, and private shuttle buses. The size of a kiss-and-ride facility depends on the demand and physical constraints of the site. Generally, space needs in the morning to drop passengers off are minimal, but in the evening peak, more space is needed as drivers must wait for passengers to arrive. If there is not dedicated space for pick-ups and drop-offs, idling vehicles can disrupt the flow of traffic.

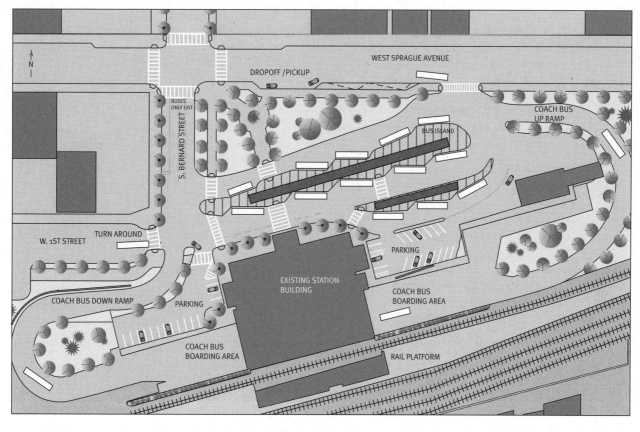

N

WEST SPRAGUE AVENUE

DROPOFF/PICKUP

COACH BUS
UP RAMP

S. BERNARD STREET

BUSES
ONLY EXIT

BUS ISLAND

TURN AROUND

W. 1ST STREET

PARKING

COACH BUS DOWN RAMP

PARKING

EXISTING STATION
BUILDING

COACH BUS
BOARDING AREA

COACH BUS
BOARDING AREA

RAIL PLATFORM

▲ **Figure 12-7**
**Design for intermodal station with
station building, bus bays, vehicle
parking, and on-street drop-off/pick-up
space (Spokane, Washington).** *Source:
Nelson\Nygaard.*

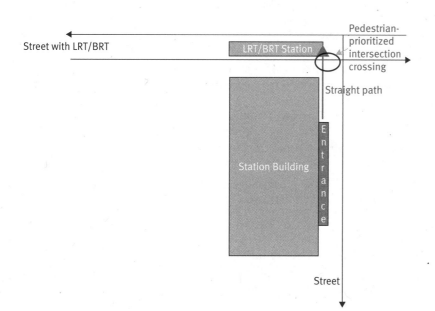

Street with LRT/BRT

LRT/BRT Station

Pedestrian-
prioritized
intersection
crossing

Straight path

Entrance

Station Building

Street

◀ **Figure 12-8**
**Direct access between station and
adjacent mode.** *Source: Nelson\
Nygaard.*

Kiss-and-rides are most effective when they are separated from other access routes, prioritizing maximum vehicle turnover, facilitating traffic flow, and avoiding traffic conflicts. Long-term parking should have a separate entrance, to facilitate vehicular egress upon completing a drop-off/pick-up. Pedestrians should be provided with an alternative route so that they can avoid walking through the kiss-and ride. The maximum walking distance between the kiss-and-ride area to the station entrance is generally no longer than 600 feet.[3] Successful kiss-and-rides should have passenger amenities such as shelters, lighting, and clear pedestrian access to the station entrance.

STATION PARKING

THE ROLE OF STATION PARKING

The primary responsibility of a transit station is to facilitate access to the transit service. One of the most convenient ways to provide station access is to provide vehicular parking. For every parking space provided, at least one person can ride the train. Add any carpools, and the volume of customers provided with station access increases even more. It's a simple formula, easy to replicate, and easy to understand. However, vehicular parking comes with tradeoffs, so providing the right amount of station parking requires the community to decide on the role of its station.

PARKING FOR REGIONAL STATIONS

Regional transit stations are intended to provide transit access for an entire region. Regional stations tend to be located in spread-out, low- to medium-density areas, with easy roadway access and few active land uses. In these areas, automobiles are the dominant mode and significant roadway space a hallmark of the transportation network. The greatest bang for the buck comes from maximizing vehicular parking at a regional station, to allow travelers from around the region to access the station.

Regional transit stations with easy-to-access parking offer an opportunity to shift commuters from long drives to urban centers into short drives to closer transit stations. Surface parking can be an opportunity when a new transit station is being planned outside, but near to, developed areas, especially where limited transit options are available (Figure 12-9). Providing lots of parking may require construction of permeable surfaces to accommodate water runoff, but the parking can provide regional access close to where people live, offering opportunities to reduce auto travel to urban centers. This approach, however, must recognize the resulting development form, travel patterns, and cost created by surrounding the station with parking.

- **Development form:** When parking is the dominant element, more active land uses cannot be present. Surrounding the station with parking therefore makes land unusable for most other activities.

- **Travel patterns:** At 200 square feet per parking space plus room for drive aisles, parking lots take up a lot of land. As described earlier, long walks through rows of parking discourage pedestrians, so the more surface parking provided, the more auto-oriented the station area will become. Co-locating parking facilities in land considered unusable for active land use (i.e., freeway interchanges or

near airports) may offer an ideal solution: a difficult land use on a difficult piece of land.

- **Cost:** At a capital cost of $10,000 per surface parking space, $20,000 per structured space, and $40,000 per below-grade space, the cost of providing a parking space for everyone who wants to access the train station becomes very high very quickly.

PARKING FOR TODS

The second dominant station type is a transit-oriented development, or TOD. *TOD* is a new term for an older phenomenon: a transit station surrounded by a mix of land uses and limited parking options, so travelers end up living, shopping, and working within a short walk of the station (Figure 12-10). The more parking is provided, the less pedestrian oriented the development can be, so TODs tend to provide the least amount of parking required to support nonstation land uses.

If vehicular parking is not a dominant station feature, other opportunities for access must be provided. As described earlier, all stations should have clear, safe, and easy pedestrian access. Without pedestrian access, a TOD is infeasible. TODs should also have significant bicycle access and storage (see later discussion), as well as connections to other transit services (bus, LRT, etc.).

REGARDLESS OF STATION TYPE, MANAGE PARKING CORRECTLY

When planning for station parking, a primary question is often how much parking should be provided. What is not considered is what to do with the parking once

Figure 12-10
Active land uses create more
interesting station areas (Oakland,
California). *Source: Nelson\Nygaard.*

it is provided. Just like any resource, parking has price, including construction,
daily operation and maintenance, and often interest payments. Even if parking is
provided at no charge to the user, the cost must still be paid by whoever agreed to
waive the user fee. Whether the parking provider is the transit agency or the local
municipality, the cost is subsidized by other funds (most likely farebox revenue
or taxes). The result of providing free parking is a reduction in other services the
agency or municipality can provide, so that drivers may park for free. The result is
also a shift in resources from the poorest of transit patrons (those who cannot afford
to own a car or who drive less than average) to the wealthiest transit patrons (those
who are most likely to drive to the station).

Deciding to price for station parking is not a yes/no decision. Different pricing mechanisms are available, depending on the different markets to be served.
The primary markets at transit stations are: short-term parkers; commuters seeking
guaranteed, reserved station parking; occasional daily commuters traveling at peak
hours; park-shop-and-ride travelers; and long-term parkers, such as those using
transit to get to the airport or intercity train station. Transit agencies have implemented different approaches to each of these markets. The following programs represent the best practices of station parking price based on these markets.

- **Tailored daily parking fees (BART):** The San Francisco Bay Area's BART charges
  daily fees at almost all of its stations, and it has criteria for raising or lowering
  parking rates based on observed occupancy. BART recognizes that setting the

right price for parking—so that a few spaces remain available at all times of day—maximizes both ridership and revenue, and helps the agency avoid the peak crowding problems associated with a lot that fills at a certain time every morning. As of April 2010, daily parking fees generated more than $8 million per year in gross revenues for BART. Nevertheless, BART's parking fees cover only a fraction of the costs of providing parking.[4]

- **Premium, monthly reserved parking (WMATA):** DC Metro offers guaranteed/reserved parking spaces at all stations with parking lots until 10:00 a.m. on weekdays for commuters who have paid a $55 monthly reserved parking permit fee. Monthly reserved permit holders are still responsible for paying daily parking fees whenever they park in a Metro facility. BART also offers a monthly reserved parking program, with fees ranging from $30 to $115 by station, based on demand. However, BART monthly reserved parking permit holders are not required to pay daily parking fees in addition to the permit fee, removing any incentive they might have to use alternative modes of station access on a day-to-day basis.

- **Short-term metered parking (TriMet):** TriMet in Portland, Oregon, reserves preferential parking spaces (near the entrance to two of its busiest park-and-ride stations) for short-term metered parking. Meter rates of $0.50 per hour, and 5-hour time limits, serve to increase turnover and consequently the total number of transit patrons using each space each day. Metered spaces also provide a station access choice for midday travelers who might otherwise have no auto access to busy stations.

- **Shared parking (TriMet):** Half of all park-and-ride facilities in the Portland, Oregon, metropolitan area, with 20 percent of the total supply of park-and-ride spaces, are in privately owned and operated facilities shared by TriMet. As a result, TriMet is able to dedicate a larger share of its capital budget to transit vehicles and facilities. In the most heavily used shared parking facilities, TriMet makes payments to the owner/operators to cover maintenance costs related to use by transit patrons.

A common theme among agencies implementing parking pricing and TOD strategies is that station parking is not an end or objective in and of itself. Rather, parking is one among several alternatives for providing and/or facilitating access to regional transit facilities and services. To ensure that policies and practices serve the primary mission of increasing ridership, parking and TOD must be planned and implemented with (1) appropriate consideration for the unique local context of each transit station and corridor, and (2) use of *cost per transit rider served* as a key metric in the evaluation of land use and station access alternatives. As stated in the *BART Access Guidelines* (2003):

> Improvements that do the most to increase ridership at the lowest cost should be prioritized. To the extent possible, costs should be compared on a consistent basis across all modes, taking into account both operating and capital expenses, land values, and the opportunity costs of foregone joint development.

CASE STUDY: WMATA'S ORANGE LINE

WMATA's Orange Line provides a comparison of station types, parking supplies, and results. The Orange Line's first five stations within Virginia serve Arlington County's Rosslyn-Ballston Corridor. These stations are all located below a prominent main street and are designed to serve individual "Transit Villages." Each village anchors a mix of land uses, higher densities than generally seen in Arlington County, frequent surface transit, and significant bicycle connectivity. A hallmark of each station area is that shared parking is permitted, whereas station-dedicated parking is not.

West of Arlington County, the Orange Line serves Fairfax County. Fairfax County's stations emphasize auto access and on-site vehicular parking. Few other land uses or activities are located within a 10-minute walk of most stations. In recent years, surface parking has been replaced with parking structures, increasing the amount of station parking available.

Figure 12-11 compares the mode of access to the stations in the Rosslyn-Ballston Corridor to the stations in Fairfax County. The results directly reflect the type of station developed. Fairfax County's auto-oriented stations simplify auto access and as a result more than half of the riders from these stations drive or are driven. R-B Corridor stations minimize commuter parking and prioritize nonmotorized access, resulting in 73 percent of boardings being from people who walked to the station. More importantly, Arlington was able to generate 27 million square feet of development since 1970 around its stations—more office space than downtown Los Angeles or Boston—and 30,000 housing units, while actual traffic numbers have remained steady for 20 years.[5] The parking policies have directly generated the travel patterns for access to these stations. Arlington exemplifies development-oriented transit as much as it exemplifies transit-oriented development.

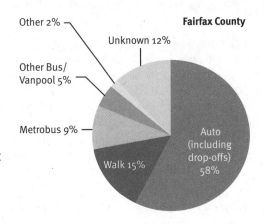

Fairfax County

Other 2%
Unknown 12%
Other Bus/Vanpool 5%
Metrobus 9%
Walk 15%
Auto (including drop-offs) 58%

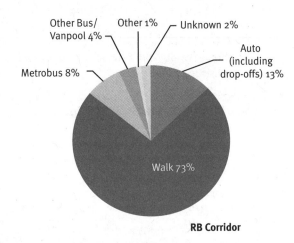

Other Bus/Vanpool 4%
Other 1%
Unknown 2%
Auto (including drop-offs) 13%
Metrobus 8%
Walk 73%

RB Corridor

Figure 12-11
Access mode to WMATA Orange Line stations, 2002. *Source: Nelson\ Nygaard/WMATA May 2002 Weekday Metrorail Ridership and Access Report.*

Taxis

A *taxi rank* is a defined area where empty taxis travel to a passenger pick-up area from an area where they have already dropped passengers off. Taxi pick-up areas should be designed to maximize efficiency, turnover, and control of passenger flows. Design elements to include are:[6]

- A clear route between the station and taxis
- A defined passenger waiting area
- Nearside taxi boarding access
- Minimization of vehicle conflicts between taxis entering and departing loading area
- Signage/information at regular points in the station, at the station exits, and at the taxi facilities
- Real-time information on taxi supply (i.e., expected wait time for passengers)
- Adequate dimensions to accommodate luggage and luggage trolleys (more important at certain stations)

A typical taxi bay can accommodate an average of fifty passengers per hour. Dimensions of taxi bays vary and depend on services, land available at the station, and type of station. The number of passengers per taxi depends on the type of station, though Transport for London recommends the following average ridership:

- Suburban: 1.3 passengers per taxi
- Intercity: 1.5 passengers per taxi
- International: 1.55 passengers per taxi

Bicycles

REGIONAL CONNECTIONS

Bicycles extend the accessible zone of a transit station from a pedestrian-based 10-minute walk to a more evenly distributed 1 to 5 miles. (Remember your high-school geometry: increasing the catchment radius from 0.5 to 3 miles increases the catchment area not six times but thirty-six times, significantly increasing ridership potential.) Encouraging this accessibility requires connecting the station area to a network of bicycle routes.

Cities that have invested in connecting their regional bicycle routes to their transit stations have achieved significant increases in transit ridership.[7] In Washington, D.C., the number of bicyclists riding the Metrorail increased by 60 percent between 2002 and 2007. At some of these stations, cyclists accounted for up to 4 percent of all passenger boardings. In Minneapolis, Metro Transit carried more than 250,000 bicycles annually and reported a doubling of bikes on buses between the spring of 2007 and fall 2008. Roughly 4 percent of Portland's MAX light rail passengers carry their bikes onto the vehicles with them. In the San Francisco Bay Area, the share of passengers accessing BART stations by bike rose from 2.5 percent in 1998 to 3.5 percent in 2008, with an average of 10,920 bike-and-ride trips per day. Of course, these U.S. figures pale in comparison to northern European levels.

BICYCLE PARKING

Bicycle storage is an integral component of developing a multimodal transit station. Bicycle storage can generally be provided in two formats. Bicycle racks accommodate more bicycles in less space but offer less protection and security and thus are less inviting to potential bicyclists. Bicycle stations require more space but offer a greater incentive to bicyclists to use transit, as the bike stations can provide security and protection from the elements. For more detail, see Chapter 7.

BICYCLE RACKS

Bicycle racks should be located within 50 feet of station entrances[8] and sited using the following guidance:

- Rack placement shall be made to avoid pedestrian conflicts.

- Bicycle racks should be installed within easy viewing distance from a main pedestrian walkway.

- When placed against station buildings or walls, bicycle racks need at least 2 feet of clear space between the rack and a parallel wall, and 2.5 feet of clear space between the rack and a perpendicular wall.

BICYCLE STATIONS

Bike stations and bike share programs are relatively new approaches to increase access to integrated, intermodal transportation options. The most successful programs to date are located at and near transportation hubs and stations, major points of employment, and tourism destinations.

Bike stations are facilities to store bicycles securely. These facilities can be aboveground, covered or uncovered, below-ground covered, open access or controlled access, free or pay-to-park, manual or automated. Bike stations provide greater security for long-term bicycle parking than standard bicycle racks, as they are traditionally staffed and monitored. Payment for use may be fee based with individual PINs, and/or automated by personal credit card or SMART card.

Bike stations vary from completely automated bike valet systems; to basic staffed facilities with some bike repair options; to places with concessions, locker rooms, and storage. Figure 12-12 shows an example of the latter.

Station Components

The Time Component: Wait Time Creates Place

Airport planners have long known that travelers waiting for a flight become short-term citizens. The more activity available within a certain proximity to each gate, the easier (and shorter) that wait is perceived as being, and the more readily that traveler will be willing to repeat the experience. Charlotte's Douglas International Airport's provision of rocking chairs in front of picturesque windows is frequently cited as a very positive part of the travel experience.[9] Happy waiters also are more willing to spend money, resulting in a micro-level example of economic

sustainability: an active, walkable place creates economic opportunity, which continues to support the active place.

Transit stations are different, but can learn from this example. Airport travelers are a captive audience who cannot bring their own drinks and have little choice but to wait for their flights, regardless of on-time performance..Transit users, who are often near home or work, and frequently have access to the car they drove, can decide to leave at any time.

Although transit riders have more travel choice, providing the right mix of uses offers them every reason to choose to remain. Also, without a security checkpoint constraining their movements, transit users have a wider walkshed to patronize nearby land uses that may not be where they wait for their train or bus. As long as the use is on their way in or out of the station, open at the correct hours, and within the line of sight of the track or bus bay, it will be considered part of that station's area. Appropriate uses should be specific to the type of travel served by the transit and the land uses surrounding the transit station. For example, for commuter rail stations that have their maximum passenger volumes during work-related travel times, uses that offer daily services are most helpful. In these cases, coffee shops, bakeries, newsstands, dry cleaners, banks, and post office/mailing services offer travelers the chance to check one more chore off their to-do lists, without adding another trip to the day. At stops near colleges and universities, uses geared toward students may include movie theaters, museums, restaurants, bars, and grocery stores. Locating municipal departments and social service agencies at any of these provides the most

Figure 12-13
Active land uses greatly enhance a station's appeal, and increase the likelihood that transit users will continue to choose transit over other modes. *Source: Nelson\Nygaard.*

likely transit riders (economically challenged and without access to a car) with the travel option they need to complete their trip (Figure 12-13).

Because the pedestrian use distance around a transit station is limited to a 5- to 10-minute walk, the amount of activity that can be accommodated is constrained. Land uses and vehicular parking then begin to compete for the limited space. It is at this point that station planners must decide what type of station they want, given what they hope to accomplish. The following case study describes BART's methodology for determining the correct balance between land uses and parking.

CASE STUDY: BART STATION REPLACEMENT PARKING

Like many transit agencies, BART once had a long-standing practice of requiring 1:1 replacement for parking at its rail stations. In other words, the developer of a BART surface lot was required to pay for new parking structures to replace all the spaces lost to on-site development. This posed a major financial obstacle for developers, reduced BART's revenue, and compromised BART's policy of reducing the share of access by single-occupant vehicle. In recognition of these issues, in 2005, the BART board adopted a new transit-oriented development policy, which provides greater flexibility in determining optimum replacement parking levels. The following station area planning effort used the new methodology developed by BART and Professor Richard Willson to determine the appropriate parking ratios specific to each site. It should be noted that the appropriate replacement parking rate varies depending on location, existing access-mode split, and density of the proposed development. There is, therefore, no single answer to what the rate should be as a comprehensive policy; the decision is based on the goals for the station and the ridership and revenue goals for the transit agency.

South Hayward Station

BART and the City of Hayward have, over the past several years, developed a plan to replace BART's parking lots at the South Hayward BART station with a TOD. This station is currently suburban in nature, serving primarily single-family homes in the surrounding neighborhoods. In 2006, BART prepared an analysis of parking replacement options regarding the existing 1,207 parking spaces, to complement the city's ongoing planning efforts in the area.[10] It documented a focused analysis of access improvements and TOD opportunities in the immediate station area. The main findings of the report were that even though some riders are lost as parking is reduced from the current supply, this is far outweighed by ridership generated by the new development that is made possible. Moreover, the development options would generate enough revenue to pay for the cost of replacement parking, a new bus intermodal facility, and placemaking investments in the transit plaza.

A developer recently entered into an exclusive negotiating agreement with BART for development of the parking lots and an adjacent parcel. The proposal includes 772 residential units and 64,680 square feet of retail space. Of the 1,207 BART-dedicated spaces, 910 will be replaced in structured parking when the project is built. Hence, the replacement parking rate is 75 percent.

What Else Does a Station Area Need?

Waiting for the bus or train is a significant part of every rider's transit experience. If stations and stops provide a comfortable waiting environment, people traveling to and from that area will be more likely to use transit. Conversely, stops without comfortable environments discourage transit use.

Within station buildings, sufficient space should be provided for both operational elements and customer convenience elements. Operating agencies will require components that make the station function: passenger waiting and boarding facilities, information distribution, and ticket purchases. If passengers are to consider the station area as a place and not just a waiting room, services (most importantly bathrooms) and retail should also be provided.

A stop classification scheme developed by the Greater Cleveland RTA can be found in Chapter 8. The scheme classifies all of RTA's stops into one of five categories by the volume of boardings, then specifies the features that should be provided for each type of stop.

Station Siting

Transit stations should be located so that they best serve the general population and maximize ridership potential. Although many nonpedestrian issues arise regarding the location of stations, a few particulars directly relate to pedestrian access and safety. Data collection and mapping are recommended to determine where people are (origin), where they want to go (destination), and where stations can be located to serve them (potential site).

A well-designed pedestrian access plan will provide a natural flow of walking customers from the surrounding area. Station planners should ask a few basic questions regarding the quality of pedestrian access: Are the pedestrian walkways leading to the station well maintained? Are they sufficiently broad to comfortably handle the expected pedestrian traffic? Are they safe and well lit? Is there adequate signage to lead individuals easily to the stations? Are there logical pedestrian connections between major origins and destinations, such as shops, schools, and workplaces?

Mapping pedestrian movements in the area of the proposed station provides the baseline data that will help shape the optimum design of the supporting pedestrian infrastructure. Just as traffic counts are an important input element of the transportation modeling process, pedestrian counts and pedestrian movements are important input parts of understanding issues regarding station access.

SERVICE ZONES

The area to be served by a transit station should be divided into *zones*. A quarter-mile to half-mile radius is traditionally recommended to determine the catchment area of each station (generally considered the furthest people will walk to catch a bus or train, respectively). If preexisting origin and destination surveys at a sufficiently small scale exist, the same zones and the same zoning codes should be used.

It is important to record travel distances from the station based on walking travel times. Maps showing areas covered in such intervals as 1 minute, 5 minutes, 10 minutes, 20 minutes, and 30 minutes not only indicate the potential catchment area for the station but may also highlight potential barriers to pedestrian access. For example, a busy roadway near the station may create severance issues for approaching pedestrians. Other impediments, such as blocked or nonexistent pavements, will become evident in a time-based mapping. Also, long signal cycles for pedestrian crossings will increase walking travel times. This type of analysis can often show areas where distances are relatively short but pedestrian travel times are lengthy.

The map in Figure 12-14 shows quarter- and half-mile radii around the Free Library of Philadelphia. Figure 12-15 shows the distance actually walked in 5 and

Center City - Parkway Parking Study

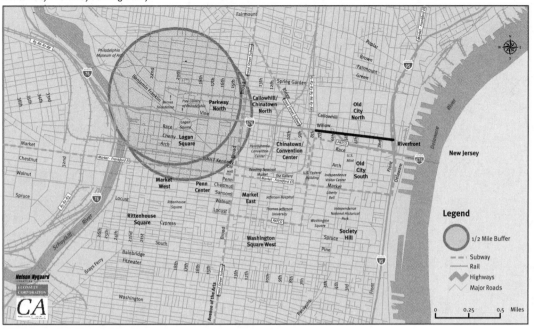

Center City - Parkway Parking Study

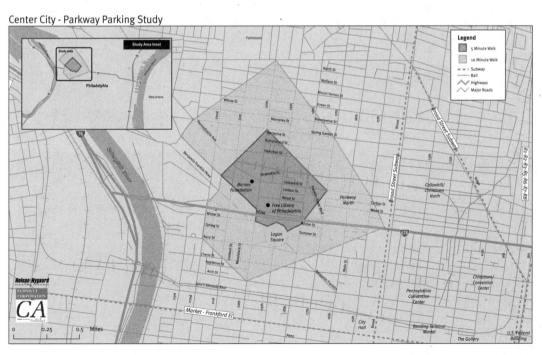

Figures 12-14 and 12-15
Measuring distance (circles) versus time (pedigrams). *Source: Nelson\ Nygaard.*

10 minutes, for a pedestrian who follow all traffic laws. Due to the presence of a wide, busy intersection, the first few minutes of the walk south was needed just to cross the first street. Walking in the opposite direction, however, allowed the walker to travel farther in the same amount of time. The result is a unique pattern, called a *pedigram*, which shows different distances walked based on physical conditions. The actual distance within a service zone is very different than the distance within a preset radial distance.

Chapter 13

Transportation Demand Management

with Jessica ter Schure and Patrick Siegman

Transportation Demand Management, or TDM, is a general term for strategies that increase overall transportation system efficiency by encouraging a shift from single-occupant vehicle (SOV) trips to non-SOV modes, or by shifting auto trips out of peak periods.

TDM strategies are often far more cost-effective than capital investments in increased roadway capacity. In fact, TDM strategies can often have a remarkable effect on traffic congestion at little to no cost. Unfortunately, TDM strategies often are not pursued, frequently because they are not well understood.

The researcher Todd Litman, at his Victoria Transport Policy Institute (VTPI) website— http://www.vtpi.org—offers a "TDM Encyclopedia" that should be required reading for all who are interested in learning more about the subject. This chapter provides a brief introduction to TDM, and addresses some of the more promising strategies at somewhat greater length.

We begin with a discussion of the nature of traffic congestion.

What Is Traffic Congestion and Why Does It Happen?

In economic terms, traffic congestion is to automobile travel what bread lines are to bread: an example of demand exceeding supply. In the case of traffic congestion, the number of motorists wanting to drive somewhere simply exceeds the roadway capacity to accommodate them. Although motorists may find the congestion annoying, many still make a choice to sit in congestion rather than avoid the trip, use another travel mode, take a different route, or change their trip pattern altogether. Just as it is difficult to live without bread, it is challenging for many families to match affordable housing, a decent job, and an easy commute.

The science of fluid dynamics is often used to help describe traffic patterns and congestion, in terms much like those used to describe the plumbing system in your house or the blood in your veins. Traffic congestion tends to form in places where you get a lot of turbulence in a liquid system, such as where a small pipe connects to a big pipe, or where pipes meet at odd angles.

Traffic itself results largely from a strong, dynamic economy, in which commerce is humming, workers are going to work, developers are building, and people are spending discretionary income on things they enjoy. For some planners, traffic congestion is merely a sign of economic "success." Indeed, the only major city in U.S. history that has ever eliminated its congestion problem is Detroit, Michigan, where congestion was eliminated by the collapse of the urban downtown as a multiuse center.

Traffic congestion is a concern largely for four reasons:

- It takes up valuable time and reduces quality of life for everyone stuck in it.

- It acts as a limit on future economic expansion. Major transportation capital projects tend to be followed by new development and economic expansion that in turn result in congestion.

- Cars stuck in congestion produce significantly more local pollution and carbon dioxide per mile than free-flowing traffic.

- As congestion reaches certain levels, the person capacity of the overall transportation network declines sharply, resulting in economic contraction until the system rebalances. That is, congestion gets so bad that people and companies simply move to other regions.

This last point is especially important. As traffic volumes increase, the vehicle throughput on a given street increases steadily until the street starts to reach capacity. At that point, throughput begins to decline rapidly—to the point where there are so many cars that none can move. When a freeway is heavily congested at peak times, it may be moving fewer cars than it does in the middle of the night. To keep people, cars, and buses moving, it is important that the street system be managed to avoid instances of severe congestion.

Where Does Congestion Happen?

In most cities, congestion tends to accumulate in predictable locations, such as:

Freeway ramps. Congestion accumulates around freeway on- and off-ramps for two main reasons:

- As the one large "pipe" of a freeway ramp meets the many small "pipes" of city streets, motorists are making many turning movements and sorting themselves out into the grid. This slows traffic movement.

- When the freeway is congested, cars heading onto the freeway back up onto city streets, reducing the ability of those streets to serve local trips.

Colliding grids. In cities with multiple street grids that misalign with each other in interesting ways, congestion inevitably accumulates at the seams between grids. This happens in part because of the awkward geometries where these grids meet and in part because some streets don't continue or are severely misaligned.

Broken grids. In many cities with nineteenth- and early twentieth-century street grids, those grids are interrupted by topography, water, railroads, freeways, and well-intentioned mid-twentieth-century interventions. In these cases, where traffic would otherwise be able to spread itself out over many streets, it is now all funneled into a few streets.

Missing grids. In many late twentieth-century cities, designers concerned with the problems of interconnected street grids intentionally eliminated through streets, creating mazes and culs-de-sac to keep through traffic from intruding upon calm residential neighborhoods. In protecting some streets, however, traffic is all funneled onto the remaining through arterials.

Major activity centers. At schools, hospitals, major employment centers, central business districts, shopping malls, and special events, a large numbers of cars tend to come and go at a fixed time to a concentrated place.

How Can We "Solve" the Congestion Problem?

Short of major demand management techniques—particularly parking pricing and roadway pricing—no city has ever "solved" its congestion problem. All successful cities have traffic congestion. The most successful cities simply locate their inevitable congestion in places where it has the least impact on local economic development, quality of life, and other goals.

San Francisco, for example, intentionally places its freeway congestion in the middle of its downtown, where the Bay Bridge meets US 101. This has the effect of making it relatively easy to drive *to* downtown, but rather difficult to drive *through* downtown. By using congestion to discourage through trips, San Francisco ironically increases the capacity of the roads to accommodate traffic into its downtown, thereby taking the most economic advantage of its freeway.

Vancouver, British Columbia, takes a different approach. It places traffic bottlenecks in a ring around the city. Traffic heading into the city from the Lion's Gate Bridge, for example, may queue for more than a mile in a retained cut through Stanley Park as it is metered into the downtown grid. The result is relatively little congestion in the city center, because of the metering effect of the bottleneck at Georgia and Denman.

Santa Monica, California, knowing there is nothing it can do to eliminate the notorious congestion of Los Angeles's Westside, has policies that intentionally place congestion where it has the least impact on residential neighborhoods and retail streets. Santa Monica accepts a high level of congestion at the first traffic signals before and after its freeway ramps, because it knows that if it eliminated congestion at these ramps, it would merely move the congestion bottleneck to the next intersection down the street. Intentional congestion points help meter the traffic to make sure that intracity traffic flows smoothly.

How Can a City Grow If It Already Has Traffic Congestion?

If there are already too many cars on the road, how can we allow more growth? Won't the city just strangle itself on more traffic?

If we want to allow more people to visit and live, work, and shop in a city with existing traffic congestion, we have no choice but to move them in more efficient ways. This is not a matter of ideology, but of *geometry*. People in cars simply take up at least ten times as much road space as people in other forms of transportation.

To influence significant numbers of people to choose more efficient travel modes, three factors merit special attention:

1. **Time.** Most people, especially working people and those with children, place a high value on their time, regardless of their income. If one way is faster than another, people will adjust their travel to use it. This is especially true for all forms of public transit—if the bus, train, ferry, or streetcar is faster than driving, most

people will choose transit over driving. This is why subways, busways, and dedicated right-of-way rail attract vastly higher ridership than mixed-traffic transit.

People also value different types of time in different ways. Some people will choose transit over driving even if transit takes longer if they can make productive use of their time on board. Awkward transfers and unreliable service, however, are maddening for most travelers—time spent waiting can have a perceived "cost" ten times higher than time spent in a vehicle.

2. **Quality.** People will avoid travel choices that do not offer a decent level of human dignity. This is often an obstacle for mixing bicycling with heavy traffic or riding a bus designed only to serve those for whom transit is a choice of last resort. Similarly, people may perceive their time spent walking as a positive part of their day if the walk is pleasant or an alternative to the gym—but if the walk is dangerous or unpleasant, the perceived time cost escalates.

3. **Cost.** The impact of cost on travel choices varies with income and is typically charted as a curved line. That is, as cost increases, travel choices are not much affected until prices get rather high; then the impact of price rapidly escalates. So, a daily parking rate of $10 may have little impact on travel choices if driving is faster than other modes, because people value their saved time as worth more than the $10 parking fee (particularly if the same commute on transit costs as much or even more). But if parking prices rise to $30, suddenly a significant share of travelers would find other ways of getting downtown. Very few would park at $60 a day.

An alternative to shifting people into more efficient travel modes is to help them avoid making the trip altogether. This means focusing on accessibility rather than mobility. *Mobility* is about adding travel lanes, bike lanes, or new bus routes to allow people to travel freely wherever they want to go. *Accessibility* is about bringing goods and services closer together so people can get what they want without needing to travel.

Cities can significantly reduce traffic by creating more complete neighborhoods, bringing a fuller array of services and retail into each neighborhood center and reducing the need for people to drive across town to conduct routine business and take care of basic needs.

Planning for Reduced Traffic

In a down economy, the number-one complaint in most communities is jobs. In an up economy, the primary complaint is traffic. Traffic, however, is a lot like the weather: Everyone always complains about it, but no one seems to be able to do anything about it. For cities fortunate enough to have sufficient economic activity to produce congestion, this chapter attempts to lay out solutions to the problem. Before we get to solutions, however, let's review projects that do *not* reduce traffic congestion, at least on their own:

• **Widen roads**. As Tom Vanderbilt explains eloquently in his book *Traffic: Why We Drive the Way We Do (and What It Says About Us)*,[1] widening roads inevitably leads to more traffic congestion, not less. Congestion is an economic problem, not an engineering problem. It is simply the result of market demand for roadway space equaling available roadway capacity. As we learned in Economics 101, if we produce more of a good (a wider road) at a lower price (less congestion), then the market demand for the good simply increases, re-creating the same congestion that the roadway widening was designed to solve in the first place. As described in more detail in Chapter 9 on motor vehicles, this traffic feedback loop is called *induced demand*.

- **New transit lines**. In the United States, many railway expansion tax measures have unfortunately been sold to commuters with the promise that the transit projects will "reduce congestion." When the resulting transit projects do not suddenly make driving easy at all times, voters understandably feel duped. Here's the dirty secret: Transit projects (almost) never result in reduced congestion. Rather, engineers' simplistic modeling tools tell us that big transit projects will result in less congestion than would otherwise be there without the transit project. Though this conclusion is true and valid in theory, it has not been demonstrated to be true or valid in practice, except in cases where the transit project is combined with strong land-use policies and other demand management tools that limit driving.

- **Bikeways**. Many northern European cities and some U.S. college towns have impressively high rates of bicycling, largely as a result of decades of investment in bicycle infrastructure and programming. As the experiences of San Francisco and other cities have shown, however, bikeway investments may create significant increases in bicycle ridership, but these may come at the expense of carpooling, walking, and transit trips. To the extent bikeways create a shift away from driving, the available capacity is simply consumed by induced demand.

It is important to remember that we build transportation capital projects not to relieve congestion, but to increase mobility, which in turn results in two big economic benefits:

- More opportunity for movement creates more opportunity for economic activity, by linking consumers to markets and residents to jobs, and increasing the overall efficiency and competitiveness of a region.

- More transportation capacity opens up new development opportunities and increases land values. A new subway line may quadruple land values around its stations, creating the market for new urban high-rises, and a new highway may change the market to allow cattle pastures to be turned into new suburban neighborhoods.

Because traffic congestion is such a large concern in so many communities, politicians and traffic engineers routinely promise that their big transportation capital projects will "relieve congestion." Strictly speaking, this is not a lie, as their overly simplistic traffic modeling tools typically ignore two critical factors:

1. *Induced demand.* When faced with having to sit in traffic congestion, many would-be travelers decide to drive outside peak hours, take transit instead, or avoid the trip altogether. When a newly widened roadway opens, motorists who

would never have driven that road during peak times suddenly decide to make the drive. The same is true of a rapid transit line: The very presence of the new, faster route causes many people to change their travel patterns, thereby "inducing" new travel demand that the model did not consider. The result is that the added construction-related delay motorists experience from a roadway-widening project is often greater than any time savings the added lanes produce.[2]

2. *Real estate market changes.* Transportation capital projects—particularly highways and rapid transit—typically result in significant real estate value impacts. Transit ridership modeling often takes these impacts into account in order to generate ridership figures to justify the project. Highway models, however, rarely do.

So, if we cannot build our way out of congestion, what can we do? The answer is quite simple: First, we need to look at both the supply and demand sides of transportation, and we need to look at transportation's relationship to land use.

Anthony Downs, the noted Brookings Institution scholar and author of such gloomily titled works as *Still Stuck in Traffic*, declares that traffic congestion is "inevitable."[3] Among economic development officials and developers, increasing motor-vehicle traffic is often perceived and described as simply the price of success. We propose a different conclusion: Traffic congestion is not inevitable. If the citizens of your city wish, traffic can be reduced. Traffic congestion is a choice, not fate. Moreover, rising traffic congestion is not simply a byproduct or unavoidable symptom of economic success. Instead, traffic congestion is typically a sign of significant economic losses. It indicates a transportation system that is not economically efficient. As a result, reducing auto traffic can often result in substantial economic gains.

However, would your city wish to make the significant changes that would be required to significantly reduce traffic, with all of the controversy that these changes might entail? This chapter cannot answer that question for your community; only the community itself can do that. It does, however, provide a toolkit of strategies that are demonstrably successful in reducing traffic, and a window into communities where remarkable changes are taking place.

Numerous cities have demonstrated that traffic and drive-alone rates can be significantly reduced. Furthermore, when a community wishes to do so, traffic can be reduced with remarkable rapidity. In Stockholm, for example (see Figure 13-1), six months into its congestion pricing trial, vehicle trips had fallen by 22 percent, far more than engineers expected.[4]

Stockholm is not an isolated case. In the following section are examples of cities, downtowns, and districts, both internationally and in the United States, that have succeeded in either: (a) significantly reducing vehicle traffic, or (b) significantly reducing drive-alone rates. In some of these examples, such as London and Stockholm, existing traffic levels have been sharply reduced from the levels of a few years ago. In many of the other examples, a major decline in the percentage of trips made by driving alone was offset by rapid growth, so that the net result was little or no increase in traffic.

The goal of this chapter is to identify a way to reduce the *existing* number of vehicle trips on your city's streets during the evening rush hour by 25 percent. Therefore, the examples in which a city merely kept traffic levels constant while

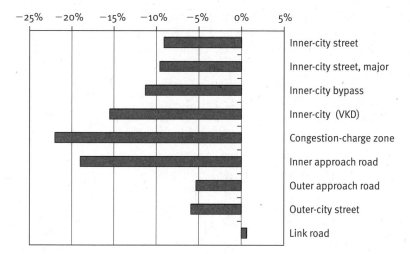

Figure 13-1
Traffic reduction during Stockholm's congestion pricing trials. *Source: "Facts and Results from the Stockholm Trials: Final Report," Stockholmsforsoket.*

the city grew rapidly—such as the addition of 250,000 workers to downtown San Francisco with no increase in traffic—are not perfect precedents. However, they do provide important lessons about how a community can reduce driving.

Where Are These Strategies Being Applied Already?

All of the transportation strategies recommended in this chapter have been implemented before. Nothing here is new or untested. Many of the recommendations are included as key steps because they appeared, over and over, as important strategies in cities that have succeeded in reducing vehicle trips. (Most of these strategies are rarely seen in communities where traffic is getting steadily worse.)

- **Arlington County, Virginia, Rosslyn-Ballston Corridor**: In the 1960s and 1970s, this suburban corridor consisted largely of tired strip malls with ubiquitous free parking, a surrounding fabric of single-family homes, and sharply declining population and retail sales. Today, development in the corridor is booming, but with little growth in traffic. Traffic counts from 1997 to 2004, for example, show that while office and residential development grew by 17.5 percent and 21.5 percent, respectively, traffic along the Rosslyn-Ballston corridor grew by only 2.3 percent. Census journey-to-work survey data show that more than 47 percent of corridor residents now take transit to work.

- **Bellevue, Washington**: In downtown Bellevue, Washington, the drive-alone commute rate fell by 30 percent from 1990 to 2000, falling from 81 percent driving alone to 57 percent.

- **Boulder, Colorado**: Between 1995 and 2008, the drive-alone rate for employees in downtown Boulder has fallen 39 percent, from 56 percent driving alone to 34 percent, while the transit mode share almost doubled from 15 percent to 29 percent.

- **Cambridge, Massachusetts**: Cambridge's Travel Demand Management ordinance requires that developers reduce the drive-alone rate for their development to 10 percent below the average rate for the census tract in which their development sits. Although the ordinance applies only to new development and building expansions, by two years after adoption of the ordinance, citywide drive-alone rates had declined, even as the state of Massachusetts as a whole experienced increasing drive-alone rates.

- **London, United Kingdom**: In its first years since beginning in 2003, congestion pricing reduced the number of vehicle trips in central London by 17 percent and person delay per mile by 26 percent, though policy changes and street reallocations raised congestion levels in 2010.[5]

- **Lloyd District, Portland, Oregon**: Between 1997 and 2006, the drive-alone rate among all Lloyd District employees fell almost 29 percent, from 60 percent to 43 percent.

- **Portland, Oregon**: In 1975, the City of Portland set a cap of roughly 40,000 parking spaces downtown; the cap was later replaced with tight maximum parking requirements. City officials credit these limits with helping to increase downtown's transit-mode split from about 20 percent in the early 1970s to 48 percent in the mid-1990s.

- **San Francisco**: Employment in downtown San Francisco doubled between 1968 and 1984, while the number of cars traveling into the downtown stayed the same.

- **Vancouver, British Columbia**: As a deliberate transportation strategy, Vancouver tremendously increased housing capacity in the downtown area to reduce commuting times and congestion in what became known as the "living-first strategy." From 1991 to 2002, the number of residents living downtown increased by 62 percent, to 76,000, but car trips into downtown remained essentially constant. In 1994, walking and cycling trips made up 20 percent of all daily trips into the downtown and together made up the third-highest used mode, behind auto and transit trips. By 1999, walking and cycling accounted for 35 percent of all daily trips and are now the most frequently used modes.

These strategies can strongly affect the number of auto trips generated in your city, giving residents better alternatives to driving alone. For the most part, they are strategies that cities can implement on their own; by contrast, congestion pricing cannot be implemented without a change in state and/or federal law. These strategies are also likely to be a useful first step before any attempt to institute congestion pricing is made. Congestion pricing, several studies have suggested, is more likely to be accepted by the public when better alternatives to driving alone are provided; the other strategies recommended in this chapter are designed to do that.

The recommendations that follow could be implemented in different variations and could also be phased in over time. As shown in Figure 13-2, the results achieved will depend greatly on how widely the strategy is applied. In general, a strategy that is purely voluntary will attract some people; a strategy that creates new incentives for those who help reduce traffic will attract more people and have more effect; and a strategy that is required will affect all those who fall within the ambit of the requirement. Strategies can also generally be applied just to new development, or to both new developments and any land use that is seeking permission to expand, or to both existing development and new development. Because the amount of new development is, typically, fairly small compared to the buildings

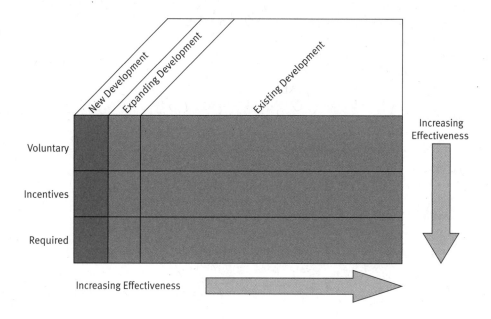

Voluntary

Incentives

Required

New Development

Expanding Development

Existing Development

Increasing Effectiveness

Increasing Effectiveness

Figure 13-2
Traffic reduction results depend on the scope of a measure. *Source: Nelson\ Nygaard.*

that already exist, applying strategies only to new development will affect only a tiny share of all development. Creating strategies that are applied to any site that seeks to expand (including both the new expansion and any existing buildings at the site) will expand the reach of a measure, and applying a strategy to all development, of course, will be the most effective.

Traffic Reduction: A How-To Guide

TDM seeks to reduce auto trips—and, it is hoped, vehicle miles traveled—by increasing travel options, by providing incentives to modify travel behavior, or by reducing the physical need to travel (through transportation-efficient land uses). TDM programs are usually implemented by public agencies or employers, or via public–private partnerships. The cumulative impact of a comprehensive set of TDM strategies can have a significant impact on travel behavior, system efficiency, and SOV rates. The strategies discussed in this chapter can reduce parking demand and traffic by more than 15 percent—sufficient to eliminate even the worst traffic congestion.

TDM strategies are some of the most cost-effective ways to allow new development in moderately dense areas without increasing traffic and parking demand or using costly supply-side methods, such as expanding roadway and parking capacity. In addition to financial savings, TDM programs can have other positive benefits, including reduced traffic congestion and air pollution, increased traffic safety, improved public health, and better urban design. The following chapter discusses, first, the regulatory framework under which a TDM program will be most effective; and, second, five TDM strategies that have proven successful in a wide variety of jurisdictions.

It is critical to mention that, for both political and practical implementation reasons, the success of TDM programs relies on the support of the private interests they affect. Good relations with the affected business community are important, because many of the most successful TDM strategies depend on the cooperation of developers and employers. Fortunately, developers and employers are generally comfortable complying with rules that improve the quality of life and regional competitiveness of the jurisdiction in which they are considering doing business, so long as they are provided some certainty as to what the rules are, they perceive regulations as being equal and fair, and any revenues generated are used to improve the business environment. In fact, most employers prefer to locate in a jurisdiction that is being proactive in addressing traffic congestion problems and investing in commute alternatives for their employees, because it increases their ability to attract and retain employees. In addition to the regulatory requirements discussed in the next section, there are three main reasons employers may choose to participate in TDM strategies:

- **Cost savings**. Many companies are finding that it costs less to pay employees not to drive than it does to provide them with free or cheap parking spaces. Offering cash to employees who choose not to drive alone to work can lead to significant reductions in parking acquisition and maintenance costs.

- **Employee attraction/retention**. Like free parking, many TDM strategies are essentially employee benefits that add to a company's appeal to potential and current employees. These benefits can also help hiring managers attract a broader range of job candidates, including working parents, students, or individuals without a car who require flexible schedules and commute options.

- **Tax incentives**. Transit subsidies can be deducted as a business expense. Pretax programs offer savings to employers as well as employees. When funds are removed from paychecks before taxes are applied, employers save on payroll taxes.

Make TDM the Law: Implement an Ordinance and Form TMAs

Although business community buy-in is important, voluntary compliance by individual companies can vary, so a TDM ordinance that includes enforcement mechanisms is important. Ultimately, legally requiring the implementation of a TDM program will benefit all stakeholders by ensuring ongoing vitality and competitiveness.

Perhaps the single most important feature of an effective TDM ordinance is mandatory membership in a Transportation Management Association (TMA). A TMA is an organization composed of representatives from an area affected by a TDM program. TMA membership should be mandatory for all new and existing employers and new commercial development, regardless of size, and overseen by a board consisting of key decisionmakers. All member employers should be required to pay an annual fee; conduct an annual employee transportation survey; and have a trained, on-site transportation coordinator to implement their TDM strategies.

TMA membership dues, combined with external revenue sources such as grants, should enable the TMA to be self-sustaining. The membership fees should be leveraged on either a per-employee or per-auto-trip basis. In the short term, jurisdictions can implement a per-employee fee to streamline immediate implementation; in the long term, a per-auto-trip fee would help achieve goals beyond merely programmatic funding by providing a financial incentive to employers to reduce trips, and would reward those employers that already have low auto trip volumes to their workplace. In either case, employers would be required to submit employee transportation survey data to measure success, monitor travel trends, and enforce program compliance.

The effectiveness of a TMA can—and should—be gauged through setting measurable program goals and expectations that are then evaluated, monitored, and enforced by the local government, which should be granted the ability to take on a greater role if the independent TMA fails to meet its goals. However, local government should play a broader role than simply serving as the enforcement arm of TDM programming: local policymakers should have *ex officio* representation on the TMA board, allowing the local government all rights of discussion, persuasion, and fiduciary responsibility in the oversight of the organization. This structure recognizes that the local government (1) is itself a major employer, (2) is a founding TMA member, (3) and has a successful TDM program that can serve as an example. But, because the local government must act as the enforcement arm for employers in the TMA, it should not be a full voting member, in order to balance the members' responsibilities.

To oversee TDM policies and programs, local governments should consider hiring a full-time transportation coordinator to manage implementation, monitoring, and enforcement of the overall program. The transportation coordinator should be accountable for achieving transportation-related goals envisioned for the area. In particular, this person should be in charge of implementing the preceding TDM recommendations, coordinating the activity of relevant municipal departments, and acting as liaison between the TMA board and staff, merchants, and residents' groups. As the city's liaison to the TMA, the transportation coordinator would also be in charge of collecting and analyzing results from an annual employee transportation survey of TMA members. The transportation coordinator should administer a similar survey for residential development, compiling and analyzing results for the annual report. This person would also be in charge of monitoring compliance and enforcing the requirements of the new TDM ordinance, including TMA membership, dues payment, annual surveys, and TDM programs.

TDM program requirements for residential development can be managed by the developer, property manager, and/or homeowners association contracting with a TMA, or through the transportation coordinator. Enforcement mechanisms include the permitting process (proof of compliance as a condition of approval, prior to issuing occupancy permits) and/or inclusion as a covenant compliance and restriction (CC&R) item.

TDM REGULATORY REQUIREMENTS TO CONSIDER

Once the regulatory and organizational framework provided by a TMA and TDM ordinance is established, localities have a substantial range of TDM strategies they can consider implementing. For example, in California, the City of Santa Monica requires employers to give cash payments to employees who do not drive; Menlo Park requires a cap on vehicle trips from some new developments; Mountain View has conditioned some new developments on the provision of free transit passes to employees; and Palo Alto requires bicycle facilities.

Every jurisdiction should carefully consider its own needs when adopting TDM strategies. As TDM programs grow and mature, jurisdictions should monitor the effectiveness of these programs, expand those that are successful, and implement new measures as needed. Broadly, however, there are five primary TDM programs universally successful enough that all jurisdictions should consider their implementation:

- Universal transit passes
- Parking cash-out
- Bicycle facility requirements
- Carsharing
- A transportation resource center[6]

CREATE UNIVERSAL TRANSIT PASSES AND REQUIRE THEM IN NEW DEVELOPMENT

In recent years, a growing number of transit agencies have teamed with universities, employers, developers, and even residential neighborhoods to provide universal transit passes. These passes typically allow unlimited rides on local or regional transit providers for low monthly fees, which are often absorbed entirely by the employer, school, or developer. This strategy serves to increase the transit mode share and reduce VMT, emissions, and congestion. This is the most basic form of financial incentive: making transit free for employees increases the likelihood that they will use it, especially if alternatives such as driving (and especially driving alone) continue to increase in cost.

The term *universal transit pass* has been used to refer to a broad range of transit programs. It is sometimes used to refer to regional pass programs, such as Metro's EZ Pass program in the Los Angeles region, which allows transit riders to purchase a pass that is good for passage on several different transit systems. It is also occasionally used to refer to electronic universal fare cards, such as the Transit Access Pass Program currently being tested by the Los Angeles MTA or the Clipper program in the San Francisco Bay Area. Both of these act as an "electronic purse," deducting fares for a number of different transit systems as the rider uses each system. The programs described here (offering deeply discounted transit passes to employers or residential developments in exchange for universal enrollment) should not be confused with these other programs.

Universal transit pass programs offer employers or residential developments the opportunity to purchase deeply discounted transit passes for their employees or residents on the condition that there is universal enrollment of all employees at a firm or all of the residences within a defined boundary (e.g., an apartment complex or a neighborhood). The principle of universal transit passes is similar to that of group insurance plans: Transit agencies can offer deep bulk discounts when selling passes to a large group, with universal enrollment, on the basis that not all those offered the pass will actually use it regularly. Employers, schools, and developers, in turn, are willing to absorb the costs because it can lower other costs like parking construction. For employees who drive, meanwhile, making existing transit free removes barriers to multimodal travel, effectively creating convenient park-and-ride shuttles to existing underused remote parking areas rather than parking in areas where it is already scarce.

Transit operators are usually supportive of universal transit passes, as such programs provide a stable source of income; increase transit ridership; and help improve cost recovery, reduce agency subsidy, and/or fund service improvements.

Universal transit pass programs can also benefit developers if implemented concurrently with reduced parking requirements, which consequently lower construction costs. Providing free transit passes for large developments constitutes an amenity that can help attract renters or home buyers as part of a lifestyle-oriented marketing campaign appealing to those seeking a "downtown lifestyle." Similarly, employers typically appreciate the program, which reduces demand for on-site parking and provides a tax-advantaged transportation benefit that can help recruit and retain employees.

Free transit passes are usually an extremely effective means to reduce the number of car trips in an area; reductions in car mode share of 4 percent to 22 percent have been documented, with an average reduction of 11 percent (see Table 13-1). By removing any cost barrier to using transit, including the need to search for spare change for each trip, people become much more likely to take transit to work or for nonwork trips. Universal transit pass programs are even more successful when passes are usable on transit systems throughout the region, rather than simply the city.

Many cities and institutions have found that trying to provide additional parking spaces costs much more than reducing parking demand by simply providing everyone with a free transit pass. For example, a study of UCLA's universal transit pass program found that a new parking space costs more than three times as much as a free transit pass ($223/month versus $71/month, respectively).

IMPLEMENTING UNIVERSAL TRANSIT PASS PROGRAMS

The critical first step in a successful universal transit pass program is to negotiate a bulk rate for the universal transit passes, to create a price structure that is at least revenue-neutral. For systems with a low mode share, the price for the passes can be quite low and still create revenue. (If huge jumps in transit ridership occur as a result of the program, the pass price can be revisited. In fact, if this occurred, it would

Table 13-1: Mode Shifts Achieved with Free Transit Passes

Location	Drive to Work		Transit to Work	
Municipalities	*Before*	*After*	*Before*	*After*
Santa Clara (VTA)[7]	76%	60%	11%	27%
Bellevue, Washington[8]	81%	57%	13%	18%
Universities				
UCLA (faculty and staff)[9]	46%	42%	8%	13%
Univ. of Washington, Seattle[10]	33%	24%	21%	36%
Univ. of British Columbia[11]	68%	57%	26%	38%
Univ. of Wisconsin, Milwaukee[12]	54%	41%	12%	26%
Colorado Univ. Boulder (students)[13]	43%	33%	4%	7%

Source: White et al., "Impacts of an Employer-Based Transit Pass Program: The Go Pass in Ann Arbor, Michigan."

probably create more benefits than downsides.) This negotiation can be led by a TMA and/or the city transportation coordinator. This negotiation should be a top priority, as other requirements depend on negotiation of an appropriate bulk price.

After a bulk rate is negotiated, it is important to the success of the program to require provision of universal transit passes to all residents and employees in the TMA or in certain areas as defined in the TDM ordinance. For occupant-owned residential units, ongoing funding for this expense could be provided through condominium or homeowners association dues, and/or by neighborhoods (as in Boulder, CO, and Santa Clara, CA, for example). For renter-occupied residential units, the property owner or manager could be responsible for collecting money for the passes through rent.

For employers, the transit pass program could be paid for by employers, managed through the partnership with the TMA, or funded through grants from environmental, public health, and transit sources (note, though, that grants usually fund pilot projects).

REQUIRE PARKING CASH-OUT

Parking cash-out is a program by which employers who offer free or reduced-price parking to their employees are required to offer an equal transportation fringe benefit to employees who use modes other than driving alone to get to work. These employees could use this money to purchase transit passes, cover carpooling expenses, or simply take the cash as additional take-home salary (if they walk to work or telecommute, for example). Essentially, parking cash-out programs ensure that all commute modes are subsidized equally and thus create incentives for commuters to carpool, take transit, and bike or walk to work.

The numerous benefits of parking cash-out include:

- Providing an equal transportation subsidy to employees who ride transit, carpool, vanpool, walk, or bicycle to work. The benefit is particularly valuable to low-income employees, who are less likely to drive to work alone.

- Providing a low-cost fringe benefit that can help individual businesses recruit and retain employees.

- Establishing a system of requirements that are simple to administer and enforce, typically requiring just one to two minutes per employee per month to administer.

In addition to these benefits, and perhaps most importantly, parking cash-out programs are proven to reduce auto congestion and parking demand. Numerous studies show that, even in suburban locations with little or no transit, financial incentives can substantially reduce parking demand. On average, a financial incentive of $70 per month reduced parking demand by more than 25 percent (see Table 13-2).

Many U.S. employers provide free or reduced-price parking (i.e., a subsidized price below lease costs and well below the full costs to build, operate, and maintain the parking) for their employees as a fringe benefit. Under a parking cash-out program, employers could either:

1. Subsidize all modes equally by continuing to offer subsidized parking on the condition that they offer the cash value of the parking subsidy to any employee who does not drive to work, ideally either as a tax-deductible transit/vanpool

Table 13-2: Effect of Financial Incentives on Parking Demand

Location	Scope of Study	Financial Incentive per Month (1995 $)	Decrease in Parking Demand
Group A: Areas with little public transportation			
Century City, CA[14]	3,500 employees at 100+ firms	$81	15%
Cornell University, NY[15]	9,000 faculty and staff	$34	26%
San Fernando Valley, CA[16]	1 large employer (850 employees)	$37	30%
Bellevue, WA[17]	1 medium-size firm (430 employees)	$54	39%
Costa Mesa, CA[18]	State Farm Insurance employees	$37	22%
Average		$49	26%
Group B: Areas with fair public transportation			
Los Angeles Civic Center[19]	10,000+ employees, several firms	$125	36%
Mid-Wilshire Blvd, LA[20]	1 mid-sized firm	$89	38%
Washington, D.C., suburbs[21]	5,500 employees at 3 worksites	$68	26%
Downtown Los Angeles[22]	5,000 employees at 118 firms	$126	25%
Average		$102	31%
Group C: Areas with good public transportation			
University of Washington[23]	50,000 faculty, staff and students	$18	24%
Downtown Ottawa[24]	3,500+ government staff	$72	18%
Average		$102	31%
Overall Average		$67	27%

subsidy, or a taxable carpool/walk/bike subsidy, equal to the value of the parking subsidy; or

2. Discontinue all subsidies by charging employees market rates to park.

Employees who opt to cash out their parking subsidies would not be eligible to receive subsidized parking from their employer, but could still drive to work sometimes if they paid the market-rate charges for parking.

The administrative and out-of-pocket costs to employers of parking cash-out are typically minimal. If an employer complies with parking cash-out by eliminating parking subsidies for employees who drive, it simply charges daily market-value rates (the current per-space lease rate) or daily cost-recovery rates (the cost to build, operate, and maintain the parking) with no monthly discount rate, which puts no additional financial burden on the employer and in fact saves it the money spent on employee parking. Employers wishing to continue to provide a parking subsidy to their employees simply must also provide an equivalent subsidy to nondriving employees.

Providing subsidies for nonparking employees is more expensive for employers in terms of out-of-pocket costs, but initial start-up costs could be reduced by using revenues from mandatory TMA membership dues (the per-employee-based dues paid by employers to the TMA), city parking revenues, or other city or TMA funds during a predefined and limited initial start-up period.

IMPLEMENTING PARKING CASH-OUT: REGULATION
In some places, parking cash-out is already required by law. Under California's "Parking Cash-Out" law, for instance, employers with fifty or more employees who

lease their parking and do not pass the full cost on to employees must provide an equivalent subsidy to employees who do not park. However, the law is not enforced at the state level, and thus it is up to local jurisdictions to enforce the program.

In areas where cash-out enforcement is left to localities, and where allowed under state law, local governments should adopt legislation that extends state parking cash-out requirements to all employers that provide free or reduced-price parking to their employees. Such an ordinance would simply require that any employer that provides subsidized parking to one or more of its employees must provide all its employees with the option to "cash out" their employee parking by taking the cash value or partial cash value of the parking subsidy. To establish the value of parking, the ordinance should define the market value of parking using the most recent estimate of the cost to add additional parking spaces to the city, including both the opportunity costs of land, and the cost to build, operate, and maintain parking itself.

To protect residential neighborhoods adjacent to major employers from potential parking spillover problems (caused by employees who may take the parking cash-out option but then drive to work and park on residential streets), local governments should implement the parking recommendations for residential districts discussed in Chapter 10.

EDUCATION AND ENFORCEMENT

To maximize compliance with and engagement in parking cash-out programs, local governments should conduct thorough, proactive education campaigns, teaching local employers about state and local cash-out laws and about how employers are affected. Such outreach programs, which can be implemented through the mechanisms of the TMA, encourage a cooperative, rather than antagonistic, relationship between those subject to the TDM requirements and those responsible for enforcing them.

Several local jurisdictions have developed enforcement mechanisms to enforce parking cash-out requirements. For example, Santa Monica, California, requires proof of compliance with the state's parking cash-out law before it will issue occupancy permits for new commercial development. Los Angeles is currently developing a parking cash-out program, including an ordinance that would allow the city council to enforce parking cash-out, and revision of the 2007 city tax forms to gather employer-leased parking information through annual tax submission.

Another available enforcement mechanism is to require employers to provide proof of compliance (via an affidavit signed by a company officer) at the same time that they receive/renew their business licenses or pay their annual business taxes. This method ensures that all employers are in compliance with parking cash-out requirements on an ongoing basis, rather than limiting proof of compliance to one-time enforcement for employers occupying new or renovated commercial buildings.

REQUIRE EXCELLENT BICYCLE FACILITIES

Bicycling is often an underutilized form of transportation. Especially in places with temperate weather and level topography, there is a great deal of potential to raise the use of bicycling as a primary mode of transportation for both residents and employees. It is worth investigating the usefulness of a revision of development standards to require provision of bicycle storage, showers, and lockers as part of development agreements to meet the following adopted goals:

- Ensure the provision of an adequate and secure supply of bicycle parking facilities at likely destinations such as transportation centers, park-and-ride lots, public institutions and major community facilities, multifamily housing, and employment centers.

- Encourage the provision of showers, clothes lockers, and other storage facilities at destinations where practical and economically feasible.

- Promote the use of bicycles for recreation, commuting, shopping, and other purposes through education, enforcement, and incentive programs.

IMPLEMENTING BICYCLE FACILITY REQUIREMENTS

Localities should consider revising development standards to include bicycle facility requirements so that both new residential and new nonresidential developments have secure, well-lit, visible, preferably ground-floor bicycle parking for both occupants and visitors. Additionally, nonresidential developments should have changing facilities with showers and lockers, and should prohibit restrictions on bringing bicycles into buildings.

General guidelines for bicycle parking requirements, as established by the American Planning Association in its *Bicycle Facility Planning Report*,[25] include recommendations that:

- Office and government buildings allocate 10 percent of the number of automobile spaces as bike facility space.

- Movie theaters, restaurants, and many other uses provide 5 percent to 10 percent of the number of automobile spaces.

As part of the TDM ordinance, development standards should be revised to include requirements for bicycle facilities and programs, including some or all of the following:

- Bicycle parking to accommodate 10 percent mode share

- Subsidies for bicycling

- Showers and lockers

- Bicycle safety classes and other bicycle programs

For more detail, see Chapter 7, "Bicycles."

PROMOTE CARSHARING

Carsharing is a hassle-free way to rent cars by the hour, eliminating the fixed costs of driving. The result is that carshare members significantly reduce their vehicle trips, while at the same time maintaining all the mobility they want.

For detail on how cities can make carsharing work as part of their overall traffic reduction strategies, see Chapter 11, "Carsharing."

CREATE A TRANSPORTATION RESOURCE CENTER

None of the TDM methods outlined in this chapter will be effective if those covered by the TDM ordinance do not understand how to make full use of them; education and outreach are therefore critical components of any comprehensive TDM program. One way to help facilitate the dissemination of information about TDM programs is to establish a Transportation Resource Center, which is a storefront office that provides personalized, comprehensive travel information about carpool matching, transit routes and schedules, pretax transit passes, bicycle routes, and other transportation options. The Transportation Resource Center would first and foremost provide "one-stop shopping" for new and existing employees and residents to get information on transportation options and services available to them.

Establishing a Transportation Resource Center that provides a wide array of individualized transportation resources to employees, residents, and visitors can be a key component to help reduce auto congestion downtown. This kind of personalized transportation planning has shown significant results in shifting trips from driving alone to other modes.

It is worth noting that outreach need not be limited to the confines of the Transportation Resource Center: social marketing and incentive programs are proving increasingly popular and effective at promoting non-SOV travel. *Social marketing* seeks to influence individuals' behavior to achieve a broad social good (in the case of TDM, reducing drive-alone trips). Awareness and educational programs, workshops, and community outreach efforts may take the form of promotional campaigns similar to product advertising. Incentive programs build on this marketing effort to frame nonmotorized and high-occupancy travel as a social norm, by offering prizes or cash rewards to residents who use non-SOV modes.

IMPLEMENTING THE TRANSPORTATION RESOURCE CENTER

Localities should consider establishing a Transportation Resource Center in a central storefront. It could be in an existing city building, such as in space shared with a public library or other government-run facility. Most importantly, it must be in a high-visibility, convenient location to ensure its use. The city's Transportation Coordinator would manage the public interface working out of the Transportation Resource Center.

The center could also house the Transportation and Parking Benefit District staff (see Chapter 10, "Parking," for more information), and could take responsibility for administering and actively marketing all demand management programs. The TMA could remain the administrator of most TDM programs, depending on the arrangement reached between the local government and the current TMA for implementation of the new TDM ordinance.

Price Your Way Out of Congestion: The Most Powerful TDM

All of the strategies discussed so far will be highly effective in reducing vehicle trips, but they will not necessarily have any impact on congestion, because of induced demand. That is, as you reduce vehicle trips in one part of the transportation system, you thereby encourage new auto trips in another part. If you want to reduce trips *and* eliminate congestion, you need to put a price on congestion. There are various ways to price congestion, all of them controversial:

- Make more of the fixed costs of driving (auto purchase, insurance, parking, etc.) variable, by promoting carsharing, pay-as-you-drive insurance, parking cash-out, and so on.

- Increase the variable costs of driving to the point where congestion diminishes, using tools such as higher fuel taxes or parking charges.

- Price congestion directly, through variable roadway tolls, either at a specific cordon line or on a per-mile basis.

A toll ring or *cordon* around a city's downtown or other natural edges is likely to be the single most successful strategy to reduce traffic within a city's most congested segments. Results from Singapore, Oslo, London, and Stockholm show how effective roadway pricing can be, at both reducing congestion and raising the necessary funds to expand the total capacity of a city's transportation network by improving walking, bicycling, and transit. In the United States, cordon pricing has been considered but not yet implemented in New York and San Francisco, among other cities, and a limited form of congestion pricing has been implemented in the form of high-occupancy toll or HOT lanes on freeways in several cities.

Cordon pricing has proven controversial, however, for a variety of reasons:

- **Economic impacts.** There is a perceived risk, and potentially a very real risk, that your city acting alone, outside a larger regional strategy, could put itself at an economic disadvantage compared to neighboring cities. In other words, if a shopper has to pay $5 to drive to your city, but it's free to drive to the next city over, you may hurt your local economy while doing nothing effective to address regional traffic congestion.

- **Legal issues.** For a congestion pricing charge to be levied in many U.S. cities, state legislation would be required.

- **Lack of transit alternatives**. One of the core objectives of most cordon pricing strategies is to improve transit services both within and connecting to the congestion pricing zone (both by providing funding for improvements as well as reducing the congestion impeding surface transit). However, a certain "chicken-and-egg" phenomenon exists in most U.S. cities, which do not provide a level of transit service commensurate with that found in international cities where cordon pricing has been successfully implemented.

- **Freedom of the road.** American culture is full of longing for the "open road." Indeed, the U.S. Supreme Court has interpreted the privileges and immunities clause of the Constitution to guarantee citizens' right to travel among the fifty states.[26] Many Americans, however, seem to equate the right to move freely about with the privilege to move free of any direct cost (that is, we should pay for our roads indirectly, through taxes, rather than directly through user fees).

- **"Something-for-nothingism."** As David Brooks of the *New York Times*[27] and others have written about extensively, there is a long-standing tendency in American politics for citizens to demand government services without having to pay for them—and for American politicians to promise this sort of wish fulfillment.

- **Privacy.** Modern approaches to cordon pricing do not establish toll booths around entrances to the city. Rather, they use license-plate recognition cameras and software to identify vehicles and charge against accounts established for those vehicles. Vehicles without accounts are sent a bill or are fined. Although these approaches make payment easy and eliminate the clutter and obstruction of toll-booths, they also raise privacy concerns among civil libertarians. Should government be able to track where its citizens are driving? Could such information be used in civil court, for example, to help demonstrate marital infidelity?

- **Equity.** Opponents of roadway pricing have derisively called HOT lanes "Lexus lanes," claiming that only the rich will be able to afford to pay roadway charges. In general, however, strategies that shift resources from support for driving to support for transit and other modes that are less expensive to use tend to be equitable by their very nature. Figure 13-3 breaks down the share of person trips by income level.

Congestion-Based Parking Pricing: A Better Approach?

The political obstacles to roadway pricing may be insurmountable in your community, but there may be a politically acceptable, yet effective, alternative. At the same time as it was studying roadway pricing, San Francisco implemented a plan to price parking as a tool for congestion management. That is, instead of pricing the trip itself, price the trip *end*. The idea is that motorists may be uncomfortable with roadway charges, but they intuitively accept parking fees. Parking, after all, is tangible: parking lots and garages take up developable land, and someone has to build and maintain them. Roads, like parks and schools, seem more in the public domain, a common resource that should be free to everyone.

San Francisco's federally funded program is called "SFpark," and it comprises several program elements:

- New parking meters that accept credit cards, debit cards, and payment by cell phone.

- In-pavement parking sensors that wirelessly network with each other and provide real-time data on parking space availability. This data is made available free to software developers.

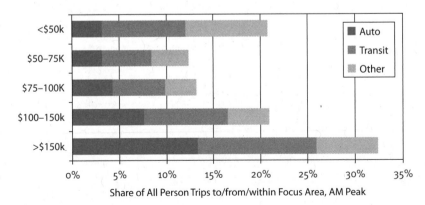

Figure 13-3
Income levels and mode of travel in downtown San Francisco. *Source: San Francisco Mobility, Access and Pricing Study, 2010, SFCTA.*

- Market-based and adjustable pricing of parking to ensure adequate parking availability at all times.

- A massive database to track utilization patterns over time, including the first census of all parking spaces in the city.

A key goal of the pilot phase is to eliminate the approximately 30 percent of traffic on city streets that consists of motorists driving around in circles trying to find an empty parking space[28]—thus the project motto "Circle Less, Live More." The project also hopes to make travel by foot, bicycle, and transit easier, in part by reducing auto congestion. More importantly, the project wants to increase economic development in the city by improving the perception of parking availability for shoppers.

To help achieve the right level of parking availability, SFpark will periodically adjust meter pricing up or down to match demand. Demand-responsive pricing encourages drivers to park in underused areas and garages, reducing demand in overused areas. With SFpark, real-time data and demand-responsive pricing work together to readjust parking patterns in the city so that parking is easier to find.

SFpark is testing its new parking management system at 6,000 of San Francisco's 25,000 metered spaces and 12,250 spaces in 15 of 20 city-owned parking garages. The pilot phase of SFpark will run through 2012.

In future phases, SFpark could use its adjustable pricing system to increase the price of parking for motorists who arrive or depart during peak congestion times. If it cost commuters twice as much to arrive at a parking space between 8:00 a.m. and 9:00 a.m. weekdays, would some arrive earlier, before the congested period, or would they choose to take transit instead? If leaving a garage during the evening peak hours cost shoppers an extra $4.00 compared to staying in the city another hour, would some shoppers grab a bite to eat and wait for the congestion period to be over? Cities around the world are eagerly awaiting San Francisco's data on motorists' price sensitivity and acceptance of such policies.

Chapter 14

Measuring Success

Transportation is not an end in itself, but rather a means by which we support a community's larger goals and aspirations. To determine the degree to which transportation investments support these goals, transportation professionals use *performance measures*, also known as *performance indicators* or *measures of success*. If it hopes to move toward sustainability, a community's transportation performance indicators must reflect all the ways the transportation system supports sustainability. This chapter explains how to ensure that your community's performance indicators reflect its sustainability policies.

Definitions

Before beginning a discussion of performance indicators, we should first define terms:

- **Goals** are self-evident public goods, something that everyone can agree is a common aspiration. They represent statements of purpose, describing long-term desired outcomes for the transportation system to support and implement a larger vision. They might not ever be achieved, but a successful campaign could be based around them. Example: Achieve world peace.

- **Objectives** describe something we want to achieve in support of a larger, long-term goal. Objectives are measurable. Example: Create a nuclear nonproliferation agreement between the United States and the Soviet Union.

- **Actions** are tasks or strategies that can be assigned, along with matching deadlines, to work toward achieving an objective. Example: Secretary of State to reserve Camp David in May.

- **Performance measurements** help determine the degree to which a goal or objective is being met. Performance measurements work best when they are quantitative, but success for many objectives must be judged qualitatively. Some measurements can be used to predict the future, as part of an evaluation process using *forecasted* data, while other measures can be used to monitor changes based on actual empirical or *observed* data. In both cases, the measurements can be done at a system level, corridor level, and/or project level, to provide the planners with a basis for evaluating alternatives, making decisions on future transportation investments, and monitoring progress over time. Example: Percent reduction in number of intercontinental ballistic missiles.

- **Targets** or *benchmarks* are performance thresholds; performance measurements reveal whether the targets have been hit. Often, targets vary by date. Example: Reduce the number of intercontinental ballistic missiles by 10 percent in 1980 and 25 percent in 1990.

- **Evaluation criteria** are performance measures that are tailored to help planners decide between one thing and another. In transportation analyses, they are used to prioritize investments or select one technology over another in a given corridor or for a specific project. Evaluation criteria are often used together, with some criteria weighted more heavily than others.

- **Screening criteria** are a short set of evaluation criteria used to reduce the number of potential projects that move forward to more detailed evaluation.

How Performance Measures Are Used

Performance measures are embedded deep in the DNA of transportation decision-making. They are used in many ways:

- To determining the optimal number of travel lanes on a specific street, balancing motorist versus pedestrian delay

- To manage intersection operations, including signal cycle length, transit prioritization, and pedestrian phasing, among other thing

- To give guidance on the degree of dedicated infrastructure provided to specific modes on specific streets, such as when a cycle track or bus-only lane is appropriate

- To establish an optimal street network, balancing the needs of all modes of transportation

- To prioritize the funding and phasing of projects

- As a basis for determining which transit routes should be subject to review for needed improvements

- In reporting to municipal authorities on progress made toward accomplishing goals and objectives

How Performance Measures Are Misused

Paradise LOSt: How Overreliance on Auto LOS Harms Cities

In the United States, the most deeply rooted flaw in transportation decisionmaking is overreliance on a single transportation performance measure: Auto Level of Service (LOS), particularly when focused on intersections. There are several methodologies for calculating LOS, and the methods vary by context. The most typical measure, from the Transportation Research Board's *Highway Capacity Manual 2000*, focuses on delays that typical motorists are projected to experience at signalized intersections (see Table 14-1). This tool uses a variety of basic data, including the number of vehicles turning, the arrangement of travel lanes at the intersection, and how the traffic signal timing is set. Designers may then make adjustments according to a long list of factors, including travel lane width, share of large trucks, grade, land-use context, and the presence of pedestrians. After running this data through

Table 14-1: Automobile Levels of Service

Level of Service (LOS)	Average Vehicle Control Delay (Seconds)	Description
A	< 10.0	Free Flow/Insignificant Delays: No approach phase is fully utilized by traffic and no vehicle waits longer than one red indication.
B	10.1–20.0	Stable Operation/Minimal Delays: An occasional approach phase is fully utilized. Many drivers begin to feel somewhat restricted within platoons of vehicles.
C	20.1–35.0	Stable Operation/Acceptable Delays: Major approach phases fully utilized. Most drivers feel somewhat restricted.
D	35.1–55.0	Approaching Unstable/Tolerable Delays: Drivers may have to wait through more than one red signal indication. Queues may develop but dissipate rapidly, without excessive delays.
E	55.1–80.0	Unstable Operation/Significant Delays: Volumes at or near capacity. Vehicles may wait through several signal cycles. Long queues form upstream from intersection.
F	> 80	Forced Flow/Excessive Delays: Represents jammed conditions. Intersection operates below capacity with low volumes. Queues may block upstream intersections.

Source: Transportation Research Board, *Highway Capacity Manual 2000.*

a complex formula, one gets an output that is a ratio of the volume of cars in the intersection compared to the capacity of that intersection. This ratio of volume to capacity is then converted to seconds of delay, using a variety of other adjustment factors. An LOS score is then assigned based on the chart in Table 14-1.

The *Highway Capacity Manual* also provides a formula for measuring Auto LOS for entire streets, not just for intersections. Its "Urban Street LOS" focuses on the difference between free-flow vehicle speed in the best conditions versus actual average speed in the whole corridor, including total delay due to red lights, stop signs, and congestion. For example, on a street where cars would go 30 mph under the best of conditions, but average only 16 mph due to stoplights and congestion, the Urban Street LOS would be C. If the designer better synchronizes the traffic lights and improves average speed to 26 mph, then the Urban Street LOS rises to A. Because it looks at the entire street and focuses on what motorists really care about—how long it takes to get from point A to point B—Urban Street LOS is more useful than Intersection LOS, but is much less used because it is more difficult to calculate.

Evaluating a Development Project's Traffic Impact

Statewide environmental analysis requirements, state traffic "concurrency standards," and local traffic impact guidelines routinely require engineers to estimate a development project's impact on nearby traffic. On its face, that may be all well and good, but because most traffic analyses are essentially a legal disclosure tool, the courts have tended to interpret transportation analyses conservatively, typically considering worst-case-scenario impacts rather than *likely* impacts. More importantly, they have tended to ignore the different travel characteristics of transit-oriented and mixed-use development (TOD and MUD), and the trip reduction effects of Transportation Demand Management (TDM) programs, unless there is a preponderance of local data to support different conclusions. Lead agencies are often reluctant to deviate from conventional practice, either because of the costs of collecting local data or, more commonly, because of the time and expense of the lawsuits that seem inevitably to result from changes to conventional practice. The consequences of this conservative approach are significant:

- **Vehicle trips are overestimated**. Typically, traffic analyses require planners to assume that vehicle trip generation rates at TODs are the same as in auto-dependent development. Lead agencies typically use the Institute of Transportation Engineers' *Trip Generation* for estimating trips for all development contexts. As noted in the *Trip Generation* users' manual, however, the data therein was collected largely at isolated, single-use locations, lacking in transit or pedestrian accommodations. Although the users' manual advises that trip rates be adjusted for mixed-use and transit-oriented development, no guidance is provided on how to make such adjustments. As noted in many studies,[1] TODs typically generate half the vehicle trips that would be predicted by the ITE manual.

- **Only local congestion is examined**. Traffic analyses typically consider traffic congestion in the immediate vicinity of the project, not downstream effects or effects on the regional transportation network.

- **Transportation impacts to cars are emphasized while impacts to people, transit, bicyclists, and other modes are ignored**. For example, a bus rapid transit or bicycle lane project that reduces vehicle capacity is typically assumed to have negative transportation impacts because it reduces capacity for cars, while the net benefits for the movement of people are ignored.

- **"Last project in" faces disproportionate burden.** Although a long history of developments may have contributed to a localized traffic congestion problem, only the project that pushes LOS across an arbitrary threshold is deemed to have had a "significant" impact. Projects that stay just under the threshold are not required to contribute anything toward mitigation; thus, a 10,000-home development may bring traffic from LOS A to LOS C, but be considered to have had "no impact." Another 10,000-home development may bring traffic from LOS C to LOS E, again with "no impact." But the last 20-home infill development that trips the LOS rating from E to F is faced with a finding of significant impact, and is required to do something to mitigate that impact.

- **Mitigations worsen the problem**. Most importantly, projects are given limited opportunities to mitigate significant negative traffic impacts. Specifically, they are usually encouraged to choose one or more of the following options, most of which do nothing to improve the situation:

  - **Widen roads**. When roads are widened, streets are typically made more hostile to pedestrians, bicyclists, and transit, because of increased vehicle speeds and pedestrian crossing distances. When vehicle trip generation is overestimated, roads are widened to a greater degree than appropriate, resulting in excess vehicle capacity that in turn induces increased vehicle demand. This mitigation method thus exacerbates the very problem it was intended to solve.

- **Reduce density**. Reducing the density of a project may reduce the total number of local vehicle trips, but at the same time it typically increases the total vehicle trip *rate*. Over time, this results in two effects: (1) Development is spread out, resulting in higher vehicle miles traveled (VMT) and a greater spread of congestion; and (2) per capita VMT is also increased, resulting in higher overall levels of traffic and decreases in air quality.

- **Move the project to a more isolated location**. Because most traffic analyses focus on local impacts rather than regional impacts, moving the project to a more isolated greenfield location produces fewer negative traffic impacts than an infill project in a location that already has some traffic. Again, this results in worsened regional traffic and has air-quality implications.

- **Implement Transportation Demand Management**. TDM programs are an option for reducing traffic impacts, yet the courts and lead agencies have historically been suspicious of such measures: How will we know for certain if they will work? What happens if there is an exceedance? As a result, despite the abundant data on the trip-reduction effects of TDM, even the most effective TDM programs are often ignored or awarded only minor discounts from the auto trip rate.

Taken together, these barriers tend to make it easier to build low-density, auto-dependent projects at the urban edge, and more difficult to do pedestrian-oriented infill projects near transit. In other words, compliance with transportation analysis conventions has tended to result in greater per capita VMT, greater regional congestion, worsened air quality, and increased carbon dioxide emissions.

SOLVING THE PROBLEM

Auto LOS is a useful measure, but it is dangerous when used excessively or inappropriately, without considering the larger implications. There are many ways in which cities can put Auto LOS in the right context.

EXEMPT CERTAIN INTERSECTIONS

San Jose and Livermore, California, realized that no matter what they did, there would always be traffic congestion in their downtowns. For Livermore, much of the traffic congestion was caused by trips without an origin or destination in the city, so Livermore could have stopped all development downtown and still have been stuck with congestion. Rather than letting cut-through traffic get in the way of the city's downtown economic development vision, the city simply accepted an LOS rating of F on its downtown streets—a choice that allowed the city to rebuild its main street with wider sidewalks and build a spectacular performing arts center without worrying about the traffic implications for cut-through drivers. San Jose took a similar approach. Other cities, like Santa Monica, have recognized that it is necessary to choose where congestion goes, locating it in places that have the least negative impact on retailers and neighborhood quality of life. Cities can not only accept LOS F at congestion chokepoints, but can also establish minimum thresholds of congestion in such locations.

EXEMPT TYPES OF PROJECTS

It is possible for most cities and transportation agencies to ignore the traffic impacts of certain types of projects, including transportation projects such as bike lanes and bus rapid transit, or developments such as affordable housing or local-serving retail. In California, transit-oriented development projects that meet specific criteria are exempt from traffic analysis under the state's environmental analysis laws.

COMPARE ALTERNATIVE LOCATIONS

Say your city wants to build a new city maintenance yard, and the traffic analysis says the trucks pulling out of the yard in the morning will create some traffic congestion. Rather than killing the project, shouldn't the analysis ask whether the proposed location for the yard works better or worse than alternate locations? After all, the city needs a maintenance yard. The same approach can be used for housing or commercial development. If there is market demand for new housing in your city, the demand is going to go somewhere. Building it in an infill location near transit may result in some traffic congestion, but likely less congestion than if the demand were pushed to a more isolated location within your city—or at the region's edge three cities over.

PROVIDE LOS FOR OTHER MODES

So, your project's traffic analysis says the project will result in an Intersection LOS E for cars, and the city says you need to mitigate that. But what if your mitigations just make everything worse for pedestrians, cyclists, and transit? It can be useful to have LOS indicators and thresholds for all modes (see the next section), so that traffic-mitigation efforts don't just produce more traffic by making it impossible to walk, bike, or ride the bus.

LOOK AT PERSON DELAY RATHER THAN VEHICLE DELAY

Intersection LOS looks only at the delay that vehicles experience. Therefore, in the analysis, a person driving alone in a car is valued forty times more than each of the forty people sitting in a bus in the adjacent lane. Pedestrians waiting to cross at the light are ignored entirely in the Auto LOS equation. So, rather than measuring vehicle delay, perhaps your city could measure *person* delay. Person delay is especially useful when setting signal timing or investing in transit priority treatments.

SUBSTITUTE WITH AUTO TRIPS GENERATED

A more holistic approach was being pursued in San Francisco at the time this book was published. The Auto Trips Generated (ATG) approach followed from a court-imposed injunction on the city's 2005 bike plan, which resulted from a citizen lawsuit. The lawsuit alleged that the city failed to do a thorough environmental analysis of the bike plan, as required under the California Environmental Quality Act (CEQA). CEQA requires that the traffic impacts of potential projects be analyzed and mitigations identified; the bike plan proposed eliminating some general travel lanes on city streets in order to stripe bike lanes in some locations. The courts agreed with the plaintiffs, and forbade all bicycle projects in San Francisco—including installing bike racks or restriping streets that had very little traffic—for 4 years, until an environmental review was complete and certified. The Environmental Impact Report (EIR), which ran to some 2,200 pages, unsurprisingly concluded that bicycle lanes generally do not have a negative impact on the environment. The analysis cost close to $1 million and took 2 years of staff time to complete—more than most of the bicycle projects in the plan combined.[2]

To avoid having to repeat the wasteful bike plan EIR, the city proposed changes to its traffic analysis criteria and thresholds. The proposal was as follows:

First, the plan is to take a citywide approach to measuring traffic and mitigating it, rather than looking at one project and one intersection at a time.

Because there is traffic congestion throughout San Francisco's street network, any project that adds a single vehicle trip would be determined to have a significant traffic impact. Projects that do not add vehicle trips, such as a rail line, bike lane, or sidewalk widening, would not be considered to have any traffic impact, even if the project reduced vehicle capacity.

To mitigate their traffic impacts, projects would pay a fee. To determine the fee, the city looked at its expected 20 years' worth of growth and created a comprehensive transportation plan to accommodate that growth, including new rail extensions, Safe Routes to Schools programs, TDM, bus frequency improvements, and so on. It then looked at the cost of these improvements and the financial resources that were likely available. Subtracting these costs, the city took the balance and allocated it across all new development in the form of an impact fee. By paying this impact fee, all projects would automatically mitigate their transportation impacts over time.

The process is fairly straightforward and in keeping with both environmental analysis and existing law. Transportation advocates have been highly supportive because they get the funding they need for their favorite projects. Developers have been supportive because they get to avoid the unpredictable and time-consuming traffic analysis process. For developers, uncertainty is risk and risk is cost: They would rather spend a certain $500,000 in impact fees than spend $200,000 in traffic consultant fees, plus two or three years of painful hearings and administrative processes. More importantly, the city is happy because it gets to pursue a systematic set of solutions to its transportation problems, rather than attempt piecemeal mitigations for individual projects as they arise.

SUBSTITUTE WITH PER CAPITA VEHICLE MILES TRAVELED

Another approach is to drop Auto LOS and replace it with per capita VMT. Like Auto Trips Generated, this approach looks at traffic holistically across the region, rather than at individual intersections. Rather than trying to accommodate traffic, this measure seeks to locate, shape, and manage development projects so that they result in the lowest possible rate of driving.

For example, your traffic analysis criteria and thresholds could be replaced with the following questions:

- Would the project result in an increase in VMT per household or per capita that is the lower of either:
  - 14,000 VMT per year per household, or
  - 70 percent of the per-household or per capita average VMT for the local jurisdiction?

- Is the project consistent with a plan adopted by an applicable state or regional agency, county, municipality, or air district, or a mayor's or governor's executive order, to reduce VMT or greenhouse gas emissions?

    Such wording has the following advantages:

- By focusing on *per capita* vehicle trips rather than *total* vehicle trips, we can identify *all* projects that put a disproportionate burden on our regional transportation systems and air quality, not just the large projects.

- Because it is based on average trip generation in the surrounding community, it does not exhibit an unfair bias for urban sites and against all rural and suburban sites. Rather, the question asks whether the project does better or worse than would be expected for the surrounding context.

- More importantly, it would no longer be possible to widen a road or reduce the size of the project to mitigate the transportation impact. Instead, the project applicant must reduce the project's trip rate, by moving the project to a more transit-friendly location, by mixing land uses, by imposing TDM programs, or by investing in pedestrian, bicycle, or transit improvements.

Measuring Success for Multiple Modes

All modes of transportation contribute toward the success of the transportation system, so sustainable cities need tools for measuring the success of each mode, and for balancing success between competing modes when there is not enough space to accommodate everything.

    LOS measures are used for each mode to describe that mode's contribution toward the efficiency of the transportation network. Alternatively, quality of service (QOS) measures might be used to describe the effectiveness of each mode from the users' perspective. Depending upon the design issue, various measures may be selected from those listed in Table 14-2 to judge the effectiveness of the design. More detailed options for measuring the success of each mode can be found in the respective mode's chapters.

Using Performance Measures to Balance Modes

The most difficult task of a street designer is deciding to what degree to inconvenience one mode in order to benefit another, particularly given a narrow street width. When is it OK to eliminate a parking lane in order to stripe a bike lane? Should a general-purpose travel lane be replaced with a bus-only lane? Can we eliminate the left-turn pockets in order to widen the sidewalk? Typically, such questions are answered through the political process, with the loudest advocates of a particular mode winning.

    Advocates for nonauto modes may complain that their city's traffic engineers care only about cars. The truth, however, is that nearly every city's transportation *performance measures* care only about cars, and the engineers have no technical

Table 14-2: Common Performance Measures

Mode	Performance Measures
Pedestrians	Sidewalk crowding (at rail stations or other major destinations)
	Average crossing delay, including average distance to crossing
	Frequency of protected crossings
	Percentage active building edge along sidewalk
	Percent sidewalk shaded
	Average block perimeter
Transit	Intersection delay
	Corridor travel time as percentage of speed limit
	On-time performance (schedule or headway adherence)
	Crowding (load factor)
	Reliability
	Frequency
	Service hours
	Customer satisfaction (as measured using surveys)
Bicyclists	Presence of bicycle lane or cycle track
	Bicycle LOS, as defined in Chapter 7
Automobiles	Roadway segment and intersection performance using urban corridor analysis techniques from the *Highway Capacity Manual 2000* for urban conditions
	Corridor travel time
	Standard deviation of average speed

guidance for balancing the needs of one mode against another. To create more space for walking, bicycling, or transit, they need to break the official rules adopted for them by their city's elected officials. To avoid having every roadway allocation turn into a political fight, cities should adopt better rules.

Step 1: Establish Priorities

Chapter 5, "Streets," describes the shortcomings of a simplistic arterial, collector, and "local" system of street typologies. Instead, you should describe your city's streets by their land-use context, and by how important each street is for each mode of transportation. This prioritization exercise becomes especially important now that it is time to establish performance measures.

Use a map to establish your priorities, and focus on one mode at a time. This exercise is easily done in a community meeting or with your elected officials. The more consensus you can build around these priorities, the easier it will be to implement your performance measures later. For practical implementation, it is usually best to rank street segments in two to four tiers for each mode.

- Pedestrian priority follows mainly from land use, with retail streets typically being of highest priority and industrial streets the lowest. Give special consideration to areas around schools and key routes that avoid such pedestrian hazards as freeway ramps, scenic corridors, and the like.

- Bicycle priority typically follows from your city's bicycle plan. If your city has no bicycle plan, work with local cyclists to determine which corridors are most important. See Chapter 7 for more detail.

- Transit priority is mainly a result of cumulative transit frequency on a given street segment. Streets with high-frequency service are first priority for transit, and streets with occasional bus service are lowest priority.

- Automobile priority is the same as your city's arterials (first priority), collectors (second priority), and locals (third priority).

- Freight priority should follow from your city's truck-route map. It is important to know where large trucks routinely travel, as travel lanes and turning radii will have to be larger on these streets, and because additional congestion on these corridors may have a greater economic impact.

- Parking priority may be usefully assigned, with on-street parking of greater importance along neighborhood retail streets, and lesser importance in industrial or office districts.

You will notice that some of your streets are of very high importance for several modes of transportation; one of these may be your "Main Street." Other streets will be of low importance for all modes. This is typical. Advocates for a particular mode may also be reluctant to assign second- and third-tier status to their mode on a particular street, thinking that their bike lane or bus signal priority project will be completely eliminated if they admit to this lower ranking. This exercise, however, only helps designers decide how much to invest in each mode relative to the others, particularly when there is not enough space to accommodate each mode perfectly or optimally.

When you are finished with this exercise, you should map the results in your city's geographic information systems (GIS) database, or publish illustrative maps online. If you are mapping in GIS, it is possible to do a composite map. More importantly, you should have your city council adopt the results as city policy.

Step 2: Establish Performance Measures

Using the guidance elsewhere in this chapter and the chapters dedicated to each mode, decide what performance measures to use for each mode, taking best advantage of available data and tailoring the measures to the issues of greatest concern in your community.

Step 3: Establish Thresholds and Targets

Now comes the tricky part. For each mode and for each priority level, you need to establish minimum and preferred LOS standards. You may also want to establish absolute minimum LOS thresholds that should not be crossed under any circumstances. There are several ways to structure these standards, and three possible approaches are described in this section. Each approach uses an A–F letter ranking system for each mode, but your city may use any system of measurement it chooses.

OPTION 1: STANDARDS BY MODE

The approach of using standards by mode references the modal priorities mapped in Step 1, and assigns LOS standards to each priority level (see Table 14-3).

OPTION 2: HYBRID SYSTEM

Table 14-4 shows a simplified hybrid system for a city that identified high-priority bicycle and transit corridors, but no second- or third-tier corridors.

Table 14-3: Sample Performance Targets by Mode

Mode	Threshold	First Priority	Second Priority	Third Priority
Pedestrians	Target	A	A	B
	Minimum	B	D	D
Bicyclists	Target	A	A	B
	Minimum	B	C	D
Transit	Target	A	A	B
	Minimum	B	C	D
Automobiles	Target	A	B	C
	Minimum	C	E	F
Freight	Target	A	B	C
	Minimum	C	E	F
Parking	Target	A	B	C
	Minimum	C	E	F

Table 14-4: Sample Performance Targets by Context

Context	Type	Target LOS	Minimum LOS	Transit Priority Corridor	Bicycle Priority Corridor
Walkable Urban	Major Street	Pedestrian: A Transit: B Bicycles: B Autos: C	Pedestrian: C Transit: D Bicycles: D Autos: E	Transit target: A Transit minimum: C	Bicycle target: A Bicycle minimum: C
	Minor Street	Pedestrian: A Transit: None Bicycles: B Autos: None	Pedestrian: B Transit: None Bicycles: C Autos: None	N/A	Bicycle target: A Bicycle minimum: B
Auto-Oriented District	Major Street	Pedestrian: B Transit: B Bicycles: B Autos: C	Pedestrian: C Transit: D Bicycles: D Autos: E	Transit target: A Transit minimum: C	Bicycle target: A Bicycle minimum: C
	Minor Street	Pedestrian: B Transit: None Bicycles: B Autos: None	Pedestrian: C Transit: None Bicycles: D Autos: None	N/A	Bicycle target: A Bicycle minimum: B

OPTION 3: INTEGRATED STREET TYPOLOGY MEASURES

The integrated street typology system shown in Table 14-5 is for a city that took its modal priority maps and grouped similar streets together into a set of typologies that integrate land-use context and all modes. In this case, the street type names are shorthand for modal priority.

Step 4: Apply the Measures

Before applying the measures, test them on a variety of actual streets to see how they work, particularly on the more challenging streets that are highest priority for more than one mode. Fine-tune the measures as necessary. When they seem optimized, adopt them as official policy, both for designers to use in implementing changes on actual streets and for planners to use in determining the transportation impacts of developments. This section provides two examples of how measures may be applied.

EXAMPLE 1: ADDING BIKE LANES TO ELM STREET

Your city's bicycle master plan includes Elm Street as a high-priority bike corridor, and the city has secured funding for a bike project there. Elm Street is currently a

Table 14-5: Sample Performance Targets by Street Type

Street Type	Level of Service	Walk	Bike	Transit	Freight	Auto	Parking
Neighborhood Retail	Priority	High	Medium	Medium	Medium	Medium	High
	Target	A	B	B	B	C	A
	Minimum	B	D	D	D	F	C
Downtown Retail	Priority	High	Medium	High	Medium	Medium	High
	Target	A	B	A	B	C	A
	Minimum	B	D	C	D	F	D
Downtown Commercial	Priority	High	Medium	High	Medium	Medium	Medium
	Target	A	B	A	B	C	B
	Minimum	B	D	C	D	F	F
Transit Boulevard	Priority	High	Medium	High	Low	Low	Low
	Target	A	B	A	C	C	C
	Minimum	B	D	C	F	F	F
Bike Boulevard	Priority	Medium	High	Low	Low	Low	Low
	Target	A	A	B	C	C	C
	Minimum	C	B	D	F	F	F
Minor Residential	Priority	High	Medium	Low	Low	Low	High
	Target	A	A	C	C	C	A
	Minimum	B	C	F	F	F	C
Residential Arterial	Priority	High	Medium	Medium	Low	Medium	Medium
	Target	A	A	B	C	C	B
	Minimum	B	C	C	D	D	F

four-lane, medium-priority auto street that runs through a residential neighborhood. There is infrequent transit service and on-street parking on both sides of the street. The city engineer has measured the performance of each mode on Elm Street and compared it against the adopted targets (Table 14-6).

According to the measurements, Elm Street is doing very well for cars, freight, and parking; adequately for walking and transit; and poorly for bikes. It is clearly out of balance, and it is appropriate to reduce LOS for cars, parking, and freight somewhat so as to improve conditions for cyclists.

Knowing that it is not appropriate to narrow sidewalks (and thereby reduce pedestrian LOS below the minimum threshold), the city engineer evaluates two options for shifting space away from cars and parking. The first option eliminates parking on one side of the street to allow bike lanes to be striped. The second eliminates two of the four general-purpose lanes and substitutes two bike lanes and left-turn pockets at each intersection. The engineer evaluates the LOS for each option (Table 14-7).

According to the analysis, the only viable plan is option 2, which provides a slight improvement in LOS for pedestrians, and a slight decrease for autos and freight. Option 1, by removing parking, also removes an important buffer between traffic and pedestrians, and it eliminates half of the on-street parking for nearby residents—both unacceptable results.

EXAMPLE 2: MAIN STREET

Main Street is the commercial heart of the city, and it is of highest priority for every mode of transportation. Bicycle advocates are demanding a bicycle lane there. The transit operator complains about congestion and is seeking bus-only lanes. Struggling merchants are demanding more on-street parking, and local citizens complain that the sidewalks are too narrow. The city engineer measures

Table 14-6: Elm Street Performance Measurements: Before

	Walk	Bike	Transit	Auto	Freight	Parking
Target	A	A	C	A	B	A
Minimum	C	C	E	D	F	C
Current Actual	C	F	C	B	B	A

Table 14-7: Elm Street Performance Measurement Options

	Walk	Bike	Transit	Auto	Freight	Parking
Option 1: Parking Removal	D	B	D	B	B	D
	Fail	Pass	Pass	Pass	Pass	Fail
Option 2: Four-to-three conversion	B	B	D	C	C	A
	Pass	Pass	Pass	Pass	Pass	Pass

performance and determines that conditions are failing or just barely passing for all modes (Table 14-8). In this situation, it is not possible simply to reallocate roadway space to bring all modes into balance. What should the city engineer do? In this case, the city engineer must look at all the tools that might benefit one mode without hurting the others. For example:

- **Pedestrians.** To improve pedestrian LOS, corner bulb-outs can be installed and landscaping improved. Perhaps the street trees and streetlights can be moved to the parking lane with minimal loss of parking spaces.

- **Bicycles.** If there is not enough room to stripe separate bicycle lanes, perhaps motor-vehicle speeds could be reduced through traffic calming, with sharrows installed in the middle of the traffic lanes. This is not a perfect solution for bicyclists, but perhaps it will meet the minimum service threshold.

- **Transit.** There is clearly not enough room for dedicated transit lanes, but perhaps the traffic signals could be interconnected and anticipate the arrivals of buses. Bus stops could be consolidated and switched from pull-outs to bulb-outs. At major bottlenecks, some on-street parking spaces may be removed to give the buses a queue jump lane. These transit improvements may have minor negative impacts on traffic, so a policy decision may be necessary about the degree to which one may be inconvenienced to benefit the other(s).

- **Autos.** Synchronizing the traffic lights or getting a smart traffic signal system can help move cars, even if little can be done to improve capacity. Removing a few parking spaces to add left- or right-turn pockets may also help.

- **Freight.** Freight will generally benefit from the auto investments. It may also be possible to designate another freight corridor so that big trucks can avoid downtown.

- **Parking.** Some of the suggested changes will result in a loss of parking. To mitigate this loss, a parking management strategy can help ensure that shoppers and commuters can still find parking space easily. (See Chapter 10 for more details.)

It may not be possible in this case to attain a passing grade for every mode, but the engineer can certainly improve conditions, and can try to make sure all modes are substandard to the same degree. This situation could also be improved by establishing *absolute* minimum service standards.

Table 14-8: Main Street Performance Measurements: Before

	Walk	Bike	Transit	Auto	Freight	Parking
Target	A	A	A	A	A	A
Minimum	C	C	C	C	C	C
Current Actual	D	F	F	D	D	C
	Fail	Fail	Fail	Fail	Fail	Pass

Citywide Transportation System Measurements

Finally, it is important to have tools to measure how well your city's transportation system meets your larger economic development, quality-of-life, ecological sustainability, and social equity goals. One approach is outlined in this section, but the approach for your city will have to be carefully tailored to your particular values and priorities.

Santa Monica Approach

As part of its efforts to update its General Plan in 2010, the City of Santa Monica, California, decided to align its transportation impact assessment tools, and overall transportation system performance measurements, with the larger goals of the General Plan. To do this, the Transportation Management Division created a multimodal *Transportation Report Card* (Table 14-9). The Report Card strives to:

- Use measures that clearly relate to the General Plan goals
- Minimize data-collection costs, by focusing on data that is already being collected or that can be regularly collected with minimal effort, or that relates to multiple goals
- Keep the Report Card simple and understandable and use the fewest possible measures that still capture all of the city's aspirations

Most of the following measures have been incorporated into Santa Monica's Transportation Report Card. Some will also be used for other purposes, including:

- *Project review.* These measures are used to help determine whether a development project must mitigate potential negative impacts on traffic and the neighborhood's overall environment.
- *Corridor review.* These measures help city engineers optimize overall mobility in the major traffic and transit corridors.

The following section provides a detailed description of the metrics that the City of Santa Monica uses to measure development-related transportation impacts during environmental review ("project review"). It also describes how to assess and/or calculate performance under each metric.

NO NET NEW VEHICULAR PM PEAK-HOUR TRIPS

Definition: The City of Santa Monica will monitor vehicular PM peak-hour trips to ensure that no new net vehicular trips are generated with a Santa Monica origin or destination.

Target: No net increase in vehicle trips in PM peak hour. Any new PM peak-hour trips are offset by a decrease in existing PM peak-hour trips.

Data Source: To precisely measure traffic generated by Santa Monica, the city could conduct annual traffic counts at a large number of specific locations throughout the city. To provide richer data at a more reasonable cost, the city is considering expanding existing data-collection efforts as follows:[3]

- **Employee trips** would be estimated using the existing data collected through employer surveys required under the city's Emissions Reduction Plan.[4]

Table 14-9: Santa Monica Transportation Report Card

Measure	Project Review	Corridor Review	Report Card
Management			
No net new Santa Monica-generated vehicular PM trips	√	√	√
Relative auto and transit travel times	√	√	√
Transit quality of service	√	√	√
Transit vs. auto capacity in selected corridors		√	
Transit vs. auto capacity in selected intersections		√	
Corridor person capacity		√	
Congestion	√	√	√
Streets			
Sidewalk completeness	√	√	√
Bike facility completeness	√	√	√
Bike parking	√		√
Signal timing			√
Environment			
VMT per capita	√	√	√
Carbon footprint (GHG emissions) per capita (for Santa Monica-generated trips)	√	√	√
City fleet with alternative fuels			√
Quality			
Quality of selected recreational transportation facilities			√
Usage by transportation mode			√
Supportive uses in the right location	√		√
Public Spaces			
Public enjoyment			√
Health			
Walk/bike trips per capita			√
Walk/bike mode share			√
Walk/bike trips by children			√
Affordability/Equity			
Household transportation expenditure			√
Unbundled parking			√
Transit availability			√
Parking cash-out			√
Economy			
Parking availability in commercial districts			√
Safety			
Crashes			√
Injuries			√
Fatalities			√
Walk/bike crashes/injuries/fatalities per usage			√
Perception of safety			√

- **Visitor and resident trips** would be estimated using periodic surveys of shoppers in neighborhood commercial districts. Such surveys would be administered in the PM peak hour and ask questions about travel choices.[5]
- **The travel demand model** would also be used to help predict changes in PM peak-hour travel behavior over time. It is sensitive to changes in transit service, mix of land uses, land-use density, and other factors that affect mode split. It would have to be updated continuously as land-use patterns change, and as new travel data becomes available.

RELATIVE AUTO AND TRANSIT TRAVEL TIMES

Definition: The City of Santa Monica will measure auto and transit travel times along key corridors within the city.

Targets: No increase in corridor travel times for cars. Transit average speed no less than 30 percent of speed limit.

Data source: GPS data will be used to track both transit and auto travel times along selected corridors (major streets with regular transit service, per input from residents and city council). To determine auto travel times, periodic pilot-car surveys will be conducted along the entire length of the corridors, calculating the ratio between transit and auto travel times. Data will be collected at specific times, including the: (1) average for PM peak hour, (2) average for Saturday peak hour, and (3) daily average or average for a typical hour to be determined.

TRANSIT QUALITY OF SERVICE

Definition: Transit QOS along transit boulevards will be measured by collecting on-board data and utilizing the GIS database. Frequency, service span, reliability, travel speed, and passenger loading are the most critical factors that will be collected from transit buses along selected transit corridors. Targets and thresholds will vary by location. For instance, transit delay is less tolerable on Wilshire than downtown; hence, a lower QOS is tolerable for downtown than for Wilshire.

Target: The target for this indicator is an improvement in QOS along these corridors.

Data source: On-board data will be used to track transit QOS. Five independent QOS measures will describe the key quantifiable features of service quality from the passenger perspective:
- **Frequency** is described by the duration of the maximum scheduled gap between consecutive buses on the route. When all service is on schedule, this gap, called the *headway*, is the maximum waiting time a customer will experience.
- **Span of service** describes the number of hours in the day that a service runs at high frequencies (every 15 minutes or better).
- **Reliability** describes the degree to which the schedule is achieved.

- **Travel speed** is average speed, not top speed. It describes how long the service takes to traverse each mile, including all sources of delay.

- **Passenger loading**, or overloading, is an important measure that provides insight into a range of issues affecting transit, including:

  - Passenger comfort, both in terms of finding a seat and crowding levels on the vehicle

  - The need from the transit operator's perspective to increase service frequency or vehicle size to improve passenger comfort

  - The risk of "pass-ups," where a transit vehicle bypasses waiting passengers because it is too full

CONGESTION

Definition: Calculated volume-to-capacity ratios will be mapped by major street segment and intersection. These ratios compare the measured or estimated volume on a given street segment or intersection with its theoretical capacity. To calculate the V/C ratio, the peak 15-minute traffic volume is divided by the lane capacity. A V/C ratio of less than 1.0 means that cars can move steadily and efficiently along a segment or through an intersection; ratios higher than 1 indicate increasing levels of delay for all motorists, as there is not enough roadway capacity to enable motorists to move steadily and efficiently.

Target: Congestion is tolerated to different degrees on different streets:

- For the first two intersections from any freeway on- or off-ramp, there are no targets. Bottlenecks will be maintained at these locations to contain congestion and keep it from spreading into nearby residential neighborhoods and commercial districts. (Expanding capacity at these intersections would invite additional regional traffic, increasing overall traffic and shifting the congestion bottlenecks to elsewhere into the city.)

- For boulevards, major avenues, secondary avenues, and commercial streets, maintain average weekday PM peak-hour volume-to-capacity ratios of 1.0 or less.

- For minor avenues, maintain average weekday PM peak-hour volume-to-capacity ratios of 0.8 or less.

- For neighborhood streets, maintain average weekday PM peak-hour volume-to-capacity ratios of 0.7 or less.

Data Source: The updated travel demand model will be used to measure volume-to-capacity ratios for intersections and segments in the city. These will be mapped by major street segment and intersection.

SIDEWALK COMPLETENESS

Definition: Sidewalk completeness is measured as the percentage of Santa Monica streets that have sufficient pedestrian facilities. Streets with walking infrastructure deficiencies will be identified and indexed in the walking and bicycling demand GIS model. This will serve as the basis for identifying and prioritizing potential improvement locations.

Target: To increase the percentage of sidewalks that have sufficient pedestrian facilities.

Data source: The walking and bicycling demand GIS model.

BIKE FACILITY COMPLETENESS

Definition: Bike facility completeness will be measured as the percentage of the bicycle network that has been completed. The walking and bicycling demand GIS model will produce an index of bicycling infrastructure deficiencies. This will serve as the basis for identifying and prioritizing potential improvement locations.

Target: To increase the percentage of the bicycle network that has been completed.

Data source: The walking and bicycling demand GIS model.

BIKE PARKING

Definition: The City of Santa Monica will track the installation of public bike parking in public or private locations.

Target: To increase the amount of public bicycle parking available in public and private locations.

Data source: As part of the project review process, the Transportation Management Division will maintain an ongoing record of required bike parking.

VEHICLE MILES TRAVELED PER CAPITA

Definition: By tracking VMT per capita, the City of Santa Monica will be able to determine if the city is bringing VMT per capita below ambient conditions or meeting SB 375 and regional targets (for Santa-Monica-generated trips). It will also enable the city to determine the effectiveness of citywide and project-specific mitigation measures in helping the city meet its established VMT per capita targets.

Target: To at least maintain and preferably reduce VMT per capita.

Data source: This data will be extracted from the travel demand model. VMT will be illustrated in maps per travel analysis zone (TAZ) or larger districts for Santa Monica trip origins (one map) and Santa Monica trip ends (one map).

CARBON FOOTPRINT (GHG EMISSIONS) PER CAPITA
(FOR SANTA-MONICA-GENERATED TRIPS)

Definition: By tracking greenhouse gas (GHG) emissions per capita, the City of Santa Monica will be able to determine if the city is bringing the carbon footprint per capita below ambient conditions or meeting SB 375 and regional targets (for Santa-Monica-generated trips). It will also enable the city to determine the effectiveness of citywide and project-specific mitigation measures in helping the city meet its established carbon footprint per capita targets.

Target: To at least maintain and preferably reduce GHG emissions per capita.

Data source: This data will be extracted from the travel demand model. GHG emissions per capita will be illustrated in maps per larger districts for Santa Monica.

Evaluating Project Alternatives

In addition to measuring modal performance on city streets, performance measures are also often used to decide between or prioritize large capital projects. London has particularly good tools for judging projects according to many different criteria. A sample London approach for evaluating and selecting transit projects—including whether to choose bus, tram, or light rail—is shown in Table 14-10.

These criteria allow planners to compare advantages and disadvantages of different projects on equal terms. First, individual projects are scored according to selected criteria, as shown in the sample evaluation "report card" in Figure 14-1.

Next, individual project scorecards can be summarized in a *Consumer Reports* style, so that different potential projects can be compared against each other in equal terms (see Figure 14-2 for an example).

Table 14-10: London Intermediate Modes Evaluation Criteria

Criteria	Subcriteria	Indicators
1. Environmental impact	Natural environment	Noise, local air pollution, global emissions, energy and fuel
2. Safety and security	Accidents and personal security	Public and private transport accidents, personal security
3. Economic	Cost, time savings, and revenue	Capital and operating costs, public and private use, public and private journey times, revenue cost benefit analysis
4. Accessibility	Public transport accessibility Accessibility to other modes	Pedestrian access to public transport, access to local centres Community severance, pedestrian space, parking and servicing access
5. Integration	Integration with other modes Accessibility impacts on regeneration and social inclusion Other local policy/plans Regional economic impact	Interface with other modes Access to development sites, access to deprived areas, access to employment Local policies, tourism National/EU objectives

Description of Scheme: Light rail from Liverpool City Centre via West Derby Road/Utting Ave East to Kirkby		Problems: High levels of deprivation in Duke St/Cornwallis, Stanley, Queens, A580, Kirkby & Parks Pathway areas. Poor public transport accessibility within corridor due to poor quality and reliability of bus and absence of rail service.		1) Total Cost of the Proposal £325m (out-turn prices, incl QRA but excluding OB)
OBJECTIVE	SUB-OBJECTIVE	QUALITATIVE IMPACTS	QUANTITATIVE MEASURE	ASSESSMENT
ENVIRONMENT	Noise	Noise introduced to environment from tram operation. Potential for some reductions in noise from reduced road traffic.		Slight Adverse
	Local Air Quality	No significant impact from light rail vehicles, car transfer results in lower emission levels.		Slight Beneficial
	Greenhouse Gases	Net reduction as saving from car transfers outweighs increases at power stations. However, overall the effects on greenhouse gas emissions is expected to be negligible.		Neutral
	Landscape	No significant impact		Neutral
	Townscape	Passes through or adjacent to nine Conservation Areas and one proposed Conservation Area. Affects urban green space and public open space. At same time, scheme can act as catalyst for urban renewal. There is a significant loss of trees in some areas which will have an impact on townscape.		Slight Adverse
	Heritage of Historic Resources	Potential impacts on archaeology and potential for impacts on setting of listed buildings.		Slight Adverse
	Biodiversity	Scheme runs adjacent to, and through, non-statutory nature conservation designations.		Neutral
	Water Environment	No significant impact.		Neutral
	Physical Fitness	Enhanced provision for pedestrians and cyclists.		Slight Beneficial
	Journey Ambience	High quality in-vehicle environment, stop facilities and travel information.		Strong Beneficial
SAFETY	Accidents	Reduction in accidents to both Merseytram car transferees and to car users remaining on the highway network.	£33m PV resulting from Merseytram car transfers.	Strong Beneficial
	Security	High visibility at stops and accesses from high quality lighting. CCTV at all stops. Park and ride site will be manned and have CCTV.		Beneficial
ECONOMY	Transport Efficiency	Strong operating ratio of 1.15:1. Full economic BCR of 1.60:1 demonstrates scheme's overall value.	Consumer Users: £535m PV Business Users & Providers: £85m PV Central Govt Cost: £236m PV Local Govt Cost: £66m PV	PVB: £483m PVB: £301m PVB: £182m (includes QRA & OB of 6%)
	Reliability	Merseytram will provide a fast reliable service through off vehicle ticket sales, a high level of segregation and priorities at on-street sections.		Strong Beneficial
	Wider Economic Impacts	The LTP strategy, where Line 1 is the highest priority scheme.developed to support the wider regeneration objectives of Merseyside.		Strong Beneficial
ACCESSIBILITY	Option Values	Serves a population of 103,687 within 800m of route, and higher number of within a bus catchment.		Beneficial
	Severance	Some severance on segregated sections–new crossings provided. Enhanced pedestrian facilities at many stops.		Neutral
	Access to Transport System	Route serves areas of high deprivation and low car ownership. All vehicles and stops are fully accessible to the mobility impaired.		Strong Beneficial
INTEGRATION	Transport Interchange	Improved interchange with: Bus - Kirkby, Croxteth, Queens Drive and City Centre, Rail - City Centre, Car - new park and ride, Cycle - facilities at stops. Interchange facilitated by integrated ticketing, network branding		Strong Beneficial
	Land Use Policy	Scheme developed as part of an integrated land use and tranport strategy to promote sustainable regeneration in Merseyside. Fully consistent with national, and regional land use poolicies.		Strong Beneficial
	Other Goverment Policies	Scheme supportive of a range of Government initiatives and themes - welfare to work, access to education, opportunity for all, reducing social exclusion and access to healthcare.		Strong Beneficial

Figure 14-1
Sample London project evaluation scorecard. *Source: Transport for London.*

RANKINGS FROM THE ROUTE PRIORITISATION

Figure 14-2
London comparison of multiple projects. *Source: Transport for London.*

Rank	Route ID	Route Name	Environment	Economy	Accessibility	Integration	Affordability	Bus Impact
1	B10a	Basildon-Laindon (via Upper Mayne)						
2	B10b	Basildon-Laindon (via Great Knightleys)						
3	B5	Basildon-Pitsea (via Broadmayne)						
4	B11	Basildon-Laindon						
5	B8	Basildon-Dry Street (via Basildon Hospital)						
6	S3b	Southend-The Ranges (via Thorpe Bay)						
7	S9	Ranges Loop						
8	B4	Basildon-Burnt Mills						
9	S3a	Southend-The Ranges (via Southchurch Boulevard)						
10	S1a	Southend-Airport (via Victoria Avenue)						
11	T3b	Lakeside-Tilbury (via Chadwell)						
12	T3a	Lakeside-Tilbury						
13	T4a	Lakeside-Purfleet (via Turrock Way)						
14	S1b	Southend-Airport (via Sutton Road)						
15	B1	Basildon-Wickford						
16	T4b	Lakeside-Purfleet (via Weston Avenue)						
17	S5a	Southend-Leigh On Sea						
18	B7	Wickford-Pitsea						
19	S5b	Southend-Leigh On Sea (via Prittlewell)						
20	S4	Southend Loop						
21	B3	Basildon-Pitsea (via Cranes)						
22	S8b	Southend-Rayleigh (via Bridgewater Drive)						
23	T2	Lakeside-Shell Haven						
24	S7	Southend-Basildon						
25	B9	Basildon-Shell Haven						
26	S8a	Southend-Rayleigh (via Eastwood Road)						
27	S2	Airport-The Ranges						
28	B2	Basildon-Rayleigh						
29	T1b	Lakeside-Basildon (via Grays)						
30	B6c	Basildon-Canvey (via Fryerns & Benfleet)						
31	S6	Southend-Canvey						
32	T1a	Lakeside-Basildon (via Arterial Road)						
33	T1c	Lakeside-Basildon (via South Stifford)						

Key

High Priority   Medium Priority   Low Priority

Additional Resources

Florida Department of Transportation. *2009 Quality/Level of Service Handbook* and Multimodal Level of Service indicators; www.dot.state.fl.us/planning/systems/sm/los/default.shtm

Transportation Research Board. *Highway Capacity Manual 2000*. TRB, 2000.

Transportation Research Board. *NCHRP Report 616: Multimodal Level of Service Analysis for Urban Streets*. TRB, 2008.

Victoria Transport Policy Institute. Multimodal Level of Service page: http://www.vtpi.org/tdm/tdm129.htm

Chapter 15

For More Information

Useful Online Resources

The following are some top sources for free information on transportation and sustainable cities available online.

Data and Research

The U.S. Census and Data.gov are a treasure trove of data, covering every imaginable aspect of America: www.census.gov and www.data.gov.

Walkscore is a very useful tool for measuring the degree to which the needs of daily life are available within walking distance of any address in the world, with better results in places where Google has found local businesses. See www.walkscore.org.

The National Center for Transit Research, housed at the University of South Florida, has volumes of data about and useful tools for transit in the United States: www.nctr.usf.edu.

The Transit Cooperative Research Program has the most useful collection of scholarly articles and analyses about transit: www.tcrponline.org/.

The Transportation Research Board compiles scholarly articles on every imaginable transportation topic. See www.trb.org.

The Federal Highway Administration maintains predictable data about roads, but also has a lot of useful information about walking and bicycling. See safety.fhwa.dot.gov/ped_bike/ and www.fhwa.dot.gov/environment/bikeped/. The FHA is also the major funder of the Pedestrian and Bicycle Information Center at www.pedbikeinfo.org/.

The Victoria Transport Policy Institute specializes in economic research, and maintains a vast encyclopedia of data on the costs of driving and the effectiveness of demand management programs in affecting travel behavior: www.vtpi.org.

Useful Advocacy with National Content

Congress for the New Urbanism. Documents and research related to urbanism: www.cnu.org.

Center for Transit Oriented Development. Abundant research on effective transit-oriented development (TOD): http://www.reconnectingamerica.org/html/TOD/index.htm.

Smart Growth America. Advocacy for and research on sustainable cities: www.smartgrowthamerica.org.

Transportation 4 America. The most effective national, sustainable transportation policy advocates in the United States: http://t4america.org/.

Journalism and Research with a Sustainable Urban Perspective

Streetfilms. If a picture is worth a thousand words, a video is worth ten thousand. Streetfilms has videos on every sustainable transport topic: http://www .streetfilms.org/.

Streetsblog. The best journalism on U.S. federal transport policy, and detail for New York, San Francisco, and Los Angeles: www.streetsblog.org.

Planetizen. Journalism on planning and urbanism: www.planetizen.com.

Especially Useful Blogs

Infrastructurist: http://www.infrastructurist.com/.

Complete Streets: http://www.completestreets.org.

Market Urbanism provides very valuable insight into planning from a non-standard view (e.g., it makes arguments that are compelling to both conservatives and libertarians): http://marketurbanism.com/.

Human Transit. The best writing anywhere on the topic of transit, including practical guidance on how to make transit work in your community: www .humantransit.org.

The Transport Politic. National journalism focused on transit infrastructure and politics: http://www.thetransportpolitic.com/.

Required Reading

The following books should be on every transportation planner's bookshelf.

Cities and Urbanism

Alexander, Christopher, Murray Silverstein, et al. *A Pattern Language.*
Caro, Robert A. *The Power Broker: Robert Moses and the Fall of New York.*
Dunham-Jones, Ellen, and June Williamson. *Retrofitting Suburbia.*
Farr, Doug. *Sustainable Urbanism: Urban Design with Nature.*
Gehl, Jan. *Life between Buildings* and *Cities for People.*
Hayden, Dolores. *A Field Guide to Sprawl.*
Jackson, Kenneth T. *Crabgrass Frontier: The Suburbanization of the United States.*
Jacobs, Jane. *Death and Life of Great American Cities.*
Mumford, Lewis. *The City in History, Its Origins, Its Transformation and Its Prospects.*
Newman, Oscar. *Defensible Space: Crime Prevention through Urban Design.*
Whyte, William H. *City: Rediscovering the Center.*

General Transportation

Grava, Sigurd. *Urban Transportation Systems.*
Newman, Peter. *Sustainability and Cities: Overcoming Automobile Dependence.*
Vuchic, Vukan. *Transportation for Livable Cities.*

Streets

Appleyard, Donald. *Livable Streets.*
Ewing, Reid. *Traffic Calming: State of the Practice.*

ITE. *Designing Walkable Urban Thoroughfares: A Context Sensitive Approach, An ITE Recommended Practice.*

Jacobs, Allan. *Great Streets.*

Cars

Downs, Anthony. *Still Stuck in Traffic: Coping with Peak-Hour Traffic Congestion*

Vanderbilt, Tom. *Traffic: Why We Drive the Way We Do.*

Bicycles

AASHTO, *Guidelines for the Development of Bicycle Facilities.*

CROW, *Design Manual for Bicycle Traffic.*

NACTO, *Urban Bikeway Design Guide*

Transit

AC Transit, "Designing with Transit."

Cervero, Robert. *The Transit Metropolis: A Global Inquiry.*

Vuchic, Vukan. *Urban Transit.*

Parking

Litman, Todd. *Parking Management Best Practices.*

Shoup, Don. *The High Cost of Free Parking.*

Useful Tools

To be a skilled transportation planner, it is important to know how to use the following tools—or at least know who to ask for help.

Google Earth

Google Earth is a free, powerful tool every planner should use regularly. In addition to showing what your house looks like from the air, Google Earth lets you:

- Compare the scale of your city to other places you know.

    Use Google Earth's "Eye Altitude" legend in the lower right corner to compare different places. For example, the Google Earth images in Figures 15-1 and 15-2 compare the historic center of Florence with the Harbor Freeway/91 interchange in Los Angeles, at the same scale.

    Figures 15-3 and 15-4 show the block patterns of Tyson's Corner, Virginia, and those of Portland, Oregon, also at the same scale as the images in Figures 15-1 and 15-2.

    Who could have imagined that six city blocks in Tyson's Corner cover the same area as well over 100 blocks in Portland? Or that most of Florence fits within a Los Angeles freeway interchange? Which places will work better for transit? Which places will work better for walking? Why?

- Measure block sizes and street widths anywhere in the world, down to the nearest foot. Google Earth is remarkably accurate—about the same as pacing out the

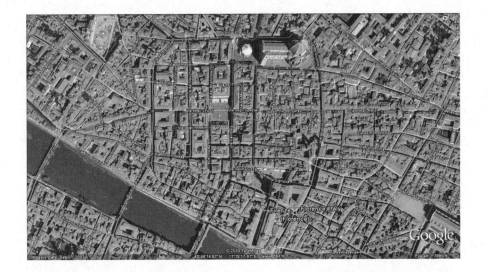

Figure 15-1
Google Earth image of Florence, Italy. *Source: Google Earth:* http://www.google.com/permissions/geoguidelines.html.

Figure 15-2
Google Earth image of Los Angeles, California (at the same scale as Figure 15-1). *Source: Google Earth:* http://www.google.com/permissions/geoguidelines.html.

actual street in the field. Field checking will always be necessary, but it's easy to see if a street's travel lanes are unnecessarily wide, if lanes can be restriped to add bike lanes, and whether there is a stop sign or signal at any intersection. Use the ruler tool to measure in the units of your choice.

From the comfort of your office, you can see that the Avenue des Champs Elysees in Paris is a very wide street, but its travel lanes are only 9 feet wide (Figure 15-5).

- Tour transportation systems around the world. Google Earth's many layers allow viewers to see rail and transit networks in any city, and see pictures of almost anything.

Your Pace and Your Shoe

How wide are the sidewalks on your favorite streets? What is the real difference between a 10-foot sidewalk and a 13-foot one? Can bike lanes be added to this street? If you know the length of your pace and your shoe, you can measure almost any street element accurately. Practice walking with a long tape measure or measuring wheel so you know the exact dimension of your typical pace, and how awkwardly you need to walk in order to pace a precise yard or meter.

Geographic Information Systems

Geographic information systems databases (simply called *GIS* in the industry) are analytical mapping tools that combine all sorts of data and show how it relates to

Figure 15-5
Using Google Earth images, you can measure street and lane dimensions anywhere in the world. *Source: Google Earth:* http://www.google.com/permissions/geoguidelines.html.

a specific place. They tie data to real-world coordinates in the form of points, lines, and polygons, making complex place-specific analysis possible. Relationships and patterns of spatial phenomena may be symbolized and displayed as maps and charts. Data visualization by geography allows for quick communication of spatial information and context to broad audiences, from policymakers and specialists to the general public. One great map can almost instantly communicate what would take pages of descriptive text and tables. Critical to any project is sourcing the most recent, accurate, and complete data available for the area of interest.

Sources of GIS and transportation-related data include:

City, county, or state governments. These entities often have GIS data available for download online, or have a GIS department that maintains and authorizes usage of their data. Similarly, regional organizations or associations of governments also collect, create, update, and disseminate GIS data.

ESRI (Environmental Systems Research Institute, Inc.), an industry leader in GIS software and data applications: http://www.esri.com/.

National Transportation Atlas Database: http://www.bts.gov/publications/national _transportation_atlas_database/2010/.

Census Transportation Planning Package (CTPP): http://www.fhwa.dot.gov/ctpp. Derived from the long form of the census, these tables provide many transportation and commuter (journey-to-work) data sets.

BatchGeo, a free, online address locator that transforms addresses into point data on Google Maps and Google Earth (which data are convertible to GIS): http://www.batchgeo.com/.

SketchUp

Another free tool available from Google, SketchUp is a powerful visualization tool that allows users to create three-dimensional (3-D) models of any part of any city (see Figure 15-6). This lets you imagine how a street might look if the buildings faced the

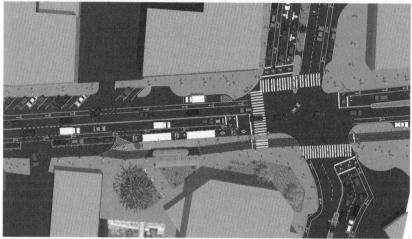

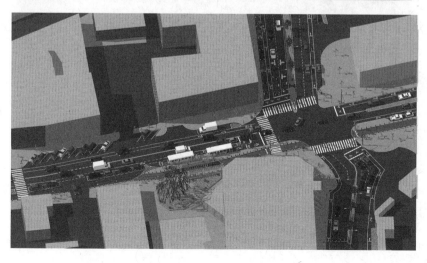

Figure 15-6
Using SketchUp and Google Earth,
it is possible to create simple 3-D
renderings, redesigning existing
spaces. *Photos: Mike Alba/Nelson\
Nygaard.*

street rather than parking lots, or if new trees were planted, or if light rail trains ran down the middle. SketchUp not only does three dimensions but also does them to scale, allowing for accuracy and precision. A huge library of everyday objects, from mailboxes to the Eiffel Tower, are available in SketchUp's 3-D warehouse.

Photoshop

Endlessly amusing for cropping photos of your family and colleagues and pasting them in unlikely places, Photoshop also serves practical purposes (see Figure 15-7).

◀ **Figure 15-7**
Using Photoshop, it is possible
to imagine how a street can be
transformed from gritty to glamorous.
*Photos: Steve Price and Dover, Kohn &
Partners.*

No tool is more useful for helping people see how changes in their community can make it better. It's one thing to describe these change verbally or in writing; it's quite another to be able to actually show people what it would actually look like.

To see some compelling examples, see Steve Price's work at www.urban-advantage.com.

Urban Land Institute Shared Parking Manual

This tool is covered in Chapter 10 on parking.

URBEMIS

This tool is covered in Chapter 10 on parking.

Endnotes

Chapter 1

1. Romolo August Staccioli, *The Roads of the Romans* (Rome: L'Erma di Bretschneider, 2003), summarized in Tom Vanderbilt, *Traffic: Why We Drive the Way We Do (and What It Says About Us)* (Knopf, 2008), 8).
2. U.S. Environmental Protection Agency. Inventory of U.S. Greenhouse Gas Emissions and Sinks: 1990–2009 (April 15, 2011). Available at http://epa.gov/climatechange/emissions/downloads11/US-GHG-Inventory-2011-Complete_Report.pdf.
3. U.S. Energy Information Administration. *Energy Annual Review 2009* (August 2010), Figure 2.0. Available at www.eia.gov/emeu/aer.

Chapter 2

1. United Nations General Assembly, *Report of the World Commission on Environment and Development: Our Common Future; Transmitted to the General Assembly as an Annex to Document A/42/427—Development and International Co-operation: Environment; Our Common Future, Chapter 2: Towards Sustainable Development; Paragraph 1* (March 20, 1987).
2. Sigalovada Sutta D. III, 188. This translation from Perry Garfinkle, *Buddha or Bust* (Three Rivers Press, 2006).
3. Taro Gomi, *Everyone Poops* (Kane/Miller, 2001).
4. A. H. Maslow, "A Theory of Human Motivation," *Psychological Review* 50, no. 4 (1943): 370–96.
5. Clayton Alderfer, *Existence, Relatedness, and Growth: Human Needs in Organizational Settings* (Free Press, 1972).
6. I. Aharon, N. Etcoff, D. Ariely, C. F. Chabris, E. O'Connor, and H. C. Breiter, "Beautiful Faces Have Reward Value: fMRI and Behavioral Evidence," *Neuron* 32 (2001): 537–51.
7. San Francisco Visitors and Convention Bureau. *2010 Visitor Profile Research* (February 2011). Summary available at http://www.sanfrancisco.travel/research/.
8. "People for Bikes: If I Ride" video (November 2, 2010); available at peopleforbikes.org.
9. Garrett Hardin, "The Tragedy of the Commons," *Science* 162, no. 3859 (December 13, 1968): 1243–48.
10. U.S. Energy Information Administration, *Annual Energy Review*, Tables 5.12a and 5.12b. Available at www.eia.gov/emeu/aer.
11. The Chevron commercials of the 1970s would have you believe that oil comes from pterodactyls, but dinosaurs generally came later.
12. U.S. Environmental Protection Agency, *Criteria Air Pollutants*, available at http://www.epa.gov/apti/course422/ap5.html.
13. Todd Litman, *Transportation Cost and Benefit Analysis II—Water Pollution*, Victoria Transport Policy Institute, 2009), available at http://www.vtpi.org/tca/.
14. Helen Pressley, "Effects of Transportation on Stormwater Runoff and Receiving Water Quality" (internal agency memo, Washington State Department of Ecology, 1991), available at www.ecy.wa.gov.
15. Ibid.
16. R. T. Bannerman, et al., "Sources of Pollutants in Wisconsin Stormwater," *Water Science Technology* 28, nos. 3–5 (1993): 247–59; Lennart Folkeson, "Highway Runoff Literature Survey" (#391; VTI, 1994), available at www.vti.se; John Sansalone, Steven Buchberger, and Margarete Koechling, "Correlations between Heavy Metals and Suspended Solids in Highway Runoff," *Transportation Research Record* 1483 (1995): 112–19, available at www.trb.org.
17. R. Field and M. O'Shea, *Environmental Impacts of Highway Deicing Salt Pollution* (EPA/600/A-92/092, 1992); Gregory Granato, Peter Church, and Victoria Stone, "Mobilization of Major and Trace Constituents of Highway Runoff in Groundwater Potentially Caused by Deicing Chemical Migration," *Transportation Research Record* 1483 (1996): 92, available at www.trb.org.
18. OPW, *Impervious Surface Reduction Study* (Olympia Public Works, 1995), available at www.ci.olympia.wa.us.
19. Entranco, *Stormwater Runoff Management Report* (Washington DOT, 2002), available at www.wsdot.wa.gov.
20. U.S. Environmental Protection Agency, *Using Smart Growth Techniques as Stormwater Best Management Practices* (2005), available free at www.epa.gov.

Chapter 3

1. A. A. Hakim, H. Petrovitch, C. M. Burchfield, G. W. Ross, B. L. Rodriguez, L. R. White, et al., "Effects of Walking on Mortality among Nonsmoking Retired Men," *New England Journal of Medicine* 338, no. 2 (January 8, 1998): 94–99.
2. Hiromi Kobayashi and Shiro Kohshima, "Evolution of the Human Eye as a Device for Communication," in *Primate Origins of Human Cognition and Behavior*, ed. T. Matsuzawa (Springer-Verlag Tokyo, 2010), 383–401.
3. Jan Gehl, *Cities for People* (Island Press, 2010), ch. 2.1, "Senses and Scale."

4. U.S. Department of Commerce, Office of Travel and Tourism Industries, "2009 United States Resident Travel Abroad," available at http://tinet.ita.doc.gov/outreachpages/download_data_table/2009_US_Travel_Abroad.pdf.

5. National Highway Traffic Safety Administration, *Traffic Safety Facts 2009* (2010). Early edition, executive summary page. Available at http://www.nhtsa.gov/.

6. Centers for Disease Control and Prevention (CDC). *Behavioral Risk Factor Surveillance System Survey Data.* Atlanta, Georgia: U.S. Department of Health and Human Services, Centers for Disease Control and Prevention, 2011. See, in particular, the compelling PowerPoint slides that CDC has compiled, which graphically show the spread of obesity over time across all states. The slides are accessible at http://www.cdc.gov/obesity/data/trends.html.

7. Michael Friedman et al., "Impact of Changes in Transportation and Commuting Behaviors During the 1996 Summer Olympic Games in Atlanta on Air Quality and Childhood Asthma," *Journal of the American Medical Association.* JAMA. 2001;285(7):897-905. doi: 10.1001/jama.285.7.897.

8. David Bassett, John Pucher, Ralph Buehler, Dixie L. Thompson, and Scott E. Crouter, "Walking, Cycling, and Obesity Rates in Europe, North America, and Australia," *Journal of Physical Activity and Health* 5 (2008): 795–814, available at http://policy.rutgers.edu/faculty/pucher/JPAH08.pdf; chart compiled by Todd Litman, in *Evaluating Public Transportation Health Benefits* (American Public Transportation Association, June 2010).

9. Excerpted from Todd Litman, *Evaluating Public Transportation Health Benefits* (American Public Transportation Association, June 2010).

10. Rochelle Dicker, Dahianna Lopez, Marci Pepper, Ian Crane, and M. Margaret Kundson, *Cost of Auto-versus-Pedestrian Injuries* (UCSF San Francisco Injury Center, March 2010).

11. Dr. Mark Fenske, "Road Rage Stressing You Out? Crank the Tunes," *Globe and Mail,* October 6, 2010, available at http://www.theglobeandmail.com/life/health/road-rage-stressing-you-out-crank-the-tunes/article1745866/.

12. National Highway Traffic Safety Administration, "Talking Points: Aggressive Driving Prosecutor's Planner," available at http://www.nhtsa.gov/people/injury/aggressive/aggproplanner/page05.htm.

13. National Highway Traffic Safety Administration, "Are You an Aggressive Driver?" available at http://www.nhtsa.gov/people/injury/aggressive/Aggressive%20Web/brochure.html.

14. Tom Vanderbilt, *Traffic: Why We Drive the Way We Do (and What It Says About Us)* (Knopf, 2008), 28.

15. SAFETEA-LU is a $244 billion transportation funding bill that was first authorized in 2005. It is a perfect example of federal acronyms that have run amok, particularly considering that the "LU" portion of the name honors Lu Young, wife of the House Transportation and Infrastructure Committee chair at the time.

16. AARP, *The Voting Behavior of Older Voters in the 2008 General Election and Prior Congressional Elections: Implications for November 2010* (2010), available at http://assets.aarp.org/rgcenter/general/voting-behavior-10.pdf.

17. U.S. Department of Transportation, Federal Highway Administration, "National Safe Routes To School" home page, http://safety.fhwa.dot.gov/saferoutes/.

18. Maya Lambiase, Heather Barry, and James Roemmich, "Effect of a Simulated Active Commute to School on Cardiovascular Stress Reactivity," *Medicine & Science in Sports & Exercise* 42, no. 8 (August 2010): 1609–16. doi:10.1249/MSS.0b013e3181d0c77b.

19. Donald Appleyard, *Livable Streets* (University of California Press, 1981), pages 15–28.

20. Ibid., page 22.

21. Ibid., page 24.

22. Ibid., page 24.

23. See, for example, P. J. Zak, A. A. Stanton, and S. Ahmadi, (2007). "Oxytocin Increases Generosity in Humans," *PLoS ONE* 2, no. 11 (2007): e1128, doi:10.1371/journal.pone.0001128. PMID 17987115; A. J. Guastella, P. B. Mitchell, and M. R. Dadds, "Oxytocin Increases Gaze to the Eye Region of Human Faces," *Biological Psychiatry* 63, no. 1 (January 2008): 3–5. doi:10.1016/j.biopsych.2007.06.026.PMID 17888410.

24. Kerstin Uvnäs Moberg, *The Oxytocin Factor: Tapping the Hormone of Calm, Love, and Healing* (Da Capo Press, 2003).

25. Michael Kosfeld, Markus Heinrichs, Paul J. Zak, Urs Fischbacher, and Ernst Fehr, "Oxytocin Increases Trust in Humans," *Nature* 435 (June 2, 2005): 673–76. doi:10.1038/nature03701.

26. J. Barton and J. Pretty, "What Is the Best Dose of Nature and Green Exercise for Improving Mental Health? A Multi-Study Analysis," *Environmental Science and Technology* (2010). doi:10.1021/es903183r.

Chapter 4

1. http://www.nywf64.com/gm07.shtml.

2. Jan Gehl, *Cities for People* (Island Press, 2010).

3. Jane Jacobs, *The Death and Life of Great American Cities* (Random House, 1961), page 15.

4. Ibid, page 56.

5. David Brooks, "The Crossroads Nation," *New York Times,* November 8, 2010.

6. Anne-Marie Slaughter, "America's Edge: Power in the Networked Century," *Foreign Affairs,* Jan/Feb 2009, available at http://www.foreignaffairs.com/articles/63722/anne-marie-slaughter/americas-edge.

Chapter 6

1. For one example, see the *Sydney CBD Public Life and Public Spaces Survey,* prepared by Gehl Architects for the City of Sydney in 2007. Data and recommendations can be found on the city's website, at http://www.cityofsydney.nsw.gov.au/development/cityimprovements/roadsandstreetscapes/PublicSpacesSurvey.asp.

2. Oscar Newman, *Defensible Space: Crime Prevention Through Urban Design* (Macmillan, 1972).

3. San Francisco Planning Department, *San Francisco Better Streets Plan.* Adopted 2010. Available at http://www.sf-planning.org/ftp/BetterStreets/index.htm.

4. Americans with Disabilities Act *Accessibility Guidelines for Buildings and Facilities,* 36 C.F.R. pts. 1190, 1991.

5. U.S. Department of Transportation, Federal Highway Administration, *Manual on Uniform Traffic Control Devices* (2009 ed.), available at mutcd.fhwa.dot.gov/.

6. Transportation Research Board, *Highway Capacity Manual* (Washington, D.C., 2000).

Chapter 7

1. D. L. Robinson, "Safety in Numbers in Australia: More Walkers and Bicyclists, Safer Walking and Bicycling," *Health Promotion Journal of Australia* 16, no. 1 (2005): 47–51; R. Elvik, "The Non-Linearity of Risk and the Promotion of Environmentally Sustainable Transport," *Accident Analysis and Prevention* 41 (2009): 849–55; J. Geyer, N. Raford, D. Ragland, and T. Pham, *The Continuing Debate about Safety in Numbers—Data from Oakland, CA* (Berkeley: Institute of Transportation Studies, UC Berkeley, 2006).

2. Peter Jacobsen, "Safety in Numbers: More Walkers and Bicyclists, Safer Walking and Bicycling," *Injury Prevention*, 9 (2003): 205–209, at page 208.

3. *2002 National Survey of Pedestrian and Bicyclist Attitudes and Behaviors*, sponsored by the U.S. Department of Transportation's National Highway Traffic Safety Administration and the Bureau of Transportation Statistics, available at http://www.bts.gov/programs/omnibus_surveys/targeted_survey/2002_national_survey_of_pedestrian_and_bicyclist_attitudes_and_behaviors/survey_highlights/entire.pdf.

4. Surveys cited in Transport Canada, "Urban Bicycle Planning," Urban Transportation Showcase Program, Case Studies in Sustainable Transportation, Issue Paper 77 (November 2008), available at http://www.tc.gc.ca/eng/programs/environment-utsp-casestudy-cs77ebikeplanning-1177.htm.

5. A. C. Nelson and David Allen, "If You Build Them, Commuters Will Use Them: Association between Bicycle Facilities and Bicycle Commuting," *Transportation Research Record* 1578 (1997): 79–83; J. Pucher and L. Dijkstra, "Promoting Safe Walking and Cycling to Improve Public Health: Lessons from the Netherlands and Germany," *American Journal of Public Health* 93, no. 9 (2003): 1509–16; Jennifer Dill and Theresa Carr, *Bicycle Commuting and Facilities in Major U.S. Cities: If You Build Them, Commuters Will Use Them—Another Look* (Transportation Research Board, 2003).

6. New Mexico: http://www.amlegal.com/nxt/gateway.dll/New%20Mexico/albuqwin/cityofalbuquerquenewmexicocodeofordinanc?f=templates$fn=default.htm$3.0$vid=amlegal:albuquerque_nm_mc; Washington: http://apps.leg.wa.gov/RCW/default.aspx?cite=46.61.770

7. S. Christmas, S. Helman, S. Buttress, C. Newman, and R. Hutchins, *Cycling, Safety and Sharing the Road: Qualitative Research with Cyclists and Other Road Users* (London: Department for Transport, 2010).

8. Surveys of cyclists in Portland, Oregon, Ashland, and other cities, by Kittleson Associates, as reported in various locations, including "Study Identifies Three Different Types of Cyclists," *The Ashland Daily Tidings*, November 6, 2010, available at http://www.dailytidings.com/apps/pbcs.dll/article?AID=/20101106/NEWS02/11060303/-1/NEWS01.

9. *London Cycling Design Standards* (Transport for London, 2005).

10. *Collection of Cycle Concepts* (Danish Road Directorate, 2000).

11. http://www.bicyclelaw.com/articles/a.cfm/legally-speaking-stop-as-yield1; http://www.legislature.idaho.gov/idstat/Title49/T49CH7SECT49-720.htm.

Chapter 8

1. Transit Cooperative Research Program, *TCRP Report 90: Bus Rapid Transit.*

2. John Niles and Lisa Callaghan Jerram, *From Buses to BRT: Case Studies of Incremental BRT Projects in North America* (Mineta Transportation Institute, 2010).

3. http://www.metro.net/projects/rapid/.

4. *Transit Waiting Environments: An Ideabook for Making Better Bus Stops* (Greater Cleveland Regional Transit Authority, June 2004).

5. U.S. Department of Transportation, Federal Highway Administration. *Summary of Travel Trends: 2009 National Household Travel Survey.* FHWA-PL-ll-022. June 2011. Table 9. Available at http://nhts.ornl.gov/.

6. *Transportation to Sustain a Community* (City of Boulder Transportation Division, 2009).

Chapter 9

1. Original advertisement published in the *Saturday Evening Post,* June 1923. Referenced in Cleveland State University's Center for Public History and Digital Humanities "Teaching + Learning Cleveland" website at: http://csudigitalhumanities.org/exhibits/items/show/1109, accessed June 25, 2011.

2. U.S. Amusement Park Attendance and Revenue History, http://www.iaapa.org/pressroom/Amusement_Park_Attendance_Revenue_History.asp.

3. Rudolph Limpert, *Motor Vehicle Accident Reconstruction and Cause Analysis*, 4th ed. (Charlottesville, VA: Michie, 1994), 663.

4. These figures are from the AASHTO Policy on the Geometric Design of Highways and Streets. Actual results may vary, depending upon personal reaction time, vehicle type, and other factors.

5. For more detail on how land-use patterns affect travel behavior, see the literature review chapter and references section of G. B. Arrington and Robert Cervero, *TCRP Report 128: Effects of TOD on Housing, Parking, and Travel* (Transportation Research Board, 2008).

6. Institute of Transportation Engineers, *Designing Walkable Urban Thoroughfares: A Context Sensitive Approach* (2010), Table 6.2.

7. Walter Kulash, *Residential Streets,* 3d ed. (National Association of Home Builders, American Society of Civil Engineers, Institute of Transportation Engineers, and Urban Land Institute, 2001), 23–25.

8. Reid Ewing and Michael King, *Flexible Design of New Jersey's Main Streets* (Rutgers University for the New Jersey Department of Transportation, n.d.).

9. Transportation Research Board, *Highway Capacity Manual* (Washington, D.C., 2000).

10. R. L. Moore and S. J. Older, "Pedestrians and Motor Vehicles Are Compatible in Today's World," *Traffic Engineering* 35, no. 12 (September 1965), as quoted in B. J. Campbell, Charles V. Zegeer, Herman H. Huang, and Michael J. Cynecki, "A Review of Pedestrian Safety Research in the United States and Abroad," FHWA-RD-03-042 (2004), 97, available at http://katana.hsrc.unc.edu/cms/downloads/Pedestrian_Synthesis_Report2004.pdf.

11. Reid Ewing, *Traffic Calming: State of the Practice* (Institute of Transportation Engineers, 1999).

12. Nancy McGuckin, with N. Contrino and H. Nakimoto. *Peak Travel in America.* 12th Conference on Transportation Planning Applications, 2009. Available at www.travelbehavior.us and based upon data in the *National Household Travel Survey,* available at http://nhts.ornl.gov/.

13. Nelson\Nygaard, *Seattle Urban Mobility Plan, Briefing,* Chapter 6, "Case Studies in Urban Freeway Removals," Available at http://www.seattle.gov/transportation/briefingbook.htm.

Chapter 10

1. Donald Shoup, *The High Cost of Free Parking* (APA Planners Press, 2005).

2. Center for Neighborhood Technology, *A Heavy Load: The Combined Housing and Transportation Burdens of Working Families* (2006); Center for Neighborhood Technology, *The Affordability Index: A New Tool for Measuring the True Affordability of a Housing Choice* (2008).

3. Donald Shoup, "Cruising for Parking," *Transport Policy* 13, no. 6 (November 2006): 479–86.

4. Mikhail Chester, Arpad Horvath, and Samer Madanat, "Parking Infrastructure: Energy, Emissions, and Automobile Life-Cycle Environmental Accounting," *Environmental Research Letters* (2010), available at http://dx.doi.org/10.1088/1748-9326/5/3/034001.

5. U.S. Housing and Urban Development, 2008.

6. *California Building Industry Association v. San Joaquin Valley Unified Air Pollution Control District,* Case No. F055448 (Cal. Ct. App. Oct. 6, 2009).

7. Nelson\Nygaard (for the Ventura Downtown Mobility and Parking Plan), "Parking Demand in Mixed-Use Main Street Districts" (2005).

8. Dan Zack, "The Downtown Redwood City Parking Management Plan." City of Redwood City, 2005. Available at http://shoup.bol.ucla.edu/Downtown%20Redwood%20City%20Parking%20Plan.pdf

9. New York City Department of Transportation "Parking in New York City" website: http://www.nyc.gov/html/dot/html/motorist/prkintro.shtml#rates.

10. Port of San Francisco website, "New Parking Meters on the Embarcadero." Accessed June 25, 2011. http://www.sfport.com/index.aspx?page=7.

11. Conor Dougherty, "The Parking Fix," *Wall Street Journal,* February 3, 2007, 1.

12. Donald Shoup, *The High Cost of Free Parking* (APA Planners Press, 2005), 516.

13. City of Westminster Visitors' Parking Scheme – FAQs. http://www.westminster.gov.uk/services/transportandstreets/parking/permits/visitorsparkingfaq/

14. Shoup, *The High Cost of Free Parking,* 435.

15. Wenyu Jia and Martin Wachs, *Parking Requirements and Housing Affordability: A Case Study of San Francisco* (University of California Transportation Center Paper No. 380, 1998); Amy Herman, *Study Findings Regarding Condominium Parking Ratios* (Sedway Group, 2001).

16. Luke Klipp, "The Real Costs of San Francisco's Off-Street Residential Parking Requirements: An analysis of parking's impact on housing finance ability and affordability." Goldman School of Public Policy, University of California at Berkeley, Masters Student paper, 2004.

17. Todd Litman, *Parking Requirement Impacts on Housing Affordability* (Victoria Transport Policy Institute, 2004).

18. Regarding legal precedent, it is worth noting that California has a long history of regulating parking prices. In the cities of Glendale, Hayward, Novato, and portions of Los Angeles, for example, it has long been illegal to charge *any* fee for residential parking in certain zones (presumably, to try to deter parking spillover problems on nearby streets). Requiring the unbundling of parking costs similarly regulates parking prices—but in the opposite direction. The fact that some cities *prohibit* parking fees, to prevent spillover parking problems in nearby curb parking, highlights the reality that effective curb parking management is an important companion to requiring a development charge for parking.

19. For detail, search online for Bellevue Ordinance No. 4822 (1995), currently at http://www.bellevuewa.gov/Ordinances/Ord-4822.pdf.

20. Shoup, *The High Cost of Free Parking,* page 127.

21. Brian Bertha, "Appendix A," in *The Low-Rise Speculative Apartment,* ed. Wallace Smith (UC Berkeley Center for Real Estate and Urban Economics, Institute of Urban and Regional Development, 1964).

Chapter 11

1. Susan Shaheen, Adam Cohen, and Elliot Martin, "Carsharing Parking Policy: A Review of North American Practices and San Francisco Bay Area Case Study," *Transportation Research Record* (March 15, 2010): 2.

2. Susan Shaheen, Adam Cohen, and Melissa Chung, *North American Carsharing: A Ten-Year Retrospective* (Institute of Transportation Studies, University of California–Davis, 2008), 4.

3. American Automobile Association, "Your Driving Costs 2010 Edition," available at http://www.aaaexchange.com/Assets/Files/201048935480.Driving%20Costs%202010.pdf.

4. Shaheen, Cohen, and Martin, "Carsharing Parking Policy," 2.

5. Nelson\Nygaard Consulting Associates, *Car-Sharing: Where and How It Succeeds* (Transit Cooperative Research Program, 2005), 4–25.

6. Shaheen, Cohen, and Chung, "North American Carsharing," 4.

7. City of Hoboken website, *Corner Cars*, available at http://www.hobokennj.org/departments/transportation-parking/corner-cars/.

8. Shaheen, Cohen, and Martin, "Carsharing Parking Policy," 14.

9. Adam Cohen, Susan Shaheen, and Ryan McKenzie, *Carsharing: A Local Guide for Planners* (Institute for Transportation Studies, University of California–Davis, 2008), 8.

10. City of Seattle Council Bill Number 116300, passed September 8, 2008.

11. National Capital Planning Commission, NCPC File No. ZC 09–16 (January 28, 2010).

12. San Francisco Planning Department, Planning Commission Resolution No. 18106 (June 10, 2010).

13. IBI Group, *On-Street Parking Carshare Demonstration Project, Final Report* (June 2009), 6, available at http://www.icommutesd.com/Transit/documents/CarshareFinalReport_ALL.pdf.

14. Around the Capital (2010), available at http://www.aroundthecapitol.com/Bills/AB_1871.

15. Nelson\Nygaard Consulting Associates, *Car-Sharing*, 5–21.

16. ABC News 10, "Davis to Subsidize Private Carsharing Firm," September 22, 2010, available at http://www.news10.net/news/local/story.aspx?storyid=96993.

17. U.S. Department of Transportation, Federal Highway Administration, *SAFETEALU 1808: CMAQ Evaluation and Assessment* (2010), available at http://www.fhwa.dot.gov/environment/air_quality/cmaq/research/safetea-lu_phase_2/chap04.cfm.

18. Northeastern University Dukakis Center, "Policy Tool: Unbundling the Price of Parking" (2010), 1, available at http://www.dukakiscenter.org/unbundled-parking/.

Chapter 12

1. Nelson\Nygaard Consulting Associates (for the Institute for Transportation and Development Policy), *Safe Routes to Transit, Bus Rapid Transit Planning Guide* (June 2005).

2. Neil Perks, "Role of Intelligent Transportation Systems (ITS) in Providing Sustainable Transport and Environmental Solutions" (Public Transport Conference, Kuching, August 4, 2010).

3. WMATA, *Station Site and Access Planning Manual* (May 2008).

4. With higher average parking fees of $3.25–$8.50 per day, WMATA is able to generate enough revenue to cover all costs of parking operations and maintenance.

5. Research prepared by Dennis Leach, Transportation Director, and Robert Brosnan, Planning Director of Arlington County in 2010. Summarized at various locations, including "40 Years of Transit Oriented Development Arlington County's Experience with Transit Oriented Development in the Rosslyn-Ballston Metro Corridor," found at http://www.fairfaxcounty.gov/dpz/projects/reston/presentations/40_years_of_transit_oriented_development.pdf.

6. "Taxi Ranks at Major Interchanges: Best Practice Guidelines," *Transport for London*, Issue 1 (March 2003).

7. John Pucher and Ralph Buehler, "Bike-Transit Integration in North America," *Journal of Public Transportation* 12, no. 3 (November 2009): 79–104.

8. Valley Transportation Authority, *Bicycle Technical Guidelines*, available at http://www.insiderpages.com/b/4229015094/charlotte-airport-charlotte.

9. Nelson\Nygaard Consulting Associates, *South Hayward BART Development, Design and Access Plan* (2006).

Chapter 13

1. Tom Vanderbilt, *Traffic: Why We Drive the Way We Do (and What It Says about Us)* (Knopf, 2008).

2. *Road Work Ahead: Is Construction Worth the Wait?* (Surface Transportation Policy Project, 1999).

3. In *Stuck in Traffic: Coping with Peak-Hour Traffic Congestion* (Brookings Institution Press, June 1992) and *Still Stuck in Traffic: Coping with Peak-Hour Traffic Congestion* (Brookings Institution Press, revised edition, April 1, 2004), Anthony Downs presents traffic congestion as an economics issue, not an engineering issue.

4. Stockholmsforsoket, *Facts and Results from the Stockholm Trials: Final Report* (2006), available at http://www.stockholmsforsoket.se/upload/Sammanfattningar/English/Final%20Report_The%20Stockholm%20Trial.pdf.

5. Transport for London website, "Congestion Charge," available at http://www.tfl.gov.uk/roadusers/congestioncharging/.

6. For a more exhaustive list of TDM strategies, see Todd Litman's *TDM Encyclopedia* at http://www.vtpi.org/tdm/.

7. Santa Clara Valley Transportation Authority (1997).

8. 1990 to 2000, available at http://www.commuterchallenge.org/cc/newsmar01_flexpass.html.

9. Jeffrey Brown et al., "Fare-Free Public Transit at Universities," *Journal of Planning Education and Research* 23 (2003): 69–82.

10. 1989 to 2002, weighted average of students, faculty, and staff, from Will Toor and Spenser W. Havlick, *Transportation and Sustainable Campus Communities* (Island Press, 2004).

11. 2002 to 2003, the effect one year after U-Pass implementation, from Sarah Adee Wu, Edo Breemen, Ida Martin, and Bryan Mark, *Transportation Demand Management: University of British Columbia (UBC) U-Pass—A Case Study* (April 2004), available at

http://www.sustain.ubc.ca/pdfs/
seedreport04/449april6upass.pdf.

12. Mode shift one year after implementation in 1994, from James Meyer et al., *An Analysis of the Usage, Impacts and Benefits of an Innovative Transit Pass Program* (Excel spreadsheet, January 14, 1998), available at www.cities21 .org/epaModeShiftCaseStudies.xls.

13. Six years after program implementation, from Francoise Poinsatte and Will Toor, *Finding a New Way: Campus Transportation for the 21st Century* (April 1999).

14. Richard W. Willson and Donald C. Shoup, "Parking Subsidies and Travel Choices: Assessing the Evidence," *Transportation* 17b (1990): 141–157, at 145.

15. Cornell University Office of Transportation Services, *Summary of Transportation Demand Management Program* (unpublished, 1992).

16. Willson and Shoup, "Parking Subsidies."

17. U.S. Department of Transportation, *Proceedings of the Commuter Parking Symposium* (USDOT Report No. DOT-T-91-14, 1990).

18. State Farm Insurance Company and Surface Transportation Policy Project, *Employers Manage Transportation* (1994).

19. Willson and Shoup, "Parking Subsidies."

20. Ibid.

21. Gerald K. Miller, *The Impacts of Parking Prices on Commuter Travel* (Metropolitan Washington Council of Governments, 1991).

22. Donald Shoup and Richard W. Willson, "Employer-Paid Parking: The Problem and Proposed Solutions," *Transportation Quarterly* 46, no. 2 (1992): 169–92, at 189.

23. Michael E. Williams and Kathleen L Petrait, "U-PASS: A Model Transportation Management Program That Works," *Transportation Research Record*, no. 1404 (1994): 73–81.

24. Willson and Shoup, "Parking Subsidies."

25. Suzan Anderson Pinsof and Terri Musser, *Bicycle Facility Planning* (American Planning Association Advisory Service Report #459; American Planning Association, 1995).

26. *Paul v. Virginia*, 75 U.S. 168 (1869); reiterated in *Saenz v. Roe*, 526 U.S. 489 (1999).

27. David Brooks, "Something for Nothing," *New York Times*, June 22, 2009.

28. Project website, www.sfpark.org.

Chapter 14

1. Most recently in G. B. Arrington and Robert Cervero, *TCRP Report 128: Effects of TOD on Housing, Parking, and Travel* (Transportation Research Board, 2008).

2. Details from San Francisco Office of the City Attorney: http://sfcityattorney.org.

3. Frequency: Employer data will be collected annually. Resident and shopper surveys: Every two or three years. Cost to monitor: Intercept surveys will cost around $15,000 but costs may be shared with other departments. Compilation of employer data may be completed by staff, but is time-consuming unless employers submit data electronically. Ongoing updates to the travel demand model will cost approximately $50,000 a year.

4. All employers of ten or more employees are required to survey employees annually to track mode split and other data. We propose to automate this effort in an online interface so that the data can be compiled and analyzed more thoroughly and efficiently. Data on total jobs by district from the Housing and Economic Development Department could be multiplied by mode split information to track total employee trips over time by district.

5. The surveys could also include questions of interest to other departments and local merchants' associations.

Index

AAA (American Automobile Association), 207–208

AARP (American Association of Retired Persons), 30

AASHTO (American Association of State Highway and Transportation Officials), 149

Accessibility, 4–5, 129, 244

Access management, 161, 162

Actions (performance indicator), 263

Active Living Research, 56

ADA, *see* Americans with Disabilities Act

Adaptability, 10–11

Aesthetics, 221–222. *See also* Beauty

Air pollution, 18, 142

All-door boarding, 110

American Association of Retired Persons (AARP), 30

American Association of State Highway and Transportation Officials (AASHTO), 149

American Automobile Association (AAA), 207–208

American Community Survey, 210

American Planning Association, 257

American Public Transit Association (APTA), 105, 137

Americans with Disabilities Act (ADA), 47, 60, 61, 69, 120

APTA (American Public Transit Association), 105, 137

Art shuttles, 126

Automobiles, *see* Motor vehicles

Auto Trips Generated (ATG) approach, 268–269

Barrier effect, 142

Beauty, 12–13, 42–43, 171, 221–222

Benchmarking, 135, 263

Bicycle lanes and paths:
  color, 83, 84, 87, 89 ·
  intersection-only, 95
  safety of, 77–78
  separated, 85, 87, 88
  types of, 79–81

Bicycle networks, 82, 83

Bicycling, 73–103
  bike parking, 76, 97–102, 234
  facilities for, 84–91, 195, 256–257
  increase in levels of, 74–75
  intersections and junctions in, 91–99

investment in, 73–74

measuring success, 101, 103

networks for, 82, 83

principles of, 76–81

as priority, 272

and stations, 233–234

in sustainable cities, 38

and traffic congestion, 245

types of cyclists, 81–82

and wayfinding, 83, 84

BIDs (business improvement districts), 183

Bike boulevards, 90

Bike racks, 98, 129, 234

Bike stations, 234

Boulevards, 90, 171

Bridges, 162–164

BRT (bus rapid transit), 112–113

Budgets, 14

Buildings, arrangement of, 36

Bunching, 109

Buses, 110–114, 123–126

Bus bays, 223–226

Business improvement districts (BIDs), 183

Bus-only lanes, 113

Bus rapid transit (BRT), 112–113

CAAA (Clean Air Act Amendments), 166

California Environmental Quality Act (CEQA), 268

Cars, *see* Motor vehicles

Carbon dioxide (CO_2) emissions, 19–21

Carbon monoxide (CO), 18

Car lanes, 153–154, 158–160

Carpooling, 195

Carsharing, 205–216
  impacts of, 207–208
  jump-starting a program for, 216
  municipal fleets, 215–216
  parking, 201, 208–210, 212
  public policies supporting, 212–215
  reducing traffic with, 257–258
  successful uses of, 208–212
  types of, 206–207

Census Transportation Planning Products (CTPP), 179

CEQA (California Environmental Quality Act), 268

Chicago Transit Authority, 109, 128

Children, 31

Choice riders, 121

Clean Air Act Amendments (CAAA), 166

ITDP (Institute for Transportation and
     Development Policy), 137
ITE, *see* Institute of Transportation Engineers
ITS (Intelligent Transportation
     System), 112

Jitneys, 120
Junctions, 91–99

Kiosks, 133
Kiss-and-ride facilities, 226, 228

Landscaping, 52, 67
Land use:
   for motor vehicles, 142
   for parking, 173
   for pedestrians, 51
   of streets, 45, 49–50
   for transit, 110
Leases, parking, 204
Level boarding, 110
Level of Service (LOS), 69–70, 101, 147, 221,
     264–268, 270
Life-cycle costing, 14
Light rail transit (LRT), 117
Limited bus service, 111–112
Loading spaces, 63
Local bus service, 111
Lockers, bicycle, 98, 99
LOS, *see* Level of Service
LRT (light rail transit), 117

Maps, transit, 130–132, 238–239
Market failure, 13–14
Measures of success, *see* Performance
     measurement
Medians, 64
Metered parking, 194–195, 260
Metro rail, 118
Mixed-use development (MUD),
     208–209, 266
Mobility, 4–5, 46, 244
Modernism, 36, 43
Motor vehicles, 139–172. *See also* Traffic
   access management for, 161, 162
   and corner radii, 158
   and corner sight distance, 156–158
   curb extensions for, 160–162
   deaths resulting from, 141
   designing cities for, 143–148
   and design manuals, 149–151
   design speed, 153
   design vehicles, 151–152
   driveways for, 161, 162
   effects on public health, 27–29, 31
   emergency, 164–165
   Four-Step Travel Demand Model for,
     166–169

and freeways, 169–172
grade separations for, 162–164
hidden costs of driving, 141–143
history of, 139–141
and intersections, 154–156
lane width for, 153–154
number of lanes for, 154
priority of, 272
right-turn lanes for, 158–160
and stations, 226–231
and streets, 45
and traffic calming, 162, 165–166
MUD (mixed-use development),
     208–209, 266
Municipal fleets, 215–216

National Association of City Transportation
     Officials (NACTO), 101
National Capital Planning
     Commission, 213
National Center for Transit Research (NCTR)
     reports, 136
National Highway Traffic Safety
     Administration (NHTSA), 29
Networks, 42–43, 82, 83
New media, 131, 133
NHTSA (National Highway Traffic Safety
     Administration), 29
Nitrogen oxide (NO_x), 18
Noise pollution, 142

Obesity, 26–27, 105
Objectives, 263
Off-street parking, 202, 203, 209, 212
Off-street paths, 84, 85
One-way couplets, 170
One-way streets, 87
On-street parking:
   and bike lanes, 87
   for carshare vehicles, 212
   potential for, 160
   proper management of, 203
Ozone (O_3) pollution, 18

PAR (Paved Accessible Route), 220
Paratransit, 120
Parking, 172–204
   of bicycles, 76, 91–99, 234
   for carsharing vehicles, 201, 208–210, 212
   cash-out for, 201, 254–256
   commercial, 189–194
   economics of, 175–176
   effects of, 173–175
   funding facilities for, 203–204
   management principles, 181–186
   metered, 194–195, 260
   minimum requirements for,
     201–203

WILEY BOOKS ON
Sustainable Design

JOHN WILEY & SONS, INC. provides must-have content and services to architecture, design and construction customers worldwide. Wiley offers books, online products and services for professionals and students. We are proud to offer design professionals one of the largest collections of books on sustainable and green design. For other Wiley books on sustainable design, visit www.wiley.com/go/sustainabledesign

♻ ENVIRONMENTAL BENEFITS STATEMENT

This book is printed with soy-based inks on presses with VOC levels that are lower than the standard for the printing industry. The paper, Rolland Enviro 100, is manufactured by Cascades Fine Papers Group and is made from 100 percent post-consumer, de-inked fiber, without chlorine. According to the manufacturer, the use of every ton of Rolland Enviro100 Book paper, switched from virgin paper, helps the environment in the following ways:

Mature trees	Waterborne waste not created	Water flow saved	Atmospheric emissions eliminated	Soiled Wastes reduced	Natural gas saved by using biogas
17	6.9 lbs.	10,196 gals.	2,098 lbs.	1,081 lbs.	2,478 cubic feet